# CLARK CLIFFORD

# CLARK CLIFFORD

## The Wise Man of Washington

JOHN ACACIA

THE UNIVERSITY PRESS OF KENTUCKY

Scholarly publisher for the Commonwealth,
serving Bellarmine University, Berea College, Centre College of Kentucky,
Eastern Kentucky University, The Filson Historical Society, Georgetown
College, Kentucky Historical Society, Kentucky State University,
Morehead State University, Murray State University, Northern Kentucky
University, Transylvania University, University of Kentucky, University of
Louisville, and Western Kentucky University.
All rights reserved.

*Editorial and Sales Offices:* The University Press of Kentucky
663 South Limestone Street, Lexington, Kentucky 40508-4008
www.kentuckypress.com

13 12 11 10 09    5 4 3 2 1

Library of Congress Cataloging-in-Publication Data

Acacia, John.
    Clark Clifford : the wise man of Washington / John Acacia.
        p. cm.
    Includes bibliographical references and index.
    ISBN 978-0-8131-2551-0 (hardcover : alk. paper)
    1. Clifford, Clark M., 1906–1998.  2. Statesmen—United States—
Biography.  3. Lawyers—United States—Biography.  4. United States—
Politics and government—1945–1989.  5. United States—Foreign
relations—1945–1989.  I. Title.
    E840.8.C55A27 2009
    973.92092—dc22
    [B]                                        2009015933

This book is printed on acid-free recycled paper meeting
the requirements of the American National Standard
for Permanence in Paper for Printed Library Materials.

Manufactured in the United States of America.

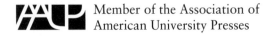 Member of the Association of
American University Presses

To my wife Karen,
the most courageous person I know

# Contents

*Photographs follow page 184*

# Introduction

# Camp David, July 1965

President Lyndon Johnson was about to make the most fateful decision of his presidency. U.S. military personnel in Vietnam had been deployed to train and assist the South Vietnamese forces and to protect the U.S. air base at Da Nang, from which Rolling Thunder, the bombing raids against North Vietnam begun the previous February, had been launched. The pretense for the bombing was retaliation for a Vietcong attack on a U.S. installation near the city of Pleiku. As of July 1965, U.S. ground forces were not engaged in combat, and the onus for a military victory lay with the corrupt and incompetent South Vietnamese army. That was about to change.

General William C. Westmoreland had just submitted a request for a massive increase in troops—100,000 men by the end of 1965, with a vague request for further troops in 1966. Johnson summoned his senior military and national security advisers, including Secretary of State Dean Rusk and Secretary of Defense Robert McNamara, to the White House to discuss Westmoreland's request.

While the White House meeting was in progress another man entered the room; Johnson waved him to an empty chair. Clark Clifford, the urbane and courtly Washington lawyer and former special counsel to President Harry S. Truman, was one of Johnson's most trusted advisers, although he was not officially a member of the administration. With the possible exception of Supreme Court Justice Abe Fortas, Clifford was Johnson's most influential "kitchen cabinet" adviser, and as the meeting began Johnson had telephoned Clifford's office, just a few blocks away from the White House, and asked him to join them immediately. As he would do frequently, Clifford promptly heeded the president's summons. Johnson had asked Clifford to familiarize himself with the situation in Vietnam back in May, in response to a recommendation from outgoing CIA director John McCone, who argued that the United States needed to sharply escalate the bombing and deploy ground troops to avoid a disastrous defeat. At the time, Clifford had responded with a letter urging caution and warning Johnson of a "quagmire" in which the United States had "no realistic hope of ultimate victory."[1] At this meeting, however, Clifford played the role of the silent observer.

Over the next few days, the president and his advisers discussed the possibility of escalation in Vietnam, culminating in a Sunday afternoon meeting on July 25, 1965, at Camp David. Clifford later described this session as a showdown between himself and McNamara, as he and the secretary of defense presented arguments for and against. Clifford, fingers steepled together in front of his face, spoke in his carefully measured cadence, a voice that exuded gravity and conviction. "I hate this war. I do not believe we can win," he said. Clifford then warned Johnson that the casualties would be high, a prediction that later proved eerily accurate: "We could lose more than 50,000 men in Vietnam."[2]

Clifford presented his case with as much passion and persuasion as he could muster, but to no avail. Johnson approved the troop deployment, thus committing the United States to a ground war from which it would take eight years to extricate itself. More than 58,000 Americans died in Vietnam. The war divided the country along generational, economic, and racial lines, and eroded the confidence the American people had in their government. Vietnam revealed the limits of U.S. power and called into question the righteousness of its foreign policy. Clifford was a central player during a watershed moment in American history; had he prevailed in 1965, one of the darkest moments in U.S. history might have been avoided.

Clark Clifford may be the most renowned presidential adviser of the twentieth century. Although he served in an official government capacity for a relatively short period of time, he cast a very long shadow. His journey from midwestern lawyer to the corridors of power in Washington is intriguing, both because of its remarkable trajectory and because of his involvement in so many pivotal moments of twentieth-century U.S. history, including the Truman Doctrine, the recognition of Israel, the improbable Democratic presidential victory in 1948, and Vietnam. His is the story of a man who was at the right place at the right time and who had the intellect, ambition, physical presence, demeanor, and confidence necessary to become a legendary adviser of American presidents. A devoted servant of four Democratic presidents, he was also extremely adept at looking after his own interests.

In addition, Clark Clifford's career traces the evolution of the modern presidency, specifically the role of the White House chief of staff or senior presidential adviser.

In the foreword to *Chief of Staff: Twenty-Five Years of Managing the Presidency,* presidential historian Richard E. Neustadt wrote, "For half a century, since Franklin Roosevelt's time, there have been in every administration some three or four senior assistants whose roles rivaled or outshone in policy significance (though not in protocol) those of even the department heads at State, Defense, Treasury or Justice, the traditional inner cabinet posts."[3] In George W. Bush's administration, for example, former senior adviser and political strategist Karl Rove was more of a household name than onetime Secretary of the Treasury John Snow. Clifford's stature in Truman's administration was comparable to that of Rove's.

The increased prominence of the president's senior staff coincided with the centralization of power and influence within the White House.[4] This trend, an important development in modern American government, continues to this day. Although George W. Bush promised during the 2000 campaign that he would utilize an "MBA" style of management, empowering the respective cabinet secretaries to run their particular departments, in reality power in his administration remained closely concentrated in the West Wing. Consider, for instance, John Snow's functioning primarily as salesman for the administration's proposals rather than formulator of policy, and Secretary of Education Rod Paige's minor role in the development of the No Child Left Behind Act.

In his 1968 book *The President's Men,* Patrick Anderson wrote that "Clifford became Truman's most influential all-around adviser and, as such, one of the four or five most important White House aides in history."[5] In the annals of American history a few names stand out as important and influential presidential advisers. Colonel Edward M. House was Woodrow Wilson's closest adviser; Harry Hopkins was Roosevelt's. Eisenhower had Sherman Adams, John F. Kennedy had his brother Robert, and Johnson had Fortas and Clifford. These men differed in terms of the nature of their relationship to the president, the role the president expected them to play, the reasons why the president confided in them, and how they were perceived by those around Washington. Hopkins, for example, according to Robert Sherwood, was "generally regarded as a sinister figure, a backstairs intriguer, an Iowan combination of Machiavelli, Svengali and Rasputin. . . . He was unquestionably a political liability to Roosevelt, a convenient target for all manner of attacks directed at the President himself, and many people wondered why Roosevelt kept him around." Roosevelt answered that particular question himself when he observed that the presidency was a lonely job because someone was always looking for something from you. He needed "somebody like Harry Hopkins who asks for nothing except to serve you."[6] As the president's brother, Robert Kennedy's loyalty was unquestioned, and despite the fact that Bobby was eight years younger, President Kennedy recognized that their different personalities complemented each other.

Abe Fortas had a more personal relationship with President Johnson than Clark Clifford did; they also differed in other respects, as Patrick Anderson noted in 1968: "The President has greater respect for Clark's political judgment than he does for Abe's. He admires Abe's warm, human qualities, but he knows Abe's heart is on fire with liberal causes, so he discounts his advice accordingly. The President likes to get advice from men like Clark who are cold and shrewd and aren't swayed by moralistic arguments. The President knows that Clark understands the nature of the Presidency—that a President may sometimes do what is right but he must always do what is necessary."[7] Clifford dispensed pragmatic advice and was composed and gentlemanly. He was loyal to the presidents he served, but never as selfless as someone like Hopkins. He understood that his role was to serve the president, but he was also ambitious enough to look after his own interests—which he did exceptionally well.

Despite his singular position as trusted adviser to both Truman and Johnson, Clark Clifford has not received a tremendous amount of attention. Douglas Frantz and David McKean have written a fine biography of Clifford (*Friends in High Places,* 1995), but it fails to examine Clifford's tenure in the Truman administration in great detail, paying more attention to the Johnson and Vietnam years, and focusing on Clifford's career as a Washington lawyer and power broker. Late in life, after publishing his long-awaited memoirs, Clifford should have enjoyed the Washington equivalent of a farewell tour, but ever the workaholic, he sought out a new and different challenge. This turned out to be a dreadful mistake. In his mid-eighties, Clifford was implicated in a scandal involving the Bank of Credit and Commerce International, or BCCI, an illicit institution whose illegal dealings included laundering drug money. The charges against Clifford were ultimately dropped because of his poor health, and his law partner and codefendant, Robert Altman, was acquitted. Despite the legal exoneration, however, Clifford's reputation was permanently damaged. Frantz and McKean covered the BCCI case as journalists, and their book's primary aim is to tell the complete story of Clifford and BCCI. In the process of setting up the BCCI story, however, they do a fine job detailing Clifford's long career as a Washington lawyer. Still, Frantz and McKean were primarily interested in seeing Clifford as a metaphor for a Washington dominated by special interests and back-room dealings. Comparing Clifford to former Secretary of State Dean Acheson, whose memoir *Present at the Creation* describes his role in the start of the Cold War, they wrote that "Clifford also was present at—and integral to—the creation of the permanent shadow govern-ment of lawyers and lobbyists who have come to dominate Wash-ington. He was a charter member of those unelected courtiers who have come to wield as much power as the men and women elected to govern the nation."[8]

Clifford's own memoir, *Counsel to the President,* was published in 1991, and while it is an invaluable source of information on his life and career, as a memoir it must be read with a healthy degree of caution. In order to properly evaluate his contribution to history, therefore, a comprehensive biography spanning his entire Washington career is warranted.

Interpretations of Clifford have changed over time, with his repu-tation generally trending downward through the years. During the Truman administration Clifford was often the subject of flattering praise. The favorable treatment he received was a function of his own care and feeding of the press, the pragmatic and politically astute counsel he provided to the president, and perhaps most of all the fact that he looked the part. In 1947 *Life* magazine described him as a "gorgeous hunk of man."[9] In 1968, just before Clifford took over for McNamara as secretary of defense, Patrick Anderson, writing for the *New York Times,* described him as follows: "The sixty-one-year-old Clifford is one of the most elegant men alive. Tall, handsome, and always beautifully attired, courtly and charming in the old school Southern manner, Clifford is one of those rare public figures, like John Kennedy, whose dazzling exterior does much to detract from the fact that he has a mind like a steel trap."[10]

Fortunately for students of history, the coverage of Clifford was usually more thoughtful than the observation that he was handsome. Cabell Phillips, in his study of the Truman presidency, wrote in 1966 that Clifford "had a mind of extraordinary scope and analytical capacity, and he expressed himself with easy, unpretentious clarity." Relative to the rest of Truman's administration Phillips singled out

Clifford as the only one who was exceptionally talented.[11] Many writers, both contemporary and historical, credited Clifford as responsible for transforming the Truman administration into an efficient, professionally run operation, and he was widely viewed as the mastermind behind Truman's miracle win in 1948. As a result of a comprehensive 1946 report that Clifford submitted to Truman on U.S.-Soviet relations he was also considered an important, albeit secondary, figure in the emergence of the Cold War.

Over time, as historians viewed Clifford with a more critical eye, it became clear that his value had been somewhat exaggerated. Alonzo Hamby, author of the 1995 Truman biography *Man of the People,* acknowledged that Clifford was Truman's "indispensable man," yet he concluded that "despite impressions that Clifford would cultivate later, he was never the master strategist of the Truman administration, never Truman's chief of staff, never quite the dominating figure in the White House."[12]

As Hamby implies, what is most striking about Clifford's career, during his time in the Truman administration and after, was his capacity for self-promotion. For that reason Clifford's years in the White House are interesting for both historians and those who follow politics because they provide a window into how Washington operates. For all of Clifford's formidable talents, the one most integral to his success was his capacity for self-promotion. During the five years he spent in the Truman administration Clifford had the good fortune to be surrounded by talented men who formulated the ideas and strategies for which he ultimately claimed or received credit. The two most prominent examples were a 1946 comprehensive evaluation of U.S.-Soviet relations, which served as a precursor to both the Truman Doctrine and the Marshall Plan, and a 1947 campaign strategy memorandum, which was widely considered to be the road map for Truman's surprise victory in 1948. In both cases Clifford did little more than some minor editing, but the most important change he made was managing to have the memorandums forwarded to the president over his signature. After Clifford left the White House to start his lucrative law practice he would frequently recount and embellish his accomplishments during the Truman administration and appropriate credit that properly belonged elsewhere. Certainly a penchant for self-promotion and a willingness to claim credit for another's intellectual property were not limited to Clifford. In a city with more inflated egos and ambition than anywhere else in America (with the possible exceptions of Wall Street and Hollywood), Clifford's success story could be considered an allegory for how Washington society operates.

Although Clifford established his legend by rather dubious means, the true measure of his character is how he ultimately put his reputation to use. When confronted with the greatest challenge of his career, Clifford rose to the occasion. Virtually alone among Johnson's senior advisers in 1965, Clifford had the wisdom and foresight to see that military intervention in Vietnam would become a quagmire and argued strenuously against escalation. In 1968 Johnson selected him as secretary of defense, and Clifford used this platform to make the case for withdrawal and a negotiated settlement. In the face of unrelenting opposition from the president and his senior advisers, Clifford steadfastly maintained that a conventional military victory in Vietnam was unattainable and not worth the cost. Although he was unable to achieve his goal, the fact that he was able to move an obstinate president in his direction was itself a tremendous accomplishment. It also permanently tarnished his reputation with Johnson, an outcome Clifford accepted as the cost of trying to extricate his country from a disastrous war.

Unfortunately for Clifford, his courageous effort to end the Vietnam War was not the climax of his Washington career. Through a combination of hubris, inattention, and naiveté, he allowed the BCCI scandal to eclipse his earlier accomplishments and irreparably damage his reputation. He deserved better.

# 1

# Special Counsel

Clark Clifford's life had many characteristics of a Hollywood movie: a handsome leading man arrives in Washington via the heartland; rises to a position of power in the White House through a combination of happenstance, talent, and hard work; participates in some of the most important events in twentieth-century U.S. history; and ultimately suffers a tragic fall. Relegated to a largely ceremonial role when he first arrived at the White House, Clifford succeeded in parlaying proximity to power into an actual position of power. When President Harry S. Truman was confronted with his first major crisis, the labor wars of 1946, Clifford's wise counsel enabled the president not only to weather the storm but also to emerge a stronger leader. Clifford helped Truman sidestep a political disaster brought on by a wayward cabinet member whom Truman had usurped as vice president and who believed that by rights the presidency should have been his. By virtue of their common Missouri background Clifford shared a bond with Truman, a bond that Clifford skillfully transformed into the role of confidante. A favorite of the news media, he was able, by association, to project an aura of competence and efficiency upon a White House that had been criticized as having neither. A master at synthesizing the ideas of others, Clifford served as a conduit for getting policy proposals to the president while burnishing his own reputation. Initially relegated to what he called the role of a "potted palm," Clifford soon ascended to a position commensurate with his talent and ambition—special counsel to the president.

Presaging the good fortune that would await him, Clark McAdams Clifford was born on Christmas Day, 1906. He was born to a respectable but not distinguished family in the fashionable west end of St. Louis. His father, Frank Clifford, was a railroad auditor with the Missouri Pacific Railroad, and his mother, Georgia Clifford, was a writer who at one time was president of the American Association of Story Tellers. *The New Republic* memorably described Clark's biography: "Clifford is one of those fortunate and rare individuals whose life story would make a heroic plot for one of those conventional romantic novels so popular at the turn of the century."[1]

Clifford was named after his maternal uncle, Clark McAdams, the crusading liberal editor of the *St. Louis Post-Dispatch*. His uncle, whom Clifford credited for much of his liberal orientation, believed that individuals and government shared a mutual responsibility to improve people's lives. The McAdams side of the family also had a profound influence on Clifford's worldview. Whereas the Cliffords were content with their lives and had little in the way of expectations, the McAdamses embodied that quintessential of American ideals: that anything was possible through effort and hard work. Throughout his life, Clifford would set high expectations for himself and pursue them single-mindedly. Despite his affinity for the McAdams side of the family, Clifford credited his father for instilling in him a work ethic—or, rather, the belief that to live was to work. His father's career also served as an example of the importance of independence. Frank had been successful in his career until his mentor died unexpectedly and was replaced by someone from a competing railroad who brought along his own people. Clifford's father could never break into this new inner circle, and his career ran into a dead end. Clifford was determined to learn from his father's mistakes and not rely on anyone but himself, and that is why he would choose to practice law.[2]

Clifford's youth reads like something out of *Ozzie and Harriet*. He attended Washington University, within walking distance of his home, where he was the Big Man on Campus. He was selected to several honor societies, played on the tennis team, led the glee club and choir, and was active in campus politics. He also tried his hand at acting and soon won leading-man roles in school plays. With his movie-star looks, it was not difficult to attract young women to play opposite him. After two years of college Clifford transferred into the Washington University law school, as was the practice at the time. He had also considered medical school, but was steered toward law by his father, and it was a decision he would never regret. During his senior year he enrolled in a seminar taught by Jacob Lashly, a partner in one of St. Louis's most distinguished firms and an outstanding trial lawyer. Clifford decided he wanted to join Lashly's firm, Holland, Lashly and Donnell, but Lashly told him there were no openings. Clifford sought out other firms throughout the city but was unable to find a position, so he went back to Lashly with a unique offer. "Sir, I would like to sit in your office library and see how this firm operates," he said. "I will work without pay, sir." Lashly was no fool and decided to take the young man up on his offer.[3]

Clifford worked for Lashly throughout the summer and was then asked to stay on for a small hourly wage. Knowing full well that it would be years before he would get to try a case, Clifford called on the court clerks in the St. Louis criminal courts and offered to represent indigent defendants (there were no public defenders at the time). Eventually he was granted the opportunity to defend an accused car thief named John Piper. Clifford devoted all his time and energy to the case and provided Piper with a stirring defense. Despite his efforts, it took the jury less than half an hour to return a guilty verdict, and Piper was sentenced to twenty-five years in prison. Clifford was devastated; yet despite the setback, and several more that followed, he was getting valuable experience.

In 1929, while traveling through Europe with a friend, he met and fell in love with the woman he would marry. Margery Kimball, who called herself Marny, was a debutante from Boston who was traveling with a group of young women from Wellesley College. Clifford convinced his traveling partner, a fellow associate from Holland, Lashly and Donnell named Louis McKeown, to alter their itinerary so they could meet up with the young ladies again. When Clark and Marny finally said good-bye, she informed him that she was engaged and that it would be improper for him to contact her again. Clifford himself had been seeing a woman named Dorothy Ladd for some time prior to his extended vacation, so it seemed highly unlikely that he and Marny would ever meet again. But, in keeping with the script of a heroic novel, Marny would enter his life again. A year later Clifford ran into an acquaintance who mentioned that, while vacationing in Maine that summer, he had met a friend of his named Marny Kimball. Clifford was greatly surprised to hear that her name was still Marny Kimball; she had broken off her engagement. It had been a year since they said their farewells in Paris, but Clifford had never stopped thinking of her. He traveled several times to Boston to court her, and they married a year later, on October 3, 1931. The couple would have three daughters, Margery, Joyce, and Randall.

Clifford's professional persistence with Holland, Lashly and Donnell paid off as well, and he made partner at the age of thirty-one, contrary to established practice at the firm. The partners at Holland et al. seldom offered partnership, but Clifford was winning cases and they were afraid to lose him. He worked long hours, driven by a personal desire to be recognized as a superior trial lawyer, and he and Marny settled into what must have been a mutually acceptable arrangement in which he dedicated himself first and foremost to his own career and ambition. He was happiest when busy and dedicated most of his nights and weekends to preparing his cases.

Success often requires more than hard work, however. Often it is a function of whom you know, and in Clifford's case his career and life would have been drastically different were it not for one man: Jake Vardaman. In one of the ironies of his career Clifford met Vardaman through his wife rather than his own lawyerly circles. Vardaman and Marny shared a love of opera, a rarity in St. Louis, and they joined together to form the Grand Opera Guild of St. Louis. This organization brought opera to the city, and through this group Clifford met Vardaman, a successful banker and businessman who also dabbled in politics. Vardaman was a financial supporter of Harry Truman in Truman's successful 1934 Senate campaign, and it was through Vardaman that Clifford first met the senator and future president. Following the attack on Pearl Harbor in December 1941 Vardaman joined the navy and asked Clifford to act as his personal attorney while he was away.[4]

Clifford served as an infantryman in the Missouri National Guard, and in April 1944 enlisted in the U.S. Naval Reserves. He did not see combat but instead worked a desk job, both in Washington, D.C., and San Francisco. By then the 1944 presidential election was heating up, and Senator Harry Truman was selected as Franklin Roosevelt's running mate, at the expense of the sitting vice president, Henry Wallace. Wallace, the liberal stalwart of the Democratic Party, was considered too far to the left, so the more conservative Truman was tapped as the nominee. Roosevelt won an unprecedented fourth term in the fall of 1944, and Truman thus became vice president. Less than four months into his new term the ailing Roosevelt died, and Harry Truman found himself the occupant of the Oval Office.

In addition to being frightened by the magnitude of the responsibility that confronted him, Truman was more than a little uncomfortable among Roosevelt's closest advisers, many of them northeastern establishment figures like the president whom they had served. Truman, for his part, was most comfortable among fellow Missourians, and one of the minor personnel changes he made was the position of naval aide to the president. His choice was Jake Vardaman.

Vardaman wasted little time before reaching out to Clifford, whom he visited while on a brief trip to San Francisco. He asked Clifford to come to Washington to be his assistant, but Clifford did not think much of the offer. When Vardaman called again, in late June, he had a better offer. Vardaman was part of the delegation that was to accompany Truman to Potsdam, where the Allied leaders would discuss the shape of postwar Europe, and he asked Clifford to temporarily stand in for him while he was away. Clifford accepted and moved to Washington, the city he would call home for the rest of his life.

Clifford's first day at the White House was July 10, 1945. Shortly after his arrival Vardaman introduced him to the president, who had not yet left for Potsdam. Although Clifford had met Truman a few years earlier, also in Vardaman's company, the president did not recall the meeting. He was busy with paperwork in the Oval Office and paused only briefly to greet Clifford. "Big fella, ain't he" was all that Truman said.[5] Despite this inauspicious first meeting with the president, over the next year Clifford would become the most important member of the White House staff.

The duties of the president's naval aide, especially one serving as a temporary stand-in, were limited. One of the most important was to serve as a "potted palm"—to stand quietly in the background during ceremonial and social occasions. Such an activity must have been torture for the workaholic Clifford. His other responsibility was to maintain the Map Room, the World War II equivalent of today's Situation Room. During Clifford's first visit to the Map Room he met a naval reserve officer named George Elsey. Elsey would become, in Clifford's words, his "closest associate and collaborator,"[6] and in addition to their tenure in Truman's White House they would find themselves working together again twenty-three years later, when Clifford became Lyndon Johnson's secretary of defense. For Clifford, Elsey was indispensable, often the author and idea man behind Clifford's proudest accomplishments.

Elsey was born on February 5, 1918, in Palo Alto, California, and grew up in Oakmont, Pennsylvania, just north of Pittsburgh. He graduated from Princeton University in 1939 with a degree in public and international affairs, but was drawn to the study of American history. He began his graduate studies at Harvard, and in 1941 was awarded one of Harvard's most prestigious awards, the Sheldon fellowship. The fellowship entailed travel, but because of World War II Europe was out of the question, so Elsey opted to pursue his studies in Washington, D.C. Elsey had more in mind than just academics, however, and the choice of Washington allowed him to pursue a commission in the naval reserve. It was a decision that would change his life. Just days after Pearl Harbor, Elsey received a commission in the Office of Naval Intelligence and was later assigned to the Map Room. The Map Room posting was incredibly fortuitous, as it afforded Elsey a "fly on the wall" view of World War II military strategy and also exposed him to classified army and navy intelligence reports. At the end of World War II these intelligence reports began to highlight the Soviet Union's aggressive efforts to establish a sphere of influence in eastern Europe. Elsey found these reports disturbing. They, and his experience in the Map Room, shaped his thinking about the Soviet Union, the subject of the Clifford-Elsey report of 1946.[7]

Clifford also was introduced to Sam Rosenman, who had been one of Franklin Roosevelt's closest advisers and was one of the few holdovers from the Roosevelt administration. Rosenman, a former judge, was special counsel to the president, a title that was somewhat misleading, as he was not the president's legal counsel. Rosenman served as an all-purpose adviser and speechwriter to both Roosevelt and Truman; after he left, Truman would name Clifford as the new special counsel. At the time of his meeting Clifford, Rosenman had a full plate and no dedicated staff, accepting help wherever he could get it. When Clifford, newly arrived in Washington, paid Rosenman an introductory courtesy call he asked the special counsel if he could be of any assistance. Rosenman jumped at the offer and gave Clifford the first of many assignments. Determined that America be better prepared for the next military conflict, Truman was an advocate of universal military training (UMT). He gave the assignment of researching and drafting a message on UMT to Rosenman, who delegated it to Clifford.

Having left the project in Clifford's hands, Rosenman joined Truman in Potsdam at the end of July. Clifford spent the better part of the next two months working on the project and delivered a memorandum with his recommendations to Rosenman on September 28. As Clifford had gleaned from his research, the program enjoyed little public or congressional support, and while it had the support of the Army chief of staff, General George C. Marshall, and Supreme Allied Commander Dwight D. Eisenhower, it did not command much support among the rest of the military. Clifford's final recommendations, seemingly obvious, were that Truman should first get the Army and Navy staffs to endorse the concept, and then devise a plan that would earn the support of both the president and the military. Clifford's recommendations, however, were not followed, and the plan languished in Congress for a year. In order to build some momentum for the proposal, Truman appointed a blue-ribbon commission to further study the idea. Their report, presented in May 1947, encountered stiff opposition, and while Truman continued to press his case, most notably in March 1948 before a joint session of Congress, the idea never got off the ground.[8]

While Clifford was helping Truman prepare for the next war, the existing one finally came to an end. On August 6, 1945, the first atomic bomb was dropped on Hiroshima, and three days later the second was dropped on Nagasaki. Within a few days the Japanese surrendered, bringing World War II to a close. Although the initial plan had been for Clifford's posting to be temporary, he had impressed Rosenman, who asked Vardaman if Clifford could stay on. Vardaman immediately agreed, and they made the proposal to Truman before the Navy could recall Clifford to San Francisco. On September 13, 1945, Clifford was formally transferred to the White House. As luck would have it, perhaps to the envy of less successful career sailors, Clifford's temporary appointment as lieutenant commander was made permanent.

In the fall of 1945 both Vardaman and Rosenman would leave the White House, presenting Clifford with an incredible opportunity. Rosenman, who had agreed to stay through the end of 1945, left for financial reasons, citing the inadequacy of the $12,000 annual salary. Clifford would offer the same explanation when he resigned from the White House staff four years later. Vardaman had grown bored with his limited responsibilities as naval aide and decided to step down, but rather than return to St. Louis he chose to remain in Washington. Vardaman was known for his abrasive manner and had alienated many of the people with whom he came in contact, including the secretary of the navy, James Forrestal, and the first lady, Bess Truman. President Truman, however, was personally indebted to Vardaman because he was one of the few businessmen to support his 1934 Senate campaign, so the president was willing to find him a job. But Vardaman did not want just any job; he wanted to be appointed as a governor of the Federal Reserve. Vardaman had been a prominent banker and businessman back in St. Louis, so he was qualified, but his relationship with the president might also have had something to do with Truman's nominating Vardaman for the position in January 1946.

After Vardaman's departure to the Federal Reserve, Truman did not immediately promote Clifford, who continued to serve informally as acting naval aide. Despite the absence of an official title, Clifford acted in Vardaman's former capacity; he also started to get many of the assignments that used to go to Rosenman. Ironically, his first high-profile assignment was to shepherd Vardaman's nomination through Congress. Vardaman's abrasive style as well as accusations that he abused the perquisites of his office ensured that his confirmation would be more than a formality. For Clifford it was his first chance to meet with the president one on one, and it also afforded him the opportunity to meet with and personally lobby members of Congress. His first major assignment was successfully accomplished: Vardaman was confirmed by a vote of 66–9 on April 3, 1946.[9]

Rosenman's departure created a void in the White House, especially in the speechwriting role, and it was not immediately clear that Clifford was up to the task. Rosenman was both experienced and a skilled writer, while Clifford had neither experience nor speechwriting skills. Rosenman later observed that Clifford "did not write well. He was quite a pedestrian writer, and although he was the principal writer after I left, he did not write with facility or with any great imagination."[10] Clifford conceded that Rosenman was correct, but suggested that his deficiencies in this area were not a problem for Truman. In fact, Clifford argued that his taking over the speechwriting was an advantage because the departure of Rosenman, who had been Roosevelt's principal speechwriter, enabled Truman to start sounding more like Harry Truman and less like Franklin Roosevelt.[11] In any case, speechwriting was not Clifford's favorite part of the job. Elsey, for one, believed that Clifford did not relish his speechwriting responsibilities. As he later recalled, "With Rosenman gone and with no staff member having any special responsibility for speech preparation, Clifford found himself—not by his initiative or by his choice, certainly not by his desire—he found himself looked to as the principal speech preparer on just about every conceivable subject that a President has to make speeches on, and he began asking me to help him in this regard."[12]

Clifford's performance during the Vardaman confirmation and his contribution to the White House staff led Truman to have a change of heart regarding a formal appointment as naval aide. Clifford received the promotion the day after the final confirmation vote for Vardaman. Along with the title came two quick promotions, first to the rank of commander and second to captain. Clifford's rapid rise in the ranks must have caused much consternation among career sailors who did not advance nearly as rapidly. The *St. Louis Post-Dispatch* observed that "the selection of Capt. Clifford as the presidential naval aide was evidence not only that the Commander in Chief prefers Missourians for his immediate associates but also indicates his preference for reserve officers over the graduates of West Point and Annapolis."[13]

Yet Clifford's military career would come to an end about two months later. Again Truman had a change of heart, this time with respect to his decision not to fill Rosenman's position as special counsel. Clifford had been serving in that capacity, though not in name, and Truman thought it best to make it official. The president likely was also looking to avoid unfavorable scrutiny, as most of the assignments Clifford worked on had nothing to do with his official responsibilities as naval aide. Getting him out of uniform and into a suit was one way to avoid that.[14] Clifford's appointment as special counsel was announced, with little fanfare, on June 27, 1946.

Clifford's role in helping resolve the labor wars of 1946 signified his arrival as Truman's premier White House adviser, and perhaps precipitated his promotion to special counsel. World War II had concentrated all of America's resources on meeting the demands of the war machine, and personal sacrifice was the order of the day as wages were held in check and consumer goods were scarce. With the war over, labor's demands could be contained no longer. In the spring of 1946, two crucial segments of the U.S. economy were in crisis. On March 31, 400,000 coal workers went on strike, and on May 18 the two major railroad unions did so also. Truman believed that in addition to crippling the economy large-scale strikes in the major energy and transportation segments also jeopardized national security. He responded to the coal strike in an authoritarian manner, issuing an executive order to seize the mines and transfer them to the control of the Department of the Interior, and ordered the miners to return to work.

Truman personally appealed to the leaders of the largest railroad unions, Alvanley Johnston and A. F. Whitney, to avert a crisis, but they refused. Truman was furious. Again Truman threatened to take authoritarian action, promising to seize the railroads in the event of a strike. Johnston and Whitney refused Truman's entreaties to negotiate a compromise and ordered their men off the job on May 23. The combined impact of the railroad strike and the coal miners who defied Truman's order to return to the mines was nothing less than devastating. In total, about one million workers went on strike. Truman was faced with his first major crisis.[15]

Truman's anger knew no bounds, and he vented his rage during a Cabinet meeting the next day. He decided to appear before a joint session of Congress to request legislation to draft the striking workers into the armed forces if they continued to threaten the national security. In order to prepare the public for this action Truman decided to address the nation via radio at 10:00 P.M. He had prepared a draft of the speech he planned to give that evening and showed it to his press secretary, Charlie Ross. Ross was horrified, but it was typical Truman. When angry the president would unleash his emotions on paper, but he almost always had the good sense never to mail the letters he wrote or read his intemperate statements in public. Nonetheless, as Alonzo Hamby observed, in this case Truman's words suggest that his rage was carrying him past the point of rationality: "I think no more of the Wall Street crowd than I do of [John L.] Lewis and Whitney. Let's give the country back to the people. Let's put transportation and production back to work, hang a few traitors, and make our own country safe for democracy. . . . Come on boys, let's do the job."[16]

Fortunately for Truman, cooler heads prevailed. Ross convinced him to have the speech rewritten. Clifford was given the difficult assignment of removing the venom from Truman's words without compromising the essential message, and he only had five hours to do it. Clifford's opening sentence suggested the gravity of the situation without the inflammatory rhetoric Truman had penned. That evening Truman declared, in Clifford's words, that the present situation was the "greatest crisis in this country since Pearl Harbor."[17] The next day, Saturday, May 25, Clifford came in early to prepare Truman's remarks for the joint session of Congress that afternoon. While he worked on the speech, John Steelman, a White House adviser who handled labor issues for Truman, worked behind the scenes with Johnston and Whitney to secure an agreement. Clifford barely completed the speech on time, handing Truman the final copy as the motorcade left for the Capitol. As Truman began his address to Congress, Clifford stepped into an anteroom, where he awaited what he hoped would be a call from Steelman. While Truman was speaking the call came in: Steelman told Clifford an agreement had been reached. Clifford scribbled a message for Truman: "Word has just been received that the railroad strike has been settled on the terms proposed by the President." Clifford handed the note to Leslie Biffle, the secretary of the Senate, who handed it to Truman just as he was reaching the climax of his speech. Truman paused to read the note, while Congress applauded his proposal to draft the striking workers into the military. In a scene that Hollywood could not have scripted any better, Truman then announced the settlement, which was greeted with thunderous applause. The railroad strike was over, and Truman had scored a major victory.

The railroad strike had been successfully resolved, but the labor dispute in the coal industry remained unsettled. John L. Lewis, the flamboyant and powerful leader of the United Mine Workers union (UMW), reneged on a temporary contract that had been agreed to in late May. Just prior to the 1946 elections he warned that if the entire contract was not renegotiated he would order 400,000 mine workers off the job. Coal was crucial to the U.S. economy: it provided more than half of all the country's electrical power and fueled the railroads. With winter approaching the sense of crisis seemed even more acute.

For Clifford, the coal strike of 1946 marked the first time he participated in a policy debate, as opposed to simply writing speeches. Truman and the Democrats had taken a beating in the midterm congressional elections, losing both the House and the Senate. Clifford was convinced that if Truman capitulated to Lewis he would be politically ruined, and he also believed that a showdown with Lewis would be an excellent opportunity to bolster the president's image. "Oh God, it was the chance of a lifetime," Clifford recalled years later. "Be right, be strong. Nobody's bigger than the President of the U.S."[18]

According to Clifford, Attorney General Tom Clark and Secretary of the Interior Julius Krug sided with him in taking a hard line against Lewis, but, "fearing [Lewis's] power, they were considerably more cautious."[19] A contemporary account in *U.S. News and World Report,* however, said that it was Krug who decided that Lewis should be opposed and that Krug brought Clifford over to his point of view.[20] Either way, they would have to convince Truman that theirs was the correct response.

Truman met with Clifford, Krug, Clark, and Steelman to discuss the situation on Saturday evening, November 16. The meeting at the White House did not start until midnight, after a black-tie reception earlier in the evening. Steelman advocated minor concessions, but Clifford strenuously disagreed and stood his ground. Clifford thought that Truman would win the battle of public opinion with Lewis and implored him to take a firm stand. "Mr. President," he said, "you have to take him on." Truman was persuaded, but warned that it would be "a fight to the finish." On Monday Attorney General Clark ordered the Justice Department to file an injunction demanding that Lewis call off the planned strike. Lewis, in response, openly defied the president and called for a nationwide strike on November 20. A few weeks later the Justice Department received a court order finding Lewis in contempt of court for violating the November injunction, and assessing an enormous fine of $3.5 million against the United Mine Workers and $10,000 against Lewis personally. Lewis had tried many times to contact the president to see if they could reach a compromise, but Clifford insisted on unconditional surrender and advised the president not to take any of the calls. For good measure, Clifford drafted a speech that was to be given on the anniversary of Pearl Harbor. In the speech Clifford compared the present strike and battle with the UMW to the Pearl Harbor attack, warning that the "present crisis has elements which make it just as ominous." By then, Lewis knew that he was beaten, and he ordered the miners back to work before Truman delivered the speech. Truman savored his latest victory. "The White House is open to anybody with legitimate business," he said, "but not to that son of a bitch."[21]

The union leader's capitulation was also a major victory for Clifford. He had taken a very visible and very vocal position in a crucial policy debate and had won the day. He had gained Truman's confidence and had scored a personal victory over Steelman, with whom he would frequently battle. Truman and Clifford also received recognition in the press. The *St. Louis Star Times* reported that the legal strategy Truman employed against Lewis was the idea of a St. Louis lawyer, Clifford. Columnists Joseph and Stewart Alsop opined that Truman had gained in stature as a result of his confrontation with Lewis, which was the product of "good advice." Just before the showdown with Lewis began they had reported that Clifford was emerging as Truman's "principal adviser."[22] Feigning dismay, Charlie Ross, the press secretary, told a reporter, "All I do around here is answer questions about the great Clark Clifford."[23] Truman biographer Robert Donovan later wrote that Clifford's instincts in the conflict with Lewis were flawless.[24]

Truman's victory over Lewis was badly needed. The elections a few weeks earlier had been a disaster, with the Republicans taking over both the House and Senate for the first time since 1928. Truman was weakened politically and looked, at best, like a caretaker president. From the left the recriminations came in waves, and Clifford was a target of criticism. Foremost were reports questioning his liberal credentials. The *Washington Daily News* reported: "There has been criticism in recent months, especially since Election Day, that the President has turned away from the New Deal, and sometimes blame is placed on Mr. Clifford. But Mr. Clifford denies that he is reactionary and doubts that he is conservative. Mr. Clifford thinks that 'Jeffersonian Democrat' might come closest to describing him. He believes in the Democratic Party, and that it, more than the Republican Party, will always be the party of the people."[25]

David Lilienthal, Truman's nominee to be the first chairman of the Atomic Energy Commission and a friend of Clifford's, noted in his journal in late December that there had been a "terrible deluge of publicity regarding Clifford."[26] *The New Republic* opined that Clifford "has somehow contrived to make Truman's swerve to the Right look as proper and dignified as a society funeral."[27] *Life* put a more favorable spin on it, suggesting that "Mr. Truman had found an associate of his own type, with grave misgivings about the New Deal, who had the courage of his convictions."[28]

A few months before the election Clifford had helped Truman with a little damage control, but the fallout had certainly contributed to the debacle in the fall elections. Henry Wallace, who had served as Roosevelt's vice president from 1941 to 1945, had been forced aside for the 1944 election that ultimately brought Truman to the Oval Office. In the interests of party unity Truman had appointed him secretary of commerce, but Wallace remained a volatile force in the administration. In September he gave a speech at Madison Square Garden during a New York gubernatorial campaign rally. In the speech he argued for a conciliatory policy toward the Soviet Union, which was inconsistent with Truman administration policy. Wallace had not cleared the speech with the State Department but instead met with Truman two days before he was scheduled to talk. Truman did not have the time to read the whole speech so Wallace ran through it quickly. Truman was apparently too preoccupied to focus on Wallace's underlying message and so did not recognize the fundamental shift in policy that Wallace was recommending. The press, having received a copy of Wallace's remarks on the day of the speech, questioned Truman about it at a press conference. He brushed off the question by claiming, incorrectly, that the speech was wholly consistent with his administration's foreign policy.

The papers the following morning revealed the magnitude of the president's blunder and suggested that he was out of touch with his own administration's foreign policy. The episode also exposed a rift in the Truman administration between Secretary of State James Byrnes and Wallace. Byrnes demanded that Wallace refrain from making statements on foreign policy and threatened to resign if he did not. Truman hoped the whole thing would blow over and also hoped that

Wallace would either retract his position or resign for the good of the administration. When he did neither, and in fact told Truman he planned to make a similar speech soon, Truman was furious. Wallace, he decided, was intentionally trying to weaken his presidency and would have to be fired.[29] A phone message to Clifford from Congressman Francis Walter of Pennsylvania revealed that Truman was not alone in his suspicions. "I have just received reliable information from a source that I am certain is correct that Mr. Wallace deliberately tried to embarrass the President with his speech," the message said.[30] Truman, without consulting with anyone on his staff, sent an angry letter to Wallace demanding his resignation. The next day he realized he had made a terrible mistake. In an effort to keep the letter from becoming public, which would have been tremendously embarrassing, Truman deputized Clifford to ask Wallace to return the letter. Clifford's personal diplomacy was successful, and Wallace returned the letter.

With the letter returned, Truman called Wallace and asked in a far more civil manner for his resignation, which Wallace immediately offered. Clifford confided to Lilienthal that he and Truman had been up much of the night discussing how to respond to Wallace's charges and how to announce that Wallace had been fired.[31] Clifford then drafted a statement for the president announcing Wallace's departure. "I am sure that Mr. Wallace will be happier in the exercise of his right to present his views as a private citizen," Truman said.[32] Wallace was gone from the Cabinet, but he would continue to haunt Truman through the 1948 elections. His departure, especially the messy way in which it transpired, was politically damaging. Wallace was the standard-bearer of the liberal wing of the Democratic Party, which thought that the White House rightfully belonged to him. At the very least the left was not energized for the midterm elections, and the Democrats expected to suffer serious losses to a revitalized Republican opposition running against a caretaker president. Wallace would make life difficult for Truman two years later when he ran as a third-party candidate in the presidential election of 1948.

In the aftermath of the 1946 midterm elections Truman and his advisers debated how to respond to the changed dynamic in Washington. James Rowe, a Washington lawyer and former Roosevelt aide who stayed active in politics, wrote a strategy memo debating whether the president should adopt a posture of cooperation or conflict vis-à-vis the Congress. Rowe, who had contacts in the Truman White House, had been asked to write the report by George Elsey and James

Sundquist of the Bureau of Budget. Rowe's lengthy report cited the Constitution, the Federalist Papers, and U.S. history and concluded that the president should not, and was indeed not obliged to, cooperate with an opposition Congress. "Because of the nature of American constitutional government and of the two-party system, it is inevitable that cooperation at a partnership level will prove unworkable," Rowe wrote. Elsey must have shared the memorandum with Clifford; a copy was found among Clifford's papers. On December 16, Clifford sent a memorandum to Truman summarizing the instances in which the president's party did not control Congress. It seems likely that he pulled this synopsis from Rowe's report, which had the same information in an appendix.[33] It would not be the last time Clifford passed along Rowe's work to the president without attribution.

It is likely that Clifford shared some of Rowe's ideas with Truman. With the exception of foreign policy, which was bipartisan and cooperative, Truman adopted a confrontational stance with the "do-nothing" Eightieth Congress. Rowe's tone was similarly confrontational. "They [Congress] have agreed generally that 'cooperation' is necessary," he wrote. "But they have made it equally plain that their definition of cooperation is abdication by the executive. . . . The probability of conflict, not cooperation, is the political reality with which the President must work for the next two years."[34]

The strategizing, of course, was not limited to Rowe. In response to the 1946 election, the liberals in the administration banded together to try to shape the course of the remaining two years of Truman's term and set strategy for 1948. At the Cabinet level most of Truman's advisers were conservatives, but the sub-Cabinet level was dominated by liberals. Oscar R. Ewing, the acting chairman of the Democratic National Committee and soon to become the administrator of the Federal Security Agency, the precursor to the Department of Health and Human Services, convened a group of these individuals to help advance the liberal agenda. The Monday Night Group, as it came to be known, met at Ewing's apartment in the Wardman Park Hotel. Also known as the Monday Night Steak Club or the Wardman Park Group, it consisted of Ewing; Clifford; Leon Keyserling, vice chairman of the president's Council of Economic Advisers; C. Girard Davidson, assistant secretary of the interior; Charles F. Brannan, assistant secretary of agriculture; David A. Morse, assistant secretary of labor; and J. Donald Kingsley, who would become Ewing's deputy at the Federal Security Agency.[35]

Clifford was actually not Ewing's first choice as a representative from the West Wing. Matthew Connelly, the president's appointments secretary, was initially asked to join, but he recommended Clifford instead. According to Ewing, Connelly "felt that Clark Clifford, who was counsel to the President, was really more involved than he was with policy matters, and that of all people in the White House Clark Clifford would be the best liaison between our group and the President. After we got started Clark Clifford carried on most of the liaison work between our group and the President."[36]

Describing his role, Clifford observed, "It was clear to the group that I was as important to the group as the group was to me, because I was their link with the President. It wouldn't do the group much good to arrive at conclusions on major issues of the day unless they felt that those views could be presented to the President."[37] Keyserling agreed, noting that "Clifford's role within the White House and his consummate skill, tact, and powers of persuasion with the president were unquestioned."[38]

The group kept no records or notes and, according to its members, met in secret. Despite the fairly high rank and number of the participants, the frequency of their meetings, and the time span over which they met, they claimed that word never leaked about the existence of the group and its agenda.[39] "It is interesting that although we met every Monday night at Ewing's apartment at the Wardman Park, had a wonderful steak dinner and then spent three or four hours together," Keyserling marveled, "there was never a single whisper of those meetings in any press in the United States to my recollection. It never got out. . . . No word of it got out."[40] According to Ewing, discretion was a paramount consideration, and that is why no notes or minutes were recorded and no one talked to the press.[41] Elsey disputes the notion that these meetings were secret. "Clark and Leon [Keyserling] in later years liked to play up the 'secrecy' of the sessions. It added to the glamour of their behind-the-scenes influence in shaping national policy. But 'Secret' they were not."[42] The importance of the group is subject to debate and is difficult to determine in the absence of documentary evidence. Alonzo Hamby thought the group was somewhat irrelevant, arguing that "from time to time [it] provided Truman with tactical ideas, rhetorical flourishes and arguments. It changed neither his basic ideological direction nor his political style."[43]

One result of the 1946 election was the rise in status of Clifford as one of Truman's important, if not the most important, White House advisers. The liberal versus conservative divide in the Truman administration was pronounced, and the success and failure of the competing factions would determine how the president governed for the remainder of his term and how he campaigned in 1948. In the White House the conservative faction was represented by Steelman, and the liberal standard-bearer was Clifford. Clifford described himself as a liberal but emphasized that his guiding philosophy was often pragmatism. In contrast to ideologically pure liberals, Clifford was driven by what was possible.[44] Clifford's associates believed that he was "unencumbered by any strong social philosophy or political conviction" and that flexibility accounted for a good deal of his influence.[45]

The competition between Steelman and Clifford was symbolic of the state of liberalism in the United States in the immediate postwar period. The greatest challenge of the time, manifested in the railroad and coal labor strikes, was to make the largest economic transition from a wartime to a peacetime economy in American history. Complicating this was the absence of a unifying force across the nation. Without the war, which had served as a unifying force, the different constituencies in the country became more focused on their own self-interest. Tempering this self-interest, however, was a pervasive fear that the Great Depression might return as the arsenal of democracy reverted back to its prewar footing. The mood of the country was thus shaped by the capitalist tendency to pursue one's self-interest, tempered by the fear that prosperity would be fleeting and that economic despair would return.[46] The challenge for liberalism was to balance the desire for a welfare state that provided the necessary safety net and a mild redistribution of income in the interests of equality while not constraining an expanding capitalist economy. As the 1946 elections demonstrated, this could be a challenging proposition.

The competition for influence between Steelman and Clifford was the result of more than ideology, however. To a large extent it was a function of how Truman administered his presidency. He had no chief of staff and essentially functioned in that role himself. In that environment and with their strong personalities, it was inevitable that Steelman and Clifford would frequently clash. According to White House staffer David Bell, "there were times in the White House when it looked as though there was a constant, continuous and rather disturbing jockeying for position and influence between Steelman and Clifford, the two senior substantive policy advisers on the President's staff."[47] Steelman's title, the assistant to the president, would suggest that he was more powerful than Clifford; but Clifford did not consider himself subordinate to anyone. The staff tended to congregate around both Steelman and Clifford, but Clifford had more influence.[48]

Clifford's rise in stature coincided with an improvement in Truman's fortunes. Although he did not have the authority of a designated and powerful chief of staff, Clifford was instrumental in instilling a sense of discipline to the administration. As an example, the embarrassment over the Wallace departure had been due to missteps on Truman's part. The entire incident could have been avoided if Wallace's speech had been vetted by staff. Truman's impatient and flippant response to a reporter's question only fanned the fire. Clifford convinced Truman to have senior staff approve all policy-related speeches by Cabinet members or other high-ranking members of the administration. He also recommended that Truman not meet with Cabinet members by himself.[49] With these changes in place, in June 1947 the *St. Louis Globe-Democrat* noted that "as the President turned more and more to his new counsel, the whole atmosphere around the West Wing seemed to change. An air of efficiency developed. Press-conference errors, such as the 'Wallace incident,' occurred less frequently." The paper also suggested that Clifford was instrumental in the improvement of Truman's polling numbers.[50] Hamby observed that "by early 1947, the entire White House seemed to be a much more professional, smoothly functioning operation. Much of the credit went to Clifford."[51]

Truman had complete confidence in Clifford, and his responsibilities as special counsel, always vaguely defined, expanded beyond speechwriting and communications. By virtue of his wise counsel in handling the Wallace situation and crushing John L. Lewis, Clifford became involved in almost every issue in the administration that was politically sensitive or dangerous. Truman often suggested that Cabinet members and other officials send their memorandums and policy recommendations directly to Clifford. "No, I don't need to see it in advance, but it's all right to check it with Clark," Truman would often say.[52]

Elsey reflected on Clifford's role in the administration and his relationship with the president:

I think the greatest value and virtue that Clifford had as a political adviser was his ability to take a long view of things. He tried not to think about tomorrow morning's headlines or what the radio commentator, or Drew Pearsons [*sic*], might say next week or so, but what effect it would have on the President, his administration, and the position of the United States over a very much longer time span. . . . Now, as to the effect, impact, of his advice, I think it would be hard to put your finger on particular pieces of advice that Clifford himself would be willing to say were *his*. He regarded his relationship with the President as being a very private, very confidential one. He would speak with the utmost candor to the President. Sometimes his advice prevailed, sometimes it did not. But he would not be one to let you know either way whether his advice had been taken or whether he had been overruled. Whatever came out of the President's Oval Office was it, that was the decision and he was, of course, completely loyal and darned effective in carrying out the President's wishes.[53]

Two or three times a week Truman and Clifford ate together in the basement lunchroom of the White House. Six to eight times a day Clifford walked the twenty paces that separated his office from Truman's door.[54] Arthur Krock, the Washington bureau chief for the *New York Times,* observed that Truman's prestige was on the rise and that "his young, able and devoted personal attorney, Clark Clifford, has been built up as the President's right arm and mentor."[55]

Clifford was a favorite with the press, which was later a source of aggravation for the president. He was a senior adviser to Truman, which in itself made him a newsworthy figure. However, the extensive attention paid to him was more than just a function of his position. Despite his proclivity for presenting himself in a modest light, Clifford sought out the press. In fact, other than Clifford himself, no one ever called him self-effacing.[56] Eben Ayers, Truman's assistant press secretary, recalled that Clifford drew attention to himself, especially relative to Clifford's successor, Charles Murphy.[57] Clifford, of course, would have quarreled with this characterization; he always presented himself as a tireless and anonymous servant of the president. When asked about his curious omission from Truman's memoirs, Clifford shrugged it off. A "staff member to a President does not expect to attain any particular place in history through the occupying of that position," he said. "You are there to *serve* the President."[58] On another occasion, Clifford told a reporter, "The talk that I am a power and an influence in the White House is a lot of bunk. I dig up and correlate material on any particular subject for the president. He does the controlling and he alone makes the decisions. Nobody makes them for him. I never knew a man who was more set in his beliefs."[59] Yet despite Clifford's disclaimer, Truman was probably weary of the speculation that Clifford was controlling his administration's agenda and exacted some measure of retribution by omitting mention of his subordinate from his memoirs.

The press was fascinated with Clifford on a number of levels. A common theme, however trivial, was the leading-man image that Clifford cut. *The New Republic* wrote, "Clifford sparkles like a jewel because of the mediocrity of those around him and because he is undoubtedly the most decorative male ever to work at 1600 Pennsylvania Avenue."[60] The *Washington Daily News* stated, "Clark Clifford is tall, blond, handsome, impressively competent and friendly."[61] The *St. Louis Globe-Democrat* described Clifford as the "'Golden Boy' of Washington," and *Life* gushed that he "has been called the most gorgeous hunk of man to hit Washington since Paul McNutt," who was administrator of the Federal Security Agency from 1939 to 1945.[62] *Life* observed that his hair looked like it had been waved with a micrometer and reported that his enemies had been spreading a nasty rumor that he had his hair curled. The source of that rumor was believed to be Steelman.[63]

Another factor driving the extensive coverage he received in the press was his role as conduit for leaked information. Arthur Krock, for example, was the recipient of many stories leaked by Clifford over more than twenty years.[64] In the crude parlance of the day, Clifford was a "Krock-sucker."[65] Later in Clifford's career, veteran reporter Jack Anderson was another beneficiary of Clifford's leaks, yet his characterization of Clifford is telling. "Clifford was a leaker," he recalled. "He knew who to leak to. He leaked to the people who could do him good or do him harm. He leaked to me when I could hurt him. Those who practiced that kind of journalism loved him. You never left his office empty handed."[66] Clifford had been in Washington for scarcely two years, yet he had learned the importance of the care and feeding of the press. Reporters are not inclined to bite the hand that feeds them, and thus treat their reliable sources with care. As a trusted source Clifford was bound to be the recipient of favorable press coverage.

The fortuitous circumstances surrounding his ascension to the corridors of power provided fertile ground for fawning press coverage. Clifford's all-American biography was itself worthy of note. Although his was not as impressive a rise as Truman's from small-town farmer to president, Clifford was not the prototype eastern Establishment figure like most of the senior officials in Roosevelt's administration. He just happened to know someone from Missouri with the right connections, which gave him the opportunity to be in the right place at the right time. The fact that he was not an Establishment figure may have worked to his advantage with respect to the press. As one reporter observed, Clifford was different from the Roosevelt White House "prima donnas who used to flit in and out the side doors of the White House during FDR's brain-trusting period."[67] After covering Roosevelt's administration for twelve years, an appealing figure from the heartland was just the type of fresh face the press wanted to write about.

The coverage was not always favorable, of course, and after the 1946 elections Clifford received a fair amount of blame from the left for leading Truman away from the New Deal and to defeat in the midterm elections, although it was not clear that one caused the other. On one occasion the press's treatment of Clifford was particularly scathing. The Gridiron Club's annual dinner was an event that mixed the press, high Washington officials, and an endless array of satirical skits. The relaxed atmosphere and the social setting were enjoyed by the senior Washington reporters and government officials in attendance, except for those who were the target of the more malicious skits. At the 1947 dinner, Clifford was a prime target. A skit that evening depicted Truman as a marionette controlled by a smug, heavily made up, and all-powerful Clifford. Mortified, Clifford gingerly approached the president Monday morning to apologize, but Truman brushed it off with a smile. "Clark, pay it no attention," he said. "That is what Washington is all about. Anyway, I am the target, not you, and they will always find something to use against me."[68] Truman's choice of words is interesting; it suggests that he may have had two objectives in mind. On the one hand he was trying to put an embarrassed staffer at ease; on the other hand he may have been trying to knock Clifford down a peg or two. "I am the target" may have been Truman's way of reminding his subordinate of their respective roles in the White House hierarchy. Clifford, after all, had been described as one who had more in common with actors than his movie-star good looks. He always seemed aware that he had an audience.[69]

Clifford's acceptance into Truman's inner circle says as much about the man as does his emergence as a White House press corps favorite. One factor, not to be underestimated, was Clifford and Truman's common heritage as Missourians. Articles that mentioned Clifford's Missouri background only to dismiss it by noting that Clifford was not an old Truman crony surely missed the point. It is true that Clifford was not a Truman crony from Missouri like Ross, Vardaman, or military aide Harry Vaughan. But as a fellow Missourian, Clifford was someone that Truman was more comfortable with than the eastern Establishment holdovers from the Roosevelt administration. According to Clifford, "The whole relationship between the President and me was a highly personal one. It developed because there was a vacuum in the White House. We were both from Missouri. He was comfortable with me."[70] David Lilienthal attributed a good deal of Clifford's enormous influence with Truman to the ability to speak and write in a language that Truman could understand. Like many midwesterners, Truman disdained the vocabulary of New Deal intellectuals.[71] Rosenman overstated his case in describing Clifford as a pedestrian writer, but either way what Rosenman considered to be a deficiency was actually an advantage for someone writing speeches for Truman. Clifford's special talent was to enable Truman to sound like Truman rather than Truman trying, and failing, to sound like FDR, as the *New York Times* reported: "It is Clifford more than anyone else . . . who convinced the President that he should not be Franklin Roosevelt, but Harry Truman, that he should no longer try to speak in the Harvard accents, but with a Missouri twang; that in place of oratory he should offer his own brand of 'common sense.' That was the trick—as simple as that—and thus far it seems to be working."[72]

In addition to speaking the same language Truman also appreciated Clifford because he was not a Roosevelt man. FDR's advisers were gradually eased out as Truman brought in individuals loyal to him. Clifford had never served under Roosevelt, so his allegiance lay indisputably with Truman. Perhaps Clifford's greatest contributions to the Truman presidency were his efforts, first, to help the president emerge from the shadow of Roosevelt and, second, to present Truman as a strong leader in his own right. The showdown with Lewis is a prime example of Clifford's recognition that Truman needed to do more than be a competent caretaker president. Truman had to convince the public that he was a strong leader, and, as the White House adviser filling the role of the modern communications office, translating that objective into action fell on Clifford's shoulders. A Roosevelt holdover could never have succeeded at that goal because comparisons between the two men would inevitably undermine the message. Rosenman was valuable to Truman, but Clifford became far more valuable because he owed his success to the opportunities presented to him in the current administration, not the previous one.

Clifford's talent for ingratiating himself with those in authority as well as those who could help him certainly contributed to his being accepted into Truman's closest circle of advisers. This is nothing new; stroking the egos of powerful individuals is not unique to Washington culture or to the Truman presidency. But Clifford's efforts went beyond mere flattery as he transformed his personality to serve his new boss. As an example, there are few things that Harry Truman enjoyed more than a stag evening of bourbon and poker. Official business (beyond political gossip) rarely intruded on these social occasions, but it was inevitable that those who were in attendance had more access to the president and thus the opportunity to transform that access into intimacy and trust. The core group of players included George Allen, a businessman, lobbyist, and influential player in the Democratic National Committee; Secretary of the Air Force Stuart Symington, a fellow Missourian and close friend of Clifford's going back to 1936; Secretary of Agriculture Clinton Anderson; and Fred Vinson, secretary of the treasury and later chief justice of the Supreme Court. Occasionally joining the game were Averell Harriman, the secretary of commerce, later the governor of New York, and a trusted adviser to three presidents; and, later, Congressman Lyndon Johnson.

Jake Vardaman, Clifford's predecessor as naval aide, did not share Truman's love of a few social drinks and friendly game of cards. After Vardaman was named naval aide Truman suggested that they celebrate with a drink, to which Vardaman responded that he did not drink. A visibly disappointed Truman then invited Vardaman to join him and "some of the boys" for a game of poker that evening. Vardaman disappointed Truman again by responding that he did not play cards either, which effectively brought their meeting to an end. No doubt unmindful of how his abrasive manner ended his tenure as naval aide, Vardaman suggested that his unwillingness to "do in Rome" accounted for his appointment as a governor of the Federal Reserve Board. "And this is the only time that clean living ever got anybody a promotion in the Truman administration," Vardaman said.[73]

Although like his predecessor he was not a poker player, Clifford did not turn down the invitation to play, first as a replacement, then as a regular. Truman also asked Clifford to assume responsibility for organizing the games, a role he did not relinquish even after resigning from the White House in January 1950. So as not to make a fool of himself, or risk losing too much money, Clifford studied the tactics and strategy of the game. "I bought a book on poker and studied it assiduously," he wrote.[74] In addition to playing and organizing the games Clifford was also the banker, responsible for distributing a $500 stack of chips to each player and for the "poverty bowl," a safety net funded by a 10 percent levy of each pot. Because they played for enough money "to keep things interesting" yet not so much that anyone could get hurt, and given the fact that they were playing with the most powerful man in the world, as the banker Clifford could find himself in some delicate situations. On one occasion Truman had a bad evening and lost $700. He took out his checkbook and began to write a check to cover his losses, but Clifford stopped him. "No checks, Mr. President," he said. "I'll take care of this and you can take care of me tomorrow."[75]

It is hard to picture someone described as "glamorous," "too good to be true," and "blessed with Southern charm, but not burdened with South political prejudices" sitting at a table playing poker and drinking bourbon. Indeed, the press reported that he did not. "He does not like cigars, bourbon whiskey, or poker playing," wrote the *St. Louis Globe-Democrat.*[76]

The president's poker evenings were typical of the relaxed relationship he had with key staff and Cabinet members. These interludes often carried over to weekend getaways and longer vacations. Truman was fond of the presidential yacht, the *Williamsburg,* and would often take his poker buddies aboard for the weekend. When it came time to vacation his favorite spots were Key West or the *Williamsburg* for an extended cruise, and he would often take along his closest aides. The usual group included Vaughan, Ross, and Clifford, among others, and Clifford continued to join the president even after he resigned from the White House. Although Truman brought staff members with him, he did little work on these trips but instead brought them for companionship. Clifford cherished these trips, not just for the interludes of leisure that they promised but also because of the opportunity to enjoy personal time with the president.

Patrick Anderson wrote insightfully that "Clifford was the only Truman aide who spoke both the language of Missouri and the language of Harvard and Wall Street as well."[77] This is indicative of one of Clifford's greatest talents. For instance, in 1949 he warned the president that in an effort to hunt down disloyalty to the government, the United States risked jeopardizing civil liberties. "I'm afraid we are moving increasingly in that direction," he wrote, "to riddle the barn door in order to hit the knothole." This ability to communicate with Truman using farm colloquialisms was a contributing factor to Clifford's success in communicating with and influencing the president. In fact, however, Clifford was born in the city of St. Louis and had never lived on a farm. Farm sayings were not second nature to him; they had to be learned and incorporated into his speech. To communicate with a boss who dismissed the political acumen of a group of reporters by claiming that "none of them has enough sense to pound sand into a rathole" or who suggested that Henry Morgenthau "did not know shit from apple butter" required learning and practicing the boss's language. Clifford did.

Clifford also ingratiated himself with the Truman family. Truman idolized his mother and adored his wife, Bess, and daughter, Margaret. For years Clifford had an uncomfortable relationship with Margaret, who did not completely trust him, but he cultivated and nurtured close relationships with Bess and Truman's mother. Clifford frequently exchanged social correspondence with Bess, especially around the holidays, which increased the level of intimacy he had with the president. In fact, others began to notice the unusual degree of closeness that Clifford enjoyed with the president, and members of the White House staff began to use him as a go-between, certain that through Clifford their ideas would receive a favorable hearing with the president.[78] Clifford would maintain a regular correspondence with Truman and Bess long after the end of Truman's presidency. He cultivated and nurtured relationships; they were the stock of his trade. According to Eben Ayers, Clifford "made contacts with the higher officials in the Government, Cabinet members and so on deliberately and where he saw it to his advantage."[79]

Clifford worked hard to protect and preserve the personal relationship he had formed with Truman. The weekly lunches, the poker games, the staff vacations, his use of farm imagery, his relationship with Bess and Truman's mother, and his Missouri background were critical to Clifford's keeping himself in Truman's good graces and ensuring that he remained a central figure in the administration. Because there was no chief of staff in the Truman White House, no one other than the president himself could limit access to the president. Clifford's work habits also assured that he had plenty of face time with the president, especially in private, and he made a point of being the last person to meet with the president at the end of the day. Clifford later wrote, "Nothing was off limits during our private discussions. It was the perfect time to reflect on the day and look ahead, and the President, who often had a bourbon and branch water as we talked, seemed to enjoy the interval between the working day and the evening. Those fifteen minutes were the most important of my day."[80] They were the most important, of course, because they afforded Clifford time with the president without the presence of other senior members of the administration. Furthermore, these meetings ensured that Clifford always got in the last word with the president at the end of the day. As a result, Clifford enjoyed a tremendous advantage over advisers with whom he had differences of opinion, such as Steelman.

By the spring of 1947, Clifford's influence in the Truman White House was unrivaled. In about a year and a half he had gone from being an understudy in the role of potted palm to one of the most powerful men in the West Wing. He was the president's speechwriter and political strategist, and he handled a good deal of the legislative work with Congress.[81] His power, however, was circumscribed by the fact that he did not possess administrative power over any executive agencies or departments. Rather, Clifford was an important figure because of his intellectual and political influence on Truman.[82] "The title of Special Counsel was grand," Clifford wrote, "but the job had no power or authority other than that conferred by the President. In a pattern that was to continue throughout my career, my value was as an adviser or counselor, and not as an administrator or bureaucrat."[83] Nor was his power unlimited. As one historian observed, despite his unquestioned executive ability and political savvy, Clifford never had extensive control over coordinating legislative planning or the broad right to speak authoritatively for the president, features that characterized the role of Kennedy and Johnson aides Theodore Sorensen, Bill Moyers, and Joseph Califano.[84]

Clifford's primary value to Truman, as mentioned earlier, was the level of professionalism and competence he instilled in the White House. Amazing, relative to the staffing levels of the modern White House, was the shadow Clifford was able to cast with only one full-time assistant, George Elsey. In addition to being intelligent and competent, Clifford was a workaholic, and this enabled him to handle the many assignments that came his way. He was also fortunate to have the tremendously capable Elsey as his deputy.

If Clifford was overworked, at least some of the blame must fall on his own shoulders. He jealously guarded many of his assignments and responsibilities and was not inclined to share them with others in the White House. "It is noticeable that Clifford takes up a variety of matters that might well be passed to other members of the staff or that should come through them," Ayers confided to his diary.[85] In addition, in what would become a pattern throughout his career, Clifford had no qualms about taking the credit for other people's work. In fact, two of his most prominent accomplishments during the Truman administration could properly be credited to someone else. Ayers recalled that "Clifford is credited with writing the speeches and had a large part in many of them, if not most of those recently, but much of the work has been done by others . . . I think he got credit for some of which perhaps others contributed the major part."[86]

Clifford's greatest strength was his talent as a presenter of other people's ideas. He was not an idea man but rather the one who brought a fully or mostly formed idea to the president. Leon Keyserling recalled Clifford's role in the Truman White House. "Now, in some ways, David Bell and David Lloyd were more 'idea men,' in a conventional sense, than Mr. Clifford was," he said. "Clifford was, without equal, the synthesizer and operator."[87] *Time* magazine concurred, noting that "one of the chief reasons for Clifford's rise has been his methodical practice of meticulously copying down the thoughts of the various men around the President, carefully sorting them out and then presenting them in a manner which suits Harry Truman to a T."[88] Clifford's smooth, confident demeanor, his deep baritone voice, his appearance, and his superior presentation skills made him a formidable champion of the policy recommendations he brought to the president. Drawing on his experience as a trial attorney, Clifford often described his preparation for an important meeting as preparing a case for the court.

In some ways it seems improbable that a man like Clifford could have brought order and efficiency to the White House. He was very territorial over his own assignments and responsibilities, yet frequently accepted credit for other people's work. He did not have, and perhaps did not want, sufficient resources to delegate his work, and he was engaged in a long-simmering feud with another senior adviser, John Steelman. It would not seem that those factors would be a recipe for efficiency, and yet Clifford did bring both efficiency and discipline to the White House. Richard E. Neustadt of the Bureau of Budget and later a professor of government at Harvard said, "It is interesting to note that divisions of responsibility within the White House were never as clearly felt or acted on as during the period of sharp tension when Clifford was counsel. In 1947/48 when power within the staff was relatively polarized and jealously guarded, staff operations probably were their most effective."[89]

Oscar Chapman, the undersecretary of the Interior Department, when asked if Clifford was valuable, replied that he was "unusual": "I don't want to belabor the question," he said, "but he's a very unusual man. First, he has a wonderful memory, remembering things; second, his word is so completely accepted as being absolutely bona fide and accurate when he tells you something. You can depend on him. . . . I soon came to believe that Mr. Clifford was one of the very top advisers to the President in his value to advising him on political matters." Respectful of Clifford's toughness, Chapman also suggested that it was better to be on Clifford's side if one got into some bureaucratic infighting.[90]

Through a combination of happenstance, tenacity, and talent, Clark Clifford had traveled from a midwestern law office to the White House. Given a unique opportunity, he soon established himself as the primary adviser to the president of the United States and the Golden Boy of Washington.

## 2

# The Elsey Report

For better or worse, the defining moment of the Truman administration was the emergence of the Cold War. The transformation of the United States and the Soviet Union from wartime allies to Cold War antagonists was one of the more significant events in twentieth-century American history. While his foreign policy contributions pale in comparison to those of Dean Acheson, George Kennan, and George Marshall, Clifford's intimacy with the president guaranteed him a place at the table. Although his contribution may have been overlooked by historians, it was not overlooked by Clifford.

Clifford believed that the Cold War began on September 24, 1946, the day he presented a report, "American Relations with the Soviet Union," to the president.[1] A synthesis of the thinking of Truman's senior foreign policy advisers, the report argued in blunt language that the Soviet Union was an expansionist power and that it posed a threat to the national security of the United States and its allies. Six months later Truman announced that "it must be the policy of the United States to give support to free peoples who are attempting to resist subjugation by armed minorities and outside forces": the Truman Doctrine.[2] In Clifford's opinion, the Clifford-Elsey report, as it has come to be known, "contained the seeds of the Marshall Plan, the seeds of NATO, and the basic principles upon which the President relied for the Truman Doctrine."[3]

It is debatable just how influential the Clifford-Elsey report was, and historians continue to argue over the exact date the Cold War began. What is not debatable is the authorship of the report. Most historians credit George Elsey as the primary author, despite Clifford's boasts that he wrote it. Perhaps more significant is that to the extent that it was important and influential, it was due to Elsey's conviction and sheer tenacity. Truman had a very limited assignment in mind when he requested the report, and that is likely the reason he gave the assignment to Clifford. Elsey convinced Clifford, who in turn convinced Truman, that a more comprehensive study was needed. The resulting exhaustive study of U.S.-Soviet relations, which Elsey compiled with minimal assistance from Clifford, is a significant historical document, whereas the simple report Truman requested would likely not have been. One of Clifford's signature accomplishments, therefore, properly belongs to George Elsey.

U.S.-Soviet relations began to deteriorate as early as the waning days of World War II. Truman's April 1945 lecture to Soviet foreign minister Vyacheslav Molotov, in which he admonished the Soviets to honor their wartime commitments, fell on deaf ears as the Soviet Union moved quickly to establish a sphere of influence and a buffer against a potentially resurgent Germany in Eastern Europe. One by one, regimes friendly to the Soviet Union assumed power in Poland, Hungary, Romania, Bulgaria, Yugoslavia, and Albania. By January 1946, a frustrated Truman told Secretary of State James Byrnes that he was "tired of babying the Soviets."[4]

George Kennan, who was temporarily running the American embassy in Moscow, prepared a lengthy analysis of Soviet-American relations in February 1946. Drawing on firsthand experience and his extensive knowledge of their history, Kennan argued that the Soviets were an expansive power antagonistic to the West. Furthermore, he argued that because of their historical insecurities and suspicion it was useless to attempt to negotiate with them. Kennan found an avid fan in Secretary of the Navy James Forrestal, who urged everyone in the administration to read the "Long Telegram," as it came to be known. According to Clifford, the Long Telegram "was probably the most important, and influential, message ever to be sent to Washington by an American diplomat."[5]

At the time he wrote the Long Telegram, however, Kennan was a virtual unknown. Less than two weeks after Kennan sent his telegram, a figure of unquestionable stature sounded the warning of an expansionist, militant Soviet Union. Winston Churchill coined the phrase "Iron Curtain" in a speech at Westminster College in Fulton, Missouri. As only a great orator could, Churchill's metaphor encapsulated the fear and suspicion of an ideologically and militarily divided Europe:

> From Stettin in the Baltic to Trieste in the Adriatic, an Iron Curtain has descended across the Continent. Behind that line

lie all the capitals of the ancient states of central and eastern Europe—Warsaw, Berlin, Prague, Vienna, Budapest, Bucharest and Sofia, all these famous cities and their populations around them lie in what I might call the Soviet sphere, and are all subject, in one form or another, not only to Soviet influence but to a very high and in some cases increasing measure of control from Moscow.[6]

Despite the ominous warnings of Churchill and Kennan, Truman continued to be hopeful of reaching an accommodation with the Soviets. During the spring and summer of 1946, however, two events began to solidify American suspicions of Soviet intentions. Stalin's refusal to remove Soviet troops from Iran by the March 2 deadline agreed to at the close of World War II and the collapse of cooperation in occupied Germany deepened Truman's fear that the Soviets could not be trusted. During a July 12 afternoon meeting, over drinks, Truman mused over the subject. Speaking to Clifford he declared that "now is the time to take a stand on Russia." He was "tired of being pushed around. Here a little, there a little, they are chiseling from us." Truman warned that the upcoming foreign ministers' conference in Paris would be "a failure if Russians want too much because we are not going to back down." Truman, Clifford recalled, "rambled on, talking and thinking aloud"; then he decided that he had to make his case of Soviet perfidy to the American people as well as the entire world.[7] With that in mind, Truman asked Clifford to prepare a report that cataloged Soviet violations of their treaties and agreements.

Truman's choice of Clifford for such an assignment is curious, given that up until then he had focused on domestic issues and had only negligible experience with foreign policy matters. The logical choice for a foreign policy study would have been someone from the State Department. Clifford is silent as to why Truman tapped him for an assignment that was clearly outside his purview. The reason is clear enough, however, in light of the fact that Truman asked only for a list of Soviet violations of their international agreements. In addition, based upon Clifford's account as well as Elsey's notes, it seems that Truman gave Clifford the assignment impulsively. Clifford's recollection of this meeting differs from Elsey's contemporary notes in one important respect: Clifford describes the meeting as a "staff meeting,"[8] whereas Elsey describes it as an afternoon meeting over drinks. The distinction is significant, as it is suggestive of Truman's expectations. Assignments made during a staff meeting would carry a higher priority than those discussed during a more casual afternoon meeting. It may be inferred from the evidence from both sources that this was indeed a casual meeting: it was over drinks and Truman was "rambling on and thinking aloud." Elsey's account seems the more credible of the two, as it is taken from notes made at the time, whereas Clifford's is based upon his recollection more than forty years later.[9]

A simple itemization of Soviet transgressions was something that could be prepared quite easily with a little help from the State Department. Clifford delegated the assignment to Elsey, who had a fair amount of exposure to national security issues as a result of his tenure as the naval reserve officer assigned to the White House Map Room. Elsey was alarmed by the steady stream of intelligence reports coming in from Europe outlining Soviet moves to consolidate their sphere of influence in Eastern Europe. He was convinced that the limited report that Truman was suggesting was insufficient. Elsey argued to Clifford that the boss was missing the point and that the violations were only a symptom of the larger problem: that Soviet-American relations were broken.[10] As Elsey said later, "I thought the whole question of our relations with the Soviet Union at that point was a much more comprehensive, much broader, matter than this technicality of agreement breaking or agreement keeping, that there were far more fundamental issues involved, that the nature of these issues didn't seem to be clearly understood in large parts of the executive branch (witness the fiasco of Henry Wallace)."[11] Instead, argued Elsey, what was needed was a report that combined a discussion of Soviet violations along with an analysis of the state of Soviet-American relations and a set of policy recommendations. He recommended that the report be based on consultations with senior officials in the foreign policy bureaucracy in order to provide Truman with a consensus opinion.

Clifford agreed to the broadened scope of the report, although Elsey's account suggests that his enthusiasm was only lukewarm. He recalled that Clifford said, "Do whatever you want. Go ahead."[12] Clifford did not have the opportunity to discuss Elsey's suggestion with Truman until four days later, by which time Elsey was already worried that the study was behind schedule. Elsey's personal notes suggest that he regretted that other priorities precluded him from starting work on the project.[13] Truman gave Clifford the go-ahead for the expanded scope, but held firm to the original due date. Truman was not anticipating an extensive position paper, as his initial expectation was simply to be given an account of Soviet violations of international agreements. As far as Truman was concerned, anything more would be nice to have, provided that Clifford and Elsey could deliver the report on time.

Elsey's eagerness for this assignment was a product of more than mere ambition. In his mind the administration was not properly focused on the Soviet issue and such a report could be used to educate those who were not in line, such as Wallace. "I tackled it with a real zeal," Elsey said, "because I felt very deeply the necessity of this kind of thing."[14] His experience in the Map Room as well as his familiarity with Kennan's Long Telegram convinced Elsey that the Soviets could no longer be considered an ally, but instead were a dangerous adversary. He also thought the report would serve to educate Clifford about the seriousness of the situation. According to Elsey, as of the summer of 1946 Clifford had been blind to the threat posed by Moscow. Since joining the Truman administration Clifford had been focused solely on domestic issues. He was a novice as far as foreign policy was concerned and had not even been thinking about it. As a close adviser to the president, Clifford, Elsey believed, had to start paying attention to the Soviet issue. "I think the principal value of that report," Elsey said, "was to educate Clark that, by God, here are some serious subjects *he's* got to start thinking about."[15]

Elsey drafted letters for Clifford's signature to the key players in the Truman foreign policy apparatus: Admiral William Leahy, who represented the Joint Chiefs of Staff; Secretary of State James Byrnes; Under Secretary of State Dean Acheson; Secretary of War Robert Patterson; Secretary of the Navy James Forrestal; Attorney General Tom Clark; and Central Intelligence group director Admiral Sydney Souers. Kennan was also consulted, as was his friend and fellow Soviet expert Charles Bohlen.[16] Clifford and Elsey met to discuss the project on July 17, but Clifford had not yet reviewed the draft letters. Elsey's impatience had been building, and he privately blamed Clifford for the delay. "I have kept prodding him this afternoon and the previous to sit down tomorrow & get into the matter of my drafts," he wrote. "So far he has done nothing." He was also more than a little annoyed when Clifford assured the president that he was working on it. "Slight exaggeration!" he wrote.[17]

Elsey was also frustrated that he and Clifford did not agree on the content and organization of the report. Elsey had thought they were on the same wavelength after their initial discussion, but it was clear five days later that such was not the case. "CMC [Clifford] then began to muse on what form our report should take," he wrote. "This was in rough form (my notes attached). It seems to me that he still does not see this as being the just all-inclusive evaluation & definition of policy that I see it."[18] Clifford's draft outline remained limited to a catalog of Soviet violations of agreements. Clifford and Elsey still failed to see eye to eye two days later, by which time the letters had already gone out. "He still does not apparently view this with the scope that I do," Elsey confided in his personal notes.[19] In the end, however, Elsey must have prevailed, as the report took shape largely as he had originally conceived it.

As Elsey and Clifford sparred over the scope of the report, they encountered some bureaucratic difficulties as well. Leahy felt slighted that a major evaluation of Soviet-American relations could be assigned without his knowing about it. Furthermore, he thought it should have been assigned to him.[20] Clifford managed both to smooth Leahy's ruffled feathers and to make clear that he was acting at the president's direction. Clifford might have avoided the embarrassment, however, had he been more attentive to the real nature of the assignment. Elsey's letters alluded to a comprehensive evaluation of U.S.-Soviet relations, but Clifford was still seeing it as a limited study of treaty violations. Had he recognized what Clifford was asking for, he might have handled the situation in a way that would have avoided stepping on toes.

Clifford also called on Secretary of State Byrnes, a man whom Clifford described as "difficult to like." Byrnes, like Henry Wallace, believed that he rightfully should have been the president. Byrnes had been the front-runner for the vice presidential nomination after Wallace was cast aside, but at the last minute Roosevelt decided to select Truman as his running mate.

As with Leahy, Byrnes was surprised and agitated that the assignment had not been given to him. Byrnes's reaction was even stronger than Leahy's, understandable since the project would logically have fallen within the State Department's jurisdiction. Byrnes, on learning of the assignment, offered his tepid assistance, with the caveat that he was not sure how helpful he could be. According to Clifford, Byrnes sarcastically asserted that he was not aware of "every agreement" Roosevelt had made with the Soviets. He claimed that some might be filed with Harry Hopkins's private papers and others "buried" in Roosevelt's papers. When Clifford recounted his conversation with Byrnes, Elsey reacted with uncharacteristic anger, saying that Byrnes had already been proven to be a liar on this subject. Byrnes had denied having had any knowledge of the Roosevelt-Stalin agreement at Yalta in February 1945 until after the Potsdam conference in August. Elsey, however, was certain that he had briefed Byrnes on it in April and May. Elsey had been responsible for filing the records of Roosevelt's wartime conferences and had personally delivered every wartime agreement to Byrnes prior to the latter's confirmation as secretary of state. "Byrnes," Elsey told Clifford, "was trying to pass off some of the blame for his lack of success in dealing with the Russians on 'secret' agreements made by Roosevelt."[21]

Truman had told Clifford that he expected the report by August 8, an unreasonably short time frame for the in-depth report Elsey had in mind but appropriate for the narrow study Truman had originally requested. When Clifford asked Elsey if the report was ready, he was again reminded that Elsey believed that a limited account of Soviet violations was only a symptom of a larger problem. "Our concern is, why the Soviet Union violates her agreements, not how," Elsey argued. "This leads us into a consideration of Soviet policy, & the nature & characteristics of Soviet leadership." Here again, Clifford seemed to be out of touch with what Elsey was thinking. Clifford was initially upset, although Elsey was finally able to persuade him of the merits of his approach.[22] What is most intriguing about this conversation is that it was even necessary. Clifford and Elsey had already had this discussion a few times, and in Elsey's mind, he had both Clifford's and Truman's approval to proceed.

Clifford went to Truman and asked for a short extension, which the president approved. The president was planning a vacation cruise on the presidential yacht the *Williamsburg* starting August 16 and hoped to read the report at that time. An extra week was not enough time; the August 16 deadline came and went. Clifford must have explained to Truman that the expanded scope would delay completion of the report. If Truman was annoyed, the anticipation of an extended vacation must have been enough of a distraction to let his mind wander to other things. In the latter part of August the president enjoyed his first extended vacation aboard the *Williamsburg,* spending two weeks cruising the Atlantic. As was his habit, he brought along his closest aides for the entire trip, including Clifford, press secretary Charlie Ross, and his military aide and Missouri crony Harry Vaughan. Other staff members came aboard for parts of the trip, and the president was also accompanied by a bevy of reporters and photographers. Despite the fact that he brought along staff and the press, Truman remained focused on the business at hand, volleyball, and little work was done.[23]

While Clifford and the president were vacationing, Elsey was back in Washington, toiling on his report. On August 21 he sent an outline of the full report along with drafts of the first two chapters to Clifford. Elsey continued his efforts to impress upon Clifford the seriousness of the emerging situation in Russia. On August 27 he forwarded a message from Elbridge Durbrow, who had replaced George Kennan as the chargé d'affaires in Moscow, which echoed the emerging tone of the report. In his cover note, Elsey wrote: "The implications and significance of this message are such that I believe you should see it in connection with our Russian study. This is a truly terrifying confirmation of some of the statements occurring in the first chapter of our report about the extent to which leaders of the Communist party dominate every phase of life and thinking of the Russian people."[24]

Clifford replied the next day, telling Elsey that Truman had changed the itinerary and that they would not return until September 1. He and Elsey would not be able to confer on the report until then. The delay did not make much of a difference, though, as Clifford had not yet even looked at the material. Perhaps looking for some assistance, Elsey forwarded some draft chapters to Kennan, who followed up with six single-spaced pages of comments. "I think the general tone is excellent and I have no fault to find with it," Kennan wrote.[25] Even after Clifford returned, Elsey continued to shoulder the entire burden. Clifford's draft copy of the full report reveals his minimal contribution, just a few minor wording changes. Elsey commented in his private notes that "this copy is particularly interesting to GME [Elsey] because it shows the *only* and *very few* things done by CMC to the report. He did nothing but change a few words."[26]

Clifford and Elsey took a few more weeks to edit the final report and send it out for printing. Clifford prepared a cover note and delivered it to the president on September 24. Clifford's home phone rang at 7:00 the next morning. The president was on the other end of the line, to Clifford's surprise. "I stayed up very late last night reading your report," he said. "Powerful stuff."

"Thank you, Mr. President," Clifford replied.

"Clark, how many copies of this memorandum do you have?"

"Twenty," Clifford replied.

"Have any been distributed yet?"

"No sir. They are all in my safe at the office."

"Well please come down to your office now, and get all twenty copies. I want them delivered to me at once."

Clifford did as instructed and brought all twenty copies to the Oval Office. Truman said that he had carefully read the report and that he found it valuable. He was concerned, however, that if the report leaked out "it would blow the roof off the White House, it would blow the roof off the Kremlin." Truman then took the copies from Clifford, and that was the end of it.[27]

The Clifford-Elsey report did not leak until it appeared in Arthur Krock's memoirs, *Sixty Years on the Firing Line,* decades later. Krock, a reporter for the *New York Times,* interviewed Truman in 1966 while compiling material for his memoirs. Truman told him about the existence of a secret report regarding U.S.-Soviet relations. Krock then approached Clifford, who had been a regular source of leaks during the Truman administration. Clifford felt that after twenty years the material was no longer sensitive, and he agreed to share the final draft copy he had in his possession on a "background basis."[28] In his oral history at the Truman Library, Clifford claims that he allowed Krock to read the report, but insisted that Krock read it in Clifford's office. "Now, whether thereafter he went out and was able to find a copy of it to put in his book, I do not know," Clifford said. "It was done without consulting me." Krock and he had a misunderstanding, said Clifford.[29]

Clifford's account strains the bounds of credibility. As he conceded, the report remained a secret until Krock's interview with Truman in 1966. The original and all known copies remained in Truman's possession; the Truman Library did not make them available to researchers until 1973. A footnote in Clifford's memoirs indicates that sixteen of the original twenty copies reside in the Truman Library and that the others are unaccounted for. It is therefore possible that Krock could have located another copy, but Clifford does not suggest from whom it might have been obtained. Furthermore, why would Krock have sought out an elusive copy if Clifford already had one? If Clifford insisted that Krock read the document under the conditions Clifford described, it would have been obvious that he would not allow Krock to publish it, and it is unlikely that a reputable reporter like Krock would have betrayed Clifford's trust by seeking out another source. But the most convincing piece of evidence that Clifford intentionally leaked the memorandum can be gleaned from a careful study of Krock's text. The report, as it appeared in Krock's memoir, was dated "September ——, 1946," not the exact date of the report as submitted, September 24, 1946. According to Elsey, Krock must have used Clifford's undated draft copy, because the final, printed copies carried the exact date, and there were only two other draft copies, both of which Elsey could account for.[30] The inescapable conclusion is that Clifford gave his draft copy of the report to Krock in order to bolster Clifford's credentials as a key figure in the early Cold War.

Clifford biographers Douglas Frantz and David McKean make the same assertion in their book *Friends in High Places*.[31]

Clifford's interest in making the report public is consistent with his proclivity for self-promotion, but in the case of the Clifford-Elsey report it is also somewhat dishonest. All of the evidence suggests that Elsey wrote the report with little to no contribution from Clifford. The drafts are all written in Elsey's precise handwriting, and the only tangible evidence of Clifford's imprint is his marked-up copy. Clifford's notations on the draft are minor wording changes at best and, as Elsey noted at the time, "He did nothing but change a few words." Clifford was out of the country when much of the drafting was done, and as of August 28 he had not even looked at it. According to Elsey, Clifford's failure to have looked at the drafts as late as August 28 indicated both a lack of interest and minimal knowledge of the subject.[32] Frantz and McKean, basing their assertions on their interviews with Clifford, claimed that he interviewed a few key figures and gave his notes to Elsey.[33] When asked about this, however, Elsey was skeptical, and said that Clifford probably misspoke. "I'm just not aware of any notes whatsoever," he said.[34] Elsey's account seems the more plausible, as there are no such notes among Elsey's papers; and, given the thoroughness of the collection, it defies logic that he would not have saved them.

Despite the fact that the report was conceived and written almost exclusively by Elsey, Clifford was quick to take credit for it. Clifford's cover note to Truman is written in the first person and makes not even a passing reference to or acknowledgment of Elsey. The note says:

> In the course of complying with your directive to prepare a summary of American relations with the Soviet Union, I have consulted the Secretary of State, the Secretary of War, the Attorney General, the Secretary of the Navy, Fleet Admiral Leahy, the Joint Chiefs of Staff, Ambassador Pauley, the Director of Central Intelligence, and other persons who have special knowledge in this field. . . . There is remarkable agreement among the officials with whom I have talked and whose reports I have studied concerning the need for a continuous review of our relations with the Soviet Union and diligent effort to improve those relations.[35]

Given the effort and passion Elsey put into this document, an acknowledgment by Clifford, especially in a memo to the president, would have been appropriate. Robert Underhill made the same observation in his book *The Truman Persuasions*. In addition, Underhill wrote, "It is almost certain that Truman knew of Elsey's involvement, but at the time he may not have realized the extent to which Clifford's assistant had prepared and shaped a product which was to have such profound consequences."[36] Krock, however, referred to Clifford as the aide who wrote the memo, so it is likely that Clifford claimed authorship while discussing the report with him.

Although he acknowledged that Elsey assisted him in this project when speaking about the report, Clifford often slipped into storytelling braggadocio. "At the President's direction," he said during an oral history interview, "I wrote a memorandum that has since received a good deal of attention, and I delivered it to him in September 1946." A few moments later he noted that "the concluding chapter was my own," thus obliquely acknowledging that he did not write the full report. During an earlier oral history interview he said, "I spent the summer of 1946 in writing the memorandum on the Soviet Union."[37] In the course of recording his oral history Clifford described the process of compiling the background information and then assembling the report:

> And then I went to work to distill it, and prepare the *essence* of it. A President doesn't have time to read the mountains of material that are sent. What you do *is* distill it and put it in as readable a form as possible. Now, I do submit that in the process, I became very interested in it, I became engrossed in it, and the memorandum that was submitted, in addition to carrying the views of these people, certainly carried my own, because you can't remain completely objective about the subject.[38]

The foregoing examples illustrate a tendency for Clifford almost absentmindedly to refer to this work as his own. It is true that the report was prepared under his auspices and tacitly under his direction, but that does not alter the fact that Clifford's contribution was minimal.

Historians have since rectified this mistake; Elsey's role was uncovered during one of his oral history interviews. During the interview, Jerry Hess of the Truman Library asked Elsey if he assisted with the report, and Elsey coyly responded that the story was plain to see from his longhand drafts within his files. "Your *longhand*. Did you write it?" Hess asked with surprise.

"All you have to do is look at the draft to get the answer to that," Elsey replied. Even with the cat out of the bag, though, Elsey was careful to correct Hess when the interviewer referred to it as Elsey's report. "It was not *my* report," said Elsey; "it was *Clifford's* report to the President."[39]

Elsey also disputes Clifford's oral history assertion, made on two separate occasions, that Clifford wrote the conclusion.[40] "He put in some language, some sentences, a few words here or there," said Elsey.[41] The absence of a draft in Clifford's hand makes either assertion impossible to prove, but the evidence favors Elsey's account.

The report itself, fifty pages long as it appeared in Krock's memoirs, is a fascinating document. Written in the early phases of the Cold War, it is amazing how much the American perception of the Soviet Union had changed in the year since the end of World War II. Although the report echoed much of what Kennan had argued in the Long Telegram, it went further than Kennan in arguing for a policy of military containment, even if Clifford and Elsey never actually used the term. (Kennan's prescription of political containment was not actually proposed until the publication of his anonymous "X" article in *Foreign Affairs* in the summer of 1947.)

The Clifford-Elsey report is broken down into several chapters, each on a separate topic: Soviet foreign policy; Soviet-American agreements, 1942–1946; violations of Soviet agreements with the United States; conflicting views on reparations; Soviet activities affecting American security; and U.S. policy toward the Soviet Union. The report opens with an ominous warning: "the gravest problem facing the United States today is that of American Relations with the Soviet Union. The solution of the problem may determine whether or not there will be a third World War."[42] Clifford and Elsey immediately emphasized the role of ideology in the conflict with the Soviet Union, establishing the notion that the Soviet-American conflict was fundamentally different from previous great-power confrontations:

> The fundamental tenet of the communist philosophy embraced by Soviet leaders is that peaceful coexistence of communist and capitalist nations is impossible. The defenders of the communist faith, as the present Soviet leaders regard themselves, assume that conflict between the Soviet Union and the leading capitalist powers of the western world is inevitable and the party leaders believe that it is their duty to prepare the Soviet Union for the inevitable conflict which their doctrine predicts. Their

basic policies, domestic and foreign, are designed to strengthen the Soviet Union and insure its victory in the predicted coming struggle between Communism and Capitalism.[43]

Clifford and Elsey warned that the Soviet Union already perceived the United States as its most likely—and most dangerous—potential enemy. Furthermore, they argued that the Soviet Union was already preparing militarily for the confrontation they considered inevitable: "Development of atomic weapons, guided missiles, materials for biological warfare, a strategic air force, submarines of great cruising range, naval mines and mine craft, to name the most important, are extending the effective range of Soviet military power well into areas which the United States regards as vital to its security."[44]

Foreshadowing the communist hysteria of the McCarthy era, the report warned that members of the U.S. Communist Party were all to be considered potential spies for the Soviet Union: "In this regard it must be remembered that every American Communist is potentially an espionage agent of the Soviet Government, requiring only the direct instruction of a Soviet superior to make the potentiality a reality." The paranoia of this statement is striking, especially as it preceded Senator Joseph McCarthy's all-out assault on communism, which began in February 1950. The Truman administration would attempt to get a political jump on the anticommunist issue in March 1947, six months after the report, with the Loyalty Program, a largely defensive measure typical of the Democrats' response throughout this period. But the Clifford-Elsey report seems to have argued for a more preemptive policy of ferreting out communists and fellow travelers than Democratic policy suggested, both during and after the Truman administration. The report also warned that the American Communist Party, presumably at the direction of the Soviet Union, was trying to subvert the U.S. armed forces, an assertion that eerily foreshadowed McCarthy's allegations in 1954.[45]

In order to counteract the mistrust and paranoia of the Soviet leadership, a positive policy of engagement was required: "The primary objective of United States policy toward the Soviet Union is to convince Soviet leaders that it is in their interest to participate in a system of world cooperation, that there are no fundamental causes for war between our nations, and that the security and prosperity of the Soviet Union, and that of the rest of the world as well, is being jeopardized by the aggressive militaristic imperialism such as that in which the Soviet Union is now engaged."[46] Clifford and Elsey were pessimistic that such an approach would succeed, however, given their belief that the Soviets viewed conflict with the United States as inevitable. The report, without specifically using the word "containment," argued for exactly that. "This government should be prepared," they argued, "while scrupulously avoiding any act which would be an excuse for the Soviets to begin a war, to resist vigorously and successfully any efforts of the U.S.S.R. to expand into areas vital to American security."[47] In contrast to the argument Kennan initiated in the Long Telegram and then more explicitly in his "X" article, Clifford and Elsey argued for a policy of military containment:

> The language of military power is the only language which disciples of power politics understand. The United States must use that language in order that Soviet leaders will realize that our government is determined to uphold the interests of its citizens and the rights of small nations. Compromise and concessions are considered, by the Soviets, to be evidence of weakness and they are encouraged by our "retreats" to make new and greater demands.
>
> The main deterrent to Soviet attack on the United States, or to attack on areas of the world which are vital to our security, will be the military power of this country.[48]

In the most chilling passage of the report, perhaps the one most widely quoted by historians, Clifford and Elsey recommend an aggressive military posture in the face of a dangerous adversary:

> Therefore, in order to maintain our strength at a level which will be effective in restraining the Soviet Union, the United States must be prepared to wage atomic and biological warfare. . . . A war with the U.S.S.R. would be "total" in a more horrible sense than any previous war and there must be constant research for both offensive and defensive weapons.[49]

The Clifford-Elsey report also argued for a proactive policy toward America's allies and other nations that might be the target of communist expansion, policies that bear a striking resemblance to the ideas articulated in the Truman Doctrine and the Marshall Plan:

> In addition to maintaining our own strength, the United States

should support and assist all democratic countries which are in any way menaced or endangered by the U.S.S.R. Providing military support in case of attack is a last resort; a more effective barrier to communism is strong economic support.[50]

The concluding paragraphs read like a synopsis of United States foreign policy for the duration of the Cold War:

In conclusion, as long as the Soviet Government adheres to its present policy, the United States should maintain military forces powerful enough to restrain the Soviet Union and to confine Soviet influence to its present area. All nations not now within the Soviet sphere should be given generous economic assistance and political support in their opposition to Soviet penetration. . . . Even though Soviet leaders profess to believe that the conflict between Capitalism and Communism is irreconcilable and must eventually be resolved by the triumph of the latter, it is our hope that they will change their minds and work out with us a fair and equitable settlement when they realize that we are too strong to be beaten and too determined to be frightened.[51]

As Truman observed, this was "powerful stuff," but did the words on the page translate into ideas that helped formulate a foreign policy to counteract the Soviet Union? On the surface, the answer would appear to be no. Clifford's anecdote of Truman's early morning phone call demonstrates that the report did not enjoy wide distribution throughout the administration and the foreign policy bureaucracy. Indeed, the evidence suggests that the report did remain locked up, literally, until Truman and Clifford brought it out into the light of day decades later. In contrast to Kennan's Long Telegram, which Forrestal considered to be required reading, or Kennan's "X" article, the close circle of individuals who read the report may not have gone beyond Clifford, Elsey, Truman, Kennan, and Leahy. Given such a small audience, it seems inconceivable that the report could have been all that influential.

Clifford argued that the Cold War officially began the day he delivered the report to Truman, so obviously he would disagree with the foregoing assessment. During one of his oral history interviews, he responded at length to the observation that the report sounded like an early version of the Marshall Plan:

Keep in mind that at the time that was written in September of '46, the Soviet Union: (a) had the most powerful ground military force in the world; (b) they had already started a period of expansionism. They had taken Latvia, Lithuania, Estonia, Poland, Bulgaria, Romania, Czechoslovakia, and Yugoslavia; the whole western periphery of the Soviet Union had been subjugated. . . . And it seemed very clear to me at the time we were the only ones who could stop this from going on. The nations of Western Europe were prostrate. England had nothing left; France had nothing left; Italy was a shambles; Belgium had nothing left. All that they had was the support of the United States. And it seemed very clear to me that we had to make it clear to the Soviet Union that they were not going to expand any more. To do so would bring them into direct confrontation with us. Now *there* is the germ of the North Atlantic Treaty Organization, which later came. In there it says too that our job is to help rebuild the nations of Western Europe to a point where they could defend themselves. Their defense wouldn't be entirely our responsibility. *There* is the Marshall plan.[52]

Clifford may have been overstating the case, but it is curious that the report hinted at the turn U.S. foreign policy would take a mere six months later with the proclamation of the Truman Doctrine and the Marshall Plan. The similarity is not a coincidence; therein lies the significance of the report. Unlike Kennan's papers, which were solo efforts, the Clifford-Elsey report was the product of extensive consultation with key members of the administration and foreign policy advisers. In fact, it was the first U.S. interdepartmental analysis of the Soviet Union, assessing that country's motives, objectives, and military strength and recommending counterstrategies. Perhaps what is most striking about the report is its authors solicited opinions outside of the State Department, particularly from the military. Truman did not want the State Department to control the debate.[53] Alonzo Hamby, author of the definitive Truman biography, *Man of the People,* argued that it "was meant primarily to be a compendium rather than a policy paper."[54] Clifford described it as a "time capsule of high-level thinking six months before the enunciation of the Truman Doctrine."[55] The significance of the Clifford-Elsey report was not a function of how many people read and were influenced by it, but by how well it summarized what the key players were already thinking. Elsey's modest assessment of the report says it best:

I think it's conceivable that having a synopsis like this, a summary, available to him *may* have been useful to the President. You see, it's important not to overemphasize the significance of this. This was a consolidation, a summary of facts, data, opinions, material already available to the President, most of which have had at one time or another been called to his attention by the Secretary of State, or the Secretary of War, or the Secretary of the Navy, or other officials, or Admiral Leahy or Harry Hopkins, in the months before he left the White House, but it's different to have things come to you piecemeal over a period of time, or having them all presented in a consistent form. The impact of having it all drawn together may have had some influence on the President.[56]

Truman buried the report not because he disagreed with the findings, but because he was worried that if it were made public Henry Wallace would accuse him of warmongering.[57] Wallace's Madison Square Garden speech and subsequent firing had been a public relations disaster, and Truman could not risk the chance of a leak. To the extent that Truman was predisposed toward taking a more aggressive posture vis-à-vis the Soviet Union, which is suggested by his meeting with Clifford, the report may have validated his position. With the assurance that his foreign policy advisers would fall into step behind him, Truman may have been more confident when he confronted the crisis in Greece and Turkey six months later.

The historical significance of the Clifford-Elsey report is open to debate. It is an exaggeration to suggest, as Clifford did, that it signified the beginning of the Cold War. Conversely, its importance should not be underestimated. In addition to its likely influence on policy making, the report is historically significant for other reasons as well.

What is especially striking is that the report was prepared by foreign policy amateurs. The knowledge and ideas Elsey gleaned from his tenure in the Map Room provided him with invaluable experience, but he remained a foreign policy novice. Clifford, who up to that point had been a domestic and political adviser, had no expertise with foreign policy. That two such inexperienced individuals could be responsible for a comprehensive analysis of U.S.-Soviet relations is one of the more curious episodes in the early Cold War. Furthermore, given its creators' relative inexperience, it is striking that the tone of the report was so hard line, even strident. After all, attitudes toward the Soviet Union were in a period of transition and, as Hamby observed, some of these newly minted anti-Soviet hard-liners, Clifford included, had previously never taken a high profile position on foreign policy.[58]

Historian Melvyn Leffler argues that the Clifford-Elsey report was more than a synopsis of the thinking among the highest levels within the Truman administration. He contends that Clifford and Elsey's intent was to establish justification for America's past, present, and future policies with respect to its superpower rival. They were not looking to prepare an objective analysis but were instead trying to establish consensus for decisive action. A more nuanced analysis would have taken into consideration the defensive imperative of establishing a cordon of buffer states between Russia and Germany. It would have focused on potential areas of agreement and cooperation between the two nations and attempted to understand the motivation for Soviet behavior. Instead, the report simplified the complex postwar situation in Europe because, Leffler argued, "Truman liked things in black and white."[59]

It is equally plausible that the Clifford-Elsey report represented an erroneous, but not intentional, misreading of Soviet intentions. In hindsight the Soviet Union was not the expansionist, ideologically motivated aggressor that was presented in the report. Rather, Stalin's primary motivation was likely to protect the Soviet Union, primarily Russia, from another invasion by surrounding his country with a buffer zone of subservient client states. Since all of the conflicts with the Soviet Union during the Cold War were fought through proxies, it is clear that the risk of total war, using weapons of mass destruction, was exaggerated. As the détente era of the 1970s demonstrated, mutual coexistence could be an effective policy, and this fact calls into question the most fundamental assumption in the report. For years Kennan argued that the containment policy he proposed was more political in nature than military and that his characterization of Russian intentions was misinterpreted. The Clifford-Elsey report, with its emphasis on military containment, was not what Kennan would have advocated.

From the standpoint of Clifford's career the report is significant in that it helped build his résumé as an important figure in the emergence of the Cold War. In later years, as a private attorney and Democratic power broker, Clifford's currency was his reputation and influence, both of which were enhanced by his credentials as a Cold War liberal. The Clifford-Elsey report, especially after it was leaked in 1968, only bolstered those credentials. Clifford took a great deal of pride in the report and his role in the early years of the Cold War, a pride that is expressed in his memoirs. According to George Elsey, however, much of this expression of pride belongs to Richard Holbrooke, special envoy to Afghanistan and Pakistan, and ghostwriter of Clifford's memoirs. During the fact-finding interviews for *Counsel to the President*, Clifford, Elsey, and Holbrooke had differences of opinion regarding the presentation of this subject. Elsey played down the significance of the report he had written, but Holbrooke was emphatic that it should be made much of.[60] Elsey lost the argument. "Although a novice," Clifford says in his memoirs, "I was given an assignment by President Truman which required me to take what amounted to a crash course with some of the nation's greatest experts on the issue that would dominate American foreign policy for almost half a century—American-Soviet relations."[61]

Clifford overstated the case. First of all, Truman did not give Clifford an assignment such as he describes; the president merely wanted a listing of recent treaties and international agreements that the Soviets had failed to abide by. Elsey was the one who later pressed the case for an extensive analysis of Soviet-American relations, while Clifford seemed to be determined to give Truman exactly what he asked for and no more. Only Elsey's perseverance ensured the report its place in history. Clifford claimed that he consulted extensively with high-level figures in the Truman administration and foreign policy bureaucracy, but the evidence suggests that he conducted only a few initial interviews to lay the groundwork for Elsey's research and to ensure that the hoped-for participants were aware that the project was being conducted at the president's behest. The notion that Clifford immersed himself in a crash course in Soviet-American relations is something of an exaggeration, especially given the fact that he was out of the country for two weeks in the middle of the project. After he returned to Washington in September, the Wallace "fiasco" no doubt occupied a good deal of his time as he scrambled to contain the fallout.[62]

If Clifford did take a "crash course" in Soviet-American relations, it could not have happened much before the second week of September, a mere two weeks before he presented the report to the president. Truman, Clifford, and the rest of the president's party did not return from their vacation until September 2, a vacation during which Clifford himself admits that little to no work was done. Upon returning to the office he doubtless would have needed a few days just to catch up and work his way through his in-box. In order to weigh in with some intelligent insight regarding a subject with which he had no expertise he would have had to do quite a bit of cramming. The report was presented to the president September 24; before that, at least a few days would have been required for final proofreading and printing. Clifford therefore clearly had little time for the "crash course" he describes, and in any event, the documentary evidence suggests that he had little input in the final report.

Historians also appear to have overemphasized Clifford's role, although most acknowledge that Elsey wrote all or most of the report. Leffler argued in his book *A Preponderance of Power* that "Clifford's intent was to present a clear, unequivocal report," because, as stated earlier, "Truman liked things in black and white." But irrespective of Truman's growing impatience with the Soviet Union, the president had not assigned Clifford the task of writing an extensive position paper, whether as a means of building a hard-line consensus against the Soviet Union or for some other purpose. Furthermore, Clifford had neither the expertise nor the passion about the subject to write, or insist upon, such a report. If Leffler is right and the intent was to write an unequivocal report to justify the administration's taking a hard line toward the Soviets, that intent would have to have been Elsey's. More than likely, Clifford did not have strong feelings on the subject at the time of the assignment; he simply did not have the knowledge and expertise sufficient to justify such conviction.

As of September 1946, Clifford was primarily a speechwriter and a domestic and political adviser focused on labor strife, food shortages, and the challenges of converting the country back to a peacetime economy. Truman's dreadful standing in the polls in mid-1946 also would have dominated most of Clifford's time. The public perception of Truman as weak and indecisive led *Time*'s congressional correspondent Frank McNaughton to remark on July 26 that Truman "could not carry Missouri now."[63] Up until the summer of 1946 Clifford's most prominent role had been in resolving the railroad strike. In short, he was not focused on foreign policy, which Elsey believed he ignored at his own peril. "I think Clifford for the first time [in mid-1946] had to pay some attention to these subjects," Elsey said. "He had been so concerned with railroad strikes and domestic turmoil . . . all the things that bubbled up and made 1946 such a God-awful mess for Truman, leading up to the disaster in November."[64]

Over time the Cold War intensified, and Clifford's feelings toward the Soviet Union became more fully formed than they were in 1946. That combined with the distortion of memory no doubt colored Clifford's recollection of the report and his role in preparing it. At the time, however, Clifford probably viewed this assignment as he would any other that the president had given him. Not possessing sufficient knowledge of the subject and lacking the time to devote to it, Clifford delegated the assignment to Elsey, whom he trusted completely. Elsey worked with diligence and passion, and the result was a quality product that Clifford proudly took credit for. Either due to a sin of omission or by design, Clifford failed to give Elsey credit for the work, although it is likely that Truman was aware of all that Elsey had done. But Clifford did not mention Elsey's role when he leaked the report twenty years later, allowing Krock to give him the credit and thus build upon the Clifford legend.

That legend grew over time and enhanced Clifford's stature as a lobbyist and power broker. Clifford's boasting in his oral history interviews was significantly toned down in his later memoirs, but his more modest tone in that book belies his pride that he was a central figure in the emergence of the Cold War. Both Clifford and Holbrooke had reasons for wanting to embellish the story, and exaggerated Clifford's role in the creation of the report "American Relations with the Soviet Union," presenting an account that is contradicted by both evidence and reason.

# 3

# Cold Warrior

The Clifford-Elsey report marked Clark Clifford's first foray into foreign policy, but over the years Clifford's counsel was sought out on a variety of foreign policy matters, both formally and informally. Clifford's proximity to the president ensured that he had a voice in some of the most significant foreign policy decisions of the early Cold War, but as with his role in the Clifford-Elsey report, his foreign policy contributions were often exaggerated. The formation of foreign policy was primarily a function of the State Department and the military. With State and the Pentagon controlling foreign policy Clifford could only influence that policy through his role as the president's primary speechwriter and also through force of will and persuasion. Clifford had no formal power or authority in matters of foreign affairs, and as a result his potential to shape policy was constrained. Where he was involved, he was often acting in the capacity of a political adviser lending his expertise to a foreign policy matter. He did play a central role in the unification of the military and the creation of the national security state, but in this capacity he was serving as an administrator and a legislative liaison, not as a foreign policy visionary.

The Clifford-Elsey report outlined a framework for the postwar relationship between the Soviet Union and the United States. In order to carry out the mission articulated in the report Truman believed it was essential to restructure the military and create the organizations and bureaucracy needed to ensure that the United States would be better prepared to fight the next war. Truman unified the military and created the Department of Defense, the National Security Council, the Central Intelligence Agency, the Air Force, and the position of chairman of the Joint Chiefs of Staff. It can be said without exaggeration that Truman created the national security state, and that legacy has outlasted even the Cold War.

"We must never fight another war the way we fought the last two,"

Truman said to Clifford. "I have the feeling that if the Army and the Navy had fought our enemies as hard as they fought each other, the war would have ended much earlier."[1] Today we take it for granted that the military is organized under a civilian secretary of defense and that one individual, the chairman of the Joint Chiefs of Staff, oversees all of the U.S. armed forces. When Truman became president in 1945, however, the Army and Navy each oversaw its own department and had a cabinet-level secretary reporting to the president. The head of the army carried the title of Secretary of War. Truman's Senate experience, especially as the chairman of a special committee charged with investigating waste and fraud in the military, gave him ample opportunity to see that the nation's military was severely constrained by interservice rivalries. Truman's vision was complete unification of the nation's military forces, on land, sea, and air. It was a massive and politically challenging task, and Truman called on Clifford to help carry it out.

In December 1945, Truman asked his secretary of war, Robert Patterson, for a military unification proposal. Patterson's plan, which Truman endorsed, called for a secretary of national defense and three assistant secretaries who would oversee the land, sea, and air forces respectively. James Forrestal, who as secretary of the navy was extremely defensive of his department's prerogatives, was reflexively antagonistic to the proposal. Deeply suspicious of the Army's motives, certain of the rightness of his position, and protected by a powerful ally in Congress, Carl Vinson of Georgia, Forrestal decided to dig in his heels. He called the president's proposal "completely unworkable" and confided to Clifford that he believed he was "fighting for the very life of the Navy." Five months later the chasm between the Army and Navy was as wide as ever, with little hope of compromise. Clifford recommended that Truman make some concessions to the Navy because he believed the plan was politically out of reach.[2]

Truman tried to broker an agreement between the two sides and asked Clifford to draft letters to Patterson, Forrestal, and the congressional leadership outlining his position on the major points of contention. Forrestal was furious over the president's letters, and in a conversation with Clifford he lashed out at the Army for its "steamroller tactics." He also threatened to resign, which would have been extremely embarrassing for Truman politically and would probably have exacerbated an already difficult situation.

The debate dragged on, with little indication that an acceptable compromise could be reached. Clifford continued to coordinate the stalled efforts between the Army, the Navy, the White House, and Congress. Beginning in the fall of 1946 Clifford and Forrestal had a standing breakfast meeting at Forrestal's home in Georgetown. These breakfasts provided an opportunity for the two men to talk candidly about unification, and Forrestal continued to view Clifford as a confidant and, as Clifford was a former naval officer, an ally. In his memoirs Clifford indicates that he supported the unification plan as proposed by Patterson and came to believe that Forrestal was being excessively rigid. Yet he must have never confided his true feelings to Forrestal, whom he described as a friend, because if he had Forrestal might have toned down his anti-Army rhetoric. In September 1946 he sent Clifford a "private and confidential" memorandum that illustrated his paranoia about the Army.[3]

Looking to break the logjam, Truman called a meeting on September 10. He told the principals that he wanted an agreement immediately and announced that Clifford and Admiral William Leahy would draft a new bill.[4] Forrestal continued to be adamant in his opposition, again threatening to resign, but Clifford worked hard to broker a compromise. He was finally successful in January 1947, and the bill was passed in July. It was a far cry from Truman's vision of a wholly unified military. The National Security Act of 1947, as the bill was called, did not provide for the position of chairman of the Joint Chiefs of Staff, and while it did establish a secretary of defense it provided no deputy and very little staff. Without the administrative and legal authority to control the different branches of the service the secretary of defense was powerless, and without a chairman of the Joint Chiefs the president would have to continue to negotiate differences among the branches. It was an imperfect compromise, but it was better than nothing. In a tactically brilliant move Truman named Forrestal the first secretary of defense, figuring that the Navy man would make life impossible for anyone else in the new position and that as defense secretary Forrestal would try to make the new arrangement work. Forrestal promised as much in a letter to Clifford two days after Congress passed the final bill, and he also praised Clifford for his tireless efforts toward effecting unification.[5]

The National Security Act did much more than unify the military, however imperfectly. It also authorized the creation of the Air Force as a separate branch of the military with its own cabinet-level secretary and established two organizations that would play central roles during the Cold War: the National Security Council and the Central Intelligence Agency. The concept of the National Security Council

(NSC) came from Forrestal who, despite his intransigence on the issue of military unification, was adamant that the United States needed to be vigilant in containing Soviet power. "What Forrestal kept pressing for—and pressing really even before the war itself came to an end—was the absolute necessity of some kind of governmental machinery which would attempt to bridge the gap between military and foreign policy," George Elsey later recalled. "He was acutely, agonizingly aware of the gap that had existed between the State Department and the military services during the war and even more significantly in the preparations for postwar conduct of foreign and military policy."[6]

Forrestal wanted the NSC to be a part of the Department of Defense, and he wanted the staff to be housed at the Pentagon. Clifford disagreed, believing that the NSC should report to the president, not the secretary of defense, and that the staff should be located close to the president. Clifford was also concerned that the NSC, as Forrestal envisioned it, would undermine the State Department.[7] Clifford carried the day; Forrestal was overruled, and the NSC became an advisory board for the president. Over time the NSC evolved into a powerful agency that overshadowed the State Department, as Clifford had feared. The staff of the NSC ballooned, and its leadership transformed from the administratively powerless position of executive secretary, as it was originally envisioned, into the powerful role of national security advisor, a position that became institutionalized under Presidents Kennedy and Johnson.[8]

The National Security Act of 1947 also established the Central Intelligence Agency. After disbanding the wartime Office of Strategic Services, Truman became dissatisfied by the disorganized and occasionally conflicting intelligence reports he was receiving. In January 1946 he asked Clifford and Leahy to study proposals submitted by the State Department and the military for intelligence coordination, and Leahy handed off the project to Clifford. Knowing next to nothing about intelligence, Clifford turned to a friend from St. Louis, Rear Admiral Sydney Souers. Souers favored the approach recommended by the military: establishing an agency that would coordinate all intelligence collected from State and the different branches of the military. Truman, however, was opposed to anything more than an informal coordinating group, and he directed Clifford to draft an executive order, which the president signed on January 22. The executive order established a director of central intelligence (DCI) who would oversee a Central Intelligence Group (CIG).[9]

The CIG thus established, Clifford pressured Souers to accept the appointment as the first director of central intelligence. Souers reluctantly accepted, but agreed to serve for only six months. After he resigned Truman named Army Air Force Lieutenant General Hoyt S. Vandenberg, the nephew of Senator Arthur Vandenberg, as the next director of central intelligence. An ambitious man, Vandenberg soon submitted a recommendation to create a new Central Intelligence Agency to replace the CIG model, which he considered unworkable. Elsey was critical of Vandenberg's recommendations, especially his abandonment of the CIG concept, which Elsey believed had been given insufficient time to show that it could work.[10] Clifford shared Elsey's criticism and was also concerned that the CIA would become involved in domestic intelligence, which was outside its mandate and properly belonged to the FBI. On July 12 he sent a memorandum to Vandenberg, in which he said, "The failure to distinguish between 'intelligence' and 'foreign intelligence' will raise a serious question in many minds as to whether the real intent of the bill is actually the same as that stated in the 'Purpose of the Act.' . . . I fear that this will lead to the suspicion that the 'National Intelligence Authority' and the 'Central Intelligence Agency' will attempt to control, with the powers granted to them in this bill, the F.B.I. and other intelligence activities."[11] Clifford also warned Vandenberg that the wording of the bill must be selected carefully in order to minimize opposition.

At this stage in the development of the CIA Clifford and Elsey disagreed on the quality of intelligence then being generated by the CIG. In response to an article by Arthur Krock praising the quality of CIG intelligence, Elsey sent Clifford a memorandum criticizing its quality. Apparently they had not spoken on the matter because Clifford was the source for the Krock article.[12]

Four days later Clifford met with Vandenberg aides Lawrence Houston and James Lay to discuss the draft legislation. Clifford bluntly asked them if the intelligence apparatus established by the president in his January executive order had proven unworkable, and they replied that it had. Clifford promised to take up the matter with Leahy and Truman, provided that the proposed CIA refrain from the domestic intelligence prerogatives of the FBI, as he had spelled out in his memo to Vandenberg.[13] Clifford brought the Vandenberg proposal to Truman, who accepted the recommendation, and in September 1946 Truman announced that legislation to create the CIA would be folded into the bill unifying the military, the National Security Act. Vandenberg became impatient that the CIA bill was appended to the one for unification, which was a higher priority for the president. Clifford and Elsey, however, preferred to keep the CIA legislation as an amendment to the unification bill, perhaps concerned about adding political complications to the overall effort. Vandenberg continued to argue for separate legislation, even during the congressional hearings on the bill, but Clifford and Elsey persevered, and the CIA was established with only the "briefest mention" in the National Security Act of 1947.[14]

The National Security Act of 1947 was an imperfect bill, relative to Truman's vision, but it was a significant step forward. The bill began the process, which was completed in 1949, of unifying the command structure of the U.S. armed forces to ensure that it could effectively fight the next war. It established the National Security Council, which coordinated the efforts of the military, the State Department, and the rest of the executive branch. And finally, it created a single agency responsible for collecting, analyzing, coordinating, and reporting foreign intelligence. The philosophical impact of the legislation, however, was greater than the changes it effected to the military and foreign policy bureaucracy. The act created a national security state, a fundamental shift for a nation that had exhibited a preference for isolationism throughout its history. As the president's agent in this endeavor, Clifford occupied a critical seat at the table during this transformative period of American history.

The emergence of the national security state permeated every facet of the American experience during the Cold War. The battle against fascism during World War II required a total mobilization of the country, but for a relatively brief four-year period. In contrast, the struggle against communism required a long-term commitment without the promise of anything comparable to the Japanese surrender at the end of World War II. Politically the national security state resulted in the election of leaders who were perceived as most diligent in defending the country from real and perceived enemies. Massive levels of military expenditure were sought and obtained, necessitating an increase in the tax burden to fund it. Communism, although personified by the Soviet Union and China, was also an ideology, and therefore a more existential threat than traditional enemies. The result was a pervasive fear and paranoia on the part of U.S. citizens that communist infiltrators might be operating within the country and looking to overthrow the government. The tangible result was the red scare of the 1950s, spearheaded by Senator Joseph McCarthy of Wisconsin. The fear of communism also permeated American culture, in movies such as the *Manchurian Candidate* and in the blacklisting of writers and artists from Hollywood and elsewhere. The national security state affected everyday life, from air raid drills in schools to the popularity of home-made bomb shelters and other civil defense preparations. Even items as benign as household appliances came to be seen as an indication of the superiority of the American economic and political model, as Vice President Richard Nixon explained to Soviet Premier Nikita Khrush-chev during the 1959 "Kitchen Debate."

The Clifford-Elsey report outlined a framework for the post-war rivalry between the Soviet Union and the United States, and the National Security Act of 1947 strengthened the command structure of the armed forces and ensured that the United States had the resources necessary to wage the Cold War. What was needed was an opportu-nity to translate the ideas expressed in the report, which represented the thinking of the president's senior foreign policy advisers, into action. That opportunity presented itself on February 21, 1947, when the British ambassador to the United States paid a call on the new secretary of state, General George C. Marshall. Marshall had already left for the weekend, but his deputy, Dean Acheson, persuaded the ambassador, Lord Inverchapel, to present the message to Acheson informally so that he could study it over the weekend.[15]

The message from Inverchapel was bleak. Great Britain no longer had the means to provide financial assistance to Greece and Turkey and was determined to remove its troops from Greece as well. The geopolitical importance of the Mediterranean was without question, and the United States was determined to contain Soviet influence there. In particular, the United States feared that the Greek communists would amass greater power in the absence of the British and would align Greece with the Soviet Union. Once firmly implanted in the east-ern Mediterranean, the communist contagion would only spread.[16] Indeed, the importance of the Middle East and the Soviet threat in that region had been emphasized in the Clifford-Elsey report:

> The Soviet Union is interested in obtaining the withdrawal of British troops from Greece and the establishment of a "friendly" government there. It hopes to make Turkey a pup-pet state which could serve as a spring-board for the dom-ination of the eastern Mediterranean. . . . The U.S.S.R is attempting to form along its Middle Eastern frontier a protec-tive zone of politically subordinate states incapable of hostile action against it and it is seeking, at the same time, to acquire for its own use in those states ports and waterways, pipelines

and oil fields. . . . The long-range Soviet aim is the economic, military and political domination of the entire Middle East.[17]

Acheson concluded his meeting with the ambassador and phoned the president to inform him of the situation. Clifford was in the Oval Office at the time for his usual end-of-the-day meeting with Truman and listened to the president's side of the conversation. It was clear from what Clifford heard that Truman would be receptive to Acheson's recommendations for substantial American aid to make up for the departure of the British. On February 27, Truman, without Clifford, met with Marshall, Acheson, and congressional leaders to discuss the situation and request their support for the appropriations legislation that Truman would be sending to the Hill. The numbers were substantial. The British estimated that $240 to $280 million would be required for Greece along with another $150 million for Turkey. To put those numbers into perspective, the total federal budget at the time was $41 billion.[18]

The congressional leaders, led by Senator Arthur Vandenberg of Michigan, the new Republican chairman of the Senate Foreign Relations Committee, listened politely to Marshall's presentation but were unmoved. Acheson, sensing that an opportunity was being squandered, asked Marshall if he could step in and proceeded to paint a doomsday scenario of expanding Soviet influence across three continents. Acheson's tactic was successful, and after a long silence Vandenberg said, "Mr. President, if you will say that to the Congress and the country, I will support you and I believe most of its members will do the same."[19] Vandenberg was also quite blunt with his recommendation, suggesting to Truman that in order to make a persuasive case to the Congress and the American people, he would have to "scare the hell out of the country."[20]

The State Department began drafting the message, but at first it was unclear whether they were to compose a legislative message or a presidential speech. Truman had left Washington on March 2 for a four-day state visit to Mexico, and while he was gone his advisers debated strategy. Clifford and Forrestal, whose hard-line views toward the Soviet Union were second to none, met on March 5. They decided to prepare a memorandum for Truman, which, as they put it, "would outline the central question of which of the two systems in moral contention would survive." Clifford's concern was that with the Democrats controlling the White House and the Republicans the Congress, the usual partisan bickering would prevent the government from adopting a bipartisan strategy to deal with the threat of communism. According to Forrestal, "Clifford said that he thought the most important thing was the development of a mechanism by which the Executive and Legislative branches of government could function. This, he thought, was particularly important because of the existing fact that different parties were in control of these two branches."[21]

The product of their discussion was a memorandum that was drafted by Forrestal aide Marx Leva and sent to Clifford on March 6 and which, according to Forrestal biographers Townsend Hoopes and Douglas Brinkley, "reads today like a first draft of the Marshall Plan, although its scope was global rather than regionally European."[22] The memorandum opened with a dire warning: "For a long time now, it has been clear that there is a serious, immediate and extraordinarily grave threat to the continued existence of this country. . . . The present danger which this country faces is at least as great as the danger which we faced during the war with Germany and Japan. Briefly stated, it is the very real danger that this country, as we know it, may cease to exist." The memorandum warned that "this country cannot afford the deceptive luxury of waging defensive warfare. As in the war of 1941–45, our victory and our survival depend on how and where we attack." Despite the militant tone of the document, the emphasis was how to channel America's "outstanding economic leadership" in order to "create the conditions under which a Free World society can live" and counteract Russia's "skillfully tailored . . . appeal to people who are in despair."[23]

The stridency of the warning combined with Forrestal's reputation as an ideologically passionate cold warrior suggest that the Leva memorandum was much more a product of Forrestal than a collaborative effort. Elsey speculated that "Forrestal drew out of his conversation with Clifford what he wanted, what he believed."[24] Forrestal had intended to send the memorandum directly to the president, but for protocol reasons decided to send it to Clifford instead, with a cover note from Leva. The memorandum received no further distribution, and it is unlikely that it played any more than a minor role in the debate over aid to Greece and Turkey.[25] Nonetheless, it is clear that both Forrestal and Clifford were comfortable with a more hard-line position relative to the Soviets.

Truman met with Clifford, Acheson, Secretary of the Treasury John Snyder, and Leahy on March 7, just prior to a full meeting with the Cabinet, and decided to ask Congress to appropriate the funds as quickly as possible. Truman then met with the full Cabinet to discuss strategy, whereupon a consensus emerged that the president should personally make the request before a joint session of Congress. Clifford said later that that was the approach both he and Acheson preferred.[26]

Elsey, upon being informed of the decision, dissented. He believed that it was premature for the president to come out strongly against the Soviet Union, and he wrote a memo to Clifford on March 8 outlining his concerns:

> I do not believe that this is the occasion for the "All-out" speech for the following reasons:
>
> 1. Insufficient time to prepare what would be the most significant speech in the President's administration. . . .
> 2. There has been no overt action in the immediate past by the U.S.S.R. which serves as an adequate pretext for the "All-out" speech. The situation in Greece is relatively abstract; there have been other instances—Iran, for example—where the occasion more adequately justified such a speech and there will be other such occasions—I fear—in the future.
> 3. The public is not prepared. . . .
>
> For these reasons, I believe that next week's message should be limited in scope. I recommend as a subject "U.S. Responsibility for European Reconstruction."[27]

Given the hard-line position he took in the Clifford-Elsey report, it was curious that Elsey would take a cautious stance here. Clifford considered Elsey's recommendations carefully, but Elsey's analysis made him more determined that it *was* the right time for an "all-out" speech. "In any crisis there are always valid reasons to consider delay or inaction," he later wrote, "but I felt it was high time to tell the American public the facts, as we had seen them for at least six months, and to ask for their support and understanding."[28]

Clifford was silent as to why Elsey opted to take a more cautious position, an issue historians have also failed to address. According to Elsey, he was unaware of the British memorandum and Britain's plans to curtail financial aid and withdraw troops. If he had known, he would not have advised caution. Elsey recalled that when he and Clifford met in Clifford's office early the next morning, Clifford fully briefed Elsey on the circumstances of the British withdrawal, at which point Elsey retracted his note of caution.[29] If Elsey is correct about this, Clifford embellished the story for his memoirs. Clifford's published account depicts him ruminating over Elsey's caution but then boldly reaching the conclusion that it was time for action. The obvious implication of Clifford's version is that if he had not stood firm and instead taken Elsey's recommendation to Truman, then the speech that articulated what became known as the Truman Doctrine might never have been given. Also, the image that Clifford conjures up is one of the wise mentor schooling his inexperienced pupil, with Clifford telling Elsey that Truman's speech would be "the opening gun in a campaign to bring people up to realization that the war isn't over by any means."[30]

If Elsey is right, Clifford looks more like a bad manager than a wise mentor. He needed Elsey's help with writing and editing the speech and yet had not fully informed him of the circumstances behind the speech, despite the fact that he had been privy to this information for a full two weeks. Either way, after their conversation on Sunday morning, March 9, Elsey was fully committed to the effort, and he and Clifford began the arduous task of reviewing and editing the State Department's draft and transforming it into a message from Truman.

The initial drafts from the State Department left something to be desired. Clifford was concerned that they were "not crisp or tough enough for a Presidential speech" and expressed his concerns to Truman, who told him to get more deeply involved. The next five drafts were a little better but still lacked focus, nor were the language and presentation consistent with a request for a substantial foreign aid appropriation. Clifford and Elsey met with State Department speechwriter Joseph M. Jones and Carl Humelsine, the director of the secretariat at State on March 8, to discuss additional ideas for improving the speech.[31]

Clifford's notes illustrate what he considered to be the important points the speech needed to emphasize. The first point was to compare the cost of a war to the amount the president was asking for. The next was the urgent need for American action, as there was no other nation that could do the job. If the United States did not act, nothing would be done, and the Soviets would expand their influence into the eastern Mediterranean. Truman also needed to emphasize that Greece needed financial support at once in order to develop a "self-sustaining domestic economy." American aid would engender hope within the hearts of the Greek people, which was vital to ensuring that they did not turn to communism. "Totalitarian regimes," Clifford believed, "are born where the people's hope dies." Clifford was also concerned that the president should make clear that the United States would control the funds in order to avoid graft, a black market created from the influx of cash, and wastage. Finally, Clifford believed that the task at hand, while grim, was preferable to the alternative.[32]

In terms of approach, Clifford and Acheson had considered three possibilities. The least confrontational was to simply request that Congress appropriate the funds for Greece, without taking a hostile posture toward the Soviet Union. The second possibility was the "all-out message," which Elsey had initially cautioned against. The compromise position, and the one agreed to, was to lay out for the Congress the dire world situation without being unnecessarily provocative.[33]

When Clifford and Elsey met Sunday morning, March 9, they reviewed the latest draft from Jones and Humelsine. Their draft incorporated the recommendations from the previous day's meeting, but the speech was still not ready for Truman. Its principal deficiency was that, as a product of the State Department, it was not written with the language and phrasing that the president would be comfortable with. It needed to be "Trumanized." The central section of the speech, as written at State and edited by Acheson, read as follows: "It is essential to our security that we assist free peoples to work out their own destiny in their own way and our help must be primarily in the form of that economic and financial aid which is essential to economic stability and orderly political processes."[34] Clifford and Elsey were satisfied with the content, but felt that it did not sound like Truman and, furthermore, lacked a memorable line—or, in today's parlance, a "sound bite." Elsey's solution was simple, yet enormously effective. He recommended breaking the paragraph into three single sentences, with each sentence beginning with the phrase "I believe that . . ." Elsey's idea was the breakthrough they needed, and in conjunction with the "well over one hundred" other changes they made that Sunday afternoon, the speech was ready for Truman to see.[35]

Truman was mostly satisfied with the speech, although he thought it still needed a little more punch. In deference to the State Department, Truman also asked Clifford to share the latest copy with Acheson. Acheson approved of most of the speech, though he objected to a couple of items, two of which were minor. The last had been inserted at Snyder's insistence, and recommended that the speech stipulate that American aid to a given country be contingent upon that nation's having a strong free enterprise system. Acheson strongly objected. He pointed out that with such a stipulation the present Labour government in Great Britain might not qualify for American aid, yet it would be ludicrous to suggest that the United States would withhold aid from its most important ally. Acheson later wrote that he invoked Marshall's name and prestige in order to convince Clifford to go along with his suggestions; Clifford claimed that he accepted Acheson's changes without any further discussion. Either way, with that issue settled, the speech was complete.[36]

Marshall, who was in Moscow for a meeting of the Council of Foreign Ministers, objected to the overall tone. Both he and State Department Soviet expert Charles Bohlen thought there "was a little too much flamboyant anti-Communism in the speech." They both also felt that the speech utilized a bit too much rhetoric. Marshall cabled his objections back to Washington, but to no avail. According to Bohlen, Marshall "received a reply that in the considered opinion of the executive branch, including the President, the Senate would not approve the doctrine without the emphasis on the Communist danger."[37] Marshall's biographer, Forrest Pogue, argued that Clifford thought that the language in the State Department's drafts was too timid. For Clifford, this speech was a perfect opportunity to improve Truman's image as a decisive leader and to assume the mantle of spokesman for the free world.[38]

Joseph Jones's account of the writing of the speech, from his 1955 book *The Fifteen Weeks,* concurs with Clifford's with respect to Acheson's three changes, but it contradicts Clifford's account in one important respect. According to Jones, "Clifford had tightened up the message further and had adapted it slightly to suit the President's delivery. Except for three additions, he had made no material change in organization, content, or phraseology."[39] Acheson makes the same observation in his memoirs, *Present at the Creation.*[40] Clifford disputes both of their accounts and argues that both Acheson and Jones gave the White House staff short shrift in crediting its contribution to the speech. Clifford suggests that Acheson and Jones were too pressed for time to compare their draft from March 9 with the heavily revised draft Clifford shared with them the next day.[41] Elsey also disputed Jones's account, which suggests that the White House staff butchered his beautifully written speech. Jones's "beautiful prose," he noted, would not have been suitable for Truman—or Acheson.[42]

Truman gave the speech on March 12, 1947, before a joint session of Congress. The Truman Doctrine, as it soon became known, would be the cornerstone of American foreign policy for the next forty years. Many years later Clifford reflected on its significance: "As I look back on it now, I think that was too broad a statement of our country's policy. . . . It could, however, very well have placed too many responsibilities upon the United States in the years that followed if the language was taken literally. . . . It did serve a very useful purpose in 1947; it brought a sense of comfort and deep encouragement to the other nations of Europe who were being very badly pressed."[43] Lest anyone forget the Clifford-Elsey report, Clifford also argued that the policy the Truman Doctrine enunciated was an outgrowth of the 1946 study and its observations about Soviet behavior. The Truman Doctrine speech, he said, sent a message to the Russians that "by God, we understood what they were up to."[44]

Clifford's contribution to the Truman Doctrine, while significant, pales in comparison to that of others, especially Acheson and Truman himself. Clifford oversaw the drafting of the speech in conjunction with Acheson, Jones, and Humelsine. The genesis of the policy must be credited to Acheson, who instantly recognized the opportunity for the United States to seize the initiative and the threat if it did not. The February 27 meeting was perhaps even more significant than the speech itself because it was then that Truman, Marshall, and Acheson convinced the congressional leadership, particularly Vandenberg, the Republican spokesman for foreign policy, to support a substantial appropriation to curtail the spread of communism. Clifford was not in attendance at that meeting, which suggests that although he was heavily involved with the phrasing of the message, he was not a player in the formulation of the policy. In short, the Truman Doctrine was fundamentally a product of the State Department, and in particular Dean Acheson.

The announcement of the Marshall Plan, in June 1947, was the next major shot in the Cold War. As with the Truman Doctrine, the concept of the Marshall Plan came from the State Department. Acheson set loose the first trial balloon on May 8 in a speech before the World Affairs Forum at Delta State Teachers College in Cleveland, Mississippi. Despite the relatively modest setting, Acheson believed it was an opportunity to alert the American people to the imminent Soviet threat. Acheson warned that "human dignity and human freedom" were at stake and that only through substantial foreign aid could Europe be sustained. Acheson's speech was only the beginning, for the State Department, this time without Clifford's help, was already drafting the speech that would launch the Marshall Plan.

Ever the savvy politician and servant of the president, Clifford knew that the emerging program would be one of the most significant of the Truman administration, and he wanted to make sure the president got the credit. He recommended that Truman himself give the speech and call the program the Truman Concept or the Truman Plan. Truman, however, was both more politically astute than Clifford and more comfortable sharing the credit with someone else. "No," he said. "We have a Republican majority in both Houses. Anything going up there bearing my name will quiver a couple of times, turn belly up, and die. Let me think about it a while." A few days later he told Clifford he was sticking to his guns. "I've decided to give the whole thing to General Marshall. The worst Republican on the Hill can vote for it if we name it after the General."[45] Years later, Clifford, who harbored resentment for Marshall stemming from their confrontation over Palestine, referred to it as the "so-called" Marshall Plan. "General Marshall took no real part in it," he said. "Then after it was created, formed, and put in final shape, it was presented to General Marshall on a silver platter."[46] Sans silver platter, Marshall gave a commencement speech at Harvard University on June 5, 1947, in which he proposed a comprehensive plan to assist Europe in recovering from the devastation of World War II.

Congress did not immediately take up the program, and Truman took a low profile in selling it.[47] But from the White House, Clifford and Elsey plotted strategy behind the scenes. In late September Elsey, who thought it had been a mistake not to consult the United Nations regarding aid for Greece and Turkey, warned against making the same mistake again. He argued that the proper approach for presenting the plan to the public and to Congress should involve public consultations with Warren Austin, the U.S. ambassador to the United Nations.[48] Clifford apparently agreed; he sent a memo to the president the very same day. "It is recommended that the President give consideration to having a short conference with Warren Austin on Monday, September 29th, to discuss the general situation," he wrote. "It is felt that this would be valuable from a public relations standpoint in demonstrating that our United Nations representative was consulted before the final decisions were made."[49] Years later, however, Clifford's recollection was different; in 1971 he said, "I would be in disagreement with him [Elsey] in that regard. I would just have to say that Mr. Elsey may have had that view and there may have been others at the time who felt that the U.N. should have been called in. I certainly did not. I'm not sure that we ever would have accomplished what President Truman accomplished if it had been taken to the U.N."[50]

Throughout the summer and fall of 1947 the situation in Europe deteriorated, and Truman's foreign policy advisers became more convinced of the critical need for emergency aid. Clifford continued his efforts to ensure congressional passage of the Marshall Plan, working most closely with Marshall; Robert Lovett, who replaced Acheson as undersecretary of state; Averell Harriman, who had replaced Wallace as secretary of commerce; and Forrestal. Clifford stressed in a memorandum to Truman that "the issues involved are of such importance as to take precedence over all other questions, and the consequences of failure are too grave to permit the President to stop anywhere short of the full use of his Constitutional powers in his efforts to meet the requirements of the situation."[51] Truman agreed, and on October 23 called Congress to say that he would call them into a special session on November 17. Clifford met with Truman on October 28 and again pressed for action on the European Recovery Program, as the Marshall Plan was also known. In order to emphasize its importance Clifford recommended that Truman personally deliver the legislation to Congress. Assistant press secretary Eben Ayers recounted the meeting in his diary: "Clifford said he thought it might be nearing the time when the president should come out with a blunt statement regarding the U.S.S.R. and its position toward the U.S. The president immediately took this up and said, very gravely, that this was a dangerous situation. He said he had talked with Marshall about it. 'I'm not ready to declare war yet,' he said."[52]

The special session met on November 17, and Truman gave a speech imploring Congress to pass an emergency appropriation for France and Italy, whose economies were in desperate shape. While Congress debated the emergency aid bill Clifford again pressed Truman on when the full Marshall Plan legislation would be ready for Congress.[53] Congress, however, had no plans to take up the Marshall Plan before it returned from its Christmas recess in January 1948. In the interim the members approved a $600 million aid package for Italy, France, and Austria.

Congress took up the Marshall Plan when it returned from its recess, but the progress was slow. The February communist coup in Czechoslovakia completely changed the equation, as it was tangible evidence of Soviet consolidation of a sphere of influence in Eastern Europe. On March 5, Lucius Clay, head of the U.S. occupation forces in Germany, sent an alarmist telegram to Washington warning that conflict with the Soviet Union could come with unexpected suddenness. These two setbacks over a short period of time took Washington by surprise, and the White House scrambled to come up with a response. Elsey believed that Truman needed to speak out publicly against the Soviet aggression, and he sent Clifford a memo on the day of the Clay telegram urging the president to use a previously scheduled speaking appointment before the Friendly Sons of St. Patrick dinner in New York to deliver the message.[54] "In the St. Patrick's Day Speech," wrote Elsey, "the President must, for his own prestige and the prestige of the United States, make a very strong speech. The speech must be strong both in content and in delivery. In the last ten days . . . especially since the fall of Czechoslovakia, demands for a stronger U.S. foreign policy have come from many sources. . . . The strongest possible speech for the President would be on Russian relations."[55]

Clifford took Elsey's recommendation to the president, but Truman wavered back and forth as to whether or not to go ahead with the speech, and if so whether it should be in New York, as Elsey suggested, or as a message to Congress. An exasperated Elsey confided to his notes that as of Tuesday, March 9, the situation was "wide open and up in the air." On March 5 Truman decided not to make the speech because "it would look political." The next day he decided to go ahead because "it would look cowardly to back out." Three days later the speech was back on, only at that point Truman wanted to speak "off the cuff" rather than deliver a formal, prepared speech. "This horrified me," Elsey wrote, "because it's stark madness for the President to make extemporaneous remarks to an audience while he is on the air! [Clifford was] also dismayed, but hesitates to speak up yet."[56]

While Truman continued to waver regarding the time and place, Clifford and Elsey began work on the speech, in conjunction with the State Department. Once again they were dissatisfied with the drafts that were coming over from Foggy Bottom. Clifford and Elsey read a March 6 draft from Lovett but thought it "totally inadequate and completely unsuitable for the President, most[ly] because it said nothing."[57] On Thursday, March 11, Clifford read the second draft from State and was still not satisfied. Clifford wanted the speech to acknowledge that the postwar recovery period was difficult, yet it was made more difficult because not all nations wanted peace, and in fact the Soviets' behavior was contrary to peace. He also wanted to draw a contrast between the United States, which was taking realistic measures to ensure peace, and the Soviet Union, whose aggression was antithetical to peace.[58]

Clifford met with Bohlen on Saturday, March 13, to discuss themes and strategy for the upcoming speech. Without a decision from Truman as to the time and place, the two men were forced to grapple with that issue as well. Further complicating the matter was their concern that the House Republicans were playing politics with the Marshall Plan. They expected that the Senate would approve the legislation that evening, but Speaker of the House Joseph Martin, among others, did not want to pass a clean bill because Truman proposed it and because they saw it as a monument to Vandenberg. Although himself a Republican, Vandenberg, an internationalist and a senator, did not have strong relations with Republicans in the House. Clifford and Bohlen anticipated that if Martin and his allies attached omnibus measures to the bill it would further delay passage until the second week of April. With that in mind, Bohlen recommended that Truman use the Friendly Sons of St. Patrick event as a trial balloon, following up with a speech before Congress on March 22. That, he believed, was the right timetable.[59] With all the obstacles the plan was encountering, Clifford must by then have been relieved that the president had not gone along with his recommendation to name it the Truman Plan.

Keeping in mind the difficulties in the House, along with Truman's earlier fear that the speech might look too political, Clifford opted to take the bipartisan high road. He wanted language in the speech saying that in a foreign policy crisis everyone in Washington needed to "thrust aside personal or political ambition," especially given that 1948 was a presidential election year. "At times like this," he wrote, "loyalty to party must give way to a greater loyalty—loyalty to country." Republicans and Democrats needed to come together because "the American people have the right to assume that political considerations will not affect our working together. They have the right to assume that we will join hands, wholeheartedly and without reservation, in our efforts to preserve peace in the world."[60]

Truman must have decided that the situation in Europe was too critical to go with a trial balloon first; he decided to give a major foreign policy address on St. Patrick's Day before a joint session of Congress. Clifford, Elsey, and the State Department continued to work on the speech, but they encountered the same difficulties as they had with the speech that became the Truman Doctrine. On March 15 Marshall sent over a draft, but both Elsey and Clifford thought it was "weak and meaningless" and they "used practically none of it." Marshall was angry that Clifford had ignored his recommendations, perhaps because a White House adviser was impinging upon his authority as secretary of state, and he lit into Clifford in the Cabinet Room the next day.[61] Marshall and Bohlen were both concerned about the rhetoric of the speech, and Bohlen asked Clifford to water it down. But Clifford would have none of it. "It had to be blunt to justify the message!" he argued. The president was going to the Hill to ask for legislation; how could he explain or justify it without blunt language? Marshall warned that an inflammatory speech by Truman might "pull the trigger—start the war."[62]

Truman went to the Capitol on March 17, almost exactly a year to the day of the creation of the Truman Doctrine, and gave a strong speech in which he laid blame for the deteriorating conditions in Europe solely at the feet of the Soviet Union. The president laid out the situation in stark terms—the confrontation with the Soviet Union was nothing short of a struggle between tyranny and freedom. In order to counter this threat, Truman called for passage of the Marshall Plan, again called for universal military training, requested a resumption of the draft, and broke a long-standing policy by suggesting that the United States might take part in a European regional defense pact, which became NATO. Apparently the House Republicans got the message, for two days later the Appropriations Committee sent the plan to the floor, recommending passage.[63] Clifford was ecstatic. "Your delivery was magnificent," he gushed in a telegram to Truman, "and the first reaction is better than we could have hoped for." He added, "I was just as proud as I could be."[64]

Like the Truman Doctrine, the Marshall Plan was conceived and formulated by the State Department, especially Dean Acheson, as Clifford took great pains to point out. Clifford's role was to serve as a White House liaison with Congress and the departments of State, Treasury, and Commerce. When it came time for Truman to publicly make the case for the urgency of the legislation, Clifford was the primary speechwriter. Clifford's contribution to the Marshall Plan, especially his role in drafting the St. Patrick's Day speech, also illuminates the nexus of electoral politics and foreign policy.

In nudging the president to take a more active role with respect to the Marshall Plan Clifford, in addition to assisting with passing the legislation and speeding relief to Europe, was functioning as image maker. Early on he recommended that the plan be named after Truman rather than Marshall. Although Clifford would later harbor resentment of Marshall, it is unlikely that his interest in naming the plan after the president was indicative of a desire to deny the credit to Marshall. Truman, who was battered in the polls and humiliated by the 1946 electoral debacle, had begun to turn things around in 1947. Pollster Elmo Roper attributed Truman's rise to his emergence from the shadow of Franklin Roosevelt and his coming to be seen as a stronger figure, especially after the departure of James Byrnes. Roper also observed that the president "began increasingly to follow his own convictions, his own judgment in preference to that of the rather hastily assembled brain trust he had previously followed. . . . In the spring an aggressive, coherent foreign policy emerged." Public support for Truman's policies was amply demonstrated by a March 1947 poll, which revealed considerable support for the Truman Doctrine, and five additional polls from July to November 1948, which showed public support for the Marshall Plan growing from 47 percent to 67 percent, with concomitantly lower disapproval numbers.[65]

As a close adviser of the president, especially one focused on domestic policy and politics, Clifford was familiar with the polls and particularly Truman's recovery in 1947. This is not to say, however, that the foreign policy merits of the plan were not important to Clifford. Since the September 1946 presentation of the Clifford-Elsey report he had become more involved with foreign policy issues and was no doubt influenced by the February 1948 Czech coup. Nonetheless, the evidence does suggest that electoral considerations played a prominent role in his thinking.

In pushing for the November 17 special session, Clifford's first priority was inflation, not foreign aid.[66] In suggesting that Truman publicly confer with UN ambassador Austin, Clifford's preeminent concern was public opinion and political strategy, not ensuring that Austin's voice was heard. The prominence of political considerations was most strongly demonstrated by the St. Patrick's Day speech. In making his case for a major foreign policy address, Elsey argued that Truman would make "Big Headline news" by publicly rejecting Wallace's conciliatory posture toward the Soviets. Although he also observed that American participation in a European defense pact would make "Bigger Headline news," Elsey recommended that the White House control the drafting of the speech so that the State Department would not "steal the President's thunder." Elsey's recommendation won the day as he and Clifford controlled the process, virtually shutting out the recommendations of the secretary of state. The day after the speech, Clifford received a memo from William L. Batt Jr., the head of the Democratic National Committee's research division. "The President's Address to Congress . . . was the best yet," Batt wrote. "The writing was clear, straightforward and forceful. . . . The presentation was forthright, unpretentious and terribly sincere. I have never heard the President do better."[67]

The Marshall Plan and the St. Patrick's Day speech were more than foreign policy statements; they were also opportunities for burnishing Truman's image as a decisive leader. That year, 1948, was a presidential election year, and Henry Wallace was expected to run as a third-party candidate. Foreign policy was the easiest way for Truman to distance himself from Wallace and, in general, it fostered a strong image for the president. Although concerned about Soviet behavior, Clifford certainly saw the opportunity to enhance Truman's image and put some wind in his electoral sails.

Clifford was apt to interject himself into a foreign policy matter when he was afraid that Truman might take a public position that would weaken him politically. In July 1946 reparations ambassador Edwin Pauley sent Truman a memorandum in which he argued that Korea was "not receiving the attention and consideration that it should" and that the Soviets were establishing a permanent presence there.[68] The State Department drafted a reply, but Clifford was concerned about the anti-Soviet language he read in the draft. Clifford, who had not yet adopted an anti-Soviet posture, cautioned Truman in a July 12, 1946, memorandum:

> I do not believe that a letter to Mr. Pauley should contain any remarks which would be embarrassing to you if the letter were published. It seems to me that some parts of the draft prepared by the Dept. of State might well be omitted. I have no reluctance in speaking frankly and bluntly about the Soviet Union on appropriate occasions, but it does not seem to me that anything could be gained by making remarks in this letter about Russia which Moscow could use for propaganda purposes if your letter were released or if it leaked.[69]

In an interesting coincidence, on the same day that he sent a memorandum to Truman advising caution, Truman gave Clifford the assignment that resulted in the stridently anti-Soviet Clifford-Elsey report. In early July 1946, however, Clifford's inexperience would have made him somewhat reluctant to speak "frankly and bluntly" about the Soviet Union.

As the president's primary political adviser, Clifford received suggestions for enhancing Truman's political stature through diplomatic measures as well as observations about the American public's reaction to foreign policy. In July 1948, during the early weeks of the Berlin Airlift, Batt sent a memorandum to Clifford suggesting that the president send General Dwight D. Eisenhower to Berlin as the president's personal representative. Two and a half weeks later Batt sent another memorandum to Clifford in which he argued that "if the pending negotiations between the Western Powers and the Soviet Union should lead to a satisfactory settlement of the major issues, particularly with regard to the situation in Berlin, it seems desirable to underscore this success of our foreign policy as emphatically as possible." And in May Batt had sent Clifford a memorandum discussing polling figures of public support for Truman's foreign policy. The numbers and findings were not terribly encouraging, showing only 30 percent approval against 40 percent disapproval and 30 percent with no opinion. Batt suggested that Clifford "ought to see them [the polls] regularly."[70]

Clifford was also quick to recognize that the escalating propaganda war between the United States and the Soviet Union could be used to the president's advantage, particularly as it provided justification for the administration's policies. Clifford provided comments to Attorney General Tom Clark concerning a speech Clark planned to make regarding Russia in May 1947. Clifford recommended a wording change, substituting the term "communist" for "totalitarian." He reasoned that if the Soviets objected, that would be an admission that they were totalitarian. In late September of that year Humelsine sent Clifford a translation of an article that had appeared in the Russian *Literary Gazette*. The article was a lengthy tirade against Truman and American imperialism, including the observation that the "clearest expression of historical ineptitude of American imperialism is precisely the figure of the man whom Wall Street has hailed as its apostle, the figure of Harry Truman, the small man in the short pants." Humelsine noted gleefully that "if this bird will write about two more articles the President will be elected without having to worry with a campaign."[71]

On other occasions when Clifford weighed in on foreign policy matters his recommendations were shaped to a great extent either by politics or in the interests of presenting the United States as the morally righteous party in the battle against the Soviet Union. One example was Clifford's involvement in a minor incident in Hungary during the closing days of 1948 and early 1949. On December 27, 1948, József Mindszenty, a Roman Catholic cardinal, was arrested in Budapest and charged with treason. The U.S. government, specifically Lovett and Truman, publicly described the arrest as a sham, the charges as false, and the incident indicative of a lack of respect for fundamental human rights. On February 8, 1949, Cardinal Mindszenty was found guilty of treason and sentenced to life imprisonment. The same day Clifford called Acheson, who had been appointed secretary of state at the beginning of Truman's second term, to discuss the matter. Clifford thought the Russians had given the United States "an excellent opportunity" and that they "had walked into a hornet's nest." According to a memo documenting Clifford's phone call, "He believe[d] that the Russians [had] made a colossal blunder and wondered if there was not some way the President could utilize this." He also argued that the affair was not a religious matter, as both Catholics and Protestants were united in their opposition to the Hungarian government's actions; rather, it was a question of "'freedom vs. tyranny.'" This incident "might provide an opportunity to dramatize the basic difference between our two philosophies," Clifford argued. Acheson agreed and drafted a presidential statement, which Truman instructed Acheson to deliver.[72]

Another example of Clifford's weighing in on the politics of a foreign policy issue concerned his comments on the State Department's China White Paper in 1949. In June 1949 Mao Zedong's Chinese Communist army defeated Chiang Kai-shek's Nationalists, forcing Chiang and his army to retreat to the island of Formosa, now known as Taiwan. The defeat in Asia was a bitter pill to swallow, especially in light of the Truman administration's successes in Europe. The political backlash was devastating, as Republicans and the so-called China Lobby, led by publishing magnate Henry Luce, mercilessly attacked the Truman administration for being pro-communist and "losing" China. The charges were outrageous, but Truman and the State Department could not sit idly by as the recriminations mounted. In response the State Department produced a 1,000-page "White Paper" to justify its policies in China.

Truman asked Clifford to read and comment on the paper before he would agree to its release. Clifford in turn gave Elsey the same assignment and received a memorandum from Elsey outlining his concerns on July 5. Because Clifford was to meet with Acheson to discuss the matter, Elsey assumed that Clifford would study the document prior to Clifford's meeting with Acheson and that Elsey's comments would simply be used to supplement Clifford's own observations. Clifford, however, had not even read the draft, as Elsey was shocked to learn and as he noted on his copy of the draft memo. Clifford made but a handful of minor wording changes to Elsey's memo and submitted it to the president the next day under his own signature.[73] The memo made a number of insightful points, yet the tone suggests that the writer's aim was to ensure the most favorable public reception of the White Paper, an assessment with which Elsey concurred.[74] "Failure to refer to Yalta in the White Paper openly and frankly would bring, I feel, so much criticism that the value of the White Paper would be seriously diminished," Elsey wrote. In conclusion, Elsey argued that "if the later chapters can be brought up to the excellent level of Chapters I and II, the White Paper will be an important historical document of far-reaching significance and wide public interest."[75]

State redrafted the paper based upon Clifford and Elsey's recommendations, and on Thursday, July 14, Clifford spoke to Elsey about the next steps. He asked Elsey to read the new draft for him, as Elsey had done for the earlier one, and emphasized that the president had taken "considerable interest" in the White Paper. According to Elsey's notes on this meeting, Clifford anticipated that extensive rewriting would still be needed and informed Truman that four teams at the State Department would be working on it under the direction of ambassador at large Philip Jessup. Clifford also observed that the "hell being raised in [the] Senate" over the loss of China was making it difficult to talk about other foreign policy priorities, such as the North Atlantic Pact (NATO) and arms for Europe.[76]

On August 2 Jessup sent a memorandum to Clifford discussing the release of the China White Paper. "In view of our emphasis upon the bipartisan approach in this whole matter," Jessup wrote, "it would be desirable to include [Senator Kenneth] Wherry and [Congressman Joseph] Martin in the distribution in addition to the eight you mentioned to me on the 'phone."[77] Wherry and Martin were the Republican minority leaders of the Senate and the House respectively, and they were both staunch isolationists.

In the case of both the China White Paper and the Mindszenty episode Clifford played the part of foreign policy spinmeister rather than that of someone actually making policy. Clifford's role with respect to the White Paper was to ensure that the document, essentially a State Department apologia, effectively presented the victory of the Chinese communists as inevitable and completely outside of Washington's control. In the case of the Hungarian cardinal, Clifford wanted to use the incident to demonstrate the tyranny of Soviet-bloc communism, and implicitly to point out the correctness of Truman's policy.

Truman biographer Robert Donovan has said that the job of the special counsel was "essentially political."[78] With that sort of mind-set Clifford was more apt to see the political angle, while members of the

State Department were not. In November 1949, Jack Beal of Time, Inc., sent Clifford a proposed article that was to appear in *Collier's* magazine. The article concerned the political shift in China some years earlier from a nation dominated by the Chinese Nationalist Party, the Kuomintang, to the temporary constitutional government that preceded the communist revolution. "No one writing official reports at that time had the kind of background that made this mean anything to him, but it may mean something to you as one who understands electoral and palace politics," Beal wrote.[79] During the time to which Beal referred, "no one" included Marshall, whom Truman had sent to China in 1946 in a failed attempt to mediate between the two sides.

The Truman Doctrine and the Marshall Plan, along with the Clifford-Elsey report, were pivotal moments in the early days of the Cold War, and Clifford played an important, although not a prominent, role in all of them. His participation in these and other foreign policy issues, as well as his closeness to Truman, spawned a certain amount of exaggeration on the part of historians—and Clifford himself—as to his importance as a foreign policy adviser. Douglas Frantz and David McKean, for example, citing a 1968 article that appeared in *Ramparts* magazine, claim that Clifford had a hand in writing NSC-68, yet that document was solely the brainchild of Paul Nitze.[80] As an ambitious and somewhat immodest man, Clifford was apt to exaggerate the part he played in these crucial foreign policy decisions. He likened his role to that of the national security advisor, although Clifford's position was not nearly as formal as that of the national security advisor under Kennedy and Johnson.[81] One of Clifford's contemporaries described his role best, observing that it was "as big as he could make it."[82]

As of the summer of 1946 Clifford had almost no involvement in foreign policy and, according to Elsey, had little interest in it. Clifford suggested otherwise: "I might say, that as I began to get into these areas, I found that the enormous, attractive, and almost magnetic force that was pulling me on was in the area of national security and foreign policy. I obviously dealt some with domestic policy, but I found out after a while that foreign policy became my major interest." On another occasion Clifford asserted that national security issues were his "main interest" and that during his first year at the White House, prior to being named special counsel, "a latent interest in this field really came into full bloom."[83] Over time, Clifford began to see himself as a foreign policy specialist. When Lyndon Johnson asked him to be attorney general Clifford turned him down, explaining that "my background and training in government falls heavily within the national security and foreign policy field, and that is where my interest lies."[84]

Clifford could claim a role in the major foreign policy issues of the day because he was the president's primary speechwriter, and speeches such as the Truman Doctrine address influenced Cold War foreign policy for decades to come. The individuals who prepare a president's remarks implicitly have some contribution to the policy itself, for the very act of stating a policy requires it to be defined. Charles Murphy, who replaced Clifford as special counsel, said that the "special counsel to the president received more assignments in the foreign policy and security fields than other members of the White House staff because of his regular responsibility for the staff work on presidential speeches and messages to Congress."[85] Elsey said of Clifford, "His major responsibility was to assist Mr. Truman in speeches. And increasingly, from 1946 on, the speeches, the messages to Congress, the special statements that Clifford had to work on, had a foreign policy emphasis."[86]

As much as he might have wanted to serve in a national security capacity, however, Clifford's job had only marginal influence in foreign policy making. According to Elsey:

> Clifford was not making foreign policy recommendations. . . . There was no National Security structure (i.e., National Security Advisor). . . . Foreign policy recommendations were made and shaped in the Department of State and such ancillary organizations as Treasury or Pentagon, and would come to the White House pretty well shaped, pretty well made. . . . Clifford wasn't making foreign policy recommendations. . . . He might have influenced how Truman handled it, what he said, or he might have shaped the phrasing of the speech.[87]

Elsey humbly described his and Clifford's role as follows:

> There were no "experts" on foreign affairs in the White House. There *were* a few of us on the White House staff who dealt on a pretty regular basis with the Department of State and the Department of Defense. I was one of them, but we did not purport to be foreign policy *makers* or foreign policy *experts*. The President looked to the Secretary of State and the Secre-

tary of Defense, the Joint Chiefs of Staff, for the advice, the opinions, the information, and the recommendations that he needed in formulating foreign policy decisions. The National Security Council was organized as a result of passage of the National Security Act of 1947 and the NSC, from the time it was created and through the remaining years of the Truman administration, was the focus of the major foreign policy discussions within the administration.[88]

According to Elsey, 90 percent of foreign policy formulation was done by the State Department and the Department of Defense, with only about 10 percent coming from the White House. He suggested that Clifford might have conceded as much later in life, especially when he was no longer in the business of impressing his clients.[89]

To the extent that Clifford was a player with respect to foreign policy, it was mainly a result of his personal contact with key individuals such as Acheson, Forrestal, and Lovett. By virtue of those contacts Clifford worked informally as a liaison between the White House, the State Department, and the military, so in this sense his role was something of a precursor to the position of national security advisor. Clifford defined his position as "a focal point in the White House to which the defense and foreign policy establishments could bring their special problems."[90] Many years later he recalled: "I remember the Secretary of State used to call me when he had something coming up and would tell me ahead of time what it was and oftentimes I would go in then, when he came over to meet with President Truman. That relationship was very definitely that way when Secretary Forrestal, who was first Secretary of the Navy, and then was the first Secretary of Defense, would come over to see the President."[91] Forrestal and Clifford would meet every Wednesday for breakfast, and Clifford said that during those meetings Forrestal pressed him to encourage Truman to take a more aggressive posture toward the Soviet Union. Walter Isaacson and Evan Thomas, authors of *The Wise Men*, described those breakfasts as early National Security Council meetings.[92]

Given Forrestal's intense feelings regarding the Soviet Union it seems plausible that he and Clifford would have discussed the proper way to deal with the Soviet Union over these breakfasts. It would be a stretch, however, to describe these weekly get-togethers as early meetings of the National Security Council. More than likely, Forrestal's primary motivation for meeting with Clifford was not to debate foreign policy but for more self-interested reasons. As the president's point man on military unification, Clifford was the person to see. In addition, Forrestal was not just the secretary of the Navy; he was also a passionate advocate of the Navy and fought hard against unification of the military services. Forrestal may well have invited Clifford to join him for breakfast at his home in order to lobby on behalf of the Navy. Clifford never shared his Forrestal breakfast conversations with Elsey, but Elsey nonetheless believed that discussions of military unification would have occupied most of their time.[93] Forrestal makes no mention of these breakfast meetings in his diary.

Clifford's relationship with Acheson was similar to his relationship with Forrestal. As a savvy bureaucratic player Acheson recognized Clifford's close relationship to Truman and concluded it was in his own best interests to keep Clifford involved and informed. But Acheson was not meeting with Clifford on matters of substance; he was merely recounting what he and Truman had talked about. Acheson recognized that it was in the State Department's best interests, as well as his own, to keep Clifford in the loop.[94] Given Truman's confidence in Acheson, as manifested in Acheson's appointment as secretary of state in 1949, Acheson would not have needed Clifford to bring his "special problems" to Truman. He could have done that himself. In the case of Clifford's relationship with Acheson, then, the term "liaison" might be a bit too strong, as Clifford was being informed by Acheson, not consulting with him.

It would also be an exaggeration to describe Clifford as an early national security advisor. Clifford described himself as such, as did Forrest Pogue, who might have simply accepted Clifford's characterization, yet most historians have not. Walter Isaacson and Evan Thomas believed that Averell Harriman, in his later position as director of the Mutual Security Agency, was the first person to serve in the capacity of national security advisor.[95] Elsey, who later served as Harriman's assistant, said that Harriman was the closest thing to a national security advisor during the Truman administration. Truman had no national security advisor, Elsey recalled. "Truman's NSC staff was minute, never more than six professionals . . . headed by an executive secretary with no more independent authority than the words 'executive secretary' imply. This man worked so anonymously," noted Elsey, that few people "recognize the name of James S. Lay, Jr."[96]

Atomic weapons, so crucial to ending World War II, became the preeminent military and national security consideration with which Truman and his successors had to grapple. Indicative of its importance to the president, Clifford informally served as Truman's liaison with the Atomic Energy Commission (AEC), the civilian organization charged with overseeing the nation's nuclear stockpile. In fact, when Truman decided to maintain civilian control over atomic weapons in 1946, Clifford was one of the first persons in whom he confided.[97] As with foreign policy, the key ingredient to Clifford's influence in a matter outside the scope of his responsibility was personal contact.

David Lilienthal, Truman's nominee to head the newly created Atomic Energy Commission, and Clifford became friends in 1946. "I have come to have a very high opinion of him—clear-headed, decisive, and with none of the maneuver complex, none discernible at least, that so marred some of his predecessors," Lilienthal confided to his diary.[98] Their friendship would become closer as a result of Lilienthal's difficult confirmation fight in early 1947. As the former head of the Tennessee Valley Authority, Lilienthal was a highly respected New Deal liberal and was assured of enthusiastic support from the Democrats. The Republicans, however, had just taken both houses of Congress in the fall of 1946, and their leaders in the Senate, Kenneth Wherry and Robert Taft, were opposed to the nomination. Lilienthal, they argued, had coddled communists during his tenure at the Tennessee Valley Authority and therefore could not be trusted to safeguard the nation's nuclear weapons. Lilienthal had little appetite for a fight and did not want to hurt the president by providing an easy target for partisan attacks. But Clifford offered assurance that "the President was in the fight to the finish," and Lilienthal decided to stick with it.[99]

As the partisan wrangling over Lilienthal's confirmation heated up, Truman began to lose his temper, which he vented—as he often did—by penning an angry screed. The letter, which he may have intended to read at a press conference, was a rant against the Republicans for taking "a low party viewpoint" throughout the confirmation hearings, which he called a "fiasco." He angrily dismissed accusations that Lilienthal was pro-communist and mocked his accusers as "peanut politicians" who were out to "ruin a good man for their personal satisfaction and the detriment of the country and the world." Press secretary Charlie Ross, and probably Clifford, interceded, convincing Truman to keep the letter private and take the more presidential high road. When the final confirmation vote was taken Lilienthal was confirmed, thanks largely to the efforts of Senator Vandenberg, who publicly opposed Taft. Clifford played a high-profile role throughout the process, a role for which he received a good deal of attention in the press.[100]

With Lilienthal confirmed, Clifford had an ally at the head of the agency in charge of safeguarding the nation's nuclear weapons. The relationship was mutual, as Lilienthal utilized Clifford as his liaison and ally in the White House. In August 1947, Clifford and Lilienthal met to discuss a report prepared by the Joint Chiefs of Staff regarding a nuclear test conducted at the Bikini atoll in the South Pacific. Both Clifford and Lilienthal were concerned that the test had reopened the issue of military versus civilian control of nuclear weapons. Clifford had been unaware of the report's existence and was, according to Lilienthal, "incredulous that the Joint Chiefs would release a report without getting Truman's approval." The following May Lilienthal contacted Clifford regarding another successful nuclear test, this time at Eniwetok island, and requested a meeting with the president. Truman was pleased with the results of the test and approved an AEC plan to apply the knowledge gained at Eniwetok to the latest weapon designs. Clifford and Lilienthal also discussed the Knowland Bill, a measure working its way through Congress that would direct the FBI to investigate presidential nominees to the AEC. In this case they came down on opposite sides of the issue. Perhaps bowing to the escalating anticommunist and loyalty fervor, Lilienthal advised the president not to veto the bill. Clifford, on the other hand, considered the bill to be an unconstitutional infringement on the executive branch. Lilienthal was "rather taken aback by the vehemence" with which Clifford opposed the legislation. "As long as I am here," Clifford said, "I shall raise my voice against approving or the signing of any such bill. It is part of an attack by the legislative upon the executive branch, a grave violation of the separation of powers." Truman followed Clifford's recommendation and vetoed the bill, a veto that the Senate narrowly sustained.[101] In August 1948 Lilienthal sent Clifford a copy of the fourth semiannual AEC report to Congress. "This tells a story of considerable progress, since the day we first talked things over," he wrote. Indicative of their growing partnership, he signed the handwritten cover note, "With gratitude and increasing respect and admiration."[102]

The news regarding atomic weapons was not always good. In late December 1948 Clifford read a proposed article by Admiral W. S. Parsons that was scheduled to appear in the *Saturday Evening Post*. In the article Parsons downgraded and deprecated the value of the atomic bomb as a military weapon. Clifford thought it would be a big mistake to allow the article to be published. "I have read the article and have the deep conviction that it would be definitely inadvisable to publish this article," he wrote. "Secretary Lovett says that it is exactly the wrong approach for us to take at this time insofar as our relations with the Soviet Union are concerned."[103] Clifford and Lovett were concerned that U.S. defense strategy would be threatened if the military efficacy of atomic weapons were called into question, particularly by a senior naval official. What Clifford does not say, but what he must have been thinking, was the risk that if the American public lost faith in the U.S. nuclear deterrent it might also lose faith in Truman's foreign policy. For those reasons, he adamantly opposed publication of Parsons's article.

Clark Clifford, who in July 1946 had no strong opinions regarding the Soviet Union, was a committed Cold War liberal by March 1947. In a position so close to the center of power during such a pivotal period of twentieth-century American history, it was inescapable that he would play an important role in the crucial decisions made from late 1946 into 1948. Clifford's role was limited, however, as he had no formal authority; and, despite his efforts to interject himself into national security matters, he was still overshadowed by such towering figures as Marshall, Acheson, and Forrestal.[104] Through personal relationships, and by virtue of his close association with President Truman, Clifford was in constant contact with key figures at the Department of Defense, the Department of State, and the Atomic Energy Commission. As the president's primary speechwriter he also had a voice in shaping what Truman said about foreign policy, more so than the presidential speechwriters of today. Two conclusions can be drawn from his forays into foreign policy. One is the propensity on the part of Clifford and some historians to exaggerate his role and influence. The other is the importance of domestic political considerations.

For Clifford, political considerations were a factor in the Truman Doctrine speech and the St. Patrick's Day speech, as both occasions presented an opportunity to present Truman as a decisive leader struggling to protect his country from a dangerous adversary. Underlining its importance to the president's image, Clifford wanted the Marshall Plan to be named after Truman. In the case of both the China White Paper and Cardinal Mindszenty's trial in Hungary, Clifford's role was to ensure the most favorable spin and to demonstrate the correctness of Truman's foreign policy. Clifford counseled the president on a foreign policy matter when he feared that the president might take a position that could hurt him politically, and he also served as a conduit for ostensible foreign policy recommendations from political operatives. Clifford's influence as a foreign policy adviser should not be overstated. Foreign policy emanated primarily from the State and Defense Departments; there was little foreign policy expertise in the West Wing. Clifford certainly had contacts in those departments and did fill an informal role as liaison, but he was not a national security advisor. His role was "as big as he could make it," both at the time and retrospectively.

# 4

## The Recognition of Israel

Clifford's memoirs begin with his May 1948 showdown with George Marshall over the question of whether Truman should grant recognition to the soon-to-be-declared State of Israel. Clifford tells the story with a dramatic flair, almost in David and Goliath terms, pointing out that Truman regarded Marshall as "the greatest living American." The implication is that Clifford's stature paled in comparison to Marshall's. While it is true that Marshall was a war hero revered by Truman, and indeed the nation, Clifford's influence with Truman was at least equal to, if not greater than, Marshall's.

According to Clifford's account, Truman and Marshall were on a "collision course over Mideast policy," which threatened the viability of the administration, not to mention Truman's reelection bid. Clifford represented the president's position in favor of recognition, while Marshall represented the consensus of the senior people in the foreign policy bureaucracy, including Robert Lovett, Charles Bohlen, George Kennan, and James Forrestal. Their position sprang from pure geopolitical realism: 30 million Arabs on one side and 600,000 Jews on the other. Furthermore, the consensus was that it would be the height of folly to antagonize the Arabs, who were sitting on the largest petroleum reserves in the world. Clifford, however, had been asked by the president to argue the case for recognition. Truman favored recognition, Clifford argued, out of moral and humanitarian concerns. Only three years had passed since Allied troops liberated the survivors from Nazi concentration camps, and Truman was sympathetic to the Zionist cause of a Jewish homeland in Palestine.[1]

Although Clifford makes the case that Truman granted recognition for humanitarian and moral reasons, some historians have accused Truman of granting recognition to Israel in a blatant pander to Jewish votes in a presidential election year. Truman's chances in 1948 were considered bleak at best, and the Jewish bloc, if energized, had the potential to be a crucial swing vote in some key states. Recognition of Israel could help to cement an important segment of the Democratic base and improve Truman's chances that fall. Clifford's playing a major role in the policy debate over recognition signaled to Marshall that domestic politics was the primary factor in the administration's support of Israel. As the president's key political advisor Clifford's motives in this debate deserve close scrutiny, but to Marshall it was an open and shut case—Clifford was demeaning the presidency and threatening U.S. national security in a naked attempt to win votes.

The Jewish vote was not numerically significant—Jews made up only 4 percent of the electorate—but it was concentrated in a few key states, particularly New York. Also contributing to the amount of influence the Jewish vote wielded within the Democratic Party, disproportionate to its numerical significance, was the fact that there were many affluent Jewish voters whom the Democrats counted upon as significant financial contributors.[2] Furthermore, the Jewish vote could not be taken for granted in 1948. The Republican nominee for president, Governor Thomas Dewey of New York, was expected to target the Jewish voter with a strong endorsement of the Zionist cause. With the largest concentration of Jewish voters in New York, then the biggest electoral prize, and Dewey running as the home-state favorite, the Jewish voter was a particularly important constituency if Truman hoped to be elected in 1948. Complicating the matter was that Truman expected a third-party challenge from the left from Henry Wallace, who also planned an appeal to the Jewish voter on the basis of the Palestine issue.

The concept of a Jewish state in Palestine had first been proposed by British foreign secretary Arthur Balfour in 1917. The League of Nations had granted the British a mandate to rule Palestine following the defeat of the Ottoman Empire in World War I. During the twenty years that separated the two world wars the British allowed Jewish immigration into Palestine, and the pace quickened with the onset of World War II. The Arab population did not welcome its new neighbors, and they were successful in pressuring the British to clamp down on Jewish immigration. Those who had already immigrated to Palestine were passionate in defense of their Zionist dream of a Jewish homeland, and they took up arms against both the British and the Arabs. Jews in the United States, to a large extent, supported the Zionist cause, and they were quite vocal in their support. Their often strident advocacy would become a point of contention with Truman, who was a supporter of the idea of a Jewish homeland, yet chafed at both the implicit and explicit threats used to garner additional support from his administration.[3]

As president, Truman's first involvement in the Palestine issue was his effort late in 1945 to convince the British to accept a large bloc of Jewish refugees into Palestine. The Zionists fixed on a number of 100,000, but the British balked, fearing the inevitable increase in Arab-Jewish violence that would accompany such a dramatic influx of displaced Jews. The British adopted a policy of delay, and by the summer of 1946 they had been unable to reach an agreement with the Zionists. That year, 1946, would see midterm elections, and American Zionists' political pressure on Truman had become intense. In New York, Governor Dewey, who had been the Republican presidential candidate in 1944, was up for reelection, and he intended to make a strong statement in support of the Zionist cause. Truman decided to preempt Dewey and issued a statement on Yom Kippur, October 4, 1946, reiterating his support for the admission of 100,000 Jewish refugees into Palestine and declaring for the first time his support for a Jewish state. Despite his efforts, however, Dewey won reelection, and the Democrats lost both the House and Senate. The Palestine issue was certainly not the deciding issue in the 1946 elections, but it did play an important role in New York City, which was normally a Democratic stronghold. At the end of 1946 the voters who were concerned about the Zionist cause sent Truman an unmistakable message that they were displeased. Apparently, despite Truman's support of the Zionist cause, they did not believe he had done enough. Truman had previously expressed his frustration at his inability to satisfy the Jews' demands. During a cabinet meeting back in July he lamented, "Jesus Christ couldn't please them when he was here on earth, so how could anyone expect that I would have any luck?"[4]

At this point Truman was both ambivalent about the Jewish leadership in the United States and abroad and uncertain what he could do to satisfy them. He also revealed more than a little self-pity. Yet circumstances in Palestine changed in 1947, and so would Truman's policies. The Jewish insurgency against the British became increasingly violent, especially among the more militant and nationalist groups. By February 1947 the British had tired of Jewish terrorist violence, and they announced that they would relinquish their mandate to the United Nations. The British move effectively dumped the problem on the doorstep of the United Nations, which would be forced to devise a solution to ensure peace in the region. It also meant that Truman would have to devote far more time and effort to the problem, as he could no longer simply cajole the British to allow refugees to immigrate into Palestine. It would be up to the UN, and principally the United States, to deal with the issue. Compounding the problem was an intensification of the political lobbying of the president by Jewish groups in America. During the latter part of 1947 Truman received approximately 135,000 cards, letters, petitions, and telegrams on the subject, the overwhelming majority of which favored the Jewish cause. Truman was becoming increasingly annoyed with the political pressure, but he could not ignore it.[5]

Around this time Clifford began to take an active interest in Palestine. Prior to that, the only evidence of his involvement with the subject was a passage in the Clifford-Elsey report concerning U.S.-Soviet interests in the Mideast. The report argued that "the U.S.S.R. is playing both sides of the Jewish situation by encouraging and abetting the emigration of Jews from Europe into Palestine, by denouncing British and American Jewish policies, and by inflaming the Arabs against these policies."[6] Clifford, as established earlier, was not the author of the report, so it is unlikely that he had a clear-cut position on the Palestine question at the time. Supporting the Zionist position were two important allies of Clifford's, David Niles and Max Lowenthal. Niles, an administrative assistant and holdover from the Roosevelt administration, was an ardent Zionist and served as Truman's eyes and ears within the Jewish-American community. Niles's portfolio was minority and civil rights issues. Lowenthal had been a counsel and advisor to Truman during his Senate days, and although he was never officially a member of the White House staff, Clifford wrote that "he came and went as he pleased."[7] Clifford, Niles, and Lowenthal were the pivotal players in the recognition of Israel, other than Truman himself. In particular, Lowenthal, who was an outsider yet had the influence and access of an insider, sent a barrage of memorandums to Clifford arguing the case in favor of recognition. To a large extent Clifford served as a conduit for Lowenthal's arguments to reach the president. Truman credited Lowenthal as the primary force behind the recognition of Israel, but because he remained outside the public eye the extent of his involvement was unknown until brought into the light of day years later by historians.[8]

Opposing Clifford and his allies was the entire foreign policy bureaucracy, especially career diplomats in the State Department, who had a strong pro-Arab bias. Clifford's primary nemesis, other than Marshall, was Loy Henderson, the director of Near Eastern and African Affairs. Clifford asserted that Henderson was heavily influenced by the British, partial to the Arabs, and anti-Semitic. Clifford may have been uncharitable in his assessment of Henderson, but he is most likely correct in asserting that Henderson had no tolerance for White House interference in what he considered his personal domain, American foreign policy in the Mideast.[9]

With the British having decided to abandon their mandate in Palestine and relinquish control to the United Nations, the policy debate became far more complicated than pushing for additional Jewish immigration. A special commission of the UN convened in the spring of 1947 to come up with a solution. In September it recommended a plan that called for the partition of Palestine into separate Jewish and Arab states. Henderson was opposed to the plan, considered it unworkable, and presciently warned that "the establishment of a Jewish State in Palestine . . . would cause much bloodshed and suffering . . . and that the continued existence of such a State could cause suffering, expense, bickering, and damage to the United States internally and internationally for many years to come."[10] Henderson put his concerns into a memorandum to Marshall, who shared it with the president. A few days after Henderson gave his memo to Marshall he was called to a meeting at the White House to explain his views to Truman, Niles, and Clifford. Clifford started the conversation by declaring, in what must have been an accusatory fashion, that it was the president's understanding that Henderson was opposed to a Jewish state in Palestine. "It would be appreciated," Clifford said, "if you would explain your reasons." After outlining his arguments, Henderson said, he was "cross-examined." Clifford's follow-up questions, if Henderson's account is to be believed, were quite condescending. "What were the sources of my views?" Henderson recalled Clifford asking him. "Were they merely my opinions which might be based on prejudice or bias? Did I think that my judgment and that of members of my office were superior to that of the intelligent group that the United Nations had selected to study and report on the Palestine problem?"[11]

As the meeting became more confrontational, Henderson grew convinced that Clifford and his allies were trying to humiliate him. Sensitive to the political implications, Henderson assured the group that he understood that the president had to consider both the domestic and international implications of the situation, but nevertheless felt that it was his responsibility to impress upon the president the likely consequences to American interests in the Mideast if he supported the creation of a Jewish state. The bickering continued until Truman had had enough. "Oh, hell," he muttered. "I'm leaving."[12]

Henderson's account of the incident is useful from a narrative perspective, but what is especially enlightening is Truman's state of mind, as Henderson perceived it. According to Henderson's later recollections, it appeared to him that Truman had not made a firm decision to support the Jewish state but feared the repercussions from his party, Congress, the press, and the general public if he withdrew his support. "He was almost desperately hoping," Henderson observed, "that the Department of State would tell him that the setting up in Palestine of Arab and Jewish States as proposed by the UN Commission would be in the interest of the United States. This, however, the State Department thus far had not been able to do."[13]

Clifford and Niles, perhaps sensing Truman's ambivalence, were determined to avoid a reversal, so they undertook some backroom lobbying to push the wavering Truman back over to their side. They enlisted the efforts of Cabinet members Robert Hannegan, the postmaster general and former chairman of the Democratic National Committee; Tom Clark; and Oscar Ewing. All three lobbied the president to push hard for a clear statement from the UN endorsing partition and the creation of a Jewish state. Failure to do so, they warned, threatened the prestige of Truman and the United States.[14] Clifford's efforts paid off—and Henderson suffered a personal defeat—when Truman instructed the State Department to endorse partition. In early October Truman met with Niles, Clifford, and Lovett to review the State Department's statement advocating partition. At that point the fight for a Jewish state in Palestine moved back to the United Nations.

As a result of intense lobbying by the United States, the partition resolution was passed by the UN in November 1947. Clifford applied pressure to wavering delegates to support the resolution. In particular he warned the Philippine ambassador to the UN that relations between the United States and the Philippines would suffer if the latter did not support partition.[15] "I was concerned that it might not go through and talked with the representatives of other nations about it," Clifford said. "We went for it. It was because the White House was for it that it went through. I kept the ramrod up the State Department's butt."[16]

The partition resolution was passed, a victory for Truman, Clifford, Niles, and Lowenthal. While its passage represented a victory for Zionists and their American supporters, it only exacerbated an already volatile situation in Palestine. The Arabs were furious over the resolution, and by early 1948 the two sides were effectively at war. Britain announced that their mandate would expire on May 15 regardless of the situation on the ground in Palestine. As the fighting escalated, the partition policy began to look like a colossal blunder. Absent a United Nations commitment to militarily enforce partition and maintain peace, it seemed that partition was just words on a page but could never become a reality. The position in the State Department changed in favor of establishing a UN trusteeship that would oversee Palestine, thus indefinitely deferring partition.

Clifford and his allies continued to hew to their position despite the objections of the overwhelming majority of the national security establishment. During one of their weekly breakfasts in 1948 Clifford and Forrestal had a frank exchange on the subject. Forrestal told Clifford, "You fellows over at the White House are just not facing up to the realities in the Middle East. There are thirty million Arabs on one side and about six hundred thousand Jews on the other. It is clear that in any contest, the Arabs are going to overwhelm the Jews. Why don't you face up to the realities? Just look at the numbers!"[17]

Clifford and Niles believed that the wall of opposition to the Zionist cause within the State Department had to be breached if they were going to succeed in convincing Truman to stay the course. They needed an ally over at Foggy Bottom, and as their candidate they selected General John Hilldring. Prior to the partition resolution Hilldring had been placed on the delegation to the UN Commission on Palestine, at Niles's suggestion. He reported directly to Niles, and thus the State Department did not know what he passed along to the White House and what instructions he was receiving. Hilldring was appointed to serve the president's interests. What is most notable about this arrangement is the level of distrust felt by Truman toward the State Department.[18] His condescending references to the "striped pants boys" over at State suggest more than a midwestern prejudice against the eastern Establishment. These references, along with the Hilldring appointment, demonstrate Truman's belief that the bureaucrats in the State Department were conducting foreign policy without regard to the president's wishes.

In February 1948, Clifford and Niles arranged for Hilldring to be transferred to Foggy Bottom to serve as a special assistant to Marshall, and with a higher rank than Henderson. The transfer had been plotted by the Wardman Park Group, the sub-Cabinet political strategy team, with Niles in attendance. Furthermore, the group also schemed to have Henderson removed so he could no longer interfere with their plans. Clifford justified his efforts to have Henderson moved out of Washington, believing that he and Niles were on the State Department's blacklist.[19] Truman concurred with the Hilldring appointment, though not with the proposal to transfer Henderson. The Hilldring plan did not work out as Clifford had planned it. Marshall and Lovett resented the obvious ploy to install a White House watchdog in the State Department, and they made it clear to Hilldring that he was not welcome. Hilldring, who revered Marshall, realized the situation was untenable, and near the end of May he tendered his resignation.[20]

Without an influential advocate at the State Department, Clifford and Niles continued to press for partition rather than a UN trusteeship. Publicly Truman was beginning to waver, and Clifford was concerned that a reversal would cost Truman politically. In fact, it did. A February special election in a heavily Democratic, predominantly Jewish district in the Bronx resulted in a humiliating defeat. Leo Isaacson, running under the banner of the American Labor Party, easily defeated the Democratic nominee, taking 56 percent of the vote in a four-person race.[21] The election was considered a rebuke of Truman's policy toward Palestine. Truman's advisors and the Democratic Party feared disaster in November. There were only three months to go until the British mandate expired. Time was running out.

The State Department and the White House continued to work at cross-purposes on the Palestine issue. At State they pushed harder for trusteeship, while at the White House Clifford continued to work toward the goal of a Jewish state. In early March Clifford sent two memos to Truman outlining his case in favor of partition and a Jewish state. Drafts of both documents are found in Lowenthal's papers, which reside at the University of Minnesota, although Clifford claimed to have written them. Also suggesting Lowenthal's authorship is the fact that Clifford had sent Lowenthal over to the office of Eliahu Epstein, the Jewish Agency representative in Washington, to gather material for the memos.[22] In both memos Lowenthal, through Clifford, argued his case in favor of partition, claiming that only partition could preserve peace in Palestine, prevent damage to U.S. prestige, and advance U.S. interests. But Clifford also tried another tactic, arguing that unless the United States pressed for partition the situation would be exploited by the Russians. He stated this explicitly in the first memo, but did not provide further explanation of his argument. In the second memo he outlined his case in greater detail.

"Partition is the only course of action with respect to Palestine that will strengthen our position vis-à-vis Russia," he wrote. Clifford's argument in support of this assertion was a bit of a stretch, as he relied on the importance of the UN to support his thesis. "The United Nations is a God-given vehicle through which the United States can build up a community of powers in Western Europe and elsewhere to resist Soviet aggression and maintain our historic interests." The UN he argued, offered the best hope for peace, and therefore anything that undermined the UN was contrary to peace. "The American people want peace," he wrote. "They fervently believe that the United Nations offers the best hope for peace." Yet that one chance for peace was being squandered, he believed, as demonstrated by the State Department's public retreat from partition.[23] Clifford was referring to UN ambassador Warren Austin's announcement on February 24 that the Security Council was authorized to use force "directed to keeping the peace and not to enforcing partition."[24]

Clifford was essentially saying that the American people's lack of confidence that peace could be preserved and World War III avoided was due to their belief that the United States was backtracking on the partition decision. He watered down this assertion somewhat by arguing that rumors that the United States would enter into military alliances external to the United Nations were contributing to the "disintegration of the United Nations."[25] But his primary point was that a reversal on the partition question would undermine both the United Nations and the American public's faith in U.S. foreign policy.

Of course Clifford had a ready solution to avoid the dark scenario he was suggesting: U.S. support for the UN partition resolution. "In order to save the United Nations for our own selfish interests, the United States must promptly and vigorously support the United Nations actions regarding Palestine," he wrote. Clifford then linked the situation in Palestine to U.S.-Soviet relations when he argued that unless the United States and the UN Security Council took steps to preserve peace in Palestine the situation would deteriorate into an all-out, bloody war. He warned, "There is no more certain way of having Russia move into the Arabian Peninsula than for us to permit war to develop between the Jews and the Arabs—and this is as certain as the rising of tomorrow's sun, less we move promptly to prevent it. Furthermore, when this happens, Russia can move in unilaterally as the defender of world peace and champion of the United Nations. To permit this to happen would be disastrous."[26]

The flaws in Clifford's argument are obvious, especially his prescription for avoiding chaos and war in Palestine. By March 1948, when Clifford sent the two memorandums, the Jews and Arabs were already at war. The State Department believed that UN trusteeship over the region would be more effective at keeping the peace because it would prevent, if only temporarily, the one thing that would inflame Arab passions the most: the declaration of a Jewish state. The threat of military force would be required to enforce partition; and, the State Department argued, the UN Security Council did not have the authority to use force to enforce partition, but only to keep the peace. Clifford's suggestions, drawn from the UN Palestine Commission, for how peace would be kept were unrealistic. He recommended that the United States cooperate with the UN's plans for establishing an international security force but argued that American participation should be limited to recruitment of volunteers. "No American troops would be involved," he promised. In fact, none of the permanent members of the Security Council would contribute forces; the volunteer force would be drawn from smaller nations. Given the solid opposition of the Arabs to a Jewish state it seems implausible that the UN Palestine Commission's plan had a reasonable chance of success, contrary to Clifford's assertion otherwise.[27]

In conclusion Clifford attacked the State Department's emphasis on the importance of Persian Gulf oil to the American economy and the threat posed to the supply due to endorsement of partition. Clifford argued that out of economic necessity the Saudis, in particular, would continue to keep the oil flowing to the United States, even if they disagreed with American foreign policy in Palestine. He also argued that appeasement of the Arabs would undermine U.S. prestige and the foreign policy achievement of the Truman Doctrine. "The most effective way to prevent Russian penetration into the Middle East and to protect vital American oil interests there is for the United States to take the initiative in the Security Council to implement the General Assembly's Palestine resolution," he opined.[28]

Despite Clifford's emphasis on the importance of steadfast support for partition and its perceived link to effective containment of Soviet influence, the domestic political implications are implicit to his argument. In the first memorandum Clifford warned that U.S. prestige was at risk and that because the government had urged partition it was "unthinkable that it should fail to back up that decision in every possible way." From that statement alone it would seem that U.S. foreign policy interests were Clifford's only concern. Yet only two sentences later Clifford advised Truman that it was important for political reasons that the United States exert sufficient pressure on the Arab states to accept partition. "Strong pressures may already have been applied, but it does not look that way to the American people," he warned. "Rather, there have been numerous examples of what appear to be acts of appeasement toward the Arabs. It is inconceivable to most Americans and to many other countries that we cannot—if we really wish to do so—exert sufficient pressure on both the Arabs and the British."[29]

Clifford's allusion to domestic politics in this first memo was subtle. He never expressly mentioned it, and the rest of the memo is concerned with his plan for implementing partition and preserving peace. Yet his observation that the American people may not be aware of the efforts already made to implement partition is telling, and suggests that his primary concern was the domestic audience rather than U.S. interests overseas. No doubt Clifford was concerned that others would interpret his recommendations as being influenced by domestic politics, so he confronted the problem directly at the beginning of his second memorandum:

> At the outset, let me say that the Palestine problem should not be approached as a Jewish question, or an Arab question, or a United Nations question. The sole question is what is best for the United States of America. Furthermore, one's judgment in advising as to what is best for America must in no sense be influenced by the election this fall. I know only too well that you would not hesitate to follow a course of action that makes certain the defeat of the Democratic Party if you thought such action were best for America. What I say is, therefore, completely uninfluenced by election considerations.[30]

Yet saying something does not necessarily make it so. Clifford's discussion of how abandonment of partition was damaging to the UN and contributing to anxiety among the American people could also be interpreted as political in nature. "All of this is causing a complete lack of confidence in our foreign policy from one end of the country to the other and among all classes of our population," he wrote. "This lack of confidence is shared by Democrats, Republicans, young people and old people. There is a definite feeling that we have no foreign policy, that we do not know where we are going, that the President and the State Department are bewildered, that the United States, instead of furnishing leadership in world affairs, is drifting helplessly." Clifford's concern, it would seem, was how Truman's foreign policy would be perceived. In another section of the memo he detailed how partition was consistent with U.S. policy going back to 1917. In making this point Clifford was attempting to answer criticism that Truman had embarked upon a new policy and convince him that despite the criticism, much of which was coming from the State Department, his policy was consistent with American interests and long-standing policy.[31]

Another factor that suggests the importance of domestic politics is the role of Lowenthal. Clifford claimed that he wrote both memos, yet the drafts found in Lowenthal's papers suggest that he was the true author. Either way, the fact that he was collaborating with Lowenthal rather than Elsey is telling. Elsey, after all, was Clifford's deputy, the man he collaborated with on all of his important assignments. Given that Palestine represented a foreign policy issue it seems logical that Clifford would have turned to the person who wrote the Clifford-Elsey report, who helped him draft the Truman Doctrine, and with whom he would be writing the St. Patrick's Day speech. Instead, Clifford turned to a freelance assistant who was an ardent Zionist and who had access to the president. This does not suggest that Lowenthal's interest was primarily political; rather, it suggests that Clifford had already made up his mind and was not looking for analysis and recommendations but simply help in framing the argument. If Clifford's interest in Palestine was limited to its foreign policy implications he would have consulted with Elsey first. Elsey, when asked during his oral history interview about the special counsel's recommendations to the president regarding Israel, deferred to Clifford. "I think it's best to ask Mr. Clifford on that," he said. "I was not privileged with Clifford's conversations with the President on this subject."[32]

While Clifford, Lowenthal, and Niles lobbied the president to continue to support partition and the creation of a Jewish state, members of the State Department worked to advance their agenda in favor of a UN trusteeship. On February 21, 1948, they sent a message to the president outlining their position. The memo urged retreat from partition, arguing that to the extent that the UN Security Council authorized the use of force in Palestine it should be limited to keeping the peace, rather than enforcing partition. The State Department then made the case for trusteeship, arguing that if neither partition nor an alternative solution could be agreed to by both parties "it would then be clear that Palestine [was] not yet ready for self-government and that some form of United Nations trusteeship for an additional period of time [would] be necessary."[33] The State Department memo outlined the policy that they planned to present to the UN, provided it had Truman's blessing. "I approve in principle this basic position," Truman cautiously replied. "I want to make it clear, however, that nothing should be presented to Security Council that could be interpreted as a recession on our part from the position we took in the General Assembly. Send final draft of Austin's remarks for my consideration."[34] Truman met with Marshall and Lovett on March 8, the same day Clifford sent his second memorandum, and both men pressed the idea of trusteeship. Truman conceded, no doubt certain that the trusteeship proposal would be seen only as a temporary measure. He misread the situation badly.

Austin gave his speech endorsing trusteeship at the UN on March 19, the very same policy Truman had, if only tacitly, already endorsed on two separate occasions. Jewish leaders both in the United States and abroad immediately denounced Truman's reversal, perceiving it as a perfidious betrayal. Apparently the temporary nature of the trusteeship plan did not resonate with Zionists, who were anxious to establish a Jewish state no matter how profound the obstacles. The Jewish response was not surprising, though Truman had failed to see it coming. What was quite unexpected was the violent reaction from Truman himself. Truman had expected that he would be consulted or informed prior to Austin's speech, whereas Marshall believed that Austin had been given the authority to go ahead with the speech at a moment of his choosing. Truman prized his relationship with Marshall, but in this case they had badly miscommunicated. The situation was exacerbated by the fact that Truman had met with Zionist leader Chaim Weizmann the day before Austin's speech and had affirmed his commitment to partition.

Truman, despite having approved the speech, was nonetheless furious at Austin and the State Department. In his mind, he had been betrayed, and he confided as much to his diary: "The State Dept. pulled the rug from under me today. . . . This morning I find that the State Dept. has reversed my Palestine policy. The first I know about it is what I see in the papers! Isn't that hell! I am now in the position of a liar and a double-crosser. . . . There are people on the third and fourth levels of the State Dept. who have always wanted to cut my throat. They've succeeded in doing so."[35]

It is unclear why Truman was so angry, but there are a number of possible explanations. At the very least, he must have believed that either Marshall or Lovett would give him advance notice of when Austin planned to deliver the speech. Perhaps he deceived himself into believing that the trusteeship recommendation merely delayed rather than superseded partition.

Truman's biographer Alonzo Hamby argued that the trusteeship debacle demonstrated how overworked Clifford was. Because there were so many other critical issues at the time, Clifford could devote only so much time to each, and because of this failed to see the train coming headlong through the tunnel.[36] Elsey's description of the chaos of March 1948 lends some credence to Hamby's thesis: "The Middle East question was—I don't want to say—down on the priority list, but it was simply one of a number of land mines around that we were trying not to step on that could explode under us. The spring of 1948 was certainly a nervous time. Then came Berlin and the blockade and the airlift. It was literally one damn thing after another."[37]

Clifford was furious as well—perhaps, as Alonzo Hamby has suggested, recognizing that he had contributed to the problem—and took the role as lead inquisitor. "Who authorized this? Heads will roll," he said ominously.[38] Clifford agreed with Truman that the State Department had intentionally embarrassed the president, although unlike Truman he believed that Marshall was to blame. "Marshall didn't know his ass from a hole in the ground," Clifford said. "Marshall left every one of those who had done this thing to the President in power. Not a hair singed. . . . But every Jew thought that Truman was a no good son-of-a-bitch."[39] His anger at the State Department was still evident a year later when he confided to Jonathan Daniels, who was conducting research for his 1950 biography *The Man of Independence:* "I was enraged by the terrible fu—ing the Boss had gotten in April."[40] Eighteen years later he was still convinced of the State Department's treachery.[41]

The White House attempted to handle the fallout over the next couple of days, but the damage had been done. Clifford's interrogation of the principals led to the inescapable conclusion that Austin's statement had been properly cleared.[42] The State Department had not intentionally tried to embarrass the president, and if anyone was to blame it was probably Truman or Clifford. All they could do was attempt to salvage the president's policy, especially in the minds of Jewish voters. With that in mind Truman called a meeting for March 24. A list of those in attendance suggests the political nature of the Palestine debate, or at the very least the importance of containing the political damage following the perceived reversal on partition. Aside from those representing the State Department, there was a distinct political character to the attendees. Among them was Oscar Ewing, the head of the Federal Security Agency, the equivalent to today's Department of Health and Human Services. Ewing had no foreign policy or national security responsibilities, but he was a high-ranking official in the Democratic National Committee (DNC) and its former acting chairman. Also attending was Senator Howard McGrath, who was not a member of the Foreign Relations Committee but was the chairman of the DNC.[43]

The political imperative of the meeting was apparent to Truman's White House advisers. In the week following the trusteeship proposal Truman's popularity took a beating, and the domestic pressures on the administration snowballed. Clifford reached out to leading Democrats to contain the damage, and they advised him that if Truman abided by the trusteeship proposal it could cost him the presidency.[44] In preparation for the meeting with the president, Bill Batt, the head of the DNC's research division, drafted a memo to Ewing, a copy of which Batt forwarded to Clifford. What is significant about Batt's note is less what he said but who was saying it and why. As an integral figure in the Democratic Party campaign machine his preeminent concern was ensuring Truman's reelection, and the Palestine issue could either help or hinder that effort.[45]

Others were aware of the political ramifications of the Palestine issue and Clifford's centrality to it. According to Thomas Schoenbaum, Dean Rusk's biographer, Clifford "was a bit too smooth and polished and Rusk distrusted him." As far as Rusk was concerned Clifford was too willing to sacrifice U.S. interests to secure the Jewish vote in the upcoming election.[46] Marshall was deeply troubled by the Palestine issue, which in his opinion had become more of an internal than an external problem. In fact, he was so disheartened by the political pressures that on one occasion he asked Henderson to deal with the undersecretary instead of him on matters related to Palestine. This was not the last or most significant incident in which Marshall decried the influence of politics on the Palestine issue, which he considered to be purely a foreign policy problem.[47]

Despite the fact that the State Department and the White House were working at cross-purposes on the Palestine issue, both parties were anxious to contain the fighting in the region. Austin presented a resolution to the UN Security Council calling for a truce, something Clifford took as a positive sign. "It is expected that this will be interpreted as an important forward step in our efforts looking toward a truce," he wrote to Truman.[48] Hopes for a truce proved elusive, however, and as the clock continued to tick toward May 15 the situation in Palestine started to build momentum on its own. On April 9 Weizmann wrote a letter to Truman declaring that partition was unavoidable and already existed on a de facto basis in much of Palestine. The only choice for the Jews, he wrote, was "between Statehood and extermination."[49]

Over the last week of March and into April the State Department continued diplomatic efforts to get the two sides to agree to a truce and a temporary trusteeship, but its efforts failed to bear fruit. Meanwhile at the White House both Truman and Clifford vacillated, certain that they wanted partition but doubtful that it could be achieved absent a significant military commitment by the United States. Elsey's private notes indicate that as of April 19 the president had not said what his view was and Clifford still had not made up his mind. Niles was unequivocal, believing that trusteeship was an abandonment of partition.[50]

Over the next two weeks both Clifford and Truman decided in favor of partition and recognition of the Jewish state that was expected to be declared on May 15. Clifford jotted down his arguments on May 4:

> Recognition is consistent with U.S. policy from the beginning.
> A separate Jewish state is inevitable. It will be set up shortly.
> As far as Russia is concerned we would do better to indicate recognition.
> We must recognize inevitably. Why not now.
> State Department resolution doesn't stop partition.[51]

Clifford and Truman discussed Palestine in their customary end-of-the-day meeting on May 7, at which time Clifford delivered the draft of a statement he wanted the president to read at his next scheduled press conference on May 13. The statement, actually drafted by Lowenthal, declared that the United States would recognize the Jewish state as soon as it was declared and would encourage other nations to do the same. Truman agreed but, sensitive to Marshall's opposition, decided to speak to him first. Clifford sat in the Oval Office as Truman telephoned the secretary of state, and it was clear from only the president's side of the conversation that Marshall continued to oppose recognition. Without giving away his hand Truman told Marshall that he wanted to have a meeting on the subject, which he scheduled for May 12, three days before the British mandate was due to expire. After hanging up Truman told Clifford that he saw some merit in Marshall's argument but nonetheless wanted to go ahead with recognition. He asked Clifford to argue the case in favor of recognition at the upcoming meeting, much in the same way a lawyer would argue a case for his client. "You know how I feel," he said. "I want you to present it just as though you were making an argument before the Supreme Court of the United States. Consider it carefully, Clark, organize it logically. I want you to be as persuasive as you possibly can be."[52]

As Clifford prepared for the biggest case of his life his primary collaborator was Max Lowenthal. His role was so significant, in fact, that it could be argued that Clifford was Lowenthal's mouthpiece. Clifford's arguments in favor of recognition were formulated and put into words by Lowenthal, who chose to remain out of the public eye. He submitted two memos to Clifford in early May arguing the case for partition. In the first, he argued the case for partition and recognition and suggested provocatively that recognition of the Jewish state would help counter Soviet influence in the region. In the second he argued that partition was a practical reality and that U.S. policy should merely recognize that, and he reiterated his belief that recognition would strengthen the United States vis-à-vis the Soviet Union.[53]

Given his audience and the fact that he was constructing Clifford's argument for the May 12 meeting with the president and the secretary of state, Lowenthal's tactics in the May 9 memo were a stroke of genius. Whereas the Palestine question had been complex only a month before, recognition had become a risk-free policy because it entailed nothing more than the mere recognition of the de facto situation on the ground. Indeed when Truman granted recognition on May 14 it was the informal de facto form of diplomatic recognition rather than the more declarative de jure. Lowenthal's ambivalent tone belied the passion with which he viewed the Zionist cause and suggested that the United States had nothing to lose in taking a strong position contrary to the interests of the overwhelming population of the region. "Since we cannot, and would not want to, reverse the reality of partition, we should derive the maximum advantage for the President and for the U.S. government from the existing situation," Lowenthal wrote.[54] It was the perfect approach to take with a president who had been agonizing over the decision for some time. In addition, the argument that prompt recognition would outflank the Soviets grounded the decision in terms of U.S. foreign policy interests and national security. With the election only six months away, Clifford's primary concern was the political implications of the decision; yet he could not have prevailed if he argued the case on the merits of politics alone, or even primarily. Lowenthal subordinated the political benefits to U.S. interests and prestige so that they could be considered an ancillary benefit.

What is particularly interesting about Clifford and Lowenthal's partnership is that it is unclear just whose ideas Lowenthal was expounding in his memos.[55] His arguments echo Clifford's notes from May 4, yet it is not clear whether Clifford shared his ideas with Lowenthal and asked him to elaborate, or whether he took the notes based on a conversation with Lowenthal. Clifford claimed the notes were prepared by him in preparation for the May 12 meeting.[56] The most plausible explanation, although it is purely conjecture, is that Clifford shared his notes of May 4 with Lowenthal as guidance in preparing their case. The linkage of the Palestine problem to the U.S.-Soviet rivalry must have come from Clifford, who was intimately familiar with Truman's thinking. Lowenthal's arguments regarding how recognition would strengthen the United States relative to Russia were too poorly formed to have originated with him. Nor did Lowenthal have any expertise on the subject of U.S.-Soviet relations. More than likely Clifford instructed him to integrate the Zionist case into the intensifying Cold War conflict with the Soviet Union, which was very much on Truman's mind following the Czech coup and the St. Patrick's Day speech.

Clifford's showdown at the White House was scheduled for 4:00 on May 12. In attendance were Truman; Clifford; Niles; Matthew Connelly, the president's appointments secretary; Marshall; Lovett; and two other men from the State Department, Fraser Wilkins and Robert McClintock. Both Henderson and Rusk were absent because Rusk believed that their presence in the same room with Clifford would be too inflammatory.[57] Immediately the meeting became confrontational. Marshall believed that Palestine was solely a foreign policy issue and therefore his responsibility. Clifford, he felt, had no business at the meeting. Truman defended Clifford with a curt rejoinder that he was there because Truman had invited him. Marshall, however, felt strongly that Clifford's attendance was inappropriate and continued to voice his complaint that Palestine policy was a serious foreign policy issue and that there should not be any domestic interference. "He said it all with a righteous God-damned Baptist tone," Clifford recalled.[58]

Lovett and Marshall presented the State Department's position: that the United States should continue to support the trusteeship resolution and defer any decision on recognition. They believed that the Jewish victories would be short-lived, and Marshall recounted a conversation with Moshe Shertok, the political representative of the Jewish Agency, from four days earlier, which Lowenthal had cited. The essence of Marshall's message, which Lowenthal ignored, was that it was "dangerous to base long-range policy on temporary military success" and that if the Jews got into trouble they should not expect the United States to bail them out. It was a blunt message.[59]

After Marshall was done it was Clifford's turn to make his case. He began by challenging the State Department's position that they were trying to secure a truce, noting correctly that while Rusk had promised on March 24 that a truce was in sight it was still not a reality. Next Clifford argued that the trusteeship proposal presupposed a single Palestine; but, as Lowenthal had argued, partition into Jewish and Arab territories was already a practical reality. Third, he argued that the president should give prompt recognition to the Jewish state even before it was declared, as this would have the advantage of restoring the president's position in favor of partition. Furthermore, it was important that the United States should grant recognition before the Soviets did. Clifford handed out a proposed statement of recognition, prepared by Elsey from Lowenthal's draft, and then reminded all present of the Balfour Declaration's promise of a Jewish state in Palestine. The Jews had waited for more than thirty years, he argued, and it was wrong to make them wait any longer. Elaborating on the moral angle, he also argued that the Jewish people had suffered many hardships throughout their history, culminating in the Holocaust. It was right for them to have a homeland of their own. Finally, he suggested that it was important in a region as strategically vital as the Middle East for there to be a nation committed to democratic government (an observation that remains true more than sixty years later).[60]

Lovett rebutted Clifford's arguments with a legalistic rejoinder. It would be "highly injurious to the United Nations to announce the recognition of the Jewish State even before it had come into existence and while the General assembly, which had been called into special session at the request of the United States, was still considering the question of a future government of Palestine." Lovett also argued that it would be "injurious to the prestige of the President" and that "it was a very transparent attempt to win the Jewish vote but . . . it would lose more votes than it would gain." Lovett also argued that premature recognition would be tantamount to "buying a pig in a poke," as there was no way to know what kind of Jewish state would be set up. Finally, Lovett dismissed Clifford's argument that it was urgent to recognize the Jewish state before Russia did so.[61]

Marshall, whose anger had been building throughout Clifford's presentation, took over after Lovett finished. Seconding Lovett's argument, Marshall concurred that a transparent attempt to win a few votes would backfire and damage the prestige of the presidency. "The counsel offered by Mr. Clifford was based on domestic political considerations, while the problem which confronted us was international," Marshall said. Then Marshall delivered what he must have believed to be the coup de grâce: "If you follow Clifford's advice and if I were to vote in the election, I would vote against you."[62]

Marshall's threat "was so shocking that it just kind of lay there for 15 or 20 seconds and nobody moved," Clifford recalled.[63] Truman, who at the very least must have been taken aback, brought the meeting to a close. Coming from Marshall, a man whom Truman revered, it must have been personally humiliating. Politically, a break with Marshall would have been crippling to Truman's chances in November. Truman replied that he "was fully aware of the difficulties and dangers in the situation, to say nothing of the political risks involved, which he, himself, would run."[64]

The May 12 showdown was a pivotal moment leading up to the birth of Israel. Marshall's warning that he would vote against the president, and the implicit threat of resignation that it carried, is frequently cited by historians. However, the question remains as to whether Truman granted recognition to Israel out of political expediency. The accounts of the meeting differ, with Clifford presenting a different picture than do Lovett and Marshall. According to Clifford, Marshall exploded in anger at him, and the threat of Marshall's refusing to vote for Truman brought a dumbfounded silence upon the room. Wilkins described Marshall's threat as jocular, although certainly with some serious intent. Wilkins's account, however, strains the bounds of credibility on at least one level: given Marshall's reputation for seriousness and rectitude, it is hard to imagine him being jocular about anything. In his book *Truman, the Jewish Vote, and the Creation of Israel,* John Snetsinger, citing an interview with McClintock, wrote that Clifford said recognition was consistent with Truman's past endorsements of a Jewish state and "emphasized that his support for such a policy was firmly based upon a consideration of the favorable political implications involved. With an election six months away, Truman should not pass up the opportunity to redeem his fallen reputation with the Jewish community."[65] According to Clifford, "Marshall's position was grossly unfair: he had no proof to sustain the charge, nor did he offer any—nor had I given him any, for I had not mentioned politics in my presentation."[66]

The truth of what really happened at the May 12 meeting is elusive as there is no independent account of what actually transpired. Clifford's recollections differ significantly from McClintock's and Wilkins's, and as all three were partisan their accounts deserve some scrutiny. Neither McClintock nor Wilkins was a senior individual in the State Department, but both were deputies to men who should have been in attendance, Rusk and Henderson. More than likely both deputies revered Marshall and would be predisposed to reflect his hostility to Clifford as well as his personal bias that Clifford's motives were solely political. Two written accounts frequently cited were written by George Elsey and McClintock. Elsey's brief notes describe a violent reaction by Marshall and have him saying that "this is just straight politics and 'you wouldn't get my vote.' CMC [Clifford] was enraged and Marshall glared at CMC," he wrote. "State had no policy except to 'wait.'" Elsey's account is not definitive, however, because he was not in attendance and was briefed by Clifford after the meeting.[67] McClintock drafted Marshall's account of the meeting. According to Clifford, Marshall was certain that history would judge him to have been correct and wanted his account to be saved for posterity; contrary to established practice, he did not water down the heated personal comments that he and Clifford exchanged.[68] Marshall and McClintock described the threat in matter-of-fact terms, yet absent the rage Clifford described: "I said bluntly that if the President were to follow Mr. Clifford's advice and if in the elections I were to vote, I would vote against the President."[69] Without a neutral account of the meeting, interpretation and speculation are the only means of gleaning what most likely occurred. Elsey helped Clifford prepare for the meeting, and his notes itemize the points the latter planned to make:

> Recognition is consistent with U.S. policy from the beginning.
> A separate Jewish State is inevitable. It will be set up in a few days.
> Other nations will recognize it. We shall have to, also, in a few months.
> It is better to recognize now—steal a march on U.S.S.R.
> The proposed State Dept action would accomplish nothing at all.[70]

Elsey's notes bear a marked resemblance to Clifford's notes from May 4, given earlier.[71] Both sets of notes, as well as Clifford's recollections, omit any discussion of politics. A close reading of Marshall's account, as drafted by McClintock, actually tells the same story. McClintock's report of Clifford's presentation is actually consistent with Clifford's own account. The only point that could be interpreted as being politically motivated is that recognition "would have distinct value in restoring the President's position for support of the partition of Palestine." More than likely Marshall and the other State Department representatives interpreted that remark as being indicative of a political preoccupation, but it could also be interpreted as concern that the president hew to a consistent message. Either way, Clifford recollected the remark almost verbatim, so he was not hiding from it. The only mention of politics in the McClintock memorandum was Marshall's and Lovett's accusation that Clifford's recommendation was a "transparent attempt to win the Jewish vote." Neither Elsey's nor McClintock's contemporaneous version of the meeting indicates that Clifford argued the case based upon electoral politics, only that Marshall and Lovett believed that he had. Wilkins's recollections years later, like Clifford's, should not be given the same weight as the two versions recorded on the very day the meeting took place.

None of this proves conclusively, one way or the other, that Clifford was motivated by political considerations. What it does prove is that Clifford did not argue the case *to the president* in the context of domestic electoral politics. The distinction is significant. Many historians, most notably Snetsinger, have argued that Truman granted recognition to Israel in a naked attempt to win Jewish votes and have used the May 12 meeting as conclusive proof of this motivation. Based upon the evidence, however, they have not made their case.

At the conclusion of their meeting Truman reached out to the still-agitated Marshall, suggesting that he understood the secretary's position and was inclined to side with him. Marshall would not even look at Clifford as he left the room; and, according to Clifford, Marshall never spoke to him again. Marshall's biographer, Forrest Pogue, says that Marshall never again even mentioned Clifford's name.[72]

Seeing the dejection on Clifford's face, Truman offered some encouragement. "Well that was rough as a cob," said the Missouri farmer turned president. "That was about as tough as it gets. But you did your best." Putting on a brave face, Clifford replied that it was not the first case he had ever lost, but in the next breath suggested that they try again. Truman agreed, but advised caution. "I can't afford to lose General Marshall," he said.[73]

For Clifford, it was no longer a question of making a persuasive case for recognition of a Jewish state; he had done that to the best of his ability. While recognition was still the objective, it could not be done at the expense of losing Marshall. Clifford would have to convince Marshall that Truman wanted to grant recognition and at the same time convince Marshall not to resign in protest or publicly disavow the president's policy. This was easier said than done, as he and Marshall were from that moment no longer on speaking terms. Clifford needed an emissary, and Lovett wasted no time in stepping into that role. He called later that afternoon to say how disturbed he was by the day's events. "It would be a great tragedy if these two men were to break over this issue," he said.

Clifford agreed, but betrayed no interest in compromising. "There isn't anything I can do at this end," he said. "The thing for you to do is persuade General Marshall that he's wrong. But, Bob, I'll tell you, he's just as wrong as he can be. This would be a terrible mistake." Perhaps hoping to negotiate a compromise, Lovett asked Clifford to stop by for a drink after work so that they could discuss the issue in private.[74]

When they met later that evening Lovett probed to see if the president would moderate his position somewhat and work with Marshall, if only to heal the wounds of that afternoon. Clifford would not budge. "Bob, there is no chance whatsoever that the President will change his mind on the basic issue. . . . So all I can say is that if anyone is going to give, it is going to have to be General Marshall, because—I can tell you now—the President is not going to give an inch." Lovett said he would see what he could do and the next morning called to suggest that as a compromise they delay the recognition announcement for a few days. Again Clifford would accept no compromise, so Lovett made a counteroffer: de facto rather than de jure recognition. Finally, this was something Clifford could agree to because the distinction, while important to the State Department, was not significant outside diplomatic circles. Besides, he could push for an upgrade to de jure recognition later, and did.[75]

The next morning Clifford and Lovett reconvened, with still no resolution in sight. Lovett and Marshall were still opposed to recognition, even given the compromise on de facto status. Hoping to close the deal, Clifford tried a different tactic. He suggested that the minimum that the president required was for Marshall to refrain from publicly opposing the decision. The meeting from two days ago was water under the bridge, and neither Truman nor Clifford required a retraction from Marshall, only a loyal silence. Lovett said he would talk to

Marshall. Time was running out, however, as the expiration of the British mandate and declaration of the Jewish state was to take place in Palestine at 12:00 A.M. on May 15, which was 6:00 P.M. on May 14 in Washington. In addition to negotiating with the State Department, Clifford also needed to coordinate the mechanics of the announcement, a task that would normally have been carried out over at Foggy Bottom. Clifford called Eliahu Epstein of the Jewish Agency and told him to submit a formal request for recognition by noon, hoping that Lovett could deliver Marshall. Epstein's letter, which was prepared before the new state had a name, simply and succinctly requested recognition for the "Jewish State." When Epstein heard the news from Palestine that the state would be called Israel he had his aide cross out the words "Jewish State" and insert the word "Israel."[76]

With no word as yet from the State Department, Clifford followed up with Lovett later that morning hoping to bring the matter to closure. Lovett recommended that they discuss the matter over lunch at the F Street Club, of which he was a member. He pleaded with Clifford for a delay of a day or two, but Clifford demanded immediate recognition. "That won't do," he said. "Let's talk plainly; while you and Secretary Marshall were away [during the March trusteeship debacle], your staff placed the president in a very unfair position. It was not of his making in any way. It was unnecessary to place him in that position."[77] Clifford again reiterated the argument about preempting the Soviets. The two men concluded their lunch without an accommodation, and the game of chicken continued. Around 4:00 Lovett called with good news. "Clark, I think we have something to work with," he said. "I have talked to the General. He cannot support the President's position, but he has agreed that he will not oppose it." Clifford was elated, but just after 5:30 State tried one more delaying tactic, which Clifford managed to fend off. Time had run out. At 6:11 P.M. Charlie Ross read a statement that Clifford had just brought him: "This government has been informed that a Jewish state has been proclaimed in Palestine. . . . The United States recognizes the provisional government as the de facto authority of the new State of Israel."[78] According to Eben Ayers, the recognition announcement took both him and Ross completely by surprise. "Neither Ross nor I had any knowledge of it before then," Ayers said. "I can still remember Clifford coming in with that statement so suddenly."[79]

For Clifford it was a triumphant success. He had faced down a figure of monumental stature and had won. The cost was Marshall's undying enmity, which on more than one occasion Clifford would reciprocate. The other cost would be lingering accusations regarding Clifford's motives. Clifford always denied that political factors were the driving force behind his position, and he may have chosen to begin his memoirs with the story of the recognition of Israel in order to refute the charges. "Although domestic considerations are in fact a legitimate part of any important foreign policy decision, I never rested the case for recognition upon politics," he wrote.[80]

Marshall, of course, thought otherwise. So did Lovett. A few days after the episode he took the unusual step of drafting a memorandum for the file so that his version of the story was saved for posterity. "On Friday afternoon [May 14] following lunch Mr. Clifford told me that the President was under unbearable pressure to recognize the Jewish state promptly," he wrote. In response to the State Department's request to temporarily delay recognition, Lovett claimed that Clifford replied that "the timing of the recognition was 'of the greatest possible importance to the President from a domestic point of view.'" Lovett closed with an accusation that is rather blunt for a document that was intended to be a part of the official record:

> In this memorandum of conversation I have omitted, for the sake of brevity, the long arguments back and forth throughout the afternoon. My protests against the precipitate action and warnings as to consequences with the Arab world appear to have been outweighed by considerations unknown to me, but I can only conclude that the President's political advisers, having failed last Wednesday afternoon to make the President a father of the new state, have determined at least to make him the midwife.[81]

In his memoirs Clifford rebutted Lovett's charge:

> It is regrettable that Lovett must have misunderstood some comment I had made. At no time did I suggest, or intend to suggest, that President Truman's major concern was domestic politics. During the luncheon we did discuss the election that would take place later that year, and three days later, when he dictated his record, it is possible that Lovett merged the two subjects. But his view that my desire to recognize Israel was motivated by political considerations was incorrect.[82]

Irrespective of motive, America's recognition of Israel was a significant event in postwar U.S. foreign policy, and for Clifford it was an impressive accomplishment. He had faced down the State Department and the immense prestige of George Marshall. Following Truman's instructions he had indeed prepared the case as if he were arguing it before the Supreme Court, and he argued it as persuasively as possible. He did not bring the State Department over to his side, but as a result of his persistence and negotiating skills he ensured that Marshall and Lovett's dissent would be silent. Second to Truman, Clifford deserves the most credit for welcoming Israel to the family of nations.

Clifford's efforts to assist the state of Israel did not end with recognition. On the same evening that Israel was born two events took place that demonstrated that the problem of Palestine was not solved and that it was an issue that would continue to occupy Clifford's time at least until the November elections. The first was the appointment by the UN General Assembly of Count Folke Bernadotte of Sweden as a mediator whose mission was to "promote a peaceful adjustment of the future situation of Palestine."[83] The second was the first Arab-Israeli War, which began when the armies of five Arab nations invaded the nascent state of Israel. In order to achieve the goal of a cessation of hostilities Bernadotte would recommend territorial adjustments that ran counter to the boundaries as spelled out in the November 1947 partition resolution. Clifford's opposition to the Bernadotte plan would again bring him into conflict with the State Department. Clifford also became involved in an effort to repeal the U.S. arms embargo, which complicated Israel's ability to defend itself. In addition, he pushed for two other measures that were the subject of intense political pressure: a promised loan to Israel of $100 million and de jure recognition.

The Bernadotte plan called for changes to the boundaries of Israel as demarcated in the November 1947 partition resolution that would effectively reduce the Jewish territory by half. It also posed a particularly troublesome problem for Truman. On September 21, 1948, Marshall made an announcement in favor of the Bernadotte plan, and the public backlash that ensued was comparable to what followed the trusteeship proposal. In addition, as with the earlier controversy, there was a State Department–White House dispute over whether Truman had approved the statement.

The secretary of state's support for the Bernadotte plan presented Thomas Dewey with an attractive political opportunity, but he waited a month to exploit it. On October 22 he published a letter in which he criticized the Truman administration's support for the Bernadotte plan. Marshall's endorsement of the plan had neutralized the political advantage that the president had enjoyed on the issue since the administration's recognition of Israel in May. Until the latest controversy, the two political parties had mutually agreed to maintain a bipartisan foreign policy, and Truman had been forced to remain silent. Once Dewey broke that truce the issue became fair game, and Clifford pounced on the opportunity. "I consider Dewey's action a serious error on his part and the best thing that has happened to us to date," he wrote to Truman. In a call to Lovett, Clifford argued that Dewey had impugned Truman's integrity by suggesting that the president had reneged on the Democratic platform. By framing the situation in those terms he effectively removed the gag that Truman had administered on himself in order to avoid a public break with Marshall. As Clifford put it to the president, "I suggested to Lovett that by reason of Dewey's action, you had no alternative but to reaffirm your support of the Democratic platform. Lovett agrees completely. I suggested to him that you would have to give out [a] statement clearly stating your position on Israel."[84] Dewey's gambit had backfired. Instead of having free rein to criticize a president silenced by loyalty to his secretary of state he had unleashed a feisty candidate who would boast of his contributions to the Zionist cause.

Truman issued a statement on Sunday, October 24, two days after the publication of Dewey's letter and nine days before the election: "I had hoped that our foreign affairs could continue to be handled on a non-partisan basis without being injected into the presidential campaign. The Republican candidate's statement, however, makes it necessary for me to reiterate my own position with respect to Palestine." The statement, drafted by Clifford, reaffirmed Truman's support for the Democratic platform, which endorsed the boundaries as delineated by the partition resolution. Furthermore, the statement also pledged that following the election of a permanent government in Israel, the United States would extend de jure recognition to the Jewish state.[85]

Because Clifford was a central figure in the debate over Palestine, his views on the issue are particularly important. Understanding his motivation is essential in explaining the policy that Truman adopted. Clifford's most extensive comments on the subject, specifically with respect to the political implications of the decisions taken, can be found in a November 1947 memorandum to Truman, which outlined a campaign strategy for 1948. The memo had this to say about the Jewish voter:

The Jewish vote, insofar as it can be thought of as a bloc, is important only in New York. But (except for Wilson in 1916) no candidate since 1876 has lost New York and won the Presidency, and its 47 [electoral] votes are naturally the first prize in any election. Centered in New York City, that vote is normally Democratic and, if large enough, is sufficient to counteract the upstate vote and deliver the state to President Truman. Today the Jewish voter is interested primarily in Palestine and will continue to be an uncertain quantity right up to the time of the election. Even though there is general approval among the Jewish people regarding the United Nations report on Palestine, the group is still torn with conflicting views and dissension. It will be extremely difficult to decide some of the vexing questions which will arise in the months to come on the basis of political expediency. In the long run, there is likely to be greater gain if the Palestine problem is approached on the basis of reaching decisions founded upon intrinsic merit.[86]

This passage is particularly noteworthy because (as will be discussed in greater detail in the next chapter) much of this memorandum was written by James Rowe, not Clifford, and Rowe's analysis and recommendation was contrary to Clifford's, given above. Rowe had written, "Unless the Palestine matter is boldly and favorably handled there is bound to be some defection on their part to the alert Dewey. It should not be overlooked, either, that much of this Jewish vote is also the 'left' vote and will go to Wallace."[87] While Clifford retained much of Rowe's original draft verbatim, he felt compelled to disregard Rowe's recommendation regarding the Jewish voter. However, Clifford may have been disingenuous here. As Truman's closest domestic advisor he was aware of Truman's determination to keep politics out of the Palestine issue, and he may simply have been telling Truman what he wanted to hear. There is no evidence to suggest that this was or was not a case of deliberate deception on Clifford's part. One can only determine Clifford's state of mind by looking at his actions with respect to Israel from November 1947 to the following November.

Indeed, the body of evidence other than what Clifford wrote in the memorandum suggests that he was indeed motivated by political concerns. For one, most of the participants were interested in the subject because of the political considerations. Aside from Elsey, who was only partially involved, many of the figures whispering in Clifford's ear were intrigued by the domestic political opportunities the issue presented vis-à-vis the Jewish voters. McGrath was chairman of the Democratic National Committee, and Ewing was the former acting chairman of the DNC and an important figure in the Democratic Party. Ewing had also convened the Wardman Park Group, whose sole purpose was to advance the Democratic agenda and electoral interests. Batt was the director of the research division of the DNC. Niles and Lowenthal were Democrats, but they were also Jewish and ardent supporters of the Zionist cause, so the political benefits would have been of secondary concern to them.

Clifford's counterargument, that it was important to preempt Russian recognition of Israel, does not stand up to scrutiny. He was the only person to argue that point in contrast to the overwhelming majority of the foreign policy bureaucracy, which opposed recognition. There is no evidence that he sought out the advice of Soviet experts, such as Kennan and Bohlen, in order to substantiate his argument. Nor did he present any facts and figures to demonstrate that a pro-Israel policy would further U.S. interests relative to the Soviet Union. He argued that the Russians would use Israel to gain a foothold in the Arabian Peninsula, but the Russians could cozy up to the Arabs to achieve the same purpose. The Clifford-Elsey report suggested as much, observing that "the U.S.S.R. is playing both sides of the Jewish situation."[88] More than likely Clifford used the Russian angle simply because he knew it would appeal to Truman.

Most telling is Clifford's conduct after recognition was granted in May 1948. His repeated attempts to coax Truman into granting de jure recognition and a loan, as well as his opposition to the Bernadotte plan, suggest that his primary motive was to bolster Truman's electoral prospects. Moreover, Clifford was Truman's primary political and domestic adviser and the key strategist for the 1948 campaign. Although he was involved in foreign policy matters, domestic issues occupied more of his time, and this was especially true in a presidential election year. Protecting and advancing the president's political interests were his paramount concern, as evidenced by his furious reaction to the trusteeship mishap. In this case he was angry because the president had been politically embarrassed, not because he believed that the State Department had compromised U.S. geopolitical interests. His giddy enthusiasm over Dewey's misstep as well as his lament that Marshall's endorsement of the Bernadotte plan had placed Truman in a difficult position illustrate the centrality of the political motive.

As far as Truman's conduct is concerned, Michael Cohen's conclusion that his motives were mixed seems to be both fair and on the mark. Truman's deep Christian faith and knowledge of Middle Eastern history imbued in him sympathy for the plight of the Jews, a sympathy intensified by their suffering during the Holocaust. Moral and humanitarian reasons were important to Truman. The fact that support for the Jewish state could be politically advantageous presented Truman with an attractive opportunity, yet it is unlikely that he would have embraced such a policy if he felt it was detrimental to U.S. interests. Clifford convinced him that it was the right policy for America, which allowed him to be true to his gut instinct from the start. Although Clifford continued to push him to take the additional steps requested by Jewish groups—granting de jure recognition, opposing the Bernadotte plan, and granting the requested loan—Truman refrained from taking any immediate action in deference to Marshall. Suggesting his true intentions, he did grant de jure recognition and approve the requested loan in January 1949, following the elections in Israel but also past the time when he could derive any political benefit from the decision.

The recognition of Israel was one of the most significant foreign policy decisions of the twentieth century and continues to have profound political and geopolitical implications to this day. Critics of Truman, such as Snetsinger, are correct in asserting that domestic politics influenced the decision. However, they are wrong in ascribing political motives to Truman. Clifford was the guilty party.

# 5

# Mastermind of the 1948 Campaign?

In November 1947, Clifford presented President Truman with a memorandum entitled "The Politics of 1948," a forty-three-page study that outlined a strategy for the 1948 presidential race. Truman was still considered a caretaker president, and his defeat by a then-unidentified Republican challenger seemed to be a foregone conclusion. Truman, however, would eventually score the greatest political upset of the twentieth century when he defeated Thomas Dewey in November 1948. The Clifford memorandum was incredibly prescient, accurately predicting that Dewey would be the Republican candidate and that Henry Wallace would run as a third-party candidate. In some cases it badly missed the mark, failing to foresee the southern backlash against Truman's civil rights policies. In addition, it is debatable how much the memo influenced Truman, whose political instincts were fairly acute; but in one respect its influence was without question: it bestowed remarkable benefits on its author.

As Truman's most trusted political adviser and the architect of his surprise victory Clifford became a celebrity within the Democratic Party. More than any other achievement during his White House career, the 1948 campaign memo established Clifford's reputation as an indispensable adviser to Democratic presidents. John F. Kennedy turned to Clifford for advice during his 1960 run for the presidency largely on the basis of Clifford's role in the last Democratic victory; Lyndon Johnson sought his counsel in 1964.[1] More than any other accomplishment during his career, the 1948 campaign made Clifford a legend and bestowed on him the credibility he needed to parlay government service into a lucrative private legal career.

The accolades bestowed on Clifford were misplaced, however, as he did not write the memo. As with the Clifford-Elsey report, "The Politics of 1948" was a document that Clifford presented to the president as his own when in fact he had done almost nothing in preparing it. This time the true author was not George Elsey but James Rowe, who had written the position paper as a way of outlining a strategy the Democrats might use in dealing with the Republican congressional majority in the aftermath of the 1946 elections. Rowe delivered his 1948 campaign strategy report in September 1947 to James Webb, Truman's budget director, because Rowe himself was not a member of the administration. Webb passed it to an aide who brought it to Clifford, who immediately recognized its value. There was a problem, however: Clifford knew that Rowe had earned the enmity of Truman because of Rowe's law partner, Thomas Corcoran. Truman personally disliked "Tommy the Cork," as he was known, and Clifford believed that the president would therefore dismiss anything coming from Rowe. With that in mind Clifford had the memo retyped; he then revised it slightly and passed it along to the president. The document he presented to Truman made no mention of Rowe.

The assessment of Clifford biographers Douglas Frantz and David McKean is particularly harsh: "The stronger evidence indicates that Clifford baldly claimed credit for an important strategy developed by someone else in order to improve his own standing with the president. After his supposed authorship of the memo had lifted him to new levels of fame, it was too late to confess."[2] As time passed, the story of the 1948 campaign began to build a momentum of its own. This was facilitated by first-generation historical accounts and also by Clifford's telling and retelling of the story. Cabell Phillips's 1966 book *The Truman Presidency* describes the memo as "one of the great dissertations on the art of politics" and "an extraordinary example of the kind of political perception that underpins a Presidential election campaign." In assessing the influence of the memo Phillips concluded that "its influence was substantial, and perhaps decisive." According to Phillips the memo was the product of the "cogent and persuasive reasoning of Clark Clifford and the secret political strategy board," yet he goes on to call it simply "the Clifford memo." There is no mention of Rowe.[3] It is worth noting that Phillips relied extensively on Clifford in writing the book; indeed, he began his acknowledgments with praise for the special counsel. "Clifford," he wrote, "was the most effective and the most heavily relied upon member of President Truman's personal staff."[4] Elsey, for his part, discounts the importance of the memorandum, arguing that Truman did not even circulate it among his staff and that it was only in 1966 that it became widely known.[5]

In 1968 Rowe received some credit for the document, but not nearly enough. In January 1968, shortly after Clifford had been named secretary of defense by President Lyndon Johnson, the *New York Times* ran a piece on Clifford in the magazine section. The article describes him as Truman's political salvation in 1948 when he submitted "a remarkable, 43-page memorandum on political strategy."[6] When Rowe read the article he was dumbfounded. "That's my memo," he told his wife. "He's getting credit for my memo." Apparently Rowe had tired of seeing his work attributed to Clifford, and he decided to set the record straight. While having lunch with James Reston, the Washington bureau chief for the *Times,* he complained that he had not received the proper credit. Reston then wrote a February 12 article questioning the authorship of the memo, which set off a series of heated telephone conversations between Rowe and Clifford. By the end of February, however, Rowe had adopted a different posture. He sent Clifford a copy of his original memo, perhaps to shame Clifford for his extensive plagiarism, but also included a conciliatory letter. He wrote, "Really I am terribly embarrassed that I embarrassed you." Rowe conceded that he was guilty of "pride of authorship," and he told Clifford that the latter could say that they collaborated on the memo or even denounce Rowe as a liar. Clifford did not respond to Reston's article, no doubt hoping that the story would die if it was not fed with additional material.[7]

The 1968 exchange between Clifford and Rowe is intriguing, and absent knowledge of their conversations it is unclear what transpired to cause Rowe to have such a change of heart. Perhaps he was trying to be patriotic and not distract Clifford from his awesome responsibility as secretary of defense during the height of the Vietnam War. Alternatively, Clifford was by that time an extremely powerful man, even apart from his status as a Cabinet member; perhaps he played hardball with Rowe and forced him to back down. The predominantly contrite tone of Rowe's letter and his offer to disavow his claims of authorship suggest that he either felt a sense of duty to Clifford or feared him. Rowe's apparent willingness to allow Clifford to publicly rebuke him, his concession that Clifford most likely improved his memo, and his apologies for giving Clifford "irrelevant problems" suggest the latter. Yet there is a subtle tone of defiance as well. "Some day," he wrote, "when we are both old men and Clifford is writing his memoirs, perhaps we can get the finished product out of the Truman Library and see what you actually did do."[8]

Rowe, and his family as well, continued to harbor a lingering resentment over what they believed to be the theft of his intellectual property. In 1981 he wrote a letter to Kenneth Hechler, who had been an administrative assistant in the Truman White House, following up on a conversation they had had at the Truman Library about the origins of the 1948 campaign memorandum. Rowe attached a copy of his original memorandum along with a published interview with Richard Neustadt, the Webb aide who had hand-delivered Rowe's memorandum to Clifford and who later became a renowned professor at Harvard. The interview correctly noted that it was Rowe who wrote the memo and described the circumstances surrounding how it came to be known as "the Clifford memo," an account that Rowe dismissed.[9] He told Hechler, "I think the explanation that Truman disliked my law partner and Clifford therefore put his name on my memorandum and took mine off, is really an afterthought. But it is so long ago there is no point in calling names."[10]

Patrick Anderson, in his 1968 book *The President's Men,* wrote that Clifford drew "upon talks with and memos from former FDR aide James Rowe and other liberal friends and political leaders."[11] There is no mention of Reston's article in Anderson's book, and that plus the fact that his book was published in the same year as Reston's article suggest that it is unlikely that Anderson consulted it. According to Anderson, Rowe was a collaborator on the memo, but played a secondary role to Clifford.

For years Clifford referred to the Rowe memorandum as his own, which is not surprising in that much of his success in private practice was built upon his reputation as the mastermind behind the stunning political upset of 1948. Furthermore, Rowe's 1968 letter probably convinced Clifford that he could continue to claim credit without fear that Rowe would assert his authorship again. During his 1971 oral history interviews with the Truman Library, Clifford referred to it on more than one occasion as the "political memorandum that I wrote." When asked about the genesis of the study he elaborated at length, beginning with the suggestion that the 1948 campaign memorandum was in many respects similar to the Clifford-Elsey report. His remarks are worth quoting at length because they suggest the extent to which he wanted people—perhaps himself included—to believe that the memorandum was a product of his own reasoning and writing:

> So, as we approached the election of 1948, I had the feeling that maybe a similar type of memorandum would be useful to

the President. Now, I did not have much of a political back-ground. . . .

In the summer of 1947 I began to have the opportunity . . . of talking to persons who had substantial political back-grounds. I'd question them and I'd get their opinions. . . .

I think that what I was engaged in was an experiment to ascertain if one, by the application of pure reason, could not reduce political imponderables to understandable equations. I found it a very interesting endeavor.

I might say in this regard, that I had to see a good many people and reach conclusions based upon, in many instances, the opinions of others. Then I would assemble it, digest it, and present it as I thought it should be digested, which after all is one of the major functions that a lawyer performs.

A lawyer is trained (hopefully) first to go out and get the facts, then to assemble them in an orderly manner, then to analyze them, to reach conclusions with reference to facts, and then to present his case in the most effective, attractive and persuasive manner. And that's about the process that I went through in preparing this memorandum.[12]

When asked specifically if Rowe helped with the preparation of the memorandum, Clifford gave a slightly evasive answer: "Yes, I drew a good deal on Jim Rowe for his interest was politics, he had been in the Roosevelt administration, and had an excellent political background. I told Jim Rowe, as I told some others, what I was in the process of doing, and so I got as much help from others as I could get."[13]

Clifford's account suggests that he devoted a great deal of time interviewing people, organizing his thoughts and notes, and writ-ing the report. He described the process of writing the Clifford-Elsey report in much the same way, yet it is clear from the evidence that his contribution to the memorandum was minimal. By the time Clif-ford made these remarks, Reston's article had called into question Clifford's assertions of authorship, so it suggests that Clifford had a good deal of hubris to craft such an account for the interviewer from the Truman Library. Or it may have simply been a matter of willful or subconscious self-deception. Clifford, after all, had told the story of the 1948 campaign so many times that he might have con-vinced himself that he had drafted the memo. When George Elsey was asked what he thought of the possibility that Clifford came to believe he had written the Rowe memorandum, as well as the Clifford-Elsey

Report, he replied in the affirmative. "That's a very perceptive remark of yours, that over time he began to think that he did. I agree with your statement."[14]

During a 1982 interview with the *Los Angeles Times,* never published, Clifford disavowed complete ownership of the memo, describing it as an "assembly job." Yet when he described the political strategists with whom he had consulted, he neglected to mention Rowe.[15] Whether this was an intentional or unconscious omission is unknowable, but it stretches the boundaries of logic to believe that he could credit others while inadvertently neglecting Rowe. Perhaps the bad blood brought to the surface by the Reston article had lingered over the ensuing fourteen years.

As late as 1989 Rowe continued to be denied credit for his work. An article in the *Washington Post National Weekly Edition,* "Clark Clifford: The Ultimate Insider and the Presidents He's Known," describes the Rowe memo as "the long memo Clifford gave to Truman that served as the guide to the campaign." It makes no mention of Rowe, nor does it specifically claim that Clifford wrote it, but the implication, especially for a reader unfamiliar with the details, was that he had. The article also describes Clifford as the "chief strategist" for the 1948 campaign.[16] This article, a primer for the publication of Clifford's memoirs two years later, would not have been subject to the same historical scrutiny as his published memoirs. With sufficient research, however, the facts surrounding the Rowe memorandum could have been uncovered. The Neustadt article and the 1968 Reston article were not the only accounts in circulation that correctly attributed the memorandum to Rowe. Hechler's memoir of the Truman administration, published in 1982, described how Rowe wrote the memo that was delivered to Clifford, who "had the good sense to recognize an excellent memorandum, dress it up for presentation and insure it got into the President's hands." Hechler also pointed out Rowe's lingering animosity over his lack of recognition, quoting Rowe as saying, "I was irritated at the time. I thought I was writing a memo for Truman. Clark [Clifford] has since gone out of his way to rectify the misunderstanding."[17]

Clifford's memoirs were published in 1991, and in that book he finally gave Rowe most of the credit he was due. Elsey, Clifford's coauthor Richard Holbrooke, and research assistant Brian VanDe-Mark convinced him that he had to come clean once and for all and put to rest all of the rumors surrounding the origins of the memo. In his published memoirs Clifford explains that the need for a comprehensive electoral strategy was discussed among the members of the Wardman Park Group, the informal team of Democratic political strategists of which Clifford was a member, but no one had the time to write it. Independent of the Wardman Park Group, Rowe shared some of his thoughts on the same subject with Webb, who suggested he document his ideas in memo form. When Webb passed the completed memo to Truman, the president passed on reading it and instead suggested that Webb give it to Clifford. Clifford shared the memorandum with the Wardman Park Group, which unanimously agreed that it both represented their views and could form the basis for a successful strategy in 1948. According to Clifford, he updated and revised the original Rowe memo after consulting with the members of the Wardman Park Group, Secretary of the Senate Leslie Biffle, and others. After his rewriting he presented the finished product to Truman, making no mention of Rowe. "There was nothing unusual about this process," Clifford wrote, "although for many years afterward, Rowe incorrectly thought the President had received and read his original memorandum."[18]

It is easy to see why Rowe believed as he did. In many respects the final product that Clifford submitted to Truman was unchanged from the version originally drafted by Rowe. At the very least it was not merely the basis for the memo for which Clifford long claimed authorship. For the most part Clifford carried over Rowe's memorandum verbatim; even the underlining and parenthetical comments were identical to the original. In those cases where Clifford substituted his own text he often said little that was substantially different than Rowe. A notable exception, as discussed in chapter 4, was Israel, where Clifford had recommended resolving the issue solely on its merits rather than basing policy on political considerations. Clifford also scrapped Rowe's section discussing high prices, another key issue for the 1948 campaign, and replaced it with his own, which was substantially shorter and did not delve into specifics, as Rowe had done. On the subject of tax reform, Rowe recommended a commission to study the issue with the intent of introducing legislation that could be passed in a bipartisan manner, thus neutralizing the issue. Instead of a commission, Clifford recommended eliminating "obvious inequities in our tax system" (which he did not specify) and "increasing personal exemptions so as to benefit those in the lowest income brackets." Another issue, Rowe warned, was the incompetent administration of aid to Greece under the auspices of the Truman Doctrine. If the initial stages of the Marshall Plan program were similarly bungled, wrote Rowe, the Republicans would have an attractive target to attack during the campaign. Clifford rewrote this section, not changing the content substantially but toning it down, perhaps so as not to offend the president, who regarded the Truman Doctrine as one of his most significant accomplishments. Clifford also substantially revised Rowe's discussion of the labor vote.

The one original contribution by Clifford was a two-paragraph section on civil rights.

Overall, Clifford could be better described as an editor rather than an author of the resulting memo. He revised the ranking of the key issues identified by Rowe and cut several paragraphs and a few sentences. The trimming resulted in a shorter memo: Rowe's original was thirty-three pages single-spaced; Clifford's was forty-three pages double-spaced. In addition, because Rowe submitted his draft in September and Clifford sent Truman his version in November, Clifford also changed some of Rowe's date references. A side-by-side analysis of the two documents leads to the inescapable conclusion that Clifford's contribution was minimal and certainly did not warrant the credit he long received as the architect of the 1948 campaign strategy. As with the Clifford-Elsey report, Clifford took credit for another individual's work.

The final memorandum, "The Politics of 1948," reiterated the basic strategy Rowe had recommended earlier, in December 1946, for dealing with an opposition Congress. Rowe advocated a policy of confrontation with the Republican Congress, foreshadowing Truman's famous attacks against the "Do-Nothing" Congress in 1948. "Insofar as it has control of the situation," Rowe wrote, "the Administration should select the issues upon which there will be conflict with the majority in Congress. It can assume it will get no major part of its program approved. Its tactics must, therefore, be entirely different than if there were any real point to bargaining and compromise."[19] The example Rowe cited was Truman's veto of the Taft-Hartley Act and, in this case at least, Clifford's counsel was decisive.

The Taft-Hartley Act, a labor bill passed in the spring of 1947, allowed the president to block a major strike by obtaining a federal injunction for an eighty-day "cooling-off" period, restricted unfair labor practices by unions, outlawed closed-shop hiring practices, and prohibited campaign contributions to candidates in federal elections. Politics were central to the issue. Truman did not want to further alienate union members by signing the bill, especially after his showdowns with the coal and railroad strikers the year before. Those who did support the bill were primarily Republican and would not have voted for Truman anyway. Therefore, the decision to veto the bill was a relatively low-risk strategy.[20] Clifford and the Wardman Park Group led the effort to secure a presidential veto. According to Leon Keyserling, he was the intellectual force behind the veto strategy, but Clifford was the one who sold it to Truman.[21] The Taft-Hartley veto was typical of Truman's confrontational relationship with the Eightieth Congress, except for foreign policy. It was also the strategy recommended by Rowe, and implicitly approved by Clifford, and it would serve Truman well in the 1948 campaign.

Another recommendation found in the Rowe memorandum was the formation of a "working committee," which was like the campaign "war rooms" of today. Clifford approved of the idea, no doubt in consultation with the Wardman Park Group, and worked with the Democratic National Committee to put Rowe's recommendation into place.[22] According to Elsey, Clifford was instrumental in setting up the working committee, which was called the Research Division. "Clifford deserves credit for that," he said. "It wouldn't have happened if he hadn't leaned on the [Democratic National] Committee."[23] The Research Division, comprising members outside the administration and headed by William Batt, served as a rapid response and opposition research team. Throughout the campaign Clifford served as a liaison between the Democratic National Committee and the White House; Batt described him as the "Father Superior" of the campaign.[24] Oddly, however (and perhaps indicative of the lingering animosity between Clifford and Rowe), when Clifford was asked during a 1971 oral history interview whose idea it had been to set up the Research Division he replied that he could not recall. Upon further reflection, he surmised that it must have originated in the Wardman Park Group.[25]

The opening shot of the presidential campaign was in January 1948, with Truman's State of the Union address. In 1948 it was not established procedure, as it is now, for the president to deliver this speech in the evening before a nationally televised audience, and there was some debate among the White House staff over whether Truman should deliver the message in person rather than releasing a written version. Clifford recognized that the State of the Union address represented an opportunity for Truman to launch his attack on the Republican Congress, as Rowe had recommended, so he strongly advised the president to deliver the message in person. The speech was not received favorably and James Reston, of the *New York Times*, criticized Clifford directly: "Clark Clifford . . . was given the task of selecting, rejecting, and providing the pattern for Mr. Truman's approval. After all this work, however, the extraordinarily chilly reception of the speech created the impression that many who heard it decided that, after all the sewing and basting, Mr. Truman was long on rags and tatters and short on pattern."[26] It was going to be a long, difficult campaign.

Truman's chances in the fall election looked bleak. A Gallup poll indicated that the president's approval rating was dismal, a mere 36 percent.[27] The press had already written him off. As if all the dark clouds on the horizon were not bad enough, in March Clifford found himself the subject of a particularly embarrassing cover story in *Time* magazine. "Only a political miracle or extraordinary stupidity on the part of the Republicans could save the Democratic party, after 16 years of power, from a debacle in November," the article asserted. It cast much of the blame on Truman, whose performance "was almost invariably awkward, uninspired and above all, mediocre." But *Time* also heaped a good deal of the blame on Clifford. Truman "was getting bad advice from people who did not know the score," *Time* wrote, and one of those giving him bad advice was Clifford, "who was strictly an amateur politician and a stranger to the President's old friends." In a particularly dismissive remark *Time* wrote that "like his boss, he is a political accident."[28] Truman dismissed the article, again reminding Clifford that "It's me they are after, not you." Reflecting upon his long rivalry with John Steelman, Clifford suspected that he was one of *Time*'s sources.[29]

Clifford had other suspects as a source for the article: senior members of Congress, especially southern Democrats, who were either angry or uncomfortable with the president's recent civil rights message.[30] On February 2 Truman had sent a message up to the Hill outlining a ten-point agenda for alleviating the scourge of racism. Truman's far-reaching plans called for the establishment of a permanent Commission on Civil Rights, a joint Congressional Committee on Civil Rights, and a Civil Rights Division in the Justice Department; the strengthening of existing civil rights laws; a federal antilynching law; voters' rights protection; creation of a permanent Fair Employment Practices Commission (FEPC), in contrast to Roosevelt's temporary FEPC; prohibition of discrimination in interstate transportation facilities; home rule and the right to vote in presidential elections for residents of the District of Columbia; statehood for Alaska and Hawaii; equal opportunity for all residents of the United States to become naturalized citizens; and the settlement of evacuation claims of Japanese-

Americans.[31] Although they were not yet aware of the depths of south-ern hostility to civil rights and how that hostility would manifest itself politically, Truman and the others in his administration would soon get a taste of it. About two weeks after the delivery of his civil rights agenda, Truman attended the annual Jefferson-Jackson Day dinner, an important event on the Democratic Party's calendar. Senator Olin Johnson of South Carolina bought an entire table directly in front of the presidential dais and then intentionally left the table empty in silent protest of Truman's policies. A few days later South Carolina's other senator, Strom Thurmond, paid a call to Senator Howard McGrath, chairman of the Democratic National Committee. He demanded that Truman withdraw "this highly controversial civil rights legislation, which tends to divide our people." When McGrath failed to satisfy his demands Thurmond marched over to the waiting press contin-gent and announced that "the present leadership of the Democratic party will soon realize that the South is no longer in the bag."[32] It was only February and already one of Rowe's premises for the 1948 campaign had been shattered: "As always, the South can be consid-ered safely Democratic. And in formulating national policy, it can be safely ignored."[33]

The ten-point agenda was not the first measure Truman had taken to advance the cause of civil rights, but it was certainly the most dra-matic. In September 1946 he had appointed a committee to study the problems of racial violence, and in early 1947 he had named a committee of prominent civil rights activists. On June 29, 1947, he became the first president to address the National Association for the Advancement of Colored People. During his speech he proclaimed that America "had reached a turning point in the long history of our coun-try's efforts to guarantee freedom and equality to all of our citizens." In a private letter Truman confided to his sister that his sentiments were genuine. "I believe what I say and I'm hopeful we may imple-ment it," he wrote. In October his Civil Rights Committee submitted a report to the president entitled *To Secure These Rights*. Unlike the myriad of federal reports that serve as a repository for dust, Truman followed through on the committee's recommendations in his Febru-ary 1948 civil rights message to Congress and in his executive orders in the summer of 1948 desegregating the armed services and ending discrimination in the civil service.[34]

Rowe, who had submitted his report in September 1947, was not privy to the Civil Rights Committee report. Clifford was familiar with the report and as a close adviser to Truman realized how important the issue was to the president. It can be inferred that Clifford had accepted Rowe's notion that the southern vote was safely Democratic; otherwise, he would have changed that section of the report, which recommended that Truman take positive measures to secure the African American vote. The memo's analysis of the civil rights issue read:

> The Republicans know how vulnerable the Democratic Party is insofar as the negro vote is concerned. They have been bending every effort to woo the negroes away from the Administration's fold. In all probability, Republican strategy at the next session will be to offer an FEPC, an anti-poll tax bill, and an anti-lynching bill. This will be accompanied by a flourish of oratory devoted to the Civil Rights of various groups of our citizens.
>
> The Administration would make a grave error if we permitted the Republicans to get away with this. It would appear to be sound strategy to have the President go as far as he feels he possibly could go in recommending measures to protect the rights of minority groups. This course of action would obviously cause difficulty with our Southern friends but that is the lesser of two evils.[35]

Rowe's discussion of the importance of the African American vote, which Clifford left unchanged, concluded that:

> A theory of many professional politicians is that the northern Negro voter today holds the balance of power in Presidential elections for the simple arithmetical reason that the Negroes not only vote in a bloc but are geographically concentrated in the pivotal, large and closely contested electoral states such as New York, Illinois, Pennsylvania, Ohio and Michigan. This theory may or may not be absolutely true, but it is certainly close enough to the truth to be extremely arguable.

Rowe also warned that Dewey's cultivation of the black vote in New York could cost Truman the state in the next year's election.[36]

Clifford, therefore, was breaking no new ground by highlighting civil rights as an important issue. It was important to Truman and it was important to African American voters, who could be a crucial bloc in some critical states and were being courted by the anticipated

Republican candidate for president. The risk that support for civil rights might alienate the South was considered acceptable, especially relative to the risk of losing New York. Clifford's integration of the civil rights issue into the campaign strategy report was not exceptional; it would have been exceptional not to have included it. Truman biographer David McCullough had this to say about Clifford's embrace of the civil rights issue:

> Of all the President's aides and Cabinet officers no one had done more than Clifford to push for a strong stand on civil rights, as part of a larger effort to, in Clifford's words, "strike for a new high ground" whenever confronting the Republican Congress. And it was a strategy based on close study, no less than moral conviction, for Clifford did nothing without careful preparation and planning. (On the golf course he was known as someone to never play behind, if it could be avoided, since he took so many practice swings before every shot.)[37]

In December 1947 Truman asked Clifford to prepare the civil rights legislation that he sent up to Congress in February 1948. Clifford delegated the assignment to Elsey, and it was ready for the president on February 1.[38]

The precedence of the political considerations associated with the civil rights issue is central in much of the correspondence in Clifford's papers. Oscar Ewing sent Clifford an undated memorandum with his comments and observations regarding the president's civil rights program. Underscoring the sensitivity of the document, the word "confidential" is written in Clifford's hand on the first page. Like Clifford and Rowe, Ewing thought that civil rights was an important campaign issue in 1948. He wrote, "Proper handling of the Civil Rights issue is of crucial importance. It can virtually assure the re-election of the President by cutting the ground out from under Wallace and gaining the enthusiastic support of the liberal and labor groups." Ewing also agreed with the prediction that Truman was not at risk in the South. "There is no danger of losing the South," he wrote. "It will neither go Republican nor vote for Wallace. In any event, however, it takes a considerable number of southern States to equal the importance of such States as New York, Pennsylvania, and Illinois." Not only did Ewing think that Truman's civil rights program presented an acceptable risk in the South, he also thought it was a completely risk-free strategy: "There is, therefore, everything to be gained and nothing

tangible to be lost by making the most forthright and dramatic statement on this issue and by backing it up with equally dramatic and
forthright action. Every attempt to compromise loses the votes which
count." Ewing also thought Truman's civil rights program did not go
far enough and that "the real pay-off will come with action to end
discrimination in the government and the armed forces."[39]

In April 1948, William Batt sent a memo to Gael Sullivan, the
executive director of the Democratic National Committee, with a
copy to Clifford, discussing the importance of the black vote. Batt was
more circumspect than Ewing, but believed there was a threat that a
significant percentage of the African American vote might be lost to
Wallace and noted that an executive order ending segregation in the
armed services would help counter that threat. He was, however, concerned about the southern backlash and thought it was important to
consult with southern congressional leaders.[40]

The poll results from the spring suggested that the confidence regarding the political saliency of the civil rights issue may have been misplaced. A March 1948 poll found that only 21 percent of non-southern
whites supported the president's program, 15 percent opposed it, and
the rest had no opinion. Another poll showed that Truman had a 57
percent disapproval rating in the South. The same poll also told a
more ominous tale regarding the upcoming election. Truman trailed
four hypothetical Republican nominees: Dewey, Arthur Vandenberg,
General Douglas MacArthur, and Governor Harold Stassen of Minnesota.[41] In addition, Truman's civil rights legislation was not going
anywhere in Congress. Truman therefore made a tactical retreat. It
was only a temporary retreat, however; at the Democratic convention in July Truman approved civil rights language in the Democratic
platform.

Clifford supported the president's civil rights stance, but he was
concerned about unnecessarily antagonizing the South. "Although I
had supported the President vigorously in his civil rights program,"
he said, "I felt that there was no need to mortify the South by pressing
for an *extreme* civil rights plank at the convention. After all, a plank
doesn't amount to very much." Clifford spoke to Truman prior to
the convention and shared his concerns with the president, suggesting a "mild approach to civil rights" so as to avoid driving the South
from the Democratic Party. As he recalled in 1971, Clifford said Truman overruled him and insisted on a stronger platform than Clifford
would otherwise have been comfortable with. Clifford recalled that
Truman said "he was not going to retreat one inch from his civil rights

program." When asked if he thought Truman pushed for a strong program out of political expediency Clifford replied, "I believe that I was concerned more with political expediency than he."[42] Clifford's account in his memoir is a little different. In *Counsel to the President* he says that he oversaw the drafting of the platform in the White House, along with support from Bill Batt and the Research Division. Although he thought it unwise politically, Clifford saw to it that the platform reflected Truman's wishes. After discussing the matter with Senator Francis Myers of Pennsylvania, chairman of the platform committee, Clifford concluded that the language needed to be softened a bit. He met with Truman and pressed his case. Truman agreed, but only because he wanted to avoid a divisive showdown at the convention, and he emphasized that his softened stance at this stage did not indicate that he was any less committed to the issue.[43]

If Truman felt he was bowing to political expediency, however, it backfired on him. The civil rights platform was the subject of heated debate at the convention and ultimately led to the defection of a bloc of southerners from the Democratic Party. Hubert Humphrey, the mayor of Minneapolis and a candidate for the U.S. Senate, felt that the plank did not go far enough and pushed for stronger language. Humphrey was successful, and against the wishes of the president the stronger language was approved by the delegates. The southerners were irate, and the Mississippi delegation and half of the Alabama delegation stormed out of the convention.

Immediately after the Democratic convention in July, Truman issued Executive Orders 9980 and 9981, which outlawed discrimination in the civil service and desegregated the armed services. According to Clifford these two dramatic measures were consistent with Truman's civil rights program, although he conceded that there may have been a political flavor to the timing. This time, however, the southern reaction was even more pronounced than the staged march off the convention floor in Philadelphia. A group of disaffected Democrats held a rival convention in Birmingham, Alabama, just after the Democratic convention ended. They proclaimed themselves the States' Rights Party; the press labeled them "Dixiecrats." The Dixiecrats nominated Strom Thurmond for president and Governor Fielding Wright of Mississippi for vice president. Ultimately the Dixiecrats carried Alabama, Mississippi, South Carolina, and Louisiana, plus one rebellious elector from Tennessee. The 1948 election marked a profound shift in American electoral politics as the South began to shift allegiance from the Democratic to the Republican Party.

Harry Truman had gone further down the road of civil rights than any president, with the exception of Lincoln. The evidence, especially candid remarks such as those found in his letter to his sister, suggests that Truman acted out of moral conviction and his belief that the United States could not be true to itself if it permanently relegated groups to the status of second-class citizens. Clifford reflected, "He would say that if our whole theory of government meant anything, that it meant that they [African Americans] were not to be different classes of citizens, that each would have the right to social, political, economic opportunity in the country, and he developed a sincere, honest and enduring attitude toward that major constitutional question."[44] George Elsey also believed that Truman's civil rights efforts were not motivated by politics. "The black vote was there. This was a subject about which he [Truman] felt very passionate," he said.[45] Although Clifford conceded that there may have been a political element to the timing of some of the president's actions, he was careful to clarify that politics did not drive the policy. "Just to recapitulate," he said, "I believe that he took the risk that his attitude on civil rights would be a political liability because of the honest conviction that he had that progress had to be made in that field."[46] According to Clifford, "The Negro vote would not at that time be considered to be the kind of vote that would be determining."[47]

Others read the political implications of the civil rights program differently. When asked about the importance of the African American vote Bill Batt responded, "Quite important. Quite important, and of course the President was very popular among Negro voters because of his strong stand on Civil Rights."[48] Philleo Nash, who was David Niles's assistant, reported to Truman just after the election that "over the country as a whole, your majority in the Negro districts is the highest ever. The *average* will be above 80%."[49] In addition, Ewing's memorandum to Clifford demonstrates his belief in the importance of the black vote.

Clifford supported the president's civil rights effort, believing it was morally right. Politically he thought it was risky and might antagonize southerners. In this regard, however, Clifford was inconsistent. When asked during a 1971 interview how he had believed the South would vote in 1948, he said, "I thought that we could hold onto them as I mentioned in the memorandum that I wrote." What he feared was that a strong civil rights platform would "mortify the South." In his memoirs he wrote that he feared that a strong civil rights platform would "provoke a crisis with the South."[50] Since both recollections were recorded many years after the fact it is impossible to determine just what Clifford thought at the time, but since both accounts describe him as trying to convince the president to water down the language it seems probable that Clifford thought the risk of a southern rebellion was very real. If that is so, his apprehension regarding the South was notably inconsistent with the Rowe memorandum. In that document, Clifford did not challenge Rowe's assumption that the South was safely Democratic; indeed, he carried over Rowe's language verbatim. The civil rights issue, therefore, provides further evidence that the memorandum that provided Clifford with a Washington meal ticket for years was the intellectual property of James Rowe.

It was at the 1948 Democratic convention that Truman called Congress back into session, the infamous "Turnip Session." The Turnip Session, so named because Truman called Congress back into session on July 26, traditionally the day that Missourians planted turnips, was consistent with the strategy articulated in the Rowe campaign memorandum. Rowe had advised Truman to run against the Republican Congress and select issues that would be at odds with the Eightieth Congress in order to highlight the differences between the parties. With that in mind Truman dramatically announced during his acceptance speech that he would call Congress back into session so they could tackle a number of pressing issues, including inflation, the housing shortage, and education funding. In essence, the strategy entailed calling the opposing party's bluff. The Republicans professed support for these issues in their party platform, but Truman was convinced that they would not take action, especially in light of the fact that they would be angry that he had called them back into session. As Rowe's memorandum had suggested, the intent was not to pass legislation but to put the issues before the American people. After the session ended, the White House released a statement itemizing the issues upon which Truman had asked Congress to take action, and next to most of the issues was the phrase "failed to act."

It is unclear where the idea for the Turnip Session originated. Batt claims that he proposed the idea to the Wardman Park Group but that they were not receptive. Undeterred, he broached the subject again, but this time only with Clifford. Perhaps looking to brush Batt off, Clifford suggested he write a memo. Again Batt was undeterred and pressed the case again. Clifford must have discussed the idea with members of the White House staff because there is a telegram from Elsey to Clifford saying that it would be unwise to call Congress back until after the conventions. According to Batt, he heard nothing further on the subject until he listened to the president's acceptance speech.[51]

Paul Taylor, an economics professor at the University of California at Berkeley, sent Clifford a memo on June 23, 1948, arguing the case for calling Congress back into session. "Nothing could put the 80th Congress on the spot quite so clearly as to be recalled to meet its responsibilities by the President," Taylor wrote.[52] It is unclear whether Taylor's memo received any circulation when it was written. Two months later Elsey forwarded the Taylor memorandum to Charles Murphy with the concession that it was "stale," which would suggest that it had not been circulated.[53]

Another memorandum, dated June 29, just six days after the Taylor memo, asks the question "Should the President call Congress back?"[54] This memorandum, found in Samuel Rosenman's papers, is both anonymous and has no identified recipient. Batt thought it might have been written either by the Research Division or by Clifford and Rosenman.[55] Rosenman thought Clifford wrote it.[56] Clifford thought it might have originated in the Wardman Park Group. Given the importance and immediacy of the subject, he surmised, the group probably would have asked the Research Division for assistance. "My guess would be that it's an assembly job. And that's why you can't find any *one* individual that says, 'Yes, I wrote the memo,'" Clifford recalled. Although he was not clear on who wrote the memo, he was certain that he supported the idea: "My recollection is, and I am reasonably clear on it, that I was in favor of calling the so-called Turnip Session. I had only one idea in mind at the time, and I think it was very clear what the idea was. I wanted to get the Congress back, ask for action in areas where we knew they were not going to give us action, and then it would help clarify the situation for the election."[57] Leon Keyserling had no specific recollection, but said that "the memo in substance is so close to the 'political' phases of the agreements reached by the Ewing group that I am confident that it may be fairly said that the memo derived from the deliberations of that group."[58] Ewing thought the idea for the special session may have originated with Clifford, but he was unsure, and he could not recall who wrote the memo.[59] Sean Savage, author of *Truman and the Democratic Party*, concluded that the idea for the special session originated in the Research Division but was supported by Clifford.[60]

The June 29 memo makes a strong argument for calling Congress back into session: "This election can only be won by bold and daring steps, calculated to reverse the powerful trend now running against us. The boldest and most popular step the President could possibly take would be to call a special session of Congress early in August."

Similar to Rowe's memorandum it suggests that the best strategy for Truman was to focus attention on Congress. "This would focus attention on the rotten record of the 80th Congress, which Dewey and [his running mate Earl] Warren and the press will try to make the country forget."[61] Truman, as stated earlier, did call Congress back into session after the convention, and this turned out to be a political stroke of genius, which contributed to his stunning victory a few months later.

It is therefore surprising that the key members of the Wardman Park Group had no recollection of the memo or the genesis of the Turnip Session. It played an important role in the biggest political upset of the century, yet Clifford, Ewing, and Keyserling could not recall discussing it among the group. Elsey also could not recall where the idea originated, although he recalled that there was plenty of speculation in the press that Truman would call Congress back into session and that might be why the idea could not be traced to any one person.[62] Clifford's recollection that the June 29 memo was probably an "assembly job" and that that is why no one claimed ownership seems the most plausible explanation, but it is still surprising that no one, other than Batt, took the credit. Although Batt may be correct that the Research Division wrote the memo, it seems unlikely that that group would have sent it over to the White House in the casual, anonymous, and unaddressed manner in which it was written. As for the memo from Taylor, it is not clear whether Clifford ever read it. Given the June 23 date on the Taylor memo, Clifford would have had little time to read it prior to the drafting of the June 29 memorandum—if indeed Clifford had drafted it.

The dramatic call for a special session of Congress signaled that the gloves were coming off for the 1948 campaign and represented the implementation of the strategy that Rowe had advocated and for which Clifford received credit. The Republican Eightieth Congress was Truman's central issue, but the delivery of the message was as central to the 1948 victory as the message itself. The extemporaneous form of speaking Truman adopted as his signature and the "whistle-stop" treks he made across the country are two of the best-known features of his campaign.

Although public speaking turned out to be one of Truman's strengths in the 1948 campaign, his public speaking skills up until then had been a liability. When delivering a speech from a prepared text he had a tendency to look down and read from the page, often in a monotone voice and sometimes with a few mistakes. When he spoke with passion, as he did during the Truman Doctrine speech, he was more effective; yet public speaking remained a weakness for him. In late 1947 Clifford suggested that Truman try another approach. In order to improve his delivery and eye contact Clifford tried writing the text on three-by-four-foot cue cards just beyond the cameras. It was no good; Truman was far too nearsighted, even with his glasses, to see the text. A few months later Clifford, Murphy, and Ross decided to try a different approach. Rather than having him read a prepared text they recommended that the president try speaking extemporaneously. The trial run would be the annual convention of the American Society of Newspaper Editors on April 17, 1948. The president's scheduled remarks were to be on the administration's efforts to combat inflation and would be broadcast live on the radio and delivered in his usual style. After the prepared speech was over and he was off the air, Truman informed the audience of newspaper editors that he wanted to speak off the record. His off-the-air remarks, on U.S. relations with the Soviet Union, were delivered extemporaneously. The subject matter was familiar to Truman and was something he was quite passionate about. The results were gratifying: the off-the-cuff remarks were received with far more enthusiasm than was his formal speech. Truman tried the off-the-cuff approach for his next three speeches and was pleased with the success.

In June Truman took his new style on the road for a test run in advance of the fall campaign. At Truman's urging Clifford had Oscar Chapman arrange an invitation for Truman to deliver a commencement address at the University of California at Berkeley and receive an honorary degree. The trip was presented to the press as an official trip, but nobody was fooled—it was clearly a political trip. Rather than fly, Truman traveled by train, making stops along the way. During the trip he gave five major speeches and about forty minor ones. The minor speeches were delivered from the rear platform of the train and were delivered in the president's new extemporaneous style. The trip was tremendously successful, both as a means of practicing Truman's off-the-cuff style and as a practice run for the fall. As Clifford recalled, "we learned a great deal about how to conduct a campaign—and these lessons were to serve us well when the final round began in September."[63] Of course Truman's journey to California infuriated the Republicans, who were outraged that the president's allegedly nonpolitical trip was being paid out of the official White House budget. Truman relentlessly exacerbated the Republicans' annoyance with frequent tongue-in-cheek references to his "nonpolitical" trip.

The 1948 presidential campaign is synonymous with Truman's whistle-stop tours. The term "whistle-stop" was immortalized by Republican senator Robert Taft, who, during the June 1948 "non-political" trip, lashed out at the president for "blackguarding Congress at every whistle-stop in the West."[64] This was a colossal blunder for the Republicans: it gave Truman the opportunity to appeal to the wounded pride of those westerners who were offended by the derisive reference to their towns as mere "whistle-stops." Taft's intemperate comment inadvertently helped the Truman campaign accomplish two of its major objectives. It allowed Truman to connect with westerners, whom Rowe identified as the important constituency for the 1948 campaign, by identifying with their issues and concerns and thus elevating them above the status of whistle-stops. It also helped Truman focus on the Republican Congress rather than Dewey, another key strategy for the campaign.

The whistle-stop trips have been romanticized by historians, but they were actually quite grueling. During one fifty-day stretch Clifford recalled spending forty days aboard the campaign train. "I lived in a little tiny stateroom where I slept and ate and wrote," he said. "My big task in the campaign was to do the writing for the President." Most evenings the president would deliver a major speech at the larger towns and cities, and during the day he would give a host of shorter, whistle-stop speeches from the platform of the train. Clifford remembered one particularly hectic day when there were fourteen whistle-stops. Elsey recalled doing sixteen whistle-stops on one day. Clifford usually drafted the major speeches while Elsey compiled the notes and outlines for the whistle-stops. Clifford recalled the train trips none too fondly: "I think I had gotten run down a little and I was besieged by an attack of boils during that whole summer. It was a nightmare. For years afterwards I'd sometimes wake up at night in a cold perspiration thinking I was back on that terrible train. It was a *real ordeal*. I don't know quite how I got through it except I was young at the time and strong and vigorous."[65]

The campaign swung into full gear just after Labor Day, when Truman departed Washington on the first of his official political campaign trips. A few weeks earlier Clifford sent Truman a memorandum reiterating strategy for the campaign. He emphasized three primary objectives. "The first objective," Clifford wrote, "is to win a large majority of the 15,000,000 independent voters who overwhelmingly followed the liberal leadership of the Democratic Party in the last four elections. This should be done by driving home to them the failure of the 80th Congress, by linking Dewey closely to the leadership of that Congress." The three important constituencies in the election, he noted, were "workers, veterans, and Negroes." The second objective was to win the support of those three groups. The final objective was to capitalize on the success and popularity of Truman's foreign policy toward the Soviet Union. "The President's policy has kept the Nation on a road leading to peace, and . . . changes in this policy may lead to war," he wrote.[66]

In order to appeal to the labor constituency, Clifford recommended that Truman call for repeal of the Taft-Hartley Act, which Congress had passed over his veto. Veterans would be drawn to Truman's own military record as well as his GI Bill of Rights. The president's civil rights program would appeal to African American voters. "The President should speak out fully on his Civil Rights record. . . . His record proves that he *acts* as well as *talks* Civil Rights," Clifford wrote. He continued to adhere to Rowe's argument from the previous fall. He wrote, "The Negro votes in the crucial states will more than cancel out any votes the President may lose in the South."[67] It is interesting that Clifford took the position that the upside of Truman's civil rights agenda outweighed the downside. Only a month earlier he had urged Truman to tone down his language on civil rights in the Democratic platform, but now he was arguing that Truman "should speak out fully" on the subject. Whereas Rowe had argued in November 1947 that the South could be ignored, the magnitude of the southern revolt was now apparent. By splitting from the Democratic Party and running under the banner of states' rights, Dixiecrat candidate Thurmond threatened to peel off a significant portion of Truman's base. Especially given his caution of just a month earlier, Clifford might have been expected to advocate caution during the campaign. Instead he made the bizarre argument that the civil rights program might have had some resonance in the South. "Even in the South," he suggested, "the Dixiecrats have raised the smoke screen of States Rights rather than openly oppose the extension of Civil Rights to the Negroes."[68] This was an absurd argument. In reality, it did not matter what label the Dixiecrats attached to their platform because the message was clear: they saw themselves as a bulwark against the repeal of segregation. It may not have been politically acceptable to openly oppose civil rights per se, but southern whites knew exactly what the Dixiecrats meant.

The 1948 election is not commonly considered one in which foreign policy was the central issue. According to Elsey, "foreign policy was not an issue on which he [Truman] intended to campaign."[69] Clifford thought otherwise; he considered foreign policy to be one of the three primary objectives of the campaign. In order "to win the 'peace' vote," he argued, Truman "should refer frequently to the Truman Doctrine and the European Recovery Program, and point out that these have been successful in maintaining the integrity of free states against Communist pressure."[70]

The balance of Clifford's memorandum focused on electoral strategy, specifically the key states and cities on which Truman should focus. Clifford's final recommendation regarding strategy proved crucial to the success of the whistle-stop tours. Truman had been embarrassed during the June "nonpolitical" trip when he mistakenly dedicated a new airport in Carey, Idaho, to a local wartime hero, Wilmer Coates. The problem was that the airport was to be named after *Wilma* Coates, a woman who had died in an airplane crash.[71] In order to avoid that type of mistake, especially during the height of the campaign when the repercussions would be magnified, Clifford recommended that Truman needed advance intelligence. "A trained observer should precede the President at every step he is scheduled to make," he wrote. "This man should prepare a brief on the town the President is scheduled to visit, explaining the local issues of importance and how they tie in to the national issues."[72] This advance intelligence was to be compiled by Batt's Research Division. Elsey recalled that:

> Every place on a presidential itinerary, every community, no matter how small or how large, was looked into by the Research Division. It prepared digests, briefs, having just the sort of the Baedeker kind of historical, geographical background—population, so on and so forth, anything notable in the history of the place. Then it would focus on the issues of 1948, material on the candidates, both for the incumbent Congressman and his opponent, material on state candidates, if that was germane, a suggestion as to what subject or what topic would be of most interest to the voters of that region.[73]

This strategy proved enormously successful during the whistle-stop campaign, with Batt's group providing exactly the type of information Truman needed to connect with the voters and discuss issues that were of concern to them.

Clifford's perceptive strategy contributed to Truman's winning in November. However, as with the previous year's memo, whose main author was James Rowe, most of Clifford's August 1948 advice on Truman's campaign was appropriated from someone else: William Batt, in conjunction with the staff of the Research Division. On August 11 Batt sent a memorandum to Clifford in which he argued that the strategy for the campaign was "to gain and solidify support from three large groups in the nation which can swing the election one way or the other, and are already predominately Democratic in their inclinations—the working people, the veterans, and the Negroes." Another objective, wrote Batt, was "to cut through all party lines by showing that the policy of the Truman administration has kept the nation on a road leading to peace, not to war."[74] Elsey had the memo retyped so that it could go out over Clifford's signature, and Clifford did some editing and a little rewriting, but the final product was substantially unchanged from Batt's original memo.[75] As with the Rowe memorandum, Clifford co-opted Batt's ideas and writing without attribution. The difference was that Clifford could make a somewhat credible argument that he needed to shield Rowe's authorship of the earlier memo from the president because Truman had no use for Rowe's law partner. This was not the case with Batt, who, as head of the Research Division of the Democratic National Committee, presumably had the president's confidence. Also, although Clifford eventually made partial acknowledgment of Rowe's authorship, the discussion of the August 1948 memorandum in *Counsel to the President* makes no reference to Batt's work; Clifford describes it as a memorandum he wrote.[76]

Although Truman did not attack the Eightieth Congress on the subject of foreign policy, and in fact collaborated with Vandenberg, foreign policy was an issue in the campaign. Using Batt's analysis, Clifford recommended that Truman capitalize on the public's confidence in the president's foreign policy by suggesting that the alternative might risk war. A number of developments in 1948 underscored the precarious state of U.S. relations with the Soviet Union, including the Czechoslovakian coup and the Berlin Airlift. Truman's political and campaign advisers, including Clifford, believed that the public's heightened concern about preserving the peace worked to Truman's advantage. Ironically, Republicans would co-opt the "whom do you trust with national security" argument for most of the Cold War, which contributed to their hold on the White House for twenty-eight out of forty-four years. In 1948, however, the Democrats believed it was an issue that accrued to their benefit.

A good deal of the correspondence Batt sent to Clifford throughout 1948 focused on foreign policy. Batt's memo of May 8 had reported the rather discouraging results of a poll concerning public opinion of Truman's foreign policy. Despite the discouraging results Batt believed that the unfavorable numbers were largely due to "a widespread ignorance" regarding the direction of American foreign policy.[77] Batt had weighed in enthusiastically after the president's St. Patrick's Day speech, but he also expressed regret that the speech did not "contain as effective a Plan for Peace as it did a Plan for Defense."[78] Shortly after the St. Patrick's Day speech Batt informed Clifford that he was planning to submit an article regarding universal military training, an issue dear to Truman, to *The Nation*. Batt was in favor of universal training and had planned to write such an article even before he joined the Research Division. Following the president's speech *The Nation* asked him if they could have the article within the week.[79] An article such as Batt's would be immensely useful and could benefit Truman by helping to sell the idea to the American people. A month later Batt notified Clifford that the campaign had lined up Dean Acheson, the former undersecretary of state, to make a few foreign policy speeches on behalf of the campaign.[80] Acheson, who Batt heard was "an excellent speaker," would succeed George Marshall as secretary of state at the beginning of Truman's second term. As far as the opposition was concerned, in August Dewey announced plans to name John Foster Dulles, the Republicans' primary foreign policy spokesman after Vandenberg, as his secretary of state. "Dewey has stated that Mr. Dulles would be the kind of Secretary of State who could say no to Joe Stalin," Batt reported.[81]

Batt also utilized Clifford as a liaison between the campaign and the State Department. In May, while collecting material for a paper on the Truman administration's peace initiatives, Batt ran into an obstacle in the person of Francis Russell, the director of the State Department's Office of Public Affairs. Russell was uncomfortable providing information to the campaign without Marshall's approval and also because he feared it might jeopardize the bipartisan cooperation on foreign policy which Truman enjoyed with the Eightieth Congress. Russell suggested that Batt have Clifford request the material from either Marshall or Lovett, which is particularly ironic because Batt sent Clifford the request on May 12, the same day of Clifford's infamous showdown with Marshall over Israel.[82]

Batt believed that it was important to tout the Truman administration's foreign policy accomplishments, especially the Truman Doctrine and the Marshall Plan. Unfortunately, the Truman Doctrine also exposed the president to the potential for bad press due to human rights abuses in Greece. Batt informed Clifford that there were reports that the Greek government had executed 160 people in retaliation for an assassination plot directed at a member of the government. Those executed were believed to be leftists who had already been imprisoned for their role in a 1944 coup attempt. Batt wrote:

> In view of the American program of aid to Greece and of the intimate linkage of President Truman's name with that program as first announced, I suggest that consideration be given at the highest level to publicly protesting these executions, if the reports of them prove to be correct.
>
> I suggest that it would be politically important for the President to denounce publicly and emphatically the excesses being committed in a country which we are aiding in the name of a common defense of democracy.[83]

The Berlin Airlift, the aerial supply operation Truman ordered in response to the Soviet land blockade of West Berlin, commenced in the summer of 1948. Because the decision was perceived as a bold stand in defiance of Soviet intransigence, Batt thought it could be beneficial to the campaign. Accordingly he recommended to Clifford that Truman send a personal envoy to Berlin, which "would be welcomed by the public as a bold step proving to the country that the President is a statesman determined to make use of the best talents in the Nation." His nominee for the position: Dwight David Eisenhower.[84] Incredibly, Batt was confident that the issues dividing the United States and the Soviet Union, particularly over Berlin, could be resolved and that the two superpowers might soon find an accommodation. Anticipating a major breakthrough as a result of the Soviet-Western power negotiations that were underway in Moscow, Batt thought it appropriate to plan for a major presidential television and radio announcement, comparable to the announcement of the Japanese surrender in 1945. He wrote, "It seems desirable to underscore this success of our foreign policy as emphatically as possible. . . . Besides inflation and housing, the fear of war is unquestionably the major concern of the American people at this time. If the President were in a position to lift this fear from their minds it would go a long way towards enhancing his prestige as the responsible leader of our foreign policy."[85]

Elsey shared Batt's optimism about the Moscow talks and thought that Truman should be prepared to announce their successful conclusion "so he capitalizes on a dramatic foreign policy matter. Otherwise, he would be lost on the public relations angle." Elsey also noted that Clifford had discussed the matter with Truman that day and would also speak to Lovett.[86] As for the Berlin Airlift, Truman made the decision without consulting Clifford or any member of his White House staff, which suggests that Truman did not always rely on Clifford's advice, at least regarding foreign policy matters. According to Elsey, "The White House staff, to the best of my knowledge, had no direct role whatsoever in any decisions or in the execution of any of the carrying out of the airlift."[87]

Clifford, Batt, and others advising the campaign believed that the foreign policy issue could work to their advantage. They also believed that Dewey would try to capitalize on it. In a memorandum to Clifford, Elsey argued that the Truman record on foreign policy was good and was "one of the strongest reasons why the Administration should be continued in office." Rather than attack the soundness of the policy itself, he believed "that Dewey's approach will consist largely of charges of 'bungling.'" Elsey went on to assert that the State Department should be responsible for responding to Dewey's charges, except those which pertained to Palestine, and should also make the case for the administration's foreign policy. The State Department should also work closely with the White House staff, he suggested. Clifford and Charles Murphy met with Matthew Connelly, the president's appointments secretary, to discuss how to sell Elsey's ideas to the president.[88]

While Dewey attacked the president from the right on foreign policy, Henry Wallace attacked from the left. Wallace remained as convinced in 1948 as he had been in 1946 that a policy of conciliation and accommodation was the only way to ensure peaceful relations with the Soviet Union. Truman's policy was to forcefully attack Wallace as being not only soft on communism, but also influenced and even in collusion with the communists. Rowe had suggested that approach in the November 1947 campaign memorandum. "The men around Wallace are motivated by the Communist Party line," he argued, and the way to defeat him was "to identify him and isolate him in the public mind with the Communists."[89] Gael Sullivan made the same argument five months earlier in a memorandum Elsey passed along to Clifford. Sullivan warned that "Wallace is a major consideration in the 1948 campaign" and that "something should be done to combat him." He argued that in order for Truman to confront Wallace's arguments and "pull the rug on him" he should broadcast a series of "fireside chats" to explain his policies, emphasize the "non-military side of the Truman Doctrine," and respond to "Wallace's fuzzy thinking . . . by clear level-headed replies—ignoring the man but answering the issue." Alternatively, Sullivan suggested that if the Democrats wanted Wallace back in the party, he should be appeased.[90] Following the Czech coup, Wallace laid the blame "on the Truman Doctrine and indicated that Russia was retaliating against U.S. aggression." In an anti-Wallace position paper forwarded to Clifford by the Democratic National Committee, the Americans for Democratic Action argued that Wallace's views regarding the Czech crisis "closely conformed to the C[ommunist] P[arty] line."[91]

The following spring, using a bit of theatrical flair, Wallace invited Soviet Premier Josef Stalin to a conference to end the Cold War and ensure a "century of peace." After Stalin issued a statement accepting Wallace's invitation Clifford asked Truman if he planned to respond. Truman replied that "nothing could or should be done at this time."[92] While Truman laid low and ignored Wallace's summit proposal, the Research Division was compiling an opposition research report about him. In June Batt sent the completed report to McGrath and Jack Redding, the publicity director for the Democratic National Committee, with a copy to Clifford. Batt recommended that "the best way to cut the ground beneath Henry Wallace is to show that Wallace is not trustworthy, has no consistent policy, and does not have the capacity to be a successful President."[93]

With only a month left before the election Truman made a potentially costly blunder, his only significant mistake of the campaign. David Noyes and Albert Carr, two campaign staffers, approached Matt Connelly with a bold idea to calm U.S.-Soviet tensions over Berlin, demonstrate to the Wallace-inclined left that Truman remained committed to peace, and also spotlight Truman's resolve in the face of Soviet aggression. Their idea was to send Chief Justice Fred Vinson to Moscow to negotiate directly with Stalin, in much the same way Roosevelt had dispatched Harry Hopkins to meet with the Soviet leader in 1945. Connelly liked the idea and immediately brought it to the president, who was back in Washington for a brief rest between campaign trips. Truman liked the idea as well. Without consulting with either Marshall, who was in Paris attending another foreign ministers conference, or Lovett, Truman instructed Charlie Ross to approach the networks with a request for air time. When Lovett, then acting secretary of state, heard about the plans he raced to the White House, literally with sirens blaring. The planned Vinson mission, he said, was a mistake, would undermine Marshall's negotiating status in Paris, and might precipitate the secretary's resignation. Truman realized that Lovett was right and told Ross to cancel the announcement. Unfortunately for Truman, however, the news leaked, presenting Dewey with an attractive opportunity to accuse Truman of playing politics with foreign policy. No doubt confident of victory, Dewey refrained from comment, thus giving Truman a free ride. In fact, Alan Harper noted, the aborted Vinson mission might have worked to Truman's benefit as it demonstrated, especially to the left, "Truman's desire to go the extra mile for peace."[94]

For the Truman campaign, the Vinson mission was nearly disastrous. For Clifford it was publicly embarrassing. According to Clifford, both he and Elsey vehemently opposed the idea, but Truman overruled them. *Time* magazine reported, incorrectly, that the Vinson mission had been Clifford's idea: "In view of the political debacle facing the Truman Administration, it was hard to understand how handsome Mr. Clifford could look so happy and knowing. He looked like a man who had something up his sleeve. In fact, he had."[95] The source of *Time*'s story is unclear, but it is understandable that Truman's political motives would be questioned so late in the campaign. And as Truman's closest political adviser, Clifford might understandably be assumed to be the source of the recommendation, especially in light of his involvement in the Palestine issue. When asked if the Vinson mission had been Clifford's idea Elsey emphatically replied, "Absolutely not! Clifford was, all of us, thought it was the Goddamnest, screwiest idea in every way, shape or form. All he did was argue against it. It didn't make any sense. To pull the Chief Justice off the Supreme Court to do anything was wrong. It would be futile; it was a grandstand play that would be seen as a grandstand play, it would backfire. It wouldn't accomplish anything anyway."[96]

As the campaign headed into the home stretch, the media was buzzing with prognostications about the upcoming election, and they all looked bleak for Truman. The press was overwhelmingly convinced that Dewey would win comfortably. Elmo Roper, the political pollster, ceased his election sampling in early September, typically the height of the campaign season. In early October *Newsweek* magazine published the results of a survey of fifty of the most respected political journalists in the country. Anticipating the publication of the results, which appeared in the October 11 issue, Clifford got off the campaign train at the first stop and headed for a newsstand. "ELECTION

FORECAST: 50 POLITICAL EXPERTS PREDICT A GOP SWEEP,"
read the headline. Clifford was dumbfounded. "That Dewey would
be favored hardly surprised me," he wrote, "but the shocker was the
vote: fifty to *nothing*. Not even one pundit out of fifty was willing to
buck conventional wisdom and predict a Truman victory."[97] Crest-
fallen, Clifford headed back to the campaign train, but in order to get
to his own cabin Clifford had to pass through the president's car. Like
a child trying to hide a racy magazine from his mother Clifford slipped
the offending magazine into his coat, but Truman was not fooled.

"What does it say, Clark?" he asked.

Clifford played dumb. "What does what say?"

"What have you got under your coat, Clark?"

"Nothing, Mr. President."

"Clark. I saw you get off the train just now, and I think that you
went in there to see if they had a newsstand with a copy of *Newsweek*.
And I think maybe you have it under your coat."

Caught, Clifford turned over the magazine to Truman, no doubt
afraid of his reaction. To his surprise, Truman seemed unfazed.
"Don't worry about that poll, Clark," he said. "I know every one of
those fifty fellows, and not one of them has enough sense to pound
sand into a rathole."[98]

Clifford did some prognosticating of his own. On October 20,
while in Washington on a short break from the campaign trail, Clifford had lunch with Arthur Krock. During their lunch Clifford tallied,
literally on the back of an envelope, his prediction of the electoral
votes by state. Clifford predicted that Truman would win 289 electoral votes; the actual tally was 303, an astonishingly close prediction.
Of the large states, Clifford missed only California, Michigan, Indiana, New Jersey, and Wisconsin. In all, he correctly predicted thirty-
six out of forty-eight states. It was a prediction he was quite proud of,
and he saved the envelope for posterity. During a 1971 oral history
interview with the Truman Library he touted the accuracy of his prediction and reviewed his electoral predictions by state with the interviewer. In his memoirs Clifford wrote that he and Krock would look
back at his "absurd predictions . . . with a combination of amusement
and amazement."[99] His prescient prediction further contributed to the
growing mystique of Clark Clifford.

Upon closer study, however, it might not be such an incredible
prediction. Clifford made his calculations while having lunch with
Krock, one of the leading political writers in the country. Krock was
convinced that Dewey would win; in fact, he had been one of the

fifty journalists who had unanimously predicted a Dewey victory. The *New York Times*, Krock's own paper, predicted the weekend before the election that Dewey would carry 345 electoral votes, a landslide.[100] Clifford's agenda for having lunch with Krock less than two weeks before the election can be inferred with a fair degree of certainty. He was applying some political spin to the journalist with the hope that he could convince him that Truman had a fighting chance. At the very least, he was looking to undermine the wave of inevitability that the Dewey campaign was planning to ride to victory. In Clifford's account of the lunch, Krock laughed when Clifford suggested that Truman had a chance to win. "Wearily," he wrote, "I took an envelope out of my pocket and wrote down the states I thought President Truman would carry. I was not convinced I was right, but I had begun to glimpse a scenario that could give the President a victory."[101] It is impossible to know what Clifford's state of mind was at the time, and whether he really believed that Truman had a realistic chance of winning. What Clifford really believed, however, is irrelevant. What is important is what he said and what he wrote on the back of that envelope. Above all other things, Clifford was loyal to Truman and if he did believe that a Dewey win was inevitable he would have never said as much to Krock, even if his comments were kept off the record. Clifford's prediction, fundamentally, was a piece of propaganda, a bit of political spin. If Clifford's prediction had been made to an ally in the campaign or the administration, it would have been more impressive. In a private chat with Elsey on October 13, Truman predicted that he would carry 340 electoral votes.[102] When Elsey shared with him the president's prediction, Clifford was incredulous. "He just shook his head," Elsey recalled.[103]

On Election Day Clifford sent Truman a personal letter, lauding his hard-fought campaign. "Win, lose or draw I want to tell you how deeply I admire the wonderful fight you have made," he wrote. "It has been a tremendous thing for the country and the party. I can't tell you how tremendously I respect and admire you for your great battle."[104] That day Truman accomplished perhaps the greatest political upset in American history. It was a victory he savored, most memorably in the famous picture of him beaming as he holds up a copy of the *Chicago Tribune* with the front-page headline "Dewey Defeats Truman." It was also a day for Clifford to savor. It represented the culmination of a long, hard-fought, and exhausting campaign. Clifford described the call he received from Truman announcing his victory as "the most gratifying" of his life.[105] Truman's victory would also be personally rewarding to Clifford, as it contributed to the aura of political genius that would follow Clifford through his final year in the Truman administration and into private practice. The 1948 campaign also introduced Clifford to Governor Robert Kerr of Oklahoma, who was then a candidate for the U.S. Senate. Near the end of the first whistle-stop tour Kerr rescued the nearly bankrupt Truman campaign by working with a group of fellow oilmen to raise the necessary funds. Kerr and Clifford would become good friends, and Clifford would support him in the 1952 presidential race. Kerr's connections also enabled Clifford to amass a small fortune in oil stocks.

Despite the accolades Clifford received, however, the author of the winning campaign strategy was James Rowe, not Clark Clifford. Clifford was certainly an important member of the campaign team. He was constantly by Truman's side, day after day, whistle-stop after whistle-stop. Along with George Elsey, he drafted Truman's off-the-cuff speeches, which required far more preparation than "off-the-cuff" would suggest. Bill Batt described Clifford's role as the "Father Superior" of the campaign. Clifford, however, was not the idea man of the campaign. According to Robert Underhill, author of *The Truman Persuasions,* "the record shows that Clifford functioned more as synthesizer of various strategies than as their originator. Some suggestions he rejected outright; others he endorsed, and in case of doubt he passed them on to the president for his consideration."[106] And sometimes Clifford took those suggestions, had them retyped, and submitted them under his own signature. His role as the master strategist for Truman's upset victory was a cornerstone of his legacy as political genius, Washington power broker, and indispensable counselor for Democratic presidents. The historical record would be incomplete if James Rowe's name was not engraved on that stone as well. Still, in the end, as Elsey said, "The mastermind strategist behind the 1948 campaign was a guy named Harry S. Truman."[107]

# 6

# One Foot out the Door

Truman's 1948 underdog victory was immensely rewarding to Clifford, on both a personal and a professional level. His loyalty and devotion to Truman were genuine, and it must have been satisfying to help Truman win the presidency in his own right. But Clifford was ready to move on. Despite the thrill of victory and the belief that he had been engaged in a "noble quest for the highest honor to which an American may aspire," Clifford also, he admitted, "found most of the actual work of a campaign tedious or inconsequential."[1] He was also under financial pressure: his $12,000 annual salary as special counsel was inadequate, and he had depleted most of his savings. Just prior to the election Clifford confided to Truman that he was weighing his options and might leave the administration to practice law. Truman was sympathetic but asked Clifford to stay on for another year, to which he agreed. But Clifford's heart was elsewhere and, while he served for all of 1949, his enthusiasm for the job was not what it used to be. According to Clifford, he "was reaching the point of diminishing returns" in his "government service."[2]

After the election and before diving back into the business of government, Truman and his staff took a well-deserved vacation in Key West. Clifford, who was usually impeccably dressed and careful to preserve his image, completely let his hair down. He donned a pair of tattered shorts, refrained from shaving for a week, and walked about barefoot. An article in *Redbook* magazine from that time wrote that he "resembled a bronzed young beachcomber." Truman was so amused with Clifford's transformation that he took to calling him "Jeeter" after an unkempt character from the play *Tobacco Road*. Truman's victory was for Clifford a personal vindication, given that he had been accused by *Time* of leading Truman to defeat. *Redbook* reported that Clifford kept a copy of the *Time* story in the top drawer of his desk: "Occasionally Clifford likes to pull out the story and read it over again. With pardonable pride he has told his friends, 'You know, I was mad when this article came out. But now I think it was a real good story. It turns out that the things it accused me of doing were the very things that helped win the election!'"[3]

The vacation was but a momentary respite from the work ahead. Awaiting Clifford upon his return to Washington was Truman's upcoming Inaugural Address and, after that, the State of the Union. Truman planned to devote the Inaugural Address to his domestic agenda and focus on foreign policy in his State of the Union speech. Just before departing for Key West Clifford asked George Elsey, who was left behind in Washington, to start gathering ideas for the two messages. While Clifford was in Key West Elsey got to work, but the more he thought about the president's instructions, the more he was convinced that Truman had it backward. Elsey believed that since it was likely that Truman would have only one opportunity to make an Inaugural Address while he would have four more State of the Union addresses, he should use the Inaugural Address as a forum to discuss foreign policy. "It would be an address far beyond just the Congress, it would be the American people and other countries, both friendly and unfriendly; whereas, the State of the Union could confine itself to domestic matters," Elsey recalled. Clifford and Elsey discussed the subject on the phone, and Elsey followed up their discussion with a long memorandum. Clifford was convinced, and after talking it over with Truman, the president came around as well.[4]

By shifting the focus of the Inaugural to foreign affairs and emphasizing that it would be a singular event, Elsey had put himself into a corner. The heightened expectations could only be satisfied with a bold new idea. In preparation for the annual State of the Union address, Clifford sent a message to the various government agencies looking for ideas. In much the same way he sent a memorandum to the State Department asking for ideas for the Inaugural, which would be "a democratic manifesto addressed to the peoples of the world, not just to the American people."[5] Elsey began work on the speech, and although most of it took shape with relative ease, it was still lacking the dramatic element he felt was needed. Unfortunately for Elsey, he was stumped and was becoming frustrated. At that point, as if in answer to a prayer, he received a call from Benjamin Hardy, who worked in the Public Affairs Department over at State and who suggested that the two arrange to meet. Elsey did not know Hardy, but he had worked with his boss, Francis Russell, on various projects, so he did not think it was unusual for Hardy to contact him. Elsey agreed to meet with Hardy, although the purpose of their meeting was not made clear.

In response to Clifford's request for ideas, Hardy had sent Russell a memorandum recommending that the United States drastically expand technical assistance to developing countries. The concept, which John F. Kennedy resurrected twelve years later with the Peace Corps and the U.S. Agency for International Development, was intended both to provide the countries in the developing world with the tools they needed to help themselves and to make that effort a major component of U.S. foreign policy. Russell had passed along Hardy's idea to Bob Lovett, but in typical bureaucratic fashion Lovett said that the idea required study. Rather than take no for an answer, Hardy totally bypassed normal bureaucratic channels, at considerable professional risk, and reached out to Elsey. When they met Hardy immediately dove into his presentation. Elsey, though surprised, was instantly taken with the idea. After the meeting Elsey brought the idea to Clifford, who also recognized that this was what they were looking for. As Clifford recalled, "this was the solution to our dilemma: while we had a speech in search of an idea, Hardy had an idea in search of a speech."[6]

In order to protect Hardy's confidentiality, given that he had taken a career risk by going outside of normal channels, Elsey informed the State Department that Truman wanted to include a plan for technical assistance to developing nations in the Inaugural Address. Despite the prodding, State not only did not mention Hardy's plan, but did not even respond. After ten days of silence from the State Department, Hardy again bypassed the normal bureaucratic channels and reached out directly to Clifford and Elsey. He informed them that the idea was being blocked by Lovett and Paul Nitze, the brilliant strategist who would later make his mark on history as the author of the famous NSC-68 paper. Nitze recalled, "Chip [Bohlen] agreed with me, and Bob Lovett signed a memorandum to the President endorsing our position [against inclusion of the technical assistance program in the Inaugural]. But Clark Clifford thought that the speech needed a humanitarian initiative and overruled us; the proposal thus went into the President's speech."[7]

Hardy's plan became known as Point Four because it was the fourth foreign policy principle Truman highlighted in his Inaugural Address, after the United Nations, the Marshall Plan, and a collective security pact that would become the North Atlantic Treaty Organization. Unfortunately for Hardy, Point Four is best known as a piece of oratory rather than as a successful government program. Although the State Department had been overruled, its opposition to the plan remained strong. Elsey recalled, "I heard all sorts of repercussions from lower staff levels in the department, people saying this was premature, the planning hadn't been done, the budgeting hadn't been done, in other words the bureaucratic red tape had not been gone through and it was a terrible mistake to put words like this in the President's mouth before the planning had been done."[8]

Clifford was convinced that given its opposition to Point Four, the program should be independent of the State Department. "I presented to the President a plan whereby the Point Four concept would be handled by an independent agency," he recalled. "I thought that in order to maintain the concept that this program was bold and new, we should bring in new people with new ideas." In order to appease his new secretary of state, Dean Acheson, who was also opposed to the idea, Truman conceded to the State Department's wish to keep the program within that organization. A disappointed Clifford later recalled, "All my worst fears about it were realized regarding the manner in which the State Department handled it. They assigned it to a man who already had another job in the State Department, so this became just a part-time responsibility of his. It was *not* pushed the way it should have been pushed."[9]

In *Counsel to the President* Clifford wrote, "I am convinced that Point Four and its offspring remain one of the noblest commitments our nation has made in this century."[10] Clifford's sentiments about Point Four may indeed have been genuine. Nonetheless, it is likely that he expended little personal capital for the idea. He presented to Truman a plan to house Point Four in an independent agency and suggested that his preference would be for a corporate executive to take a leave of absence to administer the program. He even had a candidate in mind, Paul G. Hoffman of the Studebaker Corporation. According to Clifford the two sides "really had a knock-down drag-out fight" over the issue but eventually Truman sided with the State Department, which assured him the program would get the attention it deserved.[11] Because Acheson and other senior officials in the State Department opposed the idea they did almost nothing to implement the program for a full year. Only a few weeks before Clifford resigned in January 1950, Elsey sent him a memo recommending that Truman appoint a "Special Assistant to the President" to administer Point Four. His recommendation for this position was former Senator Bob LaFollette. The same day Elsey sent a memo to White House staffer David Lloyd in which he recounted a conversation he had with Clifford that Saturday morning. They were talking about Point Four when Truman unexpectedly dropped in and joined the conversation. Truman stressed that he did not want Point Four under the auspices of State.[12]

Although the State Department assured Truman that the program would not suffer from lack of attention, the president knew that State was opposed to the idea and had attempted to kill the plan in bureaucratic red tape. Truman, however, had prominently discussed Point Four during his inaugural address, thus attaching his personal prestige to the program and raising expectations that could only be achieved with a sufficient dedication of resources. Yet despite his personal preference Truman allowed State to run the program. No doubt Truman wanted to keep his new secretary of state happy, but it is still surprising that he overruled Clifford and his own better judgment on this decision. Clifford was one of the president's most trusted advisers, and even though he was leaving, Truman still valued his counsel. The fact that Clifford was overruled suggests that he might not have fought very hard for his position.

A few months after Clifford left the administration, Elsey again sought his help. "Point Four is never going to reach the expectations that you and I had for it at its inception, so long as initiative for the program remains in the Department of State," he wrote. "It seems to me that a 'bold new program' is necessary to get our bold new program out of the mud." Elsey recommended the creation of a private corporation to raise and deploy capital for Point Four projects. He suggested that David Lilienthal would be the best person to head this company and that with "Lilienthal as a spokesman and salesman, I believe that a great many projects which are now languishing would receive a new burst of energy, and a great many projects which exist only on paper would come to life."[13] Clifford later said he spoke to the president, who agreed that "something had to be done." Elsey, however, doubted that the conversation took place. "I don't recall that he [Clifford] took any active interest in Point Four after he left office," he recalled. Elsey tried to enlist Clifford's support because Clifford was still seeing Truman regularly, primarily for social occasions, and knew that his opinion still carried great weight with the president. In fact, Elsey's suggestion that Lilienthal run the proposed corporation was a ploy to get Clifford involved. He knew that Clifford and Lilienthal were close and that Clifford held Lilienthal in high regard, and Elsey hoped that might motivate Clifford to again take an active interest in the subject. However, by this time Clifford was fully engaged in establishing his law practice and had little time for Point Four, which he later claimed to have been quite passionate about. Elsey had another theory. "To put it quite bluntly," he said, "Clifford didn't give much of a damn about 'do-gooder'" programs.[14]

Two months later Truman affixed the presidential seal to the Act for International Development, which established a Technical Cooperation Administration. In deference to Acheson and the State Department, it was placed under their auspices. The grand ambitions of Point Four were never realized until Kennedy resurrected the concept under the banner of the Peace Corps. Absent clear evidence of Clifford's advocacy of the program it could be argued that he viewed Point Four more as a rhetorical device than a foreign policy initiative. According to Eric Goldman, author of *The Crucial Decade,* "a number of friends had been saying to Truman that some State Department men were taking too much credit for the Marshall Plan and that the Inaugural Address should direct the foreign policy spotlight back on the White House."[15] If that is so, Clifford may have been acting on explicit or implied orders from Truman to put forward some foreign policy ideas for the Inaugural Address that would accomplish that objective. In a conversation with Lilienthal the day after the inauguration Clifford revealed that Point Four was only vaguely formulated, but he argued that the Marshall Plan was also introduced without sufficient planning and preparation.[16] Although Clifford is correct, it is clear that incorporating a catchy idea into the speech was his first priority, while providing real technical assistance to developing nations came second.

Point Four was also the subject of a minor historical debate among the participants. According to Acheson, he had not even heard of Point Four until Truman talked about it during the Inaugural Address.[17] In his memoir Clifford suggested otherwise, claiming that he had provided Acheson with an advance copy of the speech, including the section on Point Four, on January 16, four days before the address. A draft copy of the speech at the Truman Library bearing Acheson's handwritten comments indicates that he had seen the speech, including the section on Point Four.[18] Citing Acheson's written comments, Clifford noted that Acheson thought "that the address [was] splendid."[19] During a 1972 oral history interview, however, Clifford was asked about Acheson's claim of ignorance regarding Point Four. Specifically the interviewer was curious as to why the incoming secretary of state had heard nothing about a major program that was likely to fall under his domain. Apparently Clifford did not recall that Acheson had previously reviewed the speech because he replied that the Inaugural Address was "a personal matter that belonged within the White House." According to Clifford, the purpose of the State of the Union was to report to the people, whereas "the Inaugural Address is peculiarly a presidential and a White House matter." For those reasons, Clifford recalled, "we just didn't go out asking other people their opinions or informing them as to what was to take place."[20] Elsey was asked virtually the same question during one of his oral history interviews and, like Clifford, could not recall that Acheson had reviewed the speech beforehand. "There was no particular reason for the President to have 'cleared,' if you will, the text of his Inaugural Address with all his current or prospective Cabinet members," he replied.[21]

Although Clifford and Acheson clashed over Point Four, Clifford had been involved in Truman's selection of Acheson to replace George Marshall and had advised Acheson regarding the transition. The finalists for the position came down to Acheson and Averell Harriman, and Truman made his decision in early December. It was Clifford who informed Acheson that he would be named the next secretary of state. During their meeting Clifford explained that Truman had decided to eliminate Harriman from contention "on the ground that, though Averell had many qualifications, his gifts were not those required in the administration of the department and on dealing with the problems which the next few years would present." No doubt curious as to what set him apart from Harriman, Acheson pressed Clifford to elaborate. The president, however, had never explained to Clifford the reasoning behind his decision. "Truman did not want to appear to downgrade Averell by giving a detailed reason," Clifford said, and, in any event, the decision was "a close call."[22]

In addition to his involvement with the Acheson appointment, Clifford also advised the new secretary of state during the transition. In *Present at the Creation,* Acheson wrote that because Truman wanted to keep his appointment a secret Acheson did not have access to the briefing materials necessary to bring him up to speed. Instead he met with Lovett and Clifford, who gave him "broad instruction in a few secret meetings in their homes."[23] Acheson had left the State Department in 1947 to return to his law firm, and those meetings, Clifford recalled, gave him "the chance to ask questions: What was the background of this policy and how did we happen to reach a conclusion on that policy?"[24] As undersecretary of state Lovett was the logical choice to brief the incoming secretary because Marshall was in the hospital recovering from surgery. Clifford, who again described himself as the liaison between State and the White House, most likely offered insights as to Truman's frame of mind. Other than Acheson's brief mention of their meetings and Clifford's recollections, there is little evidence as to what they discussed. However, given that Clifford was only tangentially involved with the formation of foreign policy, it is doubtful that he could offer much of substance. Elsey was unaware of these meetings and thought it was odd that Acheson would have thought it necessary to meet with Clifford. "Acheson already had a good working relationship with Truman," he said.[25]

While Acheson was preparing to return to the battle against international communism, Clifford was preparing to go into battle against those who claimed to be fighting domestic communism. Shortly after the president enunciated the Truman Doctrine in March 1947, he issued Executive Order 9835, which established a loyalty program for federal employees. Truman made this move in response to the tremendous political pressure he was under to take offensive action against alleged communist subversives in the government. Following the 1946 Republican congressional sweep, FBI director J. Edgar Hoover and his allies on the right began to demand that Truman take immediate action to address the problem of disloyalty. Yielding to pressure, and hoping to maintain control over the process, Truman approved the executive order. As Elsey recalled, the loyalty program was intended to help the Truman administration "defend itself from the irrational, but highly emotional and very effective attacks by" the Republicans.[26] At the time Clifford did not believe that there was a loyalty problem, but felt that the program was a response to the incredible political pressure to which Truman had been subjected. Despite this conviction Clifford still acceded to inclusion of a section in the Clifford-Elsey report on the threat of domestic communism that warned "that every American Communist is potentially an espionage agent of the Soviet Government."[27] According to Clifford, this section had been included at the behest of Hoover and Attorney General Tom Clark. "As I look back on my career in government," Clifford wrote, "my greatest regret is that I did not make more of an effort to try to kill the loyalty program at its inception in 1946–47."[28]

The right was partially placated, although Hoover schemed behind the scenes to keep control over the program within the FBI. The Truman Doctrine and the loyalty program effectively neutralized an issue that the Republicans had used to their advantage in 1946. These programs ensured that the Truman administration, not the Republicans, was perceived as leading the charge against communism.[29] Truman's relentless attacks on Henry Wallace and his determination not to abandon Berlin, as manifested in the ongoing airlift, helped to inoculate him from attacks from the right.[30] After the 1948 elections, however, the right turned up the heat on the issue of anticommunism. Shocked and angered at Truman's upset victory over Dewey, the Republicans went on the offensive. Shortly after the election they began work on legislation that would further curtail the activities of the Communist Party. Within the administration there were dissenting opinions on the proposed legislation, with Clark asking Senator Patrick McCarran, Democrat of Nevada, to pass the "toughest anti-spy laws in American history." The attorney general's proposed legislation would have legalized the use of wiretaps against suspected communists and stipulated that the information gleaned from those wiretaps be admissible in court. Clifford, however, was adamantly opposed to the wiretapping provision, as he indicated in a memo entitled "The So-Called Spy Bills." "The President indicated to me a week ago yesterday that it is the Republicans who are avid for such bills . . . the hysteria-mongering bra[n]ch of the Republican party," he wrote. Measures such as wiretapping, he argued, were "disgraceful and disastrous."[31]

In March Congressman Richard Nixon and Senator Karl Mundt introduced a bill that, in the name of fighting domestic communism, further threatened civil liberties. Max Lowenthal sent a memorandum to Truman in early April warning that the Mundt-Nixon Bill, and comparable proposals, was reminiscent of the Alien and Sedition Acts of 1798–1799. Truman passed along Lowenthal's memo and asked Clifford for his comments.

Clifford submitted his memo to the president on April 29. A savvy political operator, Clifford usually did not advocate that Truman take positions that might be unpopular, and with the "red scare" just beginning to heat up, opposing these bills would not have been the politically smart move to take. In this case, however, Clifford took a strong position in opposition to the proposed legislation. "It is one thing for a nation to take basic counterespionage and security measures necessary to protect its existence," he wrote. "It is another thing to urge or tolerate heresy hunts at every stump and crossroads to smoke out and punish non-conformists of every shade and stripe of opinion different from that of the majority." Clifford presciently warned that the United States was on the verge of a slippery slope of erosion of civil liberties in an effort to stamp out communism. "With the possible exception of the days of John Adams and those of A. Mitchell Palmer, the situation is becoming more dangerous today than at any other period in American history." Citing the famous quote "Patriotism, sir, is the last refuge of a scoundrel," Clifford adroitly observed that those who cloaked their actions in the guise of patriotism were often acting purely in their own self-interest.[32] A year later Nixon won election to the U.S. Senate by maliciously slandering his opponent, Helen Gahagan Douglas, as a communist, repeatedly referring to her as a "pink lady."[33] Clifford was right.

Looking to protect Truman politically, Clifford also understood that it would be a challenge to defeat "something with nothing." To counter the bills circulating in Congress Clifford recommended that Truman resurrect an idea from the 1947 Civil Rights Commission requiring that all groups that attempted to influence public opinion register themselves with the federal government. The advantage of this approach, Clifford suggested, was that it would require all organizations, on both the right and the left, to register. Furthermore, this approach would not ban any speech or otherwise run afoul of the First Amendment.[34]

Clifford was justifiably proud to have taken the moral and constitutional high ground on this politically charged issue. The loyalty program, although politically expedient, fundamentally violated the Bill of Rights. In his memoirs he cited his April 29 memo and its defense of the First Amendment, and suggested that his observation from 1949 was equally valid today: "We gambled more than one hundred and fifty years ago, by writing the First Amendment into the Constitution, that in a free market place of opinion, the truth would prevail."[35]

In addition to their witch hunt for suspected communists and communist sympathizers, the congressional Republicans also homed in on another target—David Lilienthal. In the spring of 1949 Senator Bourke Hickenlooper, of Iowa, attacked the Atomic Energy Commission's stewardship of the nation's nuclear weapons stockpile, accusing Lilienthal and the AEC of "incredible mismanagement." Hickenlooper promised hearings before the congressional Joint Committee on Atomic Energy, hearings that he said would demonstrate that Lilienthal had not properly safeguarded the nation's atomic weapons. As a close friend of Lilienthal's and an important ally in the White House, Clifford was sent copies of the relevant correspondence. In late May Lilienthal sent Clifford a copy of a memorandum he had written to Senator Brien McMahon of Connecticut, chairman of the Select Senate Committee on Atomic Energy, in response to Hickenlooper's accusations. The personal cover note read: "Dear Clark: A reading of this may be helpful to size up the 'situation.' This is rough—but the record of real accomplishment will show through the fog of deliberate provoked fear. As ever, Dave."[36] Lilienthal turned out to be right, as Hickenlooper failed to prove anything with his investigation. In his journal Lilienthal recounted a meeting with Truman after Hickenlooper ended the hearings. "'Well, you've survived, I see,' he said grinning from ear to ear. 'I told you what you were up against: a couple fellows up for re-election and that it wouldn't turn up a thing—and it didn't. You came out of it better than ever.'"[37]

In September 1949 the United States suffered a major setback on the atomic energy front when the Soviet Union completed its first successful test of an atomic weapon. Truman made the stunning announcement on September 23, and while the American public was shocked and unsettled, there was little panic. In the White House, however, the Truman administration hunkered down for what they expected would be an onslaught of partisan sniping from congressional Republicans. Elsey thought that in order to contain some of the damage, Truman needed to take some preventive action. Specifically, in a memo to Clifford he recommended that Truman take immediate action to fill the chairmanship of the National Security Resources Board, a role which was temporarily being filled by John Steelman:

> In thinking over the implications of the President's announcement that the Russians appear to have learned how to produce an atomic explosion I have tried to decide what effect that is likely to have on the President's position politically. It seems to me that in the next week or so, we shall be faced with a torrent of articles, new stories and radio talks on the state of national security and our defenses against a Soviet atomic attack. We shall have a flood of oratory from Capitol Hill on the same subject. . . . Republicans will jump at the cue and bleat about the President's "neglect" of his duty by failing to fill the N.S.R.B. vacancy.[38]

Despite Elsey's warning, the chairmanship remained unfilled until April 1950, when Clifford confidant and secretary of the air force Stuart Symington was appointed.

Clifford first had thoughts of leaving government service following the 1948 election. He was mentally and physically exhausted from the arduous campaign, a fatigue that a week in Key West did not squelch. According to Clifford, he believed that four or five years was the extent of time one could serve at the highest levels of government before beginning to lose effectiveness.[39] He had been in the White House since July 1945, and the job was beginning to lose its excitement. "The freshness goes," Clifford recalled. "I found that everything that I would write for the President would begin to sound like something else that I had written for him. It had a stale sound to it and feel to it."[40] With a touch of bravado, Clifford also claimed that he felt he was losing some effectiveness because his close relationship to the president was making him a target of critics in the administration. "Even with the President's continued support, which I felt I could count on, I could foresee a concerted effort by some of those with whom I had disagreed to weaken my position," he wrote.[41] Clifford did not specifically name Steelman, but it was obvious to whom he was referring.

Financial pressures were also weighing on him. His $12,000 annual salary was insufficient to provide the type of comfortable living he wanted for himself and his family, and his three daughters were getting older and approaching college age. He had practically exhausted the savings from when he worked at Holland, Lashly and Donnell and from the sale of his home in St. Louis. Although he never discussed it in his oral history or in his memoirs, Clifford was also in debt. In his early White House days as naval aide, Clifford had a meeting with Alfred Lansing, a St. Louis businessman whom he had met while practicing law. During their meeting, Clifford was lamenting the difficulties of making ends meet on his navy salary of $10,000. Either out of generosity or perhaps looking to curry favor with an ally in the White House, Lansing offered to lend him money. Throughout his tenure in the White House Clifford received payments from Lansing, which were secured by nothing more than the promissory notes Clifford signed after receiving each disbursement. These payments would total almost $35,000 when he resigned as special counsel, nearly three times his annual salary. Clifford was also indebted to George Allen, the lobbyist and poker-playing confidant of Truman. Allen, who was also the secretary of the Democratic National Committee, had lent Clifford $20,000. Clifford's total debt thus exceeded $50,000, a substantial sum relative to his salary. Furthermore, as a senior White House official the propriety of accepting large loans from businessmen and lobbyists was questionable. However, the financial disclosure requirements for government officials of that time were far more lax than they are today, and Clifford never told Truman about the loans.[42]

On December 10, 1948, Clifford went to Lilienthal's house for dinner. After dinner he confided his plans for leaving to Lilienthal. "Clifford seemed tired and very thoughtful," Lilienthal wrote in his journal. "He said he was 'tired, awfully tired, not physically but emotionally, psychologically.'" Lilienthal also recorded that Clifford was disturbed by the ambition and internecine struggles within the White House. "He spoke of the awful exhibition one sees around the White House of self-seeking, etc., and seemed rather depressed by it," Lilienthal wrote. Ironically for someone who would capitalize on his contacts with powerful figures in the government for the rest of his life, Clifford also expressed his concern about the corrupting influence of government service that he saw all around him. Lilienthal recounted, "I was struck by the way he spoke of the dangers of being in the midst of such great power and influence, and its effect on people, adding, 'Every once in a while I notice it in myself, and I try to drag it out in the open.'"[43]

Clifford might have been a bit disingenuous here, as his primary motive for talking to Lilienthal was not to complain about the corrosive impact of service at the highest levels of government. He was looking for Lilienthal's blessing on the propriety of practicing law in Washington right after leaving the White House. Returning to St. Louis held no appeal for Clifford. "If I returned to St. Louis, almost none of the rare experience I have had in the past few years would be of any value to me," he told Lilienthal. Clifford's wife and daughters had grown acclimated to life in Washington, and they also wanted to stay. But Clifford recognized that it might not be appropriate to start a law practice in Washington because of the appearance that he was cashing in on his government service. Lilienthal wrote in his journal, "I knew what he had in mind: he wanted me to comment on whether it would be proper for him to practice in Washington. I said of course he shouldn't go to St. Louis, that the fact that others had been greedy and not too principled in how they practiced law didn't mean that he needed to, nor would he."[44]

That was all the encouragement and affirmation that he needed. Clifford spoke to Truman, who asked him to stay through the end of 1949. With his decision made, Clifford took the steps necessary to ensure a successful transition to private practice. He spoke to Acheson and asked if he would sponsor Clifford as a member at the Metropolitan Club, Washington's oldest and most prestigious men's club. He also spoke to Stuart Symington and George Smathers, a golf partner and senator from Florida, about joining the Burning Tree Country

Club.[45] Once he left the White House Clifford would no longer enjoy its trappings of power, and he knew that in order to impress and entertain clients, membership in these exclusive clubs was essential.

Clifford kept the promise he had made to Truman to stay at his post through 1949. However, he lacked passion for the job because he was focused on his post–White House career. Stephen Spingarn, who took over while Elsey was on a leave of absence for much of 1949, observed that "Clark's mind was preoccupied apparently—I mean, from where I sat, it seemed he was preoccupied with going into private practice." He also complained about the lack of substantive assignments from Clifford.[46]

Truman made only one attempt to entice Clifford to stay in government service. The president had the opportunity to fill two vacancies on the Supreme Court, and he casually asked Clifford if he had ever considered serving on the nation's highest court. Clifford was surprised, but by his account turned down the offer immediately. He told Truman, "I feel I am best cast as an advocate, not a judge. My training is as an advocate. I wish to be down there in the pit where the action is, and not sit up above the struggle and attempt to judge disputes. I do not think it is the right kind of career for me." According to Clifford, "Truman seemed both intrigued and a bit relieved" by his reply.[47] Despite Clifford's claim that he immediately turned down the offer, some reports at the time suggest that he was interested. The *St. Louis Globe-Democrat* reported in October that "we can name one confidant of the President who believes he has earned the job" of Supreme Court Justice.[48] Although the article did not specifically mention Clifford, it is probable that they were talking about him. For one thing, the paper had faithfully covered its native son throughout his time in the White House; for another, Clifford filed the clipping in the collection of his papers he donated to the Library of Congress.

Whether Clifford seriously considered the Supreme Court offer, or whether Truman seriously extended that offer, Clifford continued his preparations for private practice. When he told Acheson of his plans late in 1949 Acheson tried to convince Clifford to join his firm, Covington & Burling. Clifford, however, stood by his decision to start his own firm. Covington & Burling was a big firm, and Clifford did not want to share the spotlight with so many other attorneys. Clifford also received an offer from Jacob Lashly to return to his old firm, and with the offer came the promise that he would become the managing partner when Lashly retired. At one time that offer would have been all that Clifford could have hoped for, but just five years later it was not what he wanted. After roaming the corridors of power in Washington, St. Louis seemed small time. Clifford also received an offer from Stuart Symington that encouraged him to return to Missouri. Symington recommended that Clifford return to his old firm, reestablish his roots, and then make a run for the U.S. Senate. Again, Clifford politely declined.[49] Symington would run for, and win, the same seat in 1952.

Clifford's reluctance to run for office is curious, given his affinity for politics, liberal political views, and government experience. In his memoirs, Clifford dismissed the idea by noting simply that running for public office was not what he wanted to do with his life.[50] This explanation is plausible, but it is also possible that he saw elected office as not offering much of an improvement of his uncomfortable financial situation. In any case, Clifford never felt compelled to throw his own hat into the ring, but instead was content to counsel and advise those who did.

Clifford's prominence as a high-level adviser to Truman had opened the door to several high-profile opportunities after he left the White House. The U.S. Senate; the Supreme Court; senior partner in his former St. Louis firm; partnership, presumably, in one of Washington's most prestigious law firms—all were possibilities for Clifford. Yet he turned each of them down in order to establish his own firm. Of the various career possibilities open to Clifford after he left the White House, setting up his own practice was the riskiest, yet it also had the potential to be the most lucrative. He had spent the last four-and-a-half years establishing his reputation as a player in Washington's inner circles. Now he had the opportunity to capitalize on that reputation. Years later, Clifford would receive several offers to serve in the highest levels of the Kennedy and Johnson administrations; he would refuse all but one. In fact, for someone who would be regarded as the consummate Washington insider for four decades, Clifford would only return to government service for one more year.

Clifford's last day in the White House was January 31, 1950. Elsey threw him a small but elegant going-away party at the Cosmos Club, another exclusive Washington men's club. Without mentioning the farewell dinner, Clifford described himself as leaving the White House without ceremony after working "late cleaning up some loose ends." On the way out he paid a farewell call to Truman who, looking to avoid a maudlin good-bye, pretended that the visit was like any other. Instead, Clifford and Truman exchanged letters of farewell. Clifford's letter was quite personal. "During my father's lifetime," he wrote, "he and I were very close and I felt sure I would never feel toward any man what I felt toward him. I was wrong. For you now occupy that place in my heart that he held for so many years." Truman wrote two letters, one handwritten and quite informal, the other a more formal letter officially accepting his resignation. The informal letter read: "Of course I regret your leaving, but a man has responsibilities he must meet. I understand what yours are. Hope you are successful and that you'll keep your contacts here at the House. You're still a member of the 'Palace Guard.'" The second letter Clifford described as "the most treasured document in my possession." "Dear Clark," the president began, "I have now to take a step which from the bottom of my heart I wish could be indefinitely deferred."[51] Truman accepted Clifford's resignation, acknowledged the necessity of his returning to private practice, and thanked him for his service. He also lavishly praised Clifford's work:

> For all that you have given we owe you a debt impossible to pay. You had much to contribute as Special Counsel to the President because you brought to your work such great resources of legal learning and experience as a practicing lawyer. Besides this you had foresight and courage. Your reports on the various problems on which I asked you for advice were models of lucidity and logic. In the marshaling and presentation of facts your method reflected your days before the jury. Quick in the detection of spurious evidence and alert always in detecting the fallacious in the arguments of our opponents, your final opinions were always models of brevity and accuracy, as well as clarity and strength.[52]

For someone who had often passed along another's work as his own, it was somewhat ironic for Clifford to receive praise for crafting reports that were "models of lucidity and logic." But such was the reputation that Clifford had nurtured during his years in the Truman White House.

Liberals lamented his departure. *The Nation* described Clifford as "the mainstay of the Fair Deal," and *The New Republic* wrote that "Clifford's retirement as Special Counsel further weakens Our Side in the White House." *The New Republic* also credited him for the upset of the century, observing that "he and Oscar Chapman helped toward fixing the seemingly hopeless Truman 1948 campaign to the polestar of New Dealism."[53] Robert Underhill partially attributed the decline in Truman's fortunes throughout the rest of his presidency to Clifford's departure:

> After 1950 other issues arose which were beyond the solving of any president or his advisers no matter how talented they might be. The highest points in Truman's career had already been achieved. In the remaining two years the president would see his public popularity begin to fall toward the low point it reached at the end of his second term. It would be a gross error to imply that Truman's popularity rose and fell with Clifford, but likewise no explanation of Truman's success in persuasion is complete without acknowledging the role of Clifford.[54]

Eric Goldman, however, wrote that Clifford's resignation was "hardly noticed in the press."[55]

Irrespective of these differing interpretations of his impact on the Truman administration, Clifford's departure from the White House was representative of a shift from a Washington run by the Establishment, with its notions of noblesse oblige, to one in which government officials, upon leaving office, cashed in on their experience and contacts in order to make fortunes as lawyers and lobbyists. Blessed with intellectual ability, physical attractiveness, presence, and charm, Clifford would have been successful in whatever endeavor he pursued. Add to these qualities his contacts in the highest levels of government, and it was a foregone conclusion that he would become a rich and even more powerful man. According to Patrick Anderson, "he went on to start a Washington law practice that soon made him the most financially successful lawyer of his generation, probably of all time."[56]

# 7

## Washington Lawyer

Clifford's new office was at 1523 L Street, only four blocks from the White House. Clifford took on but one partner, Edward H. Miller, a lawyer from the Justice Department whom Clifford knew from St. Louis. Clifford recalled that Miller's experience in the antitrust field would complement his more extensive knowledge of the government.[1] In addition to his experience, competence, and work ethic, Miller had another attribute that made him attractive to Clifford: Miller understood his position as the unequal partner. Clifford was the marquee figure whose reputation and experience would draw clients to the new firm. Miller appealed to Clifford because he understood that he was acting in a supporting role.[2]

Although he was an avowed liberal and a former adviser to Truman, Clifford diligently worked to transform himself into someone that corporate America could be comfortable with. At least one Washington insider did not think that would be difficult. Writing in his diary, journalist Drew Pearson described Clifford "as a liberal by day and a conservative by night."[3] On November 15, 1949, a week before news of his departure was leaked to the press, Clifford gave a speech before the annual dinner of the Grocery Manufacturers Association. The speech, entitled "Business and the Government's Program," stressed his conception of a symbiotic partnership between business and government. "We can't get along without business, and I don't believe business can get along without government," he said. Rather than its being an adversary of business, Clifford argued that "one of the goals of government" was "that business should prosper." Much of the speech involved a defense and explanation of the Fair Deal as well as the Truman administration's foreign policy, but Clifford likely viewed the speech as an opportunity to present himself as an ally to the business community.[4] A week before leaving the White House Clifford appeared before the Fiduciary Counsel's Forum of New York. Clinton Davidson, the group's president, wrote that the "purpose of this meeting was to give business leaders an opportunity to get personally acquainted with Mr. Clifford."[5] According to George Elsey's notes, the purpose of the Grocery Manufacturers speech was twofold: "to win friends for the Fair Deal; [to win friends for] CMC."[6]

A few months later, after he had left the White House, Clifford gave a speech similar to the Grocery Manufacturers talk to the Executives' Club of Chicago. Again, he devoted most of his speech to a defense of the Fair Deal and Truman's foreign policy, but he also argued that the success of the Fair Deal was contingent upon an expanding economy. "I think we have to develop our economy in such a way that the ordinary people in this country can feel that they have real opportunity and real security," he suggested. Confronting directly criticisms of the Fair Deal, criticisms that were perhaps shared by some members of the Executives' Club of Chicago, Clifford argued that the Fair Deal was not leading the country toward a welfare state. On the contrary, he argued, "It is my deep conviction that the policies offered by the party in power today are acting to *preserve* the free enterprise system." According to Clifford, Truman's Fair Deal contributed to a rise in the public's standard of living and also facilitated an increase in prosperity through the expansion of the economy. In addition to promoting the Truman administration's policies, Clifford also looked to raise his stature with the business community. At the outset of the speech he proclaimed his belief in the efficacy of the free enterprise system. "I believe in it deeply," he said. "I detest Communism, I abhor Fascism, and I think that socialism is a snare and a delusion." Sensitive to the political inclinations of his audience, Clifford said that it was not his intention to make a political speech, nor was he addressing his audience as either Democrats or Republicans. In a thinly disguised sales pitch for his law firm Clifford also emphasized his experience practicing corporate law. His former St. Louis firm, he pointed out, devoted 90 percent of its practice to corporate law.[7]

Clifford was quite satisfied with his performance, which he recounted in a letter to Truman. He wrote, "My speech to the Executives Club went well but, because it was an all-out defense of you and the Fair Deal, the Chicago papers omitted any reference to it. There were approximately 900 present at the luncheon and I was highly gratified at the manner in which they received the speech."[8] Two years later he resurrected the same arguments and themes for a speech to the 50 Club of Cleveland, Ohio.[9]

Years later, a 1968 *Ramparts* magazine article, "Clark Clifford:

Attorney at War," described the 1950 speech from the perspective of New Left, revisionist historians. The article claims that Clifford argued that there were two ways to expand the economy: "first, a government-financed and militarily supported expansion of overseas markets and investments; second, a huge armaments program."[10] David Welsh and David Horowitz, the coauthors of the *Ramparts* article, appear not to have actually read the speech. Not only did Clifford not recommend a "government-financed and militarily supported expansion of overseas markets and investments," he also did not recommend a large increase in military spending. In fact, what is particularly noteworthy about this speech is that Clifford offered no plan for how to expand the economy. Using somewhat optimistic assumptions Clifford predicted that in ten years the economy would grow from $258 billion to $350 billion, or by about $90 billion. He then surmised that if half of the $90 billion increase went to the poorest third of the population, that group's average annual income of $2,000 could be doubled, to $4,000. This higher level of income and standard of living for the lower third of the economy, he argued, would constitute a new market for American products.[11] In essence, Clifford's plan for expanding the economy was to put more money into the hands of the poor. While that was certainly a plausible theory, Clifford offered no suggestions for how to channel his expected $90 billion in economic growth down to the lower classes. At best, therefore, Clifford's plan for expanding the economy was nothing more than a pie-in-the-sky dream of an expanding, yet more egalitarian, economy.

Around the same time, on February 4, 1950, Clifford appeared on the NBC news program *Meet the Press*. In response to a December invitation from Lawrence Spivak, the moderator, Clifford indicated that while he had long been interested in the program, he felt that his White House position precluded him from appearing. Since he would soon be leaving the White House, Clifford willingly accepted. The response to his appearance was favorable, with one admirer describing it as the "biggest best public relations job ever done to my knowledge. Congratulations." One viewer predicted, "Mark my words—we'll be voting for him—for President!" Spivak was also enthusiastic, writing that the "reaction to our interview with you has been unusually good." No doubt having taken the full measure of the man, Spivak anticipated his financial success and was also convinced by Clifford's public relations strategy that he was friendly to business. "Good luck to you and your new law firm," he wrote. "I hope you make a million dollars—if nothing else, to prove to your critics by example that you do believe in the free enterprise system and special reward for merit."[12] The Truman administration was similarly pleased with the performance of its former special counsel. Elsey wrote to Clifford asking for a transcript of the broadcast to help him with the nettlesome question of the difference between the Fair Deal and the New Deal.[13]

If Clifford was looking to impress members of the business community, his appearance on *Meet the Press* was a success. Clinton Davidson Jr. and his father noted Clifford's skillful handling of difficult questions. "Your performance helped us understand why you have such a good reputation as a trial lawyer," the junior Davidson wrote. Walter Lantz, the animator best known as the creator of Woody Woodpecker, wrote that "no other spot has caused quite as much comment as your appearance on 'Meet the Press' . . . but I have had at least a dozen advertising friends tell me what a magnificent job you did. This has even come from men who have been critical of the policies of the Administration and who naturally include you in their feelings."[14]

Clifford's efforts, as well as his reputation, paid off, as corporate clients began to roll in. He signed up his first client, Phillips Petroleum, due to his friendship with Senator Robert Kerr of Oklahoma. Louis Johnson, the secretary of defense who owed his position to his fund-raising prowess, put in a good word with several defense contractors.[15] One of the earliest clients to call on Clifford was none other than Howard Hughes. The multimillionaire hired Clifford on retainer to represent the three companies he controlled—Trans World Airlines, Hughes Tool Company, and the RKO Motion Picture Company—all of which relied solely on outside counsel.[16] Hughes, who was not yet the reclusive paranoid that he would become, nonetheless had a rather strange relationship with Clifford. Despite a business relationship that lasted more than twenty-five years, Clifford never actually met the famous millionaire. They always spoke by phone, although Hughes also had one, and only one, associate, Noah Dietrich, who was authorized to speak for him. Hughes, who worked unusual hours, expected his business associates to be available at any time, night or day. The combination of the three-hour time difference between Washington and California, where Hughes lived, along with Hughes's late hours, resulted in many calls to Clifford's home in the middle of the night. Yet despite Clifford's workaholic propensities he steadfastly refused to answer business calls at home, even from Hughes. Marny Clifford and Hughes became familiar telephone acquaintances, as Clifford's wife dutifully took notes each time he called and promised that Clark would return the call the following day.[17]

When Hughes called Clifford for the very first time, expressing interest in retaining the lawyer's services, Clifford politely listened. After Hughes finished, Clifford delivered a prepared speech that he used with all of his new clients, and which he quotes in his memoirs, *Counsel to the President:*

> I look forward to our association. But before we proceed, there is one point I must make clear. I do not consider that this firm will have any influence of any kind here in Washington. I cannot, and will not, represent any client before the President or before any of his staff. If you want influence, you should consider going elsewhere. What we can offer you is an extensive knowledge of how to deal with the government on your problems. We will be able to give you advice on how best to present your position to the appropriate departments and agencies of the government.[18]

According to Clifford, he gave that speech to so many clients over the years that his younger associates joked that they knew it word for word. No doubt Clifford did give that speech to all of his perspective clients, and it is also likely that on one level he believed what he said. During his *Meet the Press* interview a member of the panel asked how he would prevent clients from attempting to utilize his influence with the Truman administration and others in government. He responded with what may have been a rehearsed answer: "That decision rests with me, as to whether I shall try to prevail upon any element of relationship that I may have with persons. That is my responsibility. I do not intend to use it. Nor should I try to use it with the men who are in government today. I believe that it would be of no avail. That is the respect that I have for them."[19] In what would be a pattern throughout his career as a Washington lawyer and power broker, Clifford would never be as audacious and indiscreet as to flaunt his influence and connections in such a brazen manner. His method was far more subtle, but just as—or even more—effective. Furthermore, by exercising tact and discretion Clifford was able to maintain the confidence of the figures in government whom he courted.[20]

Other clients quickly signed up, usually on a retainer rather than a case-by-case basis. Over time his clients included some of the biggest names in corporate America, including Du Pont, Standard Oil of California, General Electric, RCA, Time, Inc., W. R. Grace Shipping, the Pennsylvania Railroad, and International Telephone & Telegraph.[21]

Despite his quick start, however, Clifford soon suffered a setback when his partner, Edward Miller, became ill and died of a heart attack in June 1950. He was only forty-three. Clifford sought out another partner, first asking Supreme Court Justice William Douglas, a personal friend. Douglas chose to remain on the court, so Clifford reached out to John J. McCloy, a Wall Street lawyer, former assistant secretary of war during World War II, and then Truman's high commissioner for Germany. McCloy was amenable to the offer, but Clifford thought it best to obtain Truman's permission before proceeding. Truman agreed that McCloy would make a splendid partner, but in order to demonstrate America's commitment to NATO Truman wanted him to remain in Germany for another year. He asked if Clifford would defer bringing him aboard until McCloy finished his service in Germany. Clifford agreed to do whatever the president asked, and Truman sent him a note the following day. "Will let you know what I'll do about that man in Europe as soon as I can," he wrote. Clifford responded with a handwritten thank-you note a few days later. "Dear Boss," he wrote, "Thank you so much for giving me the time on Tuesday. Your advise [sic] and counsel was most helpful and aided me in making an important decision." When McCloy left Germany in 1952, Clifford renewed his offer, but McCloy instead accepted the chairmanship of the Chase Manhattan Bank. With his partner's seat still unfilled, Clifford decided to bring in two associates, Carson Glass and Samuel D. McIlwain.[22]

Indicative of Clifford's continued involvement with matters in the Truman White House, he also told Truman in his thank-you note, "I was greatly encouraged by your decision to make the change you spoke about. I feel so strongly that it is correct that, if by any chance, you should wish me to perform the same function that I did in the Krug case, you have only to call upon me."[23] The "change" to which Clifford was referring was the decision to fire Louis Johnson, who had begun to clash with secretary of state Dean Acheson. The Korean War had begun two months earlier, and Truman would not tolerate dissension within his foreign policy team during a crisis. By his reference to the "Krug case" Clifford was offering to approach Johnson and demand his resignation, as he had done the previous fall with Interior Secretary Julius Krug.[24] Although Clifford no longer worked in the White House he maintained close contact with Truman on both a professional and personal level. Clifford recalled that from the time he left until Truman's term ended, "I may have had ten assignments, or fourteen, or eighteen, something of that kind. I continued to see him steadily through the period."[25]

As with his speech to the Executives' Club of Chicago, Clifford continued to be an advocate for the policies of the Truman administration. In March he contacted Elsey and asked him to ghostwrite an article for the *Saturday Evening Post* in order "to do HST good." Clifford planned to publish the article in the summer of 1950 to help counter a decline in the president's approval ratings.[26] At the beginning of 1949, after a close election, the president's approval rating was a respectable 57 percent. By January 1950, however, it had fallen to 45 percent, and a month later it was even worse. A number of factors contributed to his declining fortunes, but prior to the Korean War the hint of scandal had the most influence. Throughout his second term Truman would be dogged by allegations of corruption and influence peddling among certain members of his staff. In particular, Harry Vaughan, Truman's military aide and crony, was a conspicuous target of muckraking journalist Drew Pearson.[27] Clifford thought that some positive press for the president might help. Yet a few months later he decided not to go ahead with the article. Elsey speculated that he may have simply been too busy with his practice, especially given Miller's untimely demise.[28]

In the opening days of the Korean War, in June 1950, Clifford offered some guidance on how the war should be prosecuted. In contrast to the dovish posture he would take during the Vietnam War, Clifford advocated a hard line in Korea. In particular, he thought that Truman was making a mistake by containing the fighting below the 38th parallel, the post–World War II boundary that divided North and South Korea. Limiting the fighting to below the 38th parallel was a mistake, Clifford argued, because "we are bombing friendly people and friendly areas." Instead, in a recommendation that eerily foreshadowed the circumstances in Vietnam, he recommended that Truman take the war into North Korea: "I would like to suggest that the President issue a statement informing the world that he is going to ask the United Nations to issue an order giving the North Korean forces forty-eight hours to withdraw from South Korea. And, if the North Korean forces refuse to do so, that military forces of member nations of the United Nations will bomb military objectives in North Korea."[29] Truman replied that he thought Clifford's statement was a bit premature, but perhaps might be necessary at a later date.[30]

Truman frequently tapped his former speechwriter for assistance with crafting the administration's messages. A collection of Clifford's private papers, which resides in the Library of Congress, contains several folders of Truman's speeches and statements, indicating that even though Clifford was no longer a member of the president's inner circle, he was still an informal advisor. In October, Truman personally reached out to Clifford for assistance with an upcoming, nationally broadcast speech Truman was to give before the United Nations General Assembly.[31] A few months later, Clifford's successor as special counsel, Charles Murphy, forwarded an advance copy of the 1951 State of the Union Address for Clifford's review and comments.[32]

In 1952 Truman made one of the biggest mistakes of his presidency. On the last day of 1951 the United Steelworkers union contract with the major steel companies expired, and the companies and the union could not reach an agreement on a new contract. The companies, the union, and the Wage Stabilization Board, to which Truman had delegated the handling of the dispute, bickered for the next few months over wage and price increases but could not come to an agreement. In early April, with no agreement in sight and a strike looming that might threaten defense production during the Korean War, Truman took decisive action. He seized control of the steel companies and ordered the Department of Commerce to run the plants. Then–Secretary of Defense Robert Lovett, Murphy, and John Steelman all supported the president's action; but Clifford, who was brought in as an informal adviser, opposed it.[33] (Clifford's later recollection of the matter was vague, but he was certain that he opposed the decision.) Truman claimed the authority to seize the industry by virtue of "inherent powers of the President to take such actions in times of trouble." Clifford, however, "thought it was unwise to test the 'inherent power' issue under those circumstances" and recommended against it.[34]

Clifford's advice in the steel crisis turned out to be sound. On June 2 the Supreme Court declared the seizure unconstitutional. Clifford read the law right, and he also read the politics correctly, as the public disapproved the seizure by a 43 percent to 35 percent margin.[35] Yet one cannot help but wonder whether Clifford's position was influenced by his new career as a highly paid corporate attorney. In 1946 he advocated or supported punitive measures against the unions in order to force them back on the job, effectively siding with management. Perhaps he was simply taking a consistent position in 1952 by again advocating a position favorable to management. In any case, however, his corporate clients would not have been pleased had he endorsed a government takeover of a private industry.

Around the same time as the steelworker crisis, Truman was agonizing over the decision to run for reelection in 1952. His preference was to step down after his term ended, provided that one of his handpicked successors agreed to run. Neither of his preferences, Dwight D. Eisenhower nor Chief Justice Fred Vinson,[36] was interested in running, in Eisenhower's case on the Democratic ticket. Clifford recalled that he thought Truman should not run. "I did not think it was in either his interest, or the nation's, to seek another term as President," he wrote. "I thought it likely that the tide which he had so brilliantly turned back in 1948 would sweep over him. More important, I felt his Administration had run out of steam. He had led the nation through eight of the most tumultuous years in American history. He was wearier than he knew, and he deserved and needed a rest."[37]

Truman decided to take a short vacation in Key West in order to ponder his decision. On March 21 Clifford received a call from Truman, who was sitting on the beach. Truman asked if he could join him, apparently to discuss the matter, and Clifford caught a flight and arrived in Key West at 2:00 A.M. the next morning. Later that day the president and his former special counsel sat down to talk about the campaign. Clifford advised Truman to withdraw. Although the president had not announced his candidacy, his name had been placed on the ballot for the New Hampshire primary, and he had lost badly to Senator Estes Kefauver of Tennessee. Truman did not consider Kefauver, whom he dismissively referred to as "Cowfever," worthy of the Democratic nomination. Clifford told Truman that "the longer he waited, the weaker the party would be—whomever they nominated—in the November election." Clifford also argued that Truman would weaken himself in his remaining time in office if he remained indecisive. Clifford strongly advised the president to back out of the race as soon as possible. Perhaps considering himself indispensable during wartime, Truman wondered what impact his withdrawal might have on the war effort. Clifford assured him that the course of the Korean War "had long been established."[38]

Within the week Truman declared that he was not a candidate for president in 1952. In a personal letter Clifford told Truman that he had made the right decision and that Clifford was proud of him.[39] By Clifford's account his counsel to Truman appears to have been based on nothing more than Truman's best interests and the best interests of the Democratic Party. Upon closer examination, however, his motives appear to be somewhat self-serving. There was another potential candidate in addition to Truman and Kefauver, and he was none other than Clifford's friend Robert Kerr. Kerr harbored presidential ambitions himself and may have viewed Clifford, as the presumed architect of Truman's 1948 victory, as a critical component of a potential presidential run. During Clifford's first week in private practice Kerr had introduced him to Kenneth "Boots" Adams, the president of Phillips Petroleum. By virtue of that introduction, Clifford began a long and prosperous relationship with Phillips Petroleum. Kerr also helped Clifford sign up Standard Oil, and of course steered Kerr-McGee Oil Company's legal business to Clifford as well. The two eventually began driving to work together, and Kerr used the time to tap Clifford's brain about politics. Frantz and McKean described the relationship between the two as "the prototypical Washington relationship. Each man had something to offer the other and, contradictions aside, favors were exchanged as part of what evolved into a genuine friendship."[40]

As a means of furthering his political ambitions Kerr decided to become more involved in Washington's social scene, and he looked to Clifford for help. He approached Clifford one day, announced that he planned to host a dinner party, and asked for Clifford's help putting together a guest list. Clifford willingly agreed and assembled a group that included Symington, Senator Brien McMahon, and Speaker of the House Sam Rayburn. There was only one problem: Kerr and his wife were teetotalers and would neither serve nor allow alcoholic beverages in their home. Washington in the 1950s was a city where cocktail parties and heavy drinking were the norm, and Kerr's attitude was viewed as a little odd. Rather than forgo an evening without a little social lubrication, Symington called and invited each of the guests to his home for a drink before they went over to Kerr's. As Clifford observed, the cocktail hour at Symington's revealed a little "sociological discovery," as all the guests drank much more heavily than they normally did, knowing that they would not have the opportunity at Kerr's. The group arrived at the Kerrs' quite inebriated. In one of the typically bizarre events of the night, McMahon confessed that as a young man he had made the difficult decision to enter politics rather than become an Irish tenor. With that, he led the still-tipsy crowd in a rousing, if not aesthetically pleasing, rendition of "When Irish Eyes Are Smiling." When Kerr asked Clifford the next day how he thought the party went, Clifford told him it was a smashing success. Kerr replied knowingly, "Well, Clifford, it just goes to show—you don't have to serve liquor to have a good time."[41]

Shortly after Clifford went into private practice he had an opportunity to try to help Kerr with a piece of legislation the Oklahoma senator was sponsoring. The 1950 Kerr natural gas bill would have eliminated all federal price controls for that industry. Passage of the bill would improve the bottom line for the major gas producers, but would cause the price to rise for consumers. Truman was torn between trying to placate the liberal, northeastern segment of the Democratic Party, which opposed the bill, and those from western and southern energy-producing states, such as Rayburn, who supported it.[42] Truman forwarded the bill to Secretary of the Interior Oscar Chapman for his input. Chapman opposed the bill and recommended that Truman veto it if it passed in the Congress. "Well," Truman said, "is this another one of those give-aways to the boys?"

Chapman replied, "This is not only a give-away, Mr. President, but they've got it limited down to just a few of—one of your friends out there in Oklahoma."

Chapman and Clifford were friends, but in this case they agreed to disagree, as Clifford supported the bill. Chapman later recalled that Clifford was in favor of the bill because "he was a pretty close friend of Kerr's. He got to be pretty close to Kerr; and he was supporting anything like that for Kerr, if he could he would support it." Chapman thought it was a bad bill because it only benefited the largest gas producers, and "Kerr-McGee was among them," he said. Chapman either did not know whether Clifford personally lobbied the president or if he did know he did not say. Instead he simply pointed out that he was aware that Clifford was personally in favor of the legislation.[43] The press was less charitable, accusing Clifford of lobbying the president. Clifford, however, said it was "wholly and unequivocally untrue" that he had tried to use his influence with Truman to convince him to sign the bill.[44] Either way, Truman sided with Chapman and vetoed the bill.

In addition to his support of Kerr's gas bill, Clifford endorsed his friend's campaign for president in 1952 and attempted to convince Truman to support him as well. Kerr first confided his presidential ambitions to Clifford in 1951, and Clifford enthusiastically replied that he wanted to help. According to Clifford, Kerr believed that Clifford would be a valuable ally because of his role during the 1948 campaign. One of the first things Clifford did to help was gather together some materials he had on the subject of presidential primaries and forward them to Kerr, which he did in early January 1952.[45] Both Clifford and Kerr understood that winning Truman's endorsement was critical to the nomination, and Clifford promised to make the pitch with Truman.[46] In February he attended a dinner with Truman and his closest advisers to discuss the campaign. Truman was still on the fence about running and wanted input from his inner circle. Vinson urged Truman to run again; Murphy suggested that Truman make another attempt to convince Illinois governor Adlai Stevenson, who had previously declined, to run. Clifford argued that the president should support Kerr. Truman was not convinced, however, believing that Kerr was tainted by his financial interests in oil and gas.[47] White House staffer Kenneth Hechler thought it was odd that Clifford supported Kerr because the Oklahoma senator "smelled of oil."[48] On March 15, about two weeks before Truman withdrew from the race, Clifford sent him a letter in which he again lobbied on behalf of Kerr. Clifford did not apply a hard-sell strategy with Truman but instead emphasized the importance of knocking Kefauver out of the race and suggested that either Truman himself or Kerr was best positioned to do that. "I believe the Nebraska primary has great importance," he wrote. "If you decide to run again, I believe it would be very helpful to knock Kefauver out of the picture. On the other hand, if you do not run again, a victory by Kerr over Kefauver on April 1st would lend great impetus to Kerr's candidacy and seriously damage Kefauver's."[49]

With his ties to the oil industry and without the endorsement of the leader of the Democratic Party, Kerr's presidential run inevitably failed. While covering the Democratic convention Drew Pearson wrote a particularly scathing commentary on both Kerr's presidential run and Clifford's endorsement of the senator from Oklahoma. He wrote, "Sad sights at the Democratic Convention include: Former White House General Counsel Clark Clifford, now playing would-be kingmaker for Sen. Bob Kerr of Oklahoma. Clifford, whose law practice benefited considerably from his White House contacts, now realizes he has pulled a bull, can't get off the hook."[50]

Although Kerr's presidential run was unsuccessful, Clifford's loyalty to Kerr was personally rewarding. As he would do for many of his friends, particularly those who could provide something in return, Kerr recommended some oil and gas ventures for Clifford to invest in. Over time Clifford invested in about twenty-five separate ventures and made a fortune. Furthermore, in an industry where many wells turn out to be dry, Clifford's oil-drilling investments were uncannily close to gusher sites, suggesting that his ventures entailed far less risk than a less well connected investor could expect.[51] Clifford himself later said that he "hit it big" in the oil business.[52] Clifford and Kerr remained good friends until the senator's death in 1963, and for many years Kerr was an important source of clients for Clifford's law practice. In 1961 Kerr brought Clifford the most lucrative case of his career, a tax settlement with the Du Pont Corporation.[53]

Clifford's interest and involvement in the 1952 election was not limited to his support of Kerr. Perhaps because he was no longer in government yet still retained a strong interest in politics, Clifford was active in the campaign. There is a trove of correspondence in his papers, including letters to the candidates and high-ranking members of the Democratic Party and acknowledgments of campaign contributions.[54] No doubt Clifford was trying to sustain and nurture the relationships he had with figures in government, as they would be an invaluable asset for his law practice. Yet it is just as likely that he wanted to remain active and involved in the Democratic Party for partisan reasons. Oscar Ewing, with whom Clifford was close because of their mutual membership in the Wardman Park Group, the informal political strategizing committee, was at one point suggested as a dark horse candidate for president at the Democratic convention. He sought out Clifford's guidance as to how he should proceed. Ewing recalled, "Clark was already committed to support Senator Kerr, but he strongly advised that my name be presented to the convention because he said the picture was so confused that no one could tell who would be nominated. Clark was very close to President Truman at that time and I got the impression, whether rightly or wrongly, I do not know, that the views he expressed were those of the President."[55] After the convention Clifford sent Ewing a letter typical of the type of flattery for which he became well known. "Dear Jack," he wrote, "I wanted you to know how much I admired the way you handled yourself during the pre-convention period and the convention itself. You made a great many friends and improved immeasurably in stature in the opinion of those with whom I came into contact. Apparently it wasn't in the cards for you to get the top spot on the ticket but you ended up with increased respect and regard and a much more solid position in the Party and in the Country."[56]

The interest Clifford took in the 1952 presidential campaign was indicative of his involvement and commitment to the Democratic Party throughout the election cycle. In addition to proving his bona fides as a friend to business, Clifford's speech before the Executives' Club of Chicago also constituted a defense of the Fair Deal. In the fall of 1951 Clifford gave a purely political speech, this time in the backyard of the red-baiting senator from Wisconsin, Joseph McCarthy. Averell Harriman, then director of the Mutual Security Agency, was scheduled to deliver the speech but had to cancel. The White House scrambled to find a replacement, but Joseph Short, Truman's secretary, was unable to find anyone in the Cabinet who was available. Murphy suggested

Clifford; Truman approved, and Elsey was charged with overseeing the drafting of the speech.[57] Indicative of the importance the White House and the Democratic Party placed on this speech, Elsey contacted Charles Van Devander, the DNC's director of publicity, for some help with ideas and themes.[58] "For nearly two years," Clifford told the Democrats of Wisconsin, "I have been away from the White House, and I haven't held any official government position. But I haven't lost any of the interest I had in the questions of foreign policy and domestic policy which confront the American people." Embracing the partisan rhetoric typical of a campaign, Clifford argued that the Truman administration was "successfully leading us toward peace and the highest level of prosperity we have ever known." He continued, "I am equally convinced that our opponents have nothing to offer the American people except stubborn opposition to the progress we have made at home, and tardy, grudging acceptance of the policies we are carrying out around the world."[59] Truman was ecstatic with his performance. "Your Wisconsin speech was 'tops,'" he wrote.[60]

In June 1951 Elsey sent a letter to Clifford that seems to have been a request for help establishing an organization similar to the Research Division, which had been so successful during the campaign three years earlier. "You might be interested in knowing that we have had an increasing number of calls in recent weeks from Senators and Representatives complaining because they can't get information with which to answer Republican charges," he wrote. "In some instances, we have had to draft Congressional speeches here at the White House. That can't go on because we don't have the manpower."[61]

There was one issue in particular for which Truman sought Clifford's counsel, and that was the snowballing employee loyalty and anticommunism issue. In this regard Clifford was able to provide insight into both the legal and political aspects of an issue that would bedevil Truman and the Democrats from the late 1940s until McCarthy was censured by the Senate in 1954. In *Counsel to the President* Clifford describes the difficulties of the situation they encountered as the Democrats tried to defend themselves against the groundless attacks that they were soft on communism:

> There was great irony in the situation faced by the Truman
> Administration. Since 1946, we had sought to rally the nation
> to resist communist expansion. . . . As liberals, we saw our-
> selves as the true internationalists, the Americans who best
> understood the dangers of both communism and fascism,

while conservatives, many of whom came out of an isolation-
ist background, saw the world in grossly simplified terms.

At the same time, the "attack of the primitives" left a mark
on liberals which survives even today. In their attempt to make
anticommunism their exclusive province, the right wing often
succeeded in placing anticommunist liberals on the defensive.
On the other hand, liberals felt it was intolerable to watch the
First Amendment freedoms . . . trampled by know-nothings
masquerading as patriots.[62]

A year earlier, Clifford had taken a strong position against the
escalating witch hunt for communist subversives in the government.
By 1950 circumstances had taken a turn for the worse. The Mundt-
Nixon Bill, which was passed by the House in May 1948, had not been
acted upon in the Senate, yet the issue was gaining political momentum. In an effort to halt this freight train on a collision course with
civil liberties, Truman attempted to seize the political initiative. On
June 22, 1950, he called a meeting to discuss creating a presidential
commission on government loyalty. Clifford, who was at the meeting,
supported creating such a commission, as did the other members of
the White House staff present, except for John Steelman, who took
no position.[63] Opposing the idea were Vice President Alben Barkley,
Speaker of the House Sam Rayburn, House Majority Leader John
McCormack, and Attorney General Howard McGrath. Truman was
uncharacteristically indecisive after the meeting and planned a follow-
up session in early July, but the outbreak of the Korean War on June
25 scuttled those plans, and the commission was placed on the back
burner. Two months later Murphy sent Clifford a draft of a message
Truman was planning to deliver to Congress, which confronted the
risks to personal liberties of the proposed loyalty measures. "It has
always been difficult to draw the line between restrictions which are
proper because they are necessary for internal security, and restrictions which are improper because they violate the spirit or the letter
of the Constitution. It is clear that on certain occasions, that line has
been over-stepped," Murphy wrote in his draft.[64]

Later that summer the Senate passed the McCarran Act, otherwise
known as the Internal Security Act of 1950, a measure comparable to
the Mundt-Nixon Bill, which had been passed by the House two years
earlier but died in committee before it reached the floor of the Senate.
The bill required the Justice Department to register all members of
the Communist Party, compile a list of communist-affiliated organiza-

tions along with information about their finances and membership, and identify all of these organizations' publications as "communist." It precluded communists from working for the federal government or its defense contractors. Finally, and perhaps most absurdly, it prohibited immigration by individuals who espoused a totalitarian form of government. Prodded on by his advisers, Truman took the courageous step of vetoing the popular legislation, comparing the bill to the Alien and Sedition Acts of 1798.[65] The House and Senate promptly overrode his veto, but Truman was satisfied that he had done the right thing. In order to seize the political high ground, however, Truman's advisers again pressed for a presidential commission.[66] Elsey and Murphy, convinced that he would be able to persuade the president, asked Clifford to discuss the matter with Truman. "I talked with Clifford this afternoon," Elsey wrote to Murphy, "and unless he hears from you to contrary, he will plan to speak informally to the President on Friday/Saturday about the desirability of appointing an Internal Security Commission in the very near future. Clifford will make this an incidental matter and not the main purpose of his visit with the President."[67]

The following summer Clifford was again called in to help deal with the gathering political storm stirred up by Senator McCarthy. "Tail-Gunner" Joe had stepped onto the national scene in a February 1950 speech in Wheeling, West Virginia. That night he brandished a sheaf of papers that he claimed contained the names of 205 "known communists" in the State Department. Throughout 1950 McCarthy continued his attacks on members of the State Department, especially Dean Acheson, accusing them of coddling communists and deliberately sacrificing China to communist rule. The Republicans did well with the anticommunist issue in the 1950 midterm elections, and while they still did not control either house of Congress, they cut the Democratic majority in the Senate from twelve to two, and in the House from seventeen to twelve. In particular, they won two high-profile races with the defeat of Maryland senator Millard Tydings, a McCarthy nemesis, and the election of Richard Nixon to the Senate. The following summer McCarthy set his sights on a seemingly invulnerable target—George Marshall. It was Marshall, he charged, who was responsible for the administration's failures in China. What made the charges truly outrageous was that he accused Marshall and Acheson of being the key figures in a vast conspiracy to undermine the United States in its fight against communism.

Truman, who had expected McCarthy to use up his fifteen minutes of fame, was at a loss as to how to handle him. On February 28 Truman called a secret meeting at Blair House, which was serving as the presidential quarters while the White House was undergoing renovations, to plan strategy for how to deal with McCarthy. In attendance were Attorney General Howard McGrath, DNC chairman William Boyle, Solicitor General Philip B. Perlman, Kentucky congressman Brent Spence, and Senators Michael Monroney, Thomas Hennings, John Sparkman, and Clinton Anderson, formerly the secretary of agriculture and a poker buddy of Truman's. Also in attendance were Clark Clifford and historian John Hersey. Despite the political acumen assembled in the room, the group could come up with little to counter McCarthy's attacks. Anderson revealed that he was aware of an extensive file of embarrassing personal information that had been compiled on McCarthy, including women he had slept with, and suggested that this information be leaked to the press. Truman, however, refused to get down in the mud with McCarthy and so dismissed that recommendation. Instead he adopted a policy of "no comment."[68] It is not clear if this was Clifford's suggestion, although he had once been credited as the man who taught Truman to say, "No comment."[69]

In his fall 1951 Wisconsin speech Clifford attacked McCarthy, although not by name. He said:

> There have been some deadly serious challenges to our basic ideas of freedom in the last 2 years, and some of the most sinister of the challenges have come—not from abroad—but from right here at home. Vicious smears, reckless charges of disloyalty, and the technique of telling a bigger lie when you are caught telling a little one are bad habits that can cost us more than war itself. . . . I say that American freedom is in just as much danger from the reactionary "right" as it is from the communist "left." . . . And that is why I think Wisconsin is just as much in the "front line of freedom" as Denmark is, or Iran, or Korea.[70]

Three years later Clifford would have a personal run-in with McCarthy, this time on the eve of the infamous Army-McCarthy hearings. The "astonishingly trivial" (as Clifford described it) circumstances behind the Army-McCarthy hearings centered on the promotion and subsequent honorable discharge of an Army Reserve dentist named Irving Peress. According to McCarthy and his unscrupulous chief counsel, Roy Cohn, Peress's promotion was part of an elaborate

Clifford and Truman traveling by train to Fulton, Missouri, to attend Winston Churchill's "Iron Curtain" speech, March 5, 1946. U.S. Marine Corps, courtesy of Harry S. Truman Library.

Clifford and Truman at Winston Churchill's "Iron Curtain" speech, March 5, 1946. Terry Savage, courtesy of Harry S. Truman Library.

Clifford and Truman in Key West, Florida, on December 19, 1949. U.S. Navy, courtesy of Harry S. Truman Library.

President Kennedy and Clifford at the Distinguished Service Award ceremony in the White House Rose Garden, April 29, 1963. Cecil Stoughton, Office of the Military Aide (U.S. Army), courtesy of John F. Kennedy Presidential Library.

Clifford attending a meeting in the White House on December 23, 1963, one month into Lyndon Johnson's presidency. LBJ Library photo by Yoichi R. Okamoto.

A national security meeting on Vietnam, July 21, 1965, four days before the July 25 Camp David showdown with Secretary McNamara. LBJ Library photo by Yoichi R. Okamoto.

Meeting on Vietnam with the Joint Chiefs of Staff and Secretaries of the Armed Services, July 22, 1965. LBJ Library photo by Yoichi R. Okamoto.

Clifford at a national security meeting on Vietnam, July 26, 1965, the day after the Camp David showdown with McNamara. LBJ Library photo by Yoichi R. Okamoto.

Oval Office meeting between Clifford and President Johnson, July 14, 1967. LBJ Library photo by Yoichi R. Okamoto.

Vietnam meeting with the Wise Men on March 26, 1968, just prior to Johnson's announcement that he was dropping out of the presidential race. LBJ Library photo by Yoichi R. Okamoto.

Clifford in the Oval Office reacting to news of Martin Luther King Jr.'s assassination, April 4, 1968. LBJ Library photo by Mike Geissinger.

*Left to right:* Senator Richard Russell, Secretary of State Dean Rusk, Johnson, and Clifford meeting in the Cabinet room, October 14, 1968. LBJ Library photo by Yoichi R. Okamoto.

Clifford and Rusk at a meeting in the Oval Office, October 22, 1968. LBJ Library photo by Yoichi R. Okamoto.

Clifford and General Earle Wheeler on December 5, 1968. LBJ Library photo by Yoichi R. Okamoto.

cover-up to conceal his former membership in a left-wing organization. In February 1954 McCarthy called Peress's commander, Brigadier General Ralph W. Zwicker, before a closed hearing of his Senate subcommittee, but Zwicker refused to give him any further information. McCarthy angrily accused Zwicker of "shielding traitors" and said he was "not fit to wear that uniform." Alarmed over McCarthy's antics, Secretary of the Army Robert Stevens and Army Chief of Staff Matthew Ridgway called on Stuart Symington, then a senator from Missouri. Stevens met with Symington the following day, and after listening to his story, Symington recommended that they call Clifford. During that meeting and a subsequent meeting, this time without Symington, Clifford recommended that Stevens take a stand against McCarthy. By Clifford's reasoning, Stevens, being a Republican, was in a much better position to attack McCarthy than Symington or any other Democrat.[71]

In hindsight, Clifford's recommendation seems like the most logical choice of action, but at the time McCarthy was a man to be feared. Even President Eisenhower was unwilling to take him on, and he remained reluctant to do so even after McCarthy's malicious attacks on Marshall. Clifford had the luxury of sitting on the sidelines and suggesting that Stevens publicly confront a demagogue riding a wave of popular anxiety over alleged communist subversion. Stevens, however, was not sufficiently courageous to stand up to McCarthy, in large part because Eisenhower had all but abandoned him. Stevens agreed to order everyone involved in the Peress case to testify before McCarthy's board of inquisition. His advice ignored, Clifford said he "made no effort to contact Stevens again."[72]

The Army-McCarthy hearings began on April 22, 1954, and lasted until June 17. McCarthy publicly implicated Clifford in early June for his February meetings with Stevens and Symington. On June 5, as the *New York Times* reported, McCarthy "accused Senator Stuart Symington . . . of helping to instigate the McCarthy-Army dispute in a plot to 'destroy' President Eisenhower and the Republican party." According to McCarthy, Symington was "'running about as fast as anyone can' for the Democratic Presidential nomination." He accused Symington and Clifford of orchestrating "an insidious plot by Democrats to guide the destinies of the Republican Administration and to lead ultimately to the collapse of the G.O.P."[73] Despite his paranoia there was a kernel of truth to McCarthy's accusations. According to Clifford, the first time he and Symington discussed the Stevens case Clifford had recommended that Symington "use his personal relationship with Stevens to cut across party lines and create a backlash against McCarthy."[74] If Clifford's account in his memoirs is to be believed, it is clear that he viewed the Army-McCarthy hearings as a forum for publicly humiliating the senator from Wisconsin. McCarthy was therefore correct when he accused Clifford of conspiring in a partisan plot, but as for the idea that Clifford and Symington were intending to destroy the Eisenhower administration and the Republican Party, he was living in a paranoid fantasy land.

Two days later, in a sharp exchange with Symington, McCarthy demanded that Clifford be subpoenaed to testify:

> We find that Mr. Clark Clifford is also the advisor of Mr. Symington, and without the knowledge of this committee, the advisor of the Republican Secretary of the Army. That makes it very important, Mr. Chairman, that we have him here. . . . Clark Clifford, the chief political advisor of President Truman—and I assume the chief political advisor of a man who would be President on the Democratic ticket in 1956—is doing the advising [of Stevens], charging Mr. Cohn, [McCarthy staff director] Mr. [Frank] Carr, and myself with almost everything except murdering our great-great grandmother. . . . It may seem very clever to Senator Symington at this time that he got Clark Clifford to mislead a fine, naive, not too brilliant Republican Secretary of the Army. . . . I will ask the Chair tonight to immediately subpoena Clark Clifford.[75]

For reasons that are unclear, despite all of his posturing McCarthy had no intention of subpoenaing Clifford. The next day, after a motion had been made and seconded to call Clifford as a witness, McCarthy introduced an alternative motion, stipulating that the subcommittee adhere to its original witness list, which excluded Clifford. Symington and Clifford conferred before Symington's next appearance before the subcommittee and debated strategy. Clifford drafted a statement saying that he was available to testify, if called. Quoting McCarthy, the statement said that Clifford

> (1) was "Chief Political Advisor of Harry Truman at the time they were most vigorously fighting my attempting to expose Communists in the last administration"; (2) that I [Clifford] as "top counsel of the Democratic Party" pulled "strings from behind the scenes" to inspire the Army's charges which are the

subject of the subcommittee's current investigation; that (3) I as "top political advisor of the Democrats" connived with Senator Symington "to try to get the Republicans to commit suicide." . . . The members of your subcommittee must know that such statements are ridiculous on their face.[76]

Clifford and Symington decided not to issue the statement. Given that Symington had already indicated that Clifford was willing to testify, they believed "it would look like self-promotion." In order to clarify the matter for the record, Symington delivered a statement on June 10 explaining the circumstances that led to Clifford's involvement.[77] On June 17, the last day of the hearings, Stevens released a letter he had written to Karl Mundt, chairman of the subcommittee.[78] Clifford was never called to testify. McCarthy's bullying tactics, boorish behavior, and outrageous accusations had finally backfired on him, as Clifford and many others had hoped. The close of the Army-McCarthy hearings signaled the demise of Senator McCarthy as a political force. That December the Senate passed a resolution condemning his behavior. Three years later he drank himself into an early grave.

In addition to the extensive press coverage he received during the Army-McCarthy hearings, Clifford received a fair amount for his business dealings. On these occasions the stories were often personally embarrassing. In May 1952 Clifford's ties to the oil industry were questioned. Republican members of the House Armed Services Committee were suspicious of contacts Clifford had had with the assistant secretary of the Navy, John T. Koehler. Koehler had been responsible for overseeing the Navy's oil reserves, and the Republicans wanted to know more about a March 1950 meeting in Key West between Koehler and Clifford. Their meeting concerned the Elk Hills oil reserve, part of the Teapot Dome reserves that had become famous in the 1920s as a result of a scandal during the Warren G. Harding presidency. Standard Oil, which reportedly had agreed to a five-year retainer of $525,000 with Clifford, was interested in securing rights in the Navy's reserves, and the Republicans were understandably curious whether Koehler and Clifford had reached any secret agreement regarding their status. The fact that the reported meeting took place while President Truman was vacationing in Key West and followed a breakfast attended by Clifford, Truman, and Vinson added to the Republicans' suspicions. It was not the type of publicity either Clifford or the White House wanted.[79]

A week later, Drew Pearson, no friend of Clifford, wrote a story critical of the lawyer's lobbying on behalf of the Pennsylvania Railroad. "Lobbying in Washington ranges from subtle hints dropped at cocktail parties to bald-faced brazen campaign contributions," Pearson wrote. "It can be either ethical or smelly." Pearson's use of the word "smelly" was particularly apt, as the story focused on Clifford's efforts "on behalf of higher priced toilet facilities in railroad stations."[80] Another Pearson story a few weeks later implied that the Truman administration gave the RCA Corporation favorable treatment during an antitrust case. Pearson suggested that Truman was partial to RCA, which controlled the National Broadcasting Company, because its chairman, David Sarnoff, had given Margaret Truman, the president's daughter and an aspiring singer, a radio contract. Pearson noted that RCA hired "the lawyer closest to the White House, Clark Clifford," to handle the case.[81]

The most embarrassing and potentially damaging story of Clifford's career was also reported around this time. On June 7, 1952, the *New York Times* and the *Washington Post,* among other papers, published a story implicating Clifford in an influence-peddling scandal. The case was one of several exposed by the General Accounting Office (GAO) involving fraudulent billings to the government for war contracts. In the case involving Clifford, a Michigan trade school and two affiliates had been charged with overbilling the military by $1.3 million. Joseph Peters, the owner of the schools, believed that he had not acted improperly and needed an attorney in Washington to represent him. He had recently read that Clifford was leaving the White House to go into private practice, so he decided to hire Clifford. "I thought that if he was good enough to be the President's attorney he was good enough for us," Peters recalled. During their consultation Clifford recused himself from the case, as he had not yet left the White House, and referred the matter to his partner, Edward Miller. Peters hired Miller and agreed to pay the firm $25,000 to settle the case. According to Peters, Clifford had no direct involvement in the matter, and after Miller died there was no one to contradict Peters's statement.[82]

Two facts led the GAO to scrutinize the case. The first was the settlement amount, a paltry $125,000 against the government's calculation of $1.3 million. The second was that Clifford knew Holmes Baldridge, the assistant attorney general responsible for settling the claim, and had sponsored him for a promotion. Baldridge testified to the House Judiciary subcommittee investigating the charges that he had not disqualified himself from the case because he had never discussed the matter with Clifford. He also pointed out that Clifford was one of fifteen people who had endorsed him for the position of assistant attorney general in charge of the Claims Division. Furthermore he argued that the $1.3 million figure was overstated because there was a difference of opinion between the GAO and the Veterans Administration over how much the company had overcharged. He testified that it was the Justice Department's belief that if the case went to trial the most the government might recover would have been $141,000. Therefore, he reasoned, the $125,000 figure seemed reasonable.[83]

What Baldridge failed to mention was that Clifford had endorsed him for another promotion—for the head of the antitrust division.[84] Although Baldridge did not get that job, it suggested that his friendship with Clifford was closer than Baldridge's testimony suggested. His account of the settlement was also unconvincing, as he offered little to explain how the government's claim had been whittled down to less than 10 percent of the original amount. The more plausible explanation was what the press articles suggested: that Clifford had used his government contacts to secure a bargain settlement for his client.

For Clifford this type of press was damaging on two fronts. First, it might have threatened his relationship with Truman, the one he held most dear. With the myriad of influence-peddling scandals that plagued his second term there was the chance that Truman might cut off contact with those who threatened the integrity of his administration. Second, it jeopardized Clifford's reputation as a man of discretion. Clifford's subtle method of lobbying figures in government was far more effective than the more blatant tactics used by other Washington power brokers. It also allowed Clifford to maintain the convenient illusion, perhaps delusion, that he was not asking for favors. His reputation for discretion allowed him to give the "I have no influence" speech to his new clients while keeping a straight face.[85]

Clifford immediately took action to repair the damage. "Dear Boss," he wrote, "the smear artists have finally gotten around to me. You may have seen mention made in the papers of a case involving the settlement of conflicting claims between the Michigan Trade School and the Federal Government." He pointed out that he had no personal involvement, noting that the case had been handled by Miller. He also emphasized that he had done nothing improper. "This firm was responsible for the case and I mention the above fact only to demonstrate conclusively that no element of influence was used because I never discussed the case with any person in Government."[86]

Fortunately for Clifford, Truman believed that he had been unfairly maligned in the press. "Don't worry about these smear artists. So far as I am concerned they can't hurt you," he replied. At the bottom of the letter was a handwritten postscript that suggested how embattled Truman felt in the closing year of his administration. "Never admit anything—swing from the ground and tell 'em *to go to hell.*"[87]

Although this particular incident was not unique, it was the one most embarrassing for Clifford, at least until the BCCI scandal broke. Because there was no direct evidence that he personally participated in the case, no further investigation was warranted. Yet even though Clifford had disqualified himself, it was clear that Peters had sought out the firm because of Clifford's familiarity with the Truman administration, not because of the legal prowess of his partner. Clifford knew that he had to be very careful so as not to risk damaging the relationships he had so patiently nurtured.

His stock speech for new clients was centered on a pledge that he would not utilize his influence with individuals in government on behalf of the interests he was representing. When asked during his *Meet the Press* interview how he would respond to entreaties to lobby his former colleagues and associates, Clifford responded that his personal code of ethics was sufficient to ensure that would not happen. Yet Clifford and his clients knew that was exactly the reason they were hiring him. In 1952 Copco Steel and Engineering Company hired Clifford for help in persuading the British government to supply steel to offset the domestic shortages caused by the ongoing labor disputes and wartime mobilization in the United States. The British were facing shortages of their own, however, and were not able to provide Copco any special relief. Clifford contacted Averell Harriman at the Mutual Security Agency to see if he could provide assistance. Harriman was not the only contact Clifford had at the agency, as Elsey was then Harriman's assistant, while William Batt was chief of the Economic Cooperation Administration Mission to Great Britain. In March Elsey forwarded a memorandum to Clifford at Harriman's request, a day before Harriman was to meet with Batt. Harriman asked Batt to meet with Senators Blair Moody and Homer Ferguson of Michigan, where Copco was based, but not to do so until he had met with Clifford.[88] A month later, W. John Kenny, the deputy director for Mutual Security, sent Clifford a memorandum indicating that Batt had taken up the matter with the British government, but they remained unwilling to grant Copco any special consideration.[89] In this case, although Clifford was ultimately unsuccessful, his contacts and reputation ensured that he had an audience with the people in government who might be able to help him. Years later, while embroiled in a dispute with the steel industry, Clifford would conveniently forget his relationship with Copco and proudly claim that his firm had never represented a steel company.[90]

Truman continued to rely on Clifford from time to time on professional matters, and Clifford continued to shoulder responsibility for organizing the president's poker parties. A December 1952 note to Matthew Connelly, Truman's appointments secretary, indicates that the president had given Clifford a specific assignment to work on and that Clifford was trying to get on the president's schedule to discuss it.[91] Elsey recalled that Truman primarily used Clifford as a source for political gossip. "I don't know what kinds of assignments" Truman asked him to work on, Elsey said. "They would have been rather specific. Personal relations, talk to Bob Kerr about this or that, what does Bob Kerr think about this or that. They would have been that sort of thing. They wouldn't have been major issues, they wouldn't have been assignments to get something done. But more political gossip and their social relations. . . . Kerr and Stuart Symington specifically."[92] Their close personal correspondence continued until Truman's death. Clifford also maintained a familiar relationship with Bess Truman, although his relationship with Margaret was occasionally strained. A wealth of correspondence back and forth between the Trumans and Clifford communicates birthday and holiday wishes and acknowledges the exchange of gifts.

In order to maintain the personal relationships that he valued for professional as well as sentimental reasons, Clifford also took on more social responsibilities. Shortly after he went into private practice Clifford and Marny hosted an extravagant party for Vice President Alben Barkley and his new bride, Jane Hadley. Clifford had introduced the two during the 1948 campaign and threw the party as a wedding gift. It was estimated the party cost from $10,000 to $15,000 and was so lavish that it was written up in *Life* magazine.[93] In May 1950 Clifford purchased a new home just outside of Washington, on Rockville Pike in Bethesda, Maryland. It was a large, former farmhouse and needed extensive renovations, but it signified that Clifford was ready to graduate to the upper echelons of Washington society. Clifford and Marny also started an annual tradition that they kept up throughout the 1950s, their New Year's Day open house. The guest list for this party eventually grew to more than two hundred guests and included many of the movers and shakers in Washington. Clifford and his entire family provided the entertainment, at first only a few songs but eventually "a full-fledged show, complete with skits gently lampooning public figures and recent events." Perhaps one unintended consequence of the New Year's Day party was that it provided an opportunity for the workaholic Clifford to spend time with his family.[94] Clifford also hosted an annual birthday party for Chief Justice Fred Vinson. Truman was usually an honored guest at these affairs, and Clifford coordinated the date around Truman's schedule.[95]

Clifford also cultivated his relationships with members of Congress, especially after Truman left the White House. With Symington's election to the Senate in 1952, Clifford was close friends with three senators, Symington, Kerr, and Lyndon Johnson. Johnson rose to power quickly and became the Senate minority leader in 1953 when the Republicans reassumed control. As the demands on Johnson increased, he turned to Clifford more and more often for advice and counsel. Despite Kerr's failure in the 1952 presidential campaign, he rose to prominence in the Democratic Senate caucus. Perhaps to stay in the politicians' good graces, Clifford was always available to dispense political advice. In late December 1952 Clifford commented on a press release Kerr planned for January 1. Kerr's message was the standard promise of bipartisanship issued in response to a change of power, in this case the first Republican administration in twenty years, and at a time when the country was still entangled in the Korean War. Clifford, who must have been given an advance copy of the text, noted that he approved of Kerr's remarks. "The sole purpose [of this letter] is to congratulate you upon the excellence of your January 1st news letter," he wrote. "I believe you strike exactly the right note and that there will be general commendation for your pledge of support to Ike in the foreign policy field. I feel strongly that this is the line to follow until the time for the break comes."[96] In a September 1953 letter to Kerr, Clifford forwarded a copy of the latest American Federation of Labor (A. F. of L.) newsletter, noting, "It is particularly significant when you recall that part of the Republican strategy was to woo the A. F. of L. and develop a close political tie between the Republican Party and that organization."[97]

At the same time he was providing political advice to Kerr, Clifford was also providing legal representation to Kerr-McGee Oil. The company made an embarrassing $15 million mistake in October 1954 and turned to Clifford to bail it out. As the result of a clerical error the company had successfully bid on eight offshore oil and gas leases that it did not actually want. The tracts the company was interested in bore similar identification numbers, which accounted for the mix-up. Because of the mistake the company lost out on six other leases it coveted and for which it would have been the high bidder. Clifford wrote a letter to the Department of Interior requesting permission for Kerr-McGee to withdraw all of the bids and resubmit new bids on the sites it actually wanted. Alternatively, he suggested that if Interior was unwilling to go along with that solution they should void the original auction and offer all of the tracts at another time. If Interior was unwilling to accept either proposal, he argued that Kerr-McGee was entitled to the return of the $3 million down payment on the tracts it had inadvertently purchased. In response to Clifford's letter Interior issued a noncommittal statement noting that the matter had been referred to its lawyers "for a study of the legal aspects of its contents."[98]

The Kerr-McGee case was typical of the type of law that Clifford practiced and for which he became known. "Instead of being a broad-range law firm we were more like a boutique," Clifford recalled. "Somebody says, 'My God, I have a real tough problem. It involves Washington.' That's when they ought to come to Clifford." Clifford described his practice as "an advisory firm."[99] Personal service was important to Clifford, and for that reason he intended to keep the firm small. "Small firms retain the personal flavor and style I believe produce the best working conditions and the greatest job satisfaction," Clifford observed.[100] Perhaps another reason why Clifford wanted to keep the firm small was to keep the focus on him. What Clifford was offering his clients was more than a savvy legal mind. Courtroom experience and litigation skills were not necessarily what he was looking to sell, and in fact Clifford eschewed cases that involved complicated and time-consuming trials.[101] Instead, he offered himself as a guide to help his corporate clients navigate their ways through the often mazelike Washington bureaucracy. After having served Truman for five years Clifford understood how Washington worked and, perhaps more important, who in Washington made things work.

Above all, Clifford was looking to sell himself. Having established his reputation as Truman's most influential adviser and as the genius behind the 1948 victory, Clifford was a well-regarded figure both inside and outside of the government. Corporate leaders regularly turned to him for assistance, and most of their arrangements with his firm were on a retainer basis. Nothing says more about Clifford's practice than the fact that most of his clients paid Clifford a retainer. Under this arrangement clients were allowed to call on Clifford any time they had a problem or a concern that warranted his attention. By working on retainer Clifford also ensured that most of the time he was acting in the capacity of adviser or counselor, which was his preference and his forte. Furthermore, and perhaps most important, the retainer arrangement allowed Clifford to develop long-lasting relationships with his clients, which again played to his strength. A master at stroking and flattering powerful figures, close personal relationships were essential to his success and typical of how he ran the firm. His long-term relationship with "Boots" Adams of Phillips Petroleum, and to a lesser extent Howard Hughes, was typical.

The years in which Clifford struggled on his modest White House salary, although augmented by the personal loans from George Allen, were quickly rewarded. In his first year in private practice he earned $500,000, almost forty-two times his salary for most of his White House career.[102] In that year he paid off his debt to Allen and paid cash for the house in Bethesda. From that point on he would never earn less, and in several good years he would gross $1 million or more. In the 1950s and 1960s, that was a tremendous amount of money. His friend and confidant, David Lilienthal, recorded in his journal in April 1951 his observations about Clifford's practice and his prospects:

> Lunched with Clark Clifford. He told me the whole details of his last year, his first year of law practice after leaving the White House. It is a simply unbelievable story. He practices alone; he partner died two and a half months after they began; he hired four young lawyers; five stenographers. In this establishment—a one-man performance—he earned probably as much as any professional man in the country, amusement field included, and more than any lawyer. He said he came out even on the year, after paying off his debts . . . buying a house, outfitting a law office, etc. He was uneasy about what will happen after Truman is out, if he is; wonders if he will keep any of his clients—which is nonsense, as he is a very able man with or without Truman.[103]

Lilienthal was right: Clifford need not have worried about his prospects in the post-Truman era. Even though there was a Republican in the White House, he remained close with several key figures in the U.S. Senate. The 1954 elections returned Democratic majorities in the House and Senate, and Clifford's friend Lyndon Johnson became the Senate majority leader. In addition to his relationships with Johnson, Symington, and Kerr, Clifford cultivated relationships with many other congressional Democrats. As an active booster and contributor to the Democratic Party he was well positioned to rub elbows with both its leaders and its up-and-coming figures. The network of contacts he developed was largely due to the reputation he built during his service in the Truman administration, but it was also the product of hard work and his careful cultivation of relationships. A typical example was a 1952 congratulatory letter he wrote to John F. Kennedy upon the latter's election to the U.S. Senate. "Dear Jack," he wrote. "My heartiest congratulations to you on your wonderful victory in Massachusetts. The results of last Tuesday were so generally disheartening that your win stands out even more brightly by contrast. My sincerest wishes for a most successful tenure in office as Senator."[104]

In addition to flattery Clifford was also quick to dispense with political advice. In February 1954 he sent a report to Johnson, Symington, and Senator Earle Clements of Kentucky, the Democratic whip. The report highlighted the voting statistics for those senators who were elected in 1948 and therefore up for reelection in 1954. "These figures will indicate to some extent those races in which greater assistance will be needed than others," he wrote.[105] In September 1957 he passed along to Johnson two position papers he had written on domestic fiscal policy, one on inflation and the other on tight money and high interest rates.[106] Following the 1958 midterm elections Johnson was effusive with praise for Clifford's assistance. "I just wanted you to know how every grateful that we are for the fine work that you did," he wrote. "The Democratic victory was made up of many things. But one of the most important was the fine mind of Clark Clifford."[107]

Clifford's government contacts were not only useful in terms of advancing his business interests, but they also helped him stay out of trouble. His efforts on behalf of Phillips Petroleum had brought him before the Federal Power Commission to argue that natural gas companies had the right to raise prices for natural gas. Years later when the House Commerce Committee investigated the influence of lobbyists over regulatory agencies they discovered that Clifford had lunched with Frederick Stueck of the Federal Power Commission eight to ten times while the matter was before the commission. Clifford knew Stueck from law school days, and according to Steuck they never discussed business during those meetings, but instead talked as old friends. "We sang on the glee club together," Steuck said. Clifford was handed a subpoena to appear before the committee, but after making a few phone calls was offered a private meeting with Chairman Oren Harris, and the subpoena was forgotten.[108]

With his network of contacts in Congress and his reputation as a master political strategist, Clifford no longer needed to rely on his connection to Truman. Always the workaholic, he pushed himself ever harder in his relentless quest for success, and Lilienthal thought it was taking a toll on him. In April 1951 Lilienthal noted in his diary:

> He looks like the wrath of God, ten years older than two years ago. Troubled with his stomach, his nerves, wakes up at three A.M. How can this have happened to him, who never had any limit on how hard he could work? . . . He has a sense of insecurity (financial) that is hard to fathom, considering the facts. He is a fine man, did a great job with the President, best man in the White House since I've known about things. I told him he must remember he will be expected to render public service again, somebody must keep his hand in, as Clark Clifford, not as Harry Truman's helper.[109]

Clifford would return to government service, but only for one year, and not until 1968. The rest of the time Clifford made money, a lot of money. As Patrick Anderson observed, "Clifford, the fighting Fair Dealer of 1945–50, had gone on to become one of the richest lawyers in America."[110] He developed a reputation as a lawyer adept at helping his clients clear antitrust hurdles. "'Anything that is regulated,' said a fellow Washington lawyer, 'he can fix.'"[111] In 1961 he helped General Electric (GE) settle a series of antitrust claims against the company for price fixing and the rigging of bids for electrical equipment. The immediate victims of these schemes were the public utility companies, but since they had passed along the inflated prices the ultimate victims were the consumers. As a result of Clifford's efforts, GE was assessed a negligible fine of $430,000. Because the consumer had been defrauded, the company also faced a rash of civil suits, including a Justice Department suit claiming $70 million in damages. Although GE did not win all of the cases, Clifford was able to settle the Justice Department case for $7.7 million, or about 10 percent of the amount named in the suit. He even elicited a special dispensation from the IRS, which allowed GE to deduct its fines as a business expense. For his efforts Clifford received a fee estimated at about $2 million.[112]

On one memorable occasion Clifford boasted of the size of his fees.

He was representing Charles Revson, the head of Revlon Cosmetics, which sponsored the television game show *The $64,000 Question.* Revson was to appear before a House committee to testify about rigged quiz shows, and he hired Clifford to help prepare his testimony. For his services Clifford submitted a bill for $25,000, which was questioned by Revlon's Washington counsel. Clifford brushed off the inquiry. "When he's down at the beach at the Fontainebleau playing pinochle with his cronies, he'll boast that Clark Clifford charged him $25,000," he said. "Then it will seem worth every penny to him."[113]

When Clifford assisted another client, the FMC Corporation, with an antitrust matter he ran afoul of investigative reporter Jack Anderson. When FMC competitor Stauffer Chemical Co. attempted to purchase the American Viscose Co., the acquisition was blocked by the Justice Department on antitrust grounds. FMC was also interested in Viscose, but they had the good sense to hire Clifford before pursuing the deal. Whereas the Justice Department had acted swiftly to oppose Stauffer's purchase, they refrained from interfering with FMC's bid. This was particularly interesting to Anderson, who noted that FMC was almost twice the size of Stauffer and was therefore more of a monopoly risk. The difference, Anderson observed, was Clifford. "Why has the Justice Department hesitated to send FMC the same warnings that were sent at once to Stauffer? Insiders claim the big difference is the influence of Clark Clifford."[114] Clifford was furious but immediately shifted into damage control mode with an explanatory call to the White House. He left a lengthy phone message for then-president John F. Kennedy:

In Drew Pearson's column of Saturday, February 16, a story appears about me. The inferences and conclusions are 100% erroneous. Even the facts are 90% incorrect. An associate of mine has attended one meeting at a staff level at which time the subject was discussed.

I have not contacted, or been in touch with, any one in the Justice Department, or any one else in the government, with reference to this matter. I am sending this same memo to the Attorney General and informing him that I can confer with him, or any assistant, in order that I might demonstrate conclusively the completely erroneous nature of this story.

I ordinarily would not bother you on a matter of this kind but the —— brought your name into it.[115]

At around the same time, in February 1963, Clifford gave a speech at his alma mater, Washington University, in celebration of the university's 110th anniversary. The speech, entitled "Government and Business Today: Does the Reality Conform to the Myth?" reprised some of the themes he had addressed before the Executives' Club of Chicago in 1950 and provides some insight into his political ideology. Clifford staunchly defended the free enterprise system, which he argued was essential to defeating communism, and said that government, especially liberal government, should not be perceived as anti-business. Clifford said the notion that the government was at best a "nuisance" under Republican administrations or a "menace" under Democrats was plain wrong; rather, he said, government should be seen as the partner of business:

> I believe that the relationship between government and business has undergone such changes that the orthodox business view of government is now archaic and inadequate. . . . The orthodox business ideology on the relationship of government and business sees the growing role of government as a trend to be reversed. I submit that the trend is inevitable and irreversible, and a political or propaganda program "to get government out of business" is foredoomed to fail. Its goal is as hopeless of achievement as would be a decision by politicians to end the government's dependence on business for the accomplishment of critical national objectives. The two are permanently wedded in a partnership of necessity.[116]

The following year, in perhaps the most lucrative case in his career, Clifford saved the du Pont family an estimated $2 billion in taxes. A Supreme Court antitrust case required the company to divest itself of its 23 percent interest in General Motors. The company owned 63 million shares in GM, which had been purchased fifty years earlier for about $2 to $3 per share. Given that GM stock was selling for about $55 in 1962 and the du Ponts were in the highest tax bracket, were they to sell their stock they would face an enormous tax bill. The company lobbied Congress for special legislation to help it avoid the majority of the taxes by having the proceeds taxed as "modified capital gains." The bill was passed by Congress, largely on the terms the du Pont family wanted, and signed by President Kennedy. Clifford was instrumental in lobbying for the special-purpose legislation, instructing Du Pont's president to personally lobby more than sixty congressional and administration officials. In one particularly brazen ploy, Clifford attended a meeting in the office of Robert Knight, the general counsel for the Treasury Department. In order to counter liberal opposition to the measure, Clifford was seeking the Treasury's support. Clifford had just begun his presentation when Knight's secretary stepped in to tell him that the president was on the phone. Clifford stood up and recommended that everyone leave the room so Knight could speak to Kennedy in private, but the secretary stopped him. The call was not for Knight; it was for Clifford. It was textbook Clifford strategy because of its subtle effectiveness. Clifford did not need to tell Knight that he was close to the president; the phone call said as much. Furthermore, the call also delivered the implied message that Kennedy was on Clifford's side. As a result of Clifford's full court press, the House passed the bill a few weeks later. Despite liberal opposition in the Senate, the bill was eventually passed in that chamber as well, and the president signed the legislation. The du Pont family was ecstatic, and as in the GE case, Clifford collected a fee estimated at $2 million.[117] Clifford sent Kennedy a note thanking him for his assistance and for signing the legislation that brought such a windfall to the du Ponts. "This is to express my deep appreciation for the courtesies you extended to me with reference to the matter in which I had such a vital interest," he wrote. "Your willingness to take the time to understand the facts, and the issues involved, meant a great deal to me."[118]

The du Pont and GE cases in the early 1960s were particularly noteworthy, but Clifford was an accomplished attorney and power broker in Washington well before Kennedy became president. With his legal skills, personal charm, penchant for flattery, extensive government and business connections, and reputation as a political guru, Clifford's advice and counsel was a prized commodity. He had come a long way, from the young, eager attorney who was willing to work for free to one of the wealthiest and most powerful attorneys in Washington. Along the way he served a five-year stint in government and then capitalized on the knowledge and contacts he gained during that period. Robert S. Allen and William V. Shannon, authors of *The Truman Merry-Go-Round,* critiqued the situation of what they called "Close-up Men," focusing on the example of Clark Clifford:

> The Close-up Men are public officials who deliberately quit office to capitalize on their experience and contacts. The most recent striking example of this group is Clark Clifford. . . .

Clifford decided he could make ten times that amount in private law practice if he got out while Truman was still in the White House. He resigned in January, 1950, and his first six months of business showed he had figured it right. So many big clients rushed to hire him, they practically jostled one another going in the door.[119]

Clifford, of course, played down his status as a well-heeled lobbyist, instead suggesting he was just a lawyer, and—incredibly—still somewhat of a newcomer to Washington:

> By the sixties, I was sometimes described as a pillar of the Washington power structure, a quintessential member of the Washington establishment. I was not displeased with the compliment implicit in such a description, but at the same time it always amused me. After all, in those days Washington was still filled with alumni of the New Deal, and it was not hard to find men who even remembered the Presidency of Woodrow Wilson. I was a comparative newcomer to Washington, who, after five years of service to President Truman, resumed my profession, which I had practiced for sixteen years in St. Louis. I did not consider myself an old Washington hand. In my own mind, I was what I had always been, a lawyer.[120]

Despite the status and influence he wielded in Washington, he described himself as "an amateur in politics, a professional in the law."[121] In contrast, his biographers, Douglas Frantz and David McKean, described Clifford as he truly was: "Postwar Washington anointed Clifford as one of the most influential men of the century. He became the de facto chairman of the capital's political-legal establishment, a peerless figure in the nation's permanent government, untouchable by the electorate and out of reach of such passing fancies as term limits. He reshaped the way lobbying worked in the nation's capital, making it respectable and even desirable to trade quietly on relationships with government officials while telling clients with a straight face that he had no influence."[122]

One anecdote from Clifford's career best encapsulates the power and status he had achieved by the 1960s, if not before. As Washington legend has it, a corporate attorney once contacted Clifford for guidance regarding pending tax legislation. Three weeks later he received a telegram with Clifford's terse response: "Do nothing." Clifford followed up this counsel with a bill for $10,000. No doubt feeling that he was entitled to more than a two-word response and perhaps uncertain about why he should trust Clifford's recommendation, the lawyer asked for clarification. Clifford replied, "Because I told you so." He then sent his client a bill for an additional $5,000.[123]

# 8

# Kennedy's Consigliere

"Sue the bastard for $60 million!" former ambassador Joseph Kennedy shouted into the phone.[1] The patriarch of the Kennedy family was furious at journalist Drew Pearson for claiming that his son, Senator John F. Kennedy, was not the author of *Profiles in Courage,* the book for which he had won a Pulitzer Prize. Pearson had appeared two nights before on the *Mike Wallace Interview Show* and asserted that Kennedy had not even written the book for which he received the prestigious prize, that it had been ghostwritten for him, presumably by aide Theodore Sorensen.[2] Ambassador Kennedy had a reputation as a hothead, but in this case his anger had some foundation and not merely because he believed that Pearson had libeled his son. It was December 1957, almost three years before the next election, and Jack, unbeknownst to all but his family and closest advisers, was contemplating a run for the presidency. The accusation that Kennedy had not written *Profiles in Courage* yet had accepted the Pulitzer Prize could be devastating to his yet-undeclared candidacy as it would expose him to the American public as a fraud. And so, with his political career on the line, the would-be candidate sought out the eminent Washington attorney, Clark Clifford.

Clifford had first met Jack Kennedy when the latter was elected to Congress in 1946, and while they had seen each other socially many times, theirs was a casual relationship. In this case familiarity meant less than reputation, and Kennedy called Clifford's office and asked to see him immediately to discuss the matter. Unlike his hot-tempered father, Jack was composed as he explained the situation to Clifford. He confided that he was contemplating a run for the presidency and feared that if Pearson's charge was not refuted it would destroy his viability as a candidate. After telling Clifford his side of the story, Kennedy, ever the deferential son, asked Clifford to call his father. Joe demanded that Clifford take Pearson to court.

Clifford firmly believed that this was the wrong course of action. As satisfying as it might be to win a verdict in court and impoverish their accuser, Clifford believed that the primary objective was to protect Jack and that a protracted legal settlement would be inconsistent with that objective. The prudent course of action, he argued, was to demand and obtain a retraction. Only a retraction would settle the matter in the court of public opinion before the accusation became accepted wisdom and Kennedy's reputation was permanently compromised. A protracted legal battle, however, would keep the story alive in the media and risked an uncertain outcome. Furthermore, even if the case were decided in Kennedy's favor, the public would remain skeptical. Only a retraction would do, and Clifford believed he could obtain one.[3]

Jack believed that Clifford's approach made the most sense, but his father was not thoroughly convinced and planned to keep Clifford on a short leash. Clifford immediately arranged a meeting with Leonard Goldenson, chairman of the ABC television network, which broadcast the Wallace show. Clifford believed it was best to strike while the iron was hot and wanted the retraction issued on the following week's show, scheduled for December 14. The meeting with Goldenson would be two days earlier, on the twelfth, and Clifford planned to spend as much time in New York at the ABC offices as was necessary to secure the retraction. There would be only one opportunity to resolve the issue with the finality required to protect the young senator.

In addition to the short time, the elements were also stacked against Clifford, as a major snowfall was forecast for the day of the Goldenson meeting. Rather than risk a delayed or canceled flight, Clifford took a train to New York the prior evening. Joseph Kennedy, who as a native New Englander might have been expected to plan for the snow, was stranded at home, thus freeing Clifford to negotiate outside the shadow of the elder Kennedy. Clifford and Jack presented their case and gave Goldenson a sworn statement by Sorensen in which he categorically denied being a ghostwriter for Kennedy. After they completed their presentation Clifford issued his retraction demand, and for good measure threatened libel suits against ABC, Wallace, Pearson, and ABC's advertisers if a satisfactory agreement was not reached.

The ABC executives and attorneys were either convinced that Kennedy was in fact the author, or were concerned about being sued and agreed to issue a retraction. Clifford and ABC's lead attorney then met to hammer out and, according to Clifford, strengthen a retraction statement.[4] At the beginning of the December 14 *Mike Wallace Interview Show* an ABC Vice President, Oliver Trayz, read the following statement:

> Last Saturday night, December 7th, on this same program, Mr. Drew Pearson stated that Senator Kennedy's book, *Profiles in Courage*, which won the Pulitzer Prize, was not written by Senator Kennedy but was written by some other person, and that Senator Kennedy had never acknowledged this fact.
>
> As Vice President in charge of the Television Network of the American Broadcasting Company, I wish to state that this company has inquired into the charge made by Mr. Pearson and has satisfied itself that such charge is unfounded and that the book in question was written by Senator Kennedy.
>
> We deeply regret this error and feel it does a grave injustice to a distinguished public servant and author, to the excellent book he wrote, and to the prize he was awarded. We extend our sincere apologies to Senator Kennedy, his publishers and the Pulitzer Prize Committee.[5]

The final retraction statement was close to a handwritten Clifford draft, yet not as strong as Clifford might have wanted. Clifford wanted the retraction to start with the assertion "Mr. Pearson made a false statement, which we deeply regret," but the broadcast statement instead recounted the Pearson allegation. Clifford wanted ABC to acknowledge that Pearson's statement was "wholly false," while the actual retraction stated that Pearson's charge was "unfounded."[6] Rather than haggle over these details, Clifford and Kennedy accepted the retraction as it was ultimately crafted. Accordingly, Clifford and Kennedy signed a release, in consideration of $1, absolving ABC of any further responsibility for the matter. They might not have had to settle for such a paltry amount, however, as JFK received the news just days later that a recent New York state court decision had found that "extemporaneous remarks made over television are libel and not slander."[7] But neither Kennedy nor Clifford was interested in pursuing the matter any further; they were more than satisfied with the outcome.

Kennedy was satisfied with ABC's retraction, but to close the matter he also wanted a retraction from Pearson. After meeting with Kennedy the following month Pearson decided that he would issue a retraction, though he remained somewhat unconvinced. "Unquestionably he did conceive the idea of his book," he confided to his diary, yet Pearson also indicated that he was "still dubious as to whether he wrote too much of it in the final draft himself." Perhaps the hardheaded Pearson was susceptible to Kennedy's charm, as he tacitly admitted to himself, "Sometimes I'm a sucker for a nice guy who presents an appealing story."[8] Later Pearson issued his own retraction: "Said Norman Thomas preaching at All Souls Church the other day: 'It's easy to write about men who are dead. What we need is profiles in courage among men who are living.' Author of 'Profiles in Courage' is Sen. Jack Kennedy of Massachusetts."[9] Yet despite his unequivocal retraction, Pearson silently betrayed his lingering skepticism—he waited more than a month after his meeting with Kennedy to issue his retraction.

As far as Clifford was concerned, Pearson's retraction settled the matter once and for all. "As a result of this public statement by Mr. Pearson," he wrote to Goldenson, "the matter is concluded and you need feel no concern now about the possibility of any action on the part of Mr. Pearson. This is gratifying to Senator Kennedy and me because we were most appreciative of your understanding and cooperation."[10] To Kennedy he wrote, "It is with a very real sense of satisfaction and gratification that I close the file on the Drew Pearson–ABC Network matter. The combination of the complete refutation by the network and the categorical statement in Pearson's column of February 16th should put the matter to rest permanently."[11] Jack was particularly grateful and expressed his gratitude with gift of a Patek Philippe watch.[12]

At least one party to the *Profiles in Courage* incident, however, was highly unsatisfied with the outcome. More than twenty-five years later Mike Wallace was still angry at ABC for giving in to the Kennedys. In *Close Encounters,* his book with Gary Paul Gates, Wallace wrote:

I was furious at my employers for the way they caved in to the Kennedys. . . . [Pearson] was an influential journalist who had made a precise and measured allegation about a specific event in the career of an ambitious politician. And he was an old pro at this game; over the years Pearson had survived several libel suits with his honor intact. As for the Kennedys' libel threat, it would not have taken much fortitude to call their bluff. The last thing in the world they would have wanted was a highly publicized court fight over the question of who had written *Profiles of Courage.* The way I saw it, the ABC apology was a craven gesture and an insult to Pearson.[13]

A year later Clifford met with journalist Stewart Alsop to allay Alsop's skepticism that Kennedy wrote *Profiles in Courage* and was so convincing that Alsop wrote an article in the *Saturday Evening Post* in which he also expressed his belief that Kennedy was in fact the author. Kennedy felt that Alsop's story helped erase any lingering skepticism regarding his authorship. "I noticed in the *Saturday Evening Post* story that Stewart Alsop laid the ghost of the ghost," he wrote to Clifford. "This I know was due to you and once again I have reason to be grateful to you."[14] Clifford wrote back, "It was not only my privilege but my responsibility to stamp out any scurrilous rumor in this regard anytime I encountered it."[15]

Kennedy's critics maintained their skepticism regarding Kennedy and his Pulitzer Prize. His most recent biographer, Robert Dallek, argued that Kennedy deserves more credit than his critics are willing to give him, but less than is ordinarily attributed to the word *author*. According to Dallek, *Profiles in Courage* was the work of a committee.[16] Other Kennedy biographers have been less charitable. Herbert Parmet, author of *Jack: The Struggles of John F. Kennedy,* concluded that Sorensen and Jules Davids, Jacqueline Kennedy's professor at Georgetown University, did most of the research and drafting, and that the accolades Kennedy received were "as deceptive as installing a Chevrolet engine in a Cadillac." Gary Wills concluded that Kennedy was the "author" only in the sense that he "authorized" it and therefore should not have accepted a "writer's" award.[17]

Clifford's satisfactory resolution of Kennedy's *Profiles in Courage* problem cemented their professional and personal relationship and ensured that Kennedy would seek out his counsel again and again as he made his run for the White House and, later, during his presidency. Shortly after the *Profiles in Courage* affair, Kennedy approached Clifford for help with his upcoming speech at the March 1958 Gridiron Dinner. The annual event, an off-the-record gathering of journalists, politicians, and business leaders, was an important event on the political calendar, and Kennedy viewed it as his debut on the presidential stage. Familiar with Clifford's reputation as a "wise crack artist," Kennedy asked him for help preparing comedic material for the speech, a task for which, Kennedy wrote, Clifford was "uniquely qualified to perform." Clifford agreed and assisted Kennedy in his painstaking preparations for the speech, which was a huge success.[18]

The 1960 campaign presented Clifford with an awkward situation. As Kennedy had privately confided after the *Profiles in Courage* incident, he planned to run for president in 1960. Two of the other leading candidates were Lyndon Johnson and Senator Hubert Humphrey of Minnesota. Of the three major candidates, Clifford was close to two of them, Johnson and Stuart Symington. In January 1959 Symington had told Clifford that he too was considering a presidential run and asked for his support, which Clifford willingly agreed to give.[19] Symington, Clifford thought, was everyone's second choice for the presidential nomination, but what Clifford valued most was loyalty. He had been Symington's friend for twenty-five years and would not sacrifice that friendship to support a more expedient choice. When Kennedy asked for his support in the summer of 1959, Clifford informed him that out of loyalty he was bound to Symington. Clifford's strategy was for Symington to stay out of the primaries in the hope that the convention would be deadlocked and Symington would emerge as the untarnished, consensus second choice.

Clifford believed that Symington possessed an inherent advantage relative to the other leading candidates. In his mind, Humphrey was considered to be too liberal and prolabor for conservatives in the party. As a two-time loser Adlai Stevenson, making a third run at the presidency, faced determined opposition from those unwilling to entrust him with the party's nomination again. Ironically, from the standpoint of his later heroic efforts in the cause of civil rights and the establishment of the Great Society, Lyndon Johnson was opposed by what James Reston had termed the "extreme liberals and civil rights missionaries of the Democratic party." And Kennedy was hampered by his Roman Catholic religion. In Clifford's formulation, therefore, the strongest candidate was Symington, "a business man with a prolabor record, a border states politician acceptable to the Northern and Southern wings of the party, a handsome former Air [Force] Secretary," a candidate who wouldn't offend anybody but the intellectuals in the party who were marginalized by their continuing support of Stevenson.[20]

An important audience for Clifford's nobody-but-Symington argument was Governor Edmund G. Brown of California, who was considered a key figure in the race for the Democratic nomination. According to James Reston of the New York Times, Clifford was so effective during his trips to California to meet Brown, other influential state politicians, business leaders, and newspaper editors, it was a surprise that Brown was not endorsing Clifford for the nomination.[21]

In support of the strategy that Symington could successfully exploit his position as everyone's second choice, Clifford also believed that Symington should run a positive campaign. In early 1960 the

*New York Times* observed that in a typical presidential election year, Senate colleagues Symington and Johnson, both unannounced candidates for nomination, would be expected to discreetly attack or undermine the other. Of course that would be difficult to do when Symington's campaign adviser was publicly singing the praises of one of his primary adversaries. "I predict," said Clifford, "that when the history of 1955–60 is written, the towering figure of this period will not be Dwight David Eisenhower. It will be Lyndon Baines Johnson of Texas. The force of his intellect, the power of his personality, will leave an indelible imprint on the century."[22] Clifford's strategy would ensure that there would be no fences to mend between Johnson and Symington, and if Johnson failed to secure the nomination then his supporters would be more inclined to support Symington if there was no bad blood between the two camps. Or perhaps Clifford was simply looking to hedge his bets.

Truman, who supported Symington, echoed the Clifford strategy. Because there was no large group of voters opposed to his candidacy, Symington could ultimately emerge as the consensus candidate even without an enthusiastic following. Truman recalled that he was not the overwhelming favorite candidate in 1948, yet once the nomination was settled the party rallied behind him.[23]

The critical decision of the Symington campaign and the ultimate test of the Clifford strategy was the Indiana primary. As a midwesterner from a neighboring state Symington might have been expected to be competitive in Indiana. Kennedy campaign strategist Lawrence O'Brien believed that his candidate had to win every primary to secure the nomination, so the Kennedy camp was relieved that, "for reasons only known to God," Symington chose not to contest Indiana.[24] Clifford later said that he believed that Symington could not have risked losing a head-to-head contest with Kennedy in Indiana.[25] It is debatable whether Symington was well served by Clifford; Symington's sons believed that Clifford deliberately sabotaged their father's candidacy in order to ensure Kennedy's victory. Charles H. Brown, the chairman of the Symington campaign, blamed "that goddamned Clifford" for keeping Symington out of the Indiana primary. "His advice was just so bad," he complained. According to Clifford, Brown never spoke to him again.[26]

It might, however, have been a sound strategy. Kennedy's campaign team believed that Indiana could become a trap for Symington—if he entered the primary and then lost, it would effectively end his candidacy. As Theodore White observed in *The Making of the*

*President, 1960,* Symington's "inescapable" strategy was to avoid the "fratricidal war of the primaries" and rely on his strength as the perceived safest choice of the Democratic Party power brokers.[27] Hoping to emerge as the safe choice following a deadlocked convention may have been Symington's only strategy, but for Clifford personally, it also happened to be the safest strategy. Yet the accusation that Clifford was looking out for his own interests in the 1960 presidential race rings hollow.

Although Clifford privately had his doubts that Symington could win, he faithfully supported him and resisted Kennedy's attempt, made during the convention, to entice Symington to withdraw by dangling before him the carrot of the vice presidency. Clifford argued that Kennedy had several weaknesses, such as his age, his lack of executive experience, and his religion. He suggested that Kennedy would not fare well with the important Democratic constituency groups of farmers, African Americans, Jews, and southerners. Symington, Clifford pointed out, would be supported by those groups and also possessed the maturity, experience, and national security credentials that Kennedy was lacking. For those reasons, Clifford argued, it would be premature for Symington to withdraw and accept the second spot on the ticket, which Clifford doubted was even a valid offer.[28] If Clifford were looking out for his own interests alone, Kennedy's offer gave him the perfect opportunity. If he could persuade Symington to withdraw, Kennedy would have been indebted to him again. Clifford, however, remained loyal to Symington and refused to counsel his friend to withdraw from the race.

The expected behind-the-scenes maneuvering, as it turned out, was unnecessary: Kennedy won the nomination on the first ballot, even without Symington's delegates. The day after Kennedy won the nomination, he called for Clifford and offered Symington the number two spot on the ticket. Clifford said later that the offer surprised him, yet Kennedy had already confided to him that he favored Symington.[29] There was speculation in the press that Symington was the front runner as Kennedy's running mate. In fact, the front page of the *New York Times* that morning declared that Symington was the "heavy favorite" for the vice-presidential nomination.[30] After discussing the offer with Symington, Clifford phoned Kennedy with the news that Symington had agreed to be his running mate. But it was not to be. During the evening Kennedy had been persuaded by Speaker of the House Sam Rayburn of Texas, among others, that he could not win without Lyndon Johnson on the ticket to carry Johnson's home state of Texas. Kennedy reluctantly agreed and notified Clifford the following day that he must rescind his offer. It turned out to be the right decision, because even with Johnson on the ticket Kennedy barely won Texas and thus the election.

Perhaps as a minor consolation prize in lieu of the vice presidency, Kennedy asked Symington to chair an advisory committee to provide him with recommendations for reforming the military. The choice of Symington was based upon more than mending political fences, however. Symington had sent a military reorganization bill to the Senate Armed Services Committee in 1959, but it was never acted upon.

Clifford's loyal support for Symington did no damage to his relationship with Kennedy. A few weeks after the convention Kennedy asked Clifford to meet him for breakfast at his home in Georgetown. Perhaps looking to charm or flatter Clifford, Kennedy asked him to tell him all about the last great Democratic presidential victory. For the next two hours they discussed the 1948 campaign. Then Kennedy shifted topics and asked Clifford to take on an assignment. As a result of the Twentieth Amendment, ratified in 1933, only ten weeks would be available for executing the transfer of power from the outgoing presidential administration to the incoming one. Since 1933 only one transfer of power from one party to the other had taken place, and by all accounts the 1952 transition had been a disaster. In the interest of avoiding a repeat of that turbulent transition, the Brookings Institution had set up a committee to study presidential transitions. James Rowe, the author of the 1948 campaign strategy and now a fellow of the Brookings Institution, recommended that Kennedy dedicate someone outside the campaign to the transition effort, and he asked for that individual to represent Kennedy on the committee. Rowe recommended a few individuals for the job, but Kennedy preferred someone he knew and with whom he was comfortable. His first choice was James M. Landis, who had advised Kennedy of the New York State court libel decision during the *Profiles of Courage* matter. Rowe, however, thought Landis had insufficient experience with the executive branch, so Kennedy chose Clifford.[31]

In order to ensure that he received more than one opinion, Kennedy also asked Columbia political science professor Richard Neustadt, who had recently published the highly acclaimed book *Presidential Power: The Politics of Leadership,* to prepare an advisory memorandum for the transition. Kennedy asked Neustadt to work independently of Clifford. "When you finish," he said, "I want you to get the material back directly to me. I don't want you to send it to anybody else." Concerned about undermining Clifford, Neustadt asked, "How do you want me to relate to Clark Clifford?" Kennedy responded, "I don't want you to relate to Clark Clifford. I can't afford to confine myself to one set of advisers. If I did that, *I* would be on *their* leading strings."[32]

The transition assignment was important, but the first order of business was to win the election. Kennedy would be opposed by Richard Nixon, and the specter of a Nixon presidency galvanized the Democrats in a concerted effort to take back the White House. As a key strategist of the last Democratic victory Clifford was asked to assist in the effort, and his first order of business was to line up Truman's support. Truman had supported fellow Missourian Symington during the primaries, and his opposition to Kennedy had led him to boycott the convention. Truman's fundamental objection to Kennedy was his religion, but he questioned Kennedy's age and experience as well. He was also no fan of Joseph Kennedy. Despite Truman's early hostility to Kennedy, Clifford believed he would come around once Kennedy secured the nomination. Just days after the convention Clifford wrote Kennedy with an offer to enlist Truman's support.[33] On August 20, Kennedy paid a visit to the Truman Library, where he met with the former president. After the meeting Truman predicted a Democratic victory in the fall. Pressed to account for his dramatic change of heart, he shot back that the "Democratic National Convention settled that—and that's all there is to that."[34]

Robert F. Kennedy, who was going to run his brother's campaign, asked to meet with Clifford a few weeks after the convention to discuss Clifford's role during the campaign. Clifford suggested that the campaign needed an independent advisory group comparable to the Wardman Park Group, but Bobby was not enamored with the idea. His brother, however, thought the campaign would benefit from an infusion of energy and ideas from outside the inner circle. "I think we are in pretty good shape for August and September," the candidate wrote Clifford, "but we should come up with some new plans for programs and policy, ideas and speeches for the last four weeks," because, he confided, "I am concerned that our people may be running out of gas by that time." He asked Clifford to meet with his brother-in-law, Sargent Shriver, to discuss the matter further.[35] Shriver was much more receptive to the idea than Bobby, and the resulting group was called the Gore Group, named after one of its members, Senator Albert Gore of Tennessee.

The group comprised Gore, the father of future vice president

Albert Gore Jr.; Senator William Fulbright, the chairman of the Senate Foreign Relations Committee; Congressman Richard Bolling; and Kennedy campaign aide Frederick Dutton. The group served as a team of outside advisers that reported directly to the candidate, primarily on foreign policy matters. The group met regularly, usually at Gore's apartment in the Fairfax Hotel, and at Kennedy's insistence the group met in private.[36] According to Gore the group was effective because it was separate from the campaign. "We would try to detach ourselves from the headline of today, the pressure and emotion of the situation of today, and try to examine the campaign as it would be, likely be, three weeks from now or two months from now." The idea for the Peace Corps, the signature program of the Kennedy administration, came from the Gore Group.[37] In many respects the Peace Corps was reminiscent of Point Four, which, as described earlier, had originated during the preparations for Truman's 1949 Inaugural Address.

The Gore Group provided the Kennedy campaign with advice on a variety of foreign policy issues, including Soviet premier Nikita Khrushchev's September 1960 visit to the United States to attend the opening of the United Nations General Assembly. The Gore Group advised Kennedy to refrain from attacking Eisenhower's foreign policy during Khrushchev's visit; otherwise, it was felt, Nixon would seize the role of "defender of the flag and U.S. honor." Instead, Kennedy should seize the opportunity presented by Khrushchev's visit to issue a call for peace, while focusing primarily on domestic policy issues for the duration of Khrushchev's visit. The group also proposed a nuclear weapons policy that foreshadowed the Nuclear Test Ban Treaty of 1963, specifically a pledge to end atmospheric testing.[38] Cuba would prove to be a constant challenge to Kennedy throughout his presidency, but the Gore Group believed that the problem of Cuba represented an attractive opportunity for the Democratic candidate. Fulbright recommended that Kennedy make a major address on Cuba because he believed the Eisenhower administration was devoid of ideas on the issue. Rather than isolate Cuba, Fulbright recommended that engagement was the best option. Among the ideas he suggested was to encourage the development of a federation of all Caribbean islands, including Cuba. He also recommended U.S. support for desalination projects aimed at curbing the chronic water shortages in the region.[39]

The Gore Group also advised the Kennedy campaign on "bread and butter" domestic issues. Nixon's campaign strategy was to preach about the strength of the economy while accusing those who said otherwise of serving the ends of the communists. In order to counter that line of argument Kennedy needed to "explode the 'prosperity' thesis" and point out that the average person was not doing as well as the average banker, businessman, or manufacturer.[40] When U.S. Housing Administrator Norman Mason announced the first project to be built under a new program of direct loans for housing for the elderly, Clifford was quick to point out that the program was "conceived by Democrats and forced into law by Democrats over strenuous resistance of Republicans."[41]

The televised Kennedy-Nixon debates played a significant role in Kennedy's election, and Clifford and the other members of the Gore Group assisted with debate preparation and postdebate analysis. Following the first debate on September 26, Clifford commended Kennedy for keeping Nixon on the defensive and declared that Kennedy "clearly came out the winner." Clifford argued that Kennedy's strategy should be to highlight policy differences with Nixon, to contrast with Nixon's strategy of emphasizing the difference in means rather than ends. "The goals are very different, and he must not be permitted to create the illusion that you and he are working toward the same end," Clifford wrote. He also advised Kennedy to concentrate on projecting personal warmth during the debates, implying that Kennedy's emphasis on policy acumen and intelligence came at the expense of his charm and personal charisma. "Take advantage of every opportunity to appear with Nixon," Clifford counseled. "You are better than he is."[42] In preparation for the second debate on October 7, Dutton asked Clifford and Gore for help with some of the more difficult issues, including Nixon's charge that Americans would never tolerate a president who apologized to the Russians, Nixon's assertion that there were no fundamental differences in ideology between the parties, Kennedy's experience relative to Nixon's, and strategies for dealing with the irascible Khrushchev. Kennedy's response to the question regarding the propriety of expressing regret for the Paris conference, which had abruptly ended as a result of the U-2 incident, closely followed Clifford's proffered answer.[43]

During the second debate Kennedy suggested that the tiny islands of Quemoy and Matsu, in the Formosa Straits, were outside of the U.S. defense perimeter. By making this declaration Kennedy was serving notice to the Nationalist Chinese leader, Chiang Kai-shek, that the United States would not continue to defend him there and that he should pull his forces back to Formosa, now known as Taiwan. The Eisenhower administration had skillfully managed two separate disputes with China over these islands, and Nixon strongly disagreed with Kennedy's position. As president, Nixon declared, he would not surrender "one free inch of territory anywhere." Before pursuing this line of attack, Kennedy asked the Gore Group for some background on the Quemoy and Matsu issue. Clifford sent the materials to Larry O'Brien two days before the next debate and backed the senator's position.[44] The following day Kennedy attacked Nixon on the issue, declaring in a speech that if elected Nixon would be a "trigger-happy president" who would lead the country into war.[45]

In preparation for the fourth and final Nixon-Kennedy debate, which would focus on foreign policy, Clifford advised Kennedy to emphasize that he was a Democrat and respond with indignation to Nixon's charge that Woodrow Wilson, Roosevelt, and Truman were responsible for getting America into wars. He suggested that Kennedy emphasize his desire for peace and seize the initiative by proposing a foreign ministers' conference for early in 1961. Although the planned debate would focus on foreign policy, Clifford argued that foreign policy and domestic policy were inseparable and recommended that Kennedy reiterate his domestic policies with respect to the economy, education, and health care. As he had done after the first debate, Clifford offered several suggestions with respect to presentation. "Don't be limited by the question," he advised, especially since Nixon had already taken substantial liberties with debate questions in order to emphasize his points. He advised Kennedy to slow down his delivery, use simpler language, give down-to-earth examples more often, and present fewer points but emphasize them more. Finally, he suggested that Kennedy inject more emotion and nonverbal communication into his presentation.[46] Given that the conventional wisdom is that Kennedy won the debates on style more than substance, Clifford's advice was indicative of his strong political instincts.

The 1960 election was agonizingly close. As the returns came in, Kennedy initially built a lead, which slowly eroded as the night progressed. Clifford stayed up late watching the returns on television, but when he retired for the evening the outcome was still in doubt. Clifford slept in the following morning until he was awakened at 10:00 A.M. It was Kennedy, calling from Hyannisport. "Clark," he said, "could you send that takeover memo of yours up here right away? It looks like we're going to need it."[47]

Clifford's memo, which Kennedy had requested just after the convention, was ready for the president-elect. Running twenty-one pages, it was a broad overview of the tasks and potential pitfalls the incoming administration faced, as well as an outline for a legislative agenda. In contrast to Eisenhower, who employed Sherman Adams as a powerful chief of staff, Clifford advised Kennedy to serve as his own chief of staff, just as Truman had done. "A vigorous President in the Democratic tradition of the Presidency," Clifford wrote, "will probably find it best to act as his own chief of staff and to have no highly visible majordomo standing between him and his staff, (and, incidentally, between him and the public). It is important that all the senior professional persons on the staff should have access to the President, and the staff should consist of no more persons than can conveniently have such access on a day-to-day basis."[48] Kennedy apparently agreed with this piece of advice and announced as much on November 21 when he indicated that he would not staff Sherman Adams's position, or any comparable policy-making positions, in his own administration. He also pledged to operate with a much smaller staff than Eisenhower.[49]

Clifford's experience in the Truman administration informed much of the advice he offered Kennedy in the transition memorandum. In addition to advising Kennedy to act as his own chief of staff, Clifford advocated a small staff, just like Truman's. For Clifford, the most important White House position, unsurprisingly, was special counsel to the president, the "key policy post on the staff." Clifford's experience as naval aide was also reflected in the memo, as he described the military, naval, and air force aides as "most useful for ceremonial and housekeeping functions" but alluded to the potential of a larger role as liaison with the Pentagon depending "upon the caliber of the men."[50]

While often critical of the way Eisenhower administered his office, Clifford thought that three new jobs created during the Eisenhower administration merited staffing by Kennedy, most notably the special assistant for national security affairs. The other two positions created by Eisenhower and approved of by Clifford were the staff secretary and the secretary to the Cabinet, who served as the liaison to the Cabinet officers and agencies. Clifford, however, was critical of Eisenhower's viewing the Cabinet as a corporate board of directors who made policy that the president carried out. "This is contrary to every basic concept of the Presidency and should be junked," he recommended.[51]

The most important activity during a presidential transition is staffing the key positions in the executive branch, but Clifford outsourced development of the list of positions to the management consulting firm McKinsey & Company. His discussion of staffing was fairly limited, in places a recitation of the obvious. In the case of the Cabinet, for instance, Clifford noted that the most important posts were State, Treasury, Defense, and Attorney General, all of whom Kennedy should appoint as soon as he could select appropriate candidates. His most substantive advice on this topic was to refrain from making a big show of naming his Cabinet in December, as Eisenhower had done. Clifford argued that Eisenhower took office without an agenda and needed a Cabinet in place to provide the administration with direction. For political reasons, Clifford encouraged Kennedy to promptly name a liaison to the Council of Economic Advisers and the Bureau of Budget. Kennedy had claimed that the economy was slowing during the campaign, so he needed to demonstrate quickly that he was focused on economic issues. Clifford also anticipated that Eisenhower would charge Kennedy with abandoning fiscal restraint in order to fund Kennedy's domestic program.

Clifford was candid regarding the brevity of his memorandum, noting that he intended to present to president-elect Kennedy "a brief summary of the problems that lie ahead and suggestions for their solution" along with an offer to provide more extensive coverage at Kennedy's request.[52] In contrast, the Neustadt memo is far more detailed and contains a much more extensive discussion of the potential pitfalls to be avoided during the transition, especially with respect to the White House staff. Kennedy aide Arthur Schlesinger believed that the two memos complemented each other, as Neustadt viewed the challenges of the transition from an administrative and organizational perspective, whereas Clifford viewed it from a policy context.[53] In some respects, Kennedy preferred Neustadt's approach to Clifford's. In particular, he disliked Clifford's advice that "he see Congressmen all day long. 'I can't stand that,'" he complained to Neustadt. "'Do I have to do that? What a waste of time.'"[54] Compared to the Neustadt memo, Sorensen thought Clifford's was pretty basic. "I am never certain," said a Kennedy staff member, "whether Clifford is a genius in making the complex sound simple or in making the obvious sound profound, but either way he's a genius."[55]

After the election, the Symington Committee on the Defense Establishment presented its report. The committee advocated greater unification of the military, which for Clifford was a continuation of the effort begun during the drafting of the National Security Act of 1947. Having tangled with the Pentagon bureaucracy during the earlier effort Clifford expected intense opposition from the various branches of the military, so he recommended that the committee utilize the classic negotiating strategy of asking for much more than for what they would be willing to settle. To get "half a loaf," he argued, they "needed to ask for a whole loaf." One of the proposals the committee considered, but ultimately abandoned, would have been a visible indication of the military's unification: a single uniform for all branches of the military. Clifford readily conceded that this was a nonstarter. "Well, the navy would have died over that; the marines would have blown up the country before they ever agreed to do that," he later observed. In early December the committee presented its unanimous recommendations, calling for further centralization of power in the office of the secretary of defense. The proposals included granting the secretary of defense authority over a single congressional appropriation to the Department of Defense, rather than separate appropriations to the respective services; abolition of the separate departments of the Army, Navy, and Air Force and their respective civilian bureaucracies; and the creation of a single military adviser to the secretary of defense and president, instead of having the joint chiefs of staff. President-elect Kennedy thanked the committee, but only tepidly endorsed their recommendations. The report was "an interesting and constructive study which I know will be carefully analyzed by the Congress and the incoming administration," he said. But, like many such Washington task forces, the committee's recommendations were not fully implemented or even considered.[56]

Two days after the election Kennedy called Clifford with another assignment. In the interests of a smooth transition Eisenhower called Kennedy and asked who Kennedy's liaison to the White House would be during the transition, and Kennedy immediately chose Clifford. Clifford agreed, but stipulated that he wished to return to private practice after the transition and would not accept a position in the new administration. Clifford was silent as to his motive for forgoing a position in the Kennedy administration, but it would be safe to assume the financial motive was paramount. After eight years with a Republican president the Democrats had retaken the White House. Clifford had strong connections to the incoming administration. His practice had prospered during the Eisenhower years, but there was no doubt the next four or eight years looked even more promising. Furthermore, by assisting with the transition Clifford would garner free publicity, as Drew Pearson sarcastically noted. "Clifford performed his services without compensation from the Government," he wrote. "The sacrifice did no injury, however, to his Dun and Bradstreet rating. It is hard to conceive of a better advertising campaign for a lawyer than national publicity that he was the one who put high Federal officials behind their desks."[57]

Kennedy wasted no time announcing that Clifford would be the liaison with the outgoing Eisenhower administration, and the appointment was received favorably in the press. A profile in the *New York Times* said that "few men in the capital have so broad a knowledge of the inner workings of the White House or of how to propose and enact the liberal program of a Democratic President." James Reston opined that the choice of Clifford was a good one not only because he was an experienced and capable individual, but also because it demonstrated that Kennedy would work to unite the party. He also challenged Kennedy to select the best candidates for his administration, and to follow their advice. "For while Kennedy, like Eisenhower, has talked a lot about mobilizing the best brains of the country," he wrote, "the fact is that no Presidential candidate in history ever mobilized so many brainy characters in his campaign or used them so little."[58] As the transition coordinator a good amount of that responsibility would fall on Clifford's shoulders.

Clifford's counterpart in the Eisenhower administration was Major General Wilton "Jerry" Persons, and the two had their first meeting on November 14, 1960, during which they conferred for almost two and a half hours. The tone set during this first meeting indicated that this transition would be far more cordial and efficient than previous ones. Clifford and Persons agreed that incoming members of the Kennedy administration would have the opportunity to consult with their outgoing counterparts in the Eisenhower administration and that the department heads would prepare briefing papers for their successors. For Clifford the meeting was a bit of a homecoming, punctuated by his presentation of a ten-year-old security pass in order to gain access to the White House.[59]

Four days later Clifford and Persons had a second meeting, and afterward Clifford reported that he was satisfied "with the degree of cooperation we're getting." He also indicated that the first two meetings had been so productive that future meetings would become routine.[60] As the work of transition progressed, the pace became more hectic. Clifford's law office became a temporary base of operations for the incoming administration until they found office space. On November 20 Clifford flew down to Palm Beach, Florida, to spend three days conferring with Kennedy and his closest advisers. Kennedy, Clifford, and Kennedy's inner circle of advisers began the painstaking process of staffing the administration.

While he was down in Florida, Kennedy dispatched Clifford to handle a meeting they both believed the president-elect should avoid.

A group of Louisiana legislators came to Palm Beach hoping to meet with Kennedy to express their opposition to court-ordered school desegregation. Clifford attended the long meeting and sat patiently while the legislators vented their frustration. He took no position himself but promised that he would take their concerns to Kennedy. Kennedy and Clifford decided that the best way Kennedy could avoid getting involved in the issue would be to take the position that he would not comment on a matter before the federal courts. The delegation from Louisiana was not pleased with Kennedy's decision, and indeed this position was politically risky for Kennedy, as a group of anti-Kennedy southerners was threatening to withdraw a sufficient amount of electoral votes from Kennedy before the official electoral college certification of the vote, thus throwing the election to the House of Representatives.[61]

With respect to staffing, the first order of business was to find a spot for Bobby Kennedy. Given the central role Bobby had played during the campaign it was a foregone conclusion that he would be given a prominent spot in the administration. Jack thought that undersecretary of defense was the best position, as it would be a high-profile assignment without being so high as to provoke an outcry over nepotism. Later, after serving under a more experienced secretary of defense, Bobby could assume the top spot in his own right. Alternatively, Kennedy would find a suitable position for his brother within the White House. Joseph Kennedy, however, wanted Bobby to be the attorney general. Jack thought this would be a grave mistake. "I'm just really not comfortable with it," he said. "Bobby's bright and he has been doing a marvelous job as campaign chairman. Bobby hasn't practiced law."[62] Clifford also thought that it would be a mistake to name Bobby attorney general because he believed that the integrity of the office necessitated a nonpartisan figure. During the Truman administration he had seen firsthand the troubles that ensued when the chairman of the Democratic National Committee, Howard McGrath, became attorney general. Furthermore, Clifford had reservations about Bobby's temperament. Compared to Jack, who operated with a stiletto or a scalpel, Clifford thought Bobby worked with a meat axe.[63] Jack thought that Clifford might be able to convince his father of their position, and Clifford agreed to try. He went to New York a few days later to meet with the patriarch of the Kennedy family and made what he believed to be a persuasive presentation. The elder Kennedy allowed Clifford to make his case but was not shaken from his conviction that Bobby had to be attorney general. "Bobby is going to be Attorney General," he responded in the matter-of-fact yet cold tone that Clifford found unnerving.[64] Bobby would indeed be attorney general.

With the attorney general picked, the transition team could focus on the other top spots. The name at the top of every list was Robert Lovett, who had served as secretary of defense, deputy secretary of defense, and undersecretary of state and defense. Kennedy had been prepared to offer Lovett his choice of State, Defense, or Treasury. When O'Brien protested that Lovett was a Republican, Kennedy replied, "I don't care whether a man is a Democrat or an Igorot. I want the best fellow I can get for the particular job."[65] Kennedy asked Clifford to approach Lovett with an offer of secretary of defense, but Clifford did not think Lovett's health would permit such a taxing job. Dean Acheson told Kennedy the same thing when Kennedy paid a visit to ask for help with his choices for State, Defense, and Treasury. He informed Acheson that Clifford would be in New York presenting the job offer to Lovett, which provoked a laugh from Acheson. He told Kennedy that Lovett would never do it. "Anyway," he said, "if you want him why don't you ask him yourself? If you give warning by sending Clark up, the old rascal will have affidavits from every doctor in New York saying that he's going to drop dead." Just as Acheson had predicted, Lovett demurred when Clifford made the offer and said he had to check with his doctors. He came back from Presbyterian Hospital that same afternoon with a letter stating that due to his medical history of bleeding ulcers and the likelihood of future surgery, a high-profile job in Washington was out of the question.[66]

Kennedy refused to give up and decided to follow Acheson's advice, although in reverse. He asked Lovett to come down to Washington for lunch, and Lovett jumped on the first plane. But Lovett resisted Kennedy's charm offensive and said that his ulcer troubles precluded another stint of government service. He did, however, recommend the two individuals who would eventually serve as secretary of state and secretary of defense, Dean Rusk and Robert McNamara. After Lovett declined his offer, Kennedy selected C. Douglas Dillon, who had served as Eisenhower's undersecretary of state, as treasury secretary.

With the key positions of State, Defense, and Treasury staffed, Clifford and the rest of the Kennedy transition team could focus on the remainder of the appointments. One position that Clifford was decisive in filling was the director of the Bureau of Budget. For this position Clifford nominated David Bell, with whom he had worked in the Truman administration. Kennedy's inner circle from Boston considered it an "audacious" choice on Clifford's part, given Bell's youth. At best, they were considering him for associate director, but Clifford nominated him for the top spot and prevailed.

By Christmas, Clifford would report that he was satisfied with the selections for the Cabinet and other senior positions. "I am immensely pleased at the progress that is being made," he wrote Kennedy. "Your Cabinet selections have received universal acclaim and you are off to a wonderful start. All is going smoothly at this end."[67] Not everyone was pleased, however. The hostess of a dinner party that Clifford attended was less than thrilled with the guests with whom she would be socializing over the next four years. She leaned close to Clifford and lamented, "This Cabinet sure doesn't have much glamour." Clifford, however, was thinking about more than dinner parties. "I don't want any mercurial, flashy, brilliant men in there. I want men who can make things run right, men who can carry out the orders of the boss."[68]

During the transition Kennedy had two face-to-face meetings with Eisenhower, a significant improvement from the bad blood that characterized the Truman-Eisenhower transition. The first, on December 6, began with a private meeting between the president and president-elect. Following that meeting Kennedy received briefings from the outgoing secretaries of State, Defense, and Treasury, and Clifford sat in on those meetings as Kennedy's sole aide.[69]

The second meeting of Kennedy and Eisenhower was on January 19, the day before the inauguration. This meeting was confined mostly to a discussion of the most urgent foreign policy issues the new president would be confronted with the following day, most significantly Laos and Cuba. Laos had been a concern since the breakup of the French colonial empire in Indochina and the tentative resolution of the Indochina War as embodied in the 1954 Geneva Accords. In the ensuing civil war the United States sided with the Royal Laotian Government while the Soviets sided with the communist Pathet Lao. During the early weeks of 1961 the Pathet Lao scored some significant military victories, threatening the survival of the Royal Laotian Government. Outgoing Secretary of State Christian Herter indicated it was his opinion that if a political settlement could not be reached, the United States would be forced to intervene militarily. Eisenhower agreed, warning of the threat to Thailand, Cambodia, and South Vietnam if the communists prevailed. Even more ominously, he suggested that if the United States could not convince its Southeast Asia Treaty

Organization (SEATO) allies to participate, then he would be willing, "as a last desperate hope, to intervene unilaterally." On the subject of Cuba, Eisenhower said it was the policy of his government to assist guerrilla forces who were opposed to President Fidel Castro. He also informed Kennedy that the United States was helping to train anti-Castro forces in Guatemala and recommended that these efforts continue.[70] Three months later these anti-Castro guerrillas would be spectacularly defeated at the Bay of Pigs, and Kennedy would have to handle the fallout.

The following day Kennedy was inaugurated, the Camelot era officially began, and Clifford returned to his law practice. As Drew Pearson had predicted, Clifford's service during the transition had done much to increase his stature as a Washington power broker. The day after the inauguration Kennedy appeared at the annual dinner of the Alfalfa Club, a men's-only organization for which Clifford was to be elected president. Kennedy praised Clifford for his service during the campaign and transition and noted that, unlike other supplicants looking for favors from the new administration, Clifford asked for nothing. "All he asks in return is that we advertise his law firm on the back of one-dollar bills," Kennedy joked.[71]

Clifford had stipulated at the beginning of the transition that he would not serve in the administration, but Kennedy did want him to serve, if only in a limited capacity. A couple of days after the inauguration Kennedy called Clifford with a job offer: chief disarmament negotiator with the Soviet Union. During the Eisenhower administration there had been no arms reduction agreements, and Kennedy was looking to jump-start the process. Applying a little presidential persuasion, Kennedy told Clifford that he was having a press conference the next day and hoped to announce the appointment at that time. Clifford promised to discuss the matter with John McCloy, Kennedy's disarmament adviser, but told the president it was questionable whether he could accept the assignment. Kennedy promised not to make any precipitous announcements.[72] Clifford, however, never seriously considered the assignment. By his account he "had no expertise in the field of arms negotiations" and also wanted to establish a precedent in which transition chiefs completed the task at hand and then returned to the private sector.[73] Clifford may have been completely honest in his reasons for turning down the assignment, but it just as likely that he did not want to be away from his law practice while he commuted back and forth between Washington and Geneva.

Clifford was probably just as happy not to serve in the Kennedy administration because it is likely that he would have never achieved as high a stature under Kennedy as under Truman. For one thing, Clifford was fifty-four at the time Kennedy became president, and his age might not have fit in with the youthful, energetic image Kennedy was looking to present in his administration. When Lovett rejected the Cabinet offers he said he could never keep up with "a bunch of forty-year-old touch-football players."[74] The other thing that would have been difficult for Clifford was the unusually close and exclusionary relationship between Kennedy and his inner circle of Massachusetts advisers. As Clifford observed, there was a tendency among the group, especially on the part of Kennedy aide Kenneth O'Donnell, to exclude those they considered outsiders. On more than one occasion O'Donnell prevented Clifford from getting in to see the president to follow up on assignments the president had given him. This problem became so bad that Clifford eventually decided to bypass O'Donnell altogether and schedule meetings with the president directly through Kennedy's secretary, Evelyn Lincoln.[75]

Always one to cultivate an important relationship, Clifford maintained a regular correspondence with Kennedy and liberally applied the type of fawning and flattery for which he was known. In late July 1961, he sent Kennedy a letter praising the president for his first six months in office and requesting an autographed picture. He wrote, "My confidence in your ability to handle the job has grown steadily these last six months, as has my admiration for your courage and fortitude."[76] Two days later he sent Kennedy a letter commending him on his nationally televised speech during the Berlin crisis. "Your speech was magnificent. It was firm without being belligerent and it was realistic without being hopeless or discouraging. You have rendered a great service to the American people and I know they will rally around you."[77] On another occasion he complimented Kennedy on his magnanimous attitude toward his political rivals. He wrote, "I have noted with interest and gratification your attitude, since becoming President, toward those who opposed your candidacy. You have, time and again, changed opponents into supporters." Abraham Lincoln had pledged to make his enemies into friends once he became president, Clifford noted, a not very subtle favorable comparison of Kennedy to arguably the greatest president the country had ever had.[78]

Kennedy, for his part, relied on Clifford's advice and business connections on a variety of issues. When Justice Charles Whittaker retired in the spring of 1962 Kennedy consulted Clifford for help with his first Supreme Court appointment. Bobby Kennedy was strongly advocating William Henry Hastie, who if nominated would have been the first African American on the Supreme Court. Clifford, however, was unimpressed by Hastie's record and believed that Kennedy should make his first appointment solely on merit alone. "I thought it demeaned the court just to reach out and get a black and put him on the court," Clifford said, "like it would demean the court to reach out and get a woman or reach out and get a Jew or a Catholic. I was against all that."[79] Although it was only a year into Kennedy's presidency Clifford was taking the long view and considering how the appointment would shape Kennedy's legacy. In his opinion Truman's appointments were undistinguished, and that represented a black mark on his presidency. Clifford argued that Hastie would be seen as a political appointment, made perhaps as a response to the promise made by Henry Cabot Lodge, Nixon's running mate, that an African American would serve in Nixon's cabinet.[80] Clifford also thought such a choice would especially be a mistake in an election year. Perhaps in a year or two, he suggested, but not now. He also warned Kennedy that the appointment of Hastie would be stalled in the Judiciary Committee, which was chaired by James Eastland of Mississippi. Eastland had advocated the appointment of his friend and college roommate, William Howard Cox, to a federal judgeship. An avowed racist, Cox in open court had referred to black plaintiffs as a "bunch of niggers . . . acting like a bunch of chimpanzees." No doubt Clifford feared that Eastland would make a spectacle of a Hastie nomination.[81]

Kennedy took Clifford's advice, partially. Clifford had recommended Paul Freund, a professor at Harvard Law School, who had also been recommended by both National Security Advisor McGeorge Bundy and Sorensen. Clifford's own name also appeared on the short list.[82] Instead of Hastie or Freund, Kennedy selected Byron White, the deputy attorney general. While Clifford was satisfied that Kennedy had heeded his advice with respect to Hastie, he felt that Kennedy had ignored the spirit of his overall recommendation that the president select the most distinguished candidate available rather than a political choice or someone he knew and with whom he felt most comfortable. In Clifford's estimation White was not sufficiently distinguished, but rather was someone already in Kennedy's administration. In addition, White could be attacked as a political appointment, given that he had been the head of the Citizens for Kennedy organization during the 1960 campaign. "So I felt as though I had labored like in the mountains, do you see," Clifford lamented.[83] But he did not tell Kennedy of his reservations. "The appointment of Byron White has been very well received," he wrote. "A check indicates his confirmation should proceed uneventfully. Your administration is strengthened by it, and I am more convinced of the wisdom of your decision."[84]

Kennedy's administration was also strengthened as a result of a showdown with the steel industry, and Clifford was instrumental in the victory. Roger Blough, the president of U.S. Steel, asked for a private meeting with Kennedy in the spring of 1962. At the meeting Blough notified Kennedy that U.S. Steel was about to announce a price increase of six dollars per ton of steel. The other major steel producers soon followed. Kennedy was shocked and infuriated. He viewed Blough's announcement as a betrayal of an agreement they had just reached. In January 1962, Kennedy had met secretly with Blough; David McDonald, the head of the steelworkers union; and Labor Secretary Arthur Goldberg. The steelworkers' contract was up for renewal, and the union was clamoring for wage increases that Big Steel—the large U.S. steel companies—was resisting. Kennedy feared that a sizable change in steel prices posed a major threat to price stability and was determined to contain wage increases and avert a potential strike, which he believed would be devastating to the economy. During their meeting Kennedy implored the two sides to enter into early negotiations to reach a noninflationary agreement. The negotiations continued into early April, and the result was an agreement that produced a ten cent per hour increase in pension contributions and promises to reduce unemployment among steelworkers in exchange for a hold on wages. Kennedy viewed the price increase as a breach of faith and was determined to use any means available to him to force Big Steel to rescind it.[85] "My father always told me that all business men were sons-of-bitches, but I never believed it till now," Kennedy complained.[86]

The following day, April 11, Kennedy blasted Big Steel in a statement he made at the beginning of a press conference:

> In this serious hour in our nation's history when we are confronted with grave crises in Berlin and South East Asia, when we are devoting our energies to economic recovery and stability . . . and asking union members to hold down their wage requests at a time when wage restraint and sacrifice are being asked of every citizen, the American people will find it hard, as I do, to accept a situation in which a tiny handful of steel executives whose pursuit of private power and profit exceed their sense of public responsibility, can show such utter contempt for the interest of 185,000,000 Americans.[87]

Kennedy brought Clifford into the situation, believing that with his clients in the business world Clifford might be able to convince Big Steel to reverse the price increase. Kennedy told Clifford that Goldberg had been meeting all day with Robert Tyson, the chair of U.S. Steel's finance committee, but the meetings had gone nowhere. He asked Clifford to meet in secret with Tyson before Tyson returned to New York. Clifford and Tyson met that evening at a location out of view of reporters, aboard the U.S. Steel airplane, which was parked at National Airport. Clifford says he was firm with Tyson and told him that Kennedy would use all means at his disposal to force the steel companies to reverse their decision. Tyson protested that there had been a misunderstanding, that U.S. Steel had never promised not to raise prices. Clifford responded that it was only the president's perception of events that mattered, and the president was convinced that he had been double-crossed.[88]

Kennedy then sent Clifford and Goldberg up to New York to meet with Blough, ordering them to stay until they reached a deal. According to Clifford, both he and Goldberg were firm that there would be no compromise and that the president was determined to take any and all steps to force the steel companies to rescind the price increase. Among the threats proffered were tax audits, antitrust investigations, and cancellations of Defense Department steel contracts with all steel manufacturers participating in the price increase. Goldberg recalled the meeting somewhat differently, although he did recall that Clifford warned Blough of possible antitrust investigations. "Mr. Clifford played a conciliatory role in the discussion and seemed to want to probe me as well as the industry to see if further adjustments could be in order," he said.[89]

The tide finally turned against U.S. Steel when word that Bethlehem Steel, the second largest producer, about half the size of U.S. Steel, announced that they would roll back the price increase. At that point Goldberg knew that U.S. Steel would back down, yet he said that Clifford continued to make "mediatory statements," which Goldberg dismissed. "I thought this had gone far enough and now we ought to focus our attention on when U.S. Steel would make its announcement," Goldberg said.[90] Following the meeting Clifford called Kennedy and, quoting Oliver Hazard Perry following a victory over the British during the War of 1812, reported, "We have met the enemy and they are ours. They have capitulated, Mr. President."[91]

While Clifford may have exaggerated his unwillingness to compromise, it is clear that he played a pivotal role in the negotiations with U.S. Steel. Bobby Kennedy recalled that Clifford played an intimate role, although, like Clifford himself, he gave most of the credit to President Kennedy.[92] The president confided to his friend Paul Fay that Clifford's role was pivotal: "If any one person deserves the credit for having the steel companies see the light, it has to be Clark Clifford. Since he represents so many of them here in Washington, he has immediate entrée. Can't you just see Clifford outlining the possible courses of action the Government should take if they showed signs of not moving?"[93]

A contemporary newspaper account described Clifford in the role of the good cop who presented himself as a friend of the steel industry, while at the same time saying that he was one hundred percent in agreement with a president who felt that he had been double-crossed. It also stated that Clifford and Goldberg offered no threats or inducements. Rather, the tactic Clifford employed was to warn of the "abysmal" outlook for the industry if the steel companies persisted with the price increase. The implication, as Clifford framed it, was that the economy as a whole would suffer and the steel industry would be blamed.[94] Of course the contemporary account should be read with some degree of skepticism. Clifford was an inveterate leaker, and it is likely that he was one of the sources of the story and therefore might have influenced how he was portrayed.

A year later Kennedy was confronted with another price increase in the steel industry. This time, however, the risk to the economy was not considered as serious. The increase was announced by the Wheeling Steel Corporation, a much smaller company than U.S. Steel, and it was not followed by others in the industry. The president convened the group that had been so effective in dealing with the last steel crisis, but unlike the prior year he maintained relative silence on the issue. Clifford advised the president against an aggressive response, which he argued had "rankled badly" the first time, and argued that in this case a price increase was justified. Curiously, despite his endorsement of the president's 1962 assault on the industry, he argued that even that price increase was justified. Clifford also warned Kennedy about the perception that the president was singling out the steel industry.[95]

What is most striking in accounts of the 1962 steel crisis is the incongruity between Clifford's telling and the other historical sources. Clifford contends that he was firm with the steel executives, warning them not to cross the president. Goldberg's recollection, however, is that Clifford was far more accommodating, even as the momentum shifted in Kennedy's favor. Clifford's saying in 1963 that the prior year's price increase was "warranted" suggests that he was more conciliatory to the industry than he might have wanted readers of his memoirs to think.

The battle with Big Steel was an example of how Clifford's contacts in the business community were an asset to the president. Clifford's contacts in the press also worked to the president's advantage. In one instance, Clifford's relationships with the press helped keep a damaging story from appearing in the *Washington Post*. The incident involved the Communications Satellite Corporation, or COMSAT, a quasi-private corporation created by Congress with the passage of the Communications Satellite Act of 1962. COMSAT was part of a partnership between government and private industry formed to administer the nation's satellite communications. Kennedy selected Phillip Graham, the publisher of the *Washington Post* and a friend of Clifford, as chairman of COMSAT but asked Clifford to "keep an eye on the operation." Clifford thought it was wise that Kennedy asked him to become involved because, although Kennedy did not know it at the time, Graham had begun to suffer an "emotional erosion," later diagnosed as bipolar disorder.[96] The company itself had been a popular target of liberals since the legislative floor debate; it was accused that COMSAT would rely too much on government outlays for research while the company's shareholders, not the general public, would enjoy the profits. Those same liberals were determined to exercise stringent oversight of the company.

In early March 1963, Clifford phoned a distraught Kennedy. Graham had sent a reporter to Clifford's office with a copy of an article that was to appear in the paper two days later. The article was about COMSAT, and Graham wanted to show it to Clifford as a courtesy before it appeared in the paper. "It's murderous," Kennedy lamented as he tried to figure out a way to keep the article out of the paper. "How do we try to prevent him from doing it?" he asked Clifford. "It would be a hell of a headache for me which may be part of his mixed up purpose, but very bad for the corporation and the directors and everybody." While Kennedy waited on the phone Clifford spoke to Jerry Siegel of the *Post*. "Did they say that he has decided to print it or that he is susceptible to reasoning on it?" Kennedy asked. Clifford continued speaking to Siegel and then reported to the president that Graham was determined to print the story before congressional hearings on COMSAT started that Monday. He promised to read the story, speak to Siegel, and then report back to the president. There is no record of what Clifford said to Siegel, or possibly Graham, but the *Post* did not publish the story.[97]

Clifford refused all offers from Kennedy to serve in his administration, but he did accept a part-time position as a member of the President's Foreign Intelligence Advisory Board (PFIAB). The PFIAB was an organization originally created by Eisenhower, although under a different name, and seemed to be the type of bureaucratic agency that Kennedy would look to eliminate once he was in office. The Bay of Pigs disaster and Kennedy's subsequent loss of confidence in CIA director Allen Dulles, however, convinced Kennedy that he needed an independent assessment of the country's intelligence-gathering activities. "I doubt my Presidency could survive another catastrophe like this," he confided to Clifford, referring to the Bay of Pigs fiasco.[98] With that in mind Kennedy gave the PFIAB a mandate to study the nation's foreign intelligence operations and make recommendations from the standpoint of organization, operations, and budget. Clifford served on the PFIAB, for five years as its chairman. The most noteworthy recommendation made during Clifford's tenure was that the position of director of Central Intelligence be separated from the Central Intelligence Agency, a change not implemented until the aftermath of the terrorist attacks of September 11, 2001.[99]

Clifford became the chairman of the PFIAB in May 1963 following the resignation of James R. Killian Jr. The appointment was met with hostility by the *New York Times,* which believed that Clifford was not suited for the job: "Mr. Clifford has a brilliant mind, but, as a long-time trouble-shooter for the Democratic party, he is inextricably associated with partisan politics. He replaces a skilled and objective scientist-administrator. The selection is at best unfortunate. It is bound to give the impression that our intelligence activities will now be monitored—not by a chairman who is an expert in the field—but by one who is essentially a politician."[100]

Killian rushed to Clifford's defense: "He has staunchly supported the independence of the board and its tough-minded insistence that it be fully informed and free of political or policy influence—an insistence that has been unfailingly honored."[101] Bundy advised Kennedy that Clifford was a good choice, noting that having him succeed Killian was the preference of Clifford's colleagues on the PFIAB. Bundy also thought that Clifford was a good choice because he would work well with the president. "This is one place where we want a man with whom you can work in the closest personal trust, rather than a fashionable piece of window dress which requires constant therapy," he wrote.[102]

Presidential advisory boards often function as window dressing, depending upon the level of commitment from the president and the relative importance of the issues they are assigned. In this case, it is difficult to fully evaluate the significance of the PFIAB because the documentary evidence is not fully available. At the very least, as both a member and chairman Clifford had access to a good deal of classified intelligence material. Not surprisingly, Clifford thought the PFIAB played a very important role in the Kennedy administration. "The board [PFIAB] performed a very useful service," he said. "It was wise to have a board operating directly under the president, looking at our foreign intelligence operations. There had been a lot of free wheeling going on and practically no supervision."[103]

Despite Clifford's long tenure on the PFIAB, his greatest value to Kennedy was not his experience as a member and chairman of that board, but his political acumen. In the summer of 1963, when James Landis ran into some difficulties because of unpaid taxes, Kennedy consulted Clifford on how the situation should be handled. At the time Landis was working in the private sector as an attorney, but he had served as special counsel to Kennedy back in 1961 and had also served in the Roosevelt and Truman administrations. The problem for Kennedy was that Landis had not filed a tax return in five years and, although he had finally paid the back taxes, the issue was whether he should be prosecuted. Clifford believed that there were two arguments for not prosecuting: Landis's voluntary disclosure to the Internal Revenue Service and payment of back taxes, and what Clifford described as both a drinking problem and "psychiatric disturbances." However, Clifford was concerned that if Landis were not prosecuted and Kennedy attempted to bury the story, it would come back to haunt him. Therefore, he believed that Kennedy had no choice but to prosecute. Bobby Kennedy, the attorney general, sharply disagreed with Clifford, but in this case Clifford was persuasive. Landis was indicted and pled guilty a week later.[104]

The Landis matter was not the only occasion where Clifford and Bobby Kennedy took opposing sides. Another occasion concerned conflict-of-interest allegations against Fred Korth, the secretary of the Navy. Korth had been president of Continental National Bank of Fort Worth before joining the government, but while serving as Navy secretary he had continued to take an active role in bank matters. The actions Korth took on behalf of the bank were extensively documented in a series of letters, all on his Navy stationery. In one instance he had invited some of the bank's most important clients for an evening cruise on the Navy yacht *Sequoia*. He also arranged an appointment with naval procurement officers for a Houston company, a Continental National client that wanted to do business with the Navy. Bobby Kennedy thought that Korth's continuing involvement in the bank was inappropriate and believed that the letters could be especially embarrassing to the administration. Bobby believed that Korth should resign even though his actions did not constitute a direct conflict of interest, whereas Clifford believed he should not resign. In this case, Bobby's recommendation prevailed. Following his resignation, Korth returned to Continental National.[105]

The Blauvelt affair was an episode in which the personal became political. In this case, Clifford was called in to help the president contain the damage caused by an erroneous record in an obscure family genealogy. An unexplained error in a privately published family genealogy indicated that the president had been married to a woman named Durie Malcolm, whom Clifford had known socially when he lived in St. Louis. An unknown individual had passed the information to a few reporters, and the rumors started to circulate in Washington and in a few minor publications. Kennedy called Clifford in early 1962 and asked him to help contain the story. Clifford, after having discussed the matter with Kennedy, was satisfied that the rumor was false. He then called Malcolm who, while flattered, assured Clifford that the rumor was indeed false. She corroborated Kennedy's account that they had casually dated but denied that they ever had a serious relationship, much less that they had married. The story lingered throughout the year, kept alive in right-wing publications, until it was picked up nationally in September. A September 19 article in the *New York Times* reported that the newspaper had first heard the story in August 1961, but had concluded that the rumors were false. However, when a letter to *Parade,* a nationally circulated Sunday newspaper supplement, appeared asking whether the rumors were true, the *Times* decided it had to run a story. The story, which mirrored a similar account in *Newsweek,* concluded that the rumor was groundless.[106]

In addition to Clifford's role as an informal presidential adviser he also represented the Kennedys in several legal matters and assisted Jackie Kennedy in her endeavor to refurnish the White House. Clifford developed a close relationship with the first lady, which began when he represented them in a real estate matter. The Kennedys were interested in obtaining a weekend residence in the Virginia countryside and fell in love with a four-hundred-acre estate named Glen Ora.

Unfortunately for the Kennedys the owner, a widow named Gladys Tartiere, did not wish to sell or rent the property to them. Not to be dissuaded, Jackie asked Clifford to speak to Ms. Tartiere again, and again. According to Clifford, he promised the owner that if the Kennedys rented the property they would take good care of the house and would return it in better shape then before, but she still refused. He then tried again, and was this time apparently successful, by making the absurd argument that for national security reasons it was important that the Kennedys be allowed to rent the estate. Only during a time of heightened Cold War tension could such an argument be effective, but Clifford claimed that the nation would be more secure if the president had a retreat from the burdens of his office.[107] The evidence suggests, however, that Clifford was willing to use more than hollow appeals to patriotism to secure what his client wanted. Clifford's papers contain a handwritten set of notes in which he formulated his strategy, including the sympathy appeal that Kennedy needed the house as a retreat. Following that were the more conniving suggestions to "get something on her" or "bribe her" with a job for her son or a committee appointment for her.[108] In any case, Tartiere agreed to rent the property to the Kennedys for a year.

It is not clear which of Clifford's arguments was the persuasive one, but a drawing found in Clifford's papers suggests that he was willing to use either the carrot or the stick. Jackie had been so grateful to Clifford for obtaining the property that she drew Clifford a picture as a thank-you note. The caption at the top of the drawing reads "The Legal Profession" and the bottom "Establishing a Relationship." The picture itself depicts a smiling, wavy-haired, elegantly dressed Clifford carrying flowers and a bottle of champagne in one hand. All very charming, but the other hand is holding a briefcase with documents entitled "List of Jails," "Tortures," and "Places of Exile." (Clifford said the picture showed him going to "beard" the landlady.) Tartiere is seen in the background, pushing aside a curtain to watch Clifford as he approaches the house. She is depicted not quite in Edvard Munch style, but not in a flattering way either. Clifford described the drawing as the "most treasured 'payment'" he ever received from a client, but is silent as to whether Jackie meant it to be tongue-in-cheek. When their lease expired, Tartiere told the press that she was sorry to see the Kennedys go.[109]

Clifford assisted the Kennedys with their purchase of a home in Atoka, Virginia, to replace Glen Ora. As it was a relatively ordinary real estate matter, although one involving a year-long effort to secure the easements necessary to ensure ingress and egress to the estate,

Clifford staffed it out to one of his firm's associates, Sam McIlwain. Although the transaction itself was simple, the fact that the client was the president of the United States meant that Clifford would have to make sure to avoid anything that could be politically embarrassing. Accordingly, both McIlwain and Clifford advised the Secret Service that no government funds should be spent building the necessary access road to the estate.[110]

Jackie Kennedy was grateful for Clifford's help with the family's real estate matters, but it was his collaboration with her on the White House renovation project that brought them close together. Undeniably, Jacqueline Kennedy brought an element of glamour to the White House by her very presence. When she first moved into the White House, however, she was unimpressed with the surroundings. Much of the décor was rather undistinguished, and the interior was, by her standards, run down. In particular, she was struck by the absence of furnishings of historical importance. With that observation, Jackie began a project to transform the White House into the "First House in the Land." As her plans began to take shape it was clear that the effort would cost several million dollars and provoke a public backlash. Undeterred, she formulated a plan to raise the necessary funds from private donations. In order to ensure that she would not run afoul of the law or political pitfalls, she asked Clifford to come to lunch with her to discuss it.

"Clark," she asked, "how many people go through the White House every year?"

Clifford wasn't sure. "A lot," he answered. "Maybe one or two million. I think I could find out. But why do you want to know?"

Jackie stayed on the offensive. "Before I answer your questions you answer mine," she responded. "Do any of these leave money at the White House?"

"No. The White House is public property," Clifford answered. "People don't pay to go on tour. Why should they?"

"They shouldn't," said Jackie. "But we should make available something tangible that they can buy as a memento. We could use the money because, in effect, my goal is the make the White House 'the First House in the Land.'"

"Well, that's certainly a laudable goal," Clifford responded, perhaps patronizingly. "I've read about your renovation project, Jackie, and I'm all for it. I'll continue to think about it."

"Don't let's think about," Jackie replied. "Let's do something about it."[111]

Clifford was cautious, recalling the furor that greeted Truman when he authorized the addition of a balcony, forever known as "Truman's Balcony," to the south portico. "You just can't make any changes in the White House," he cautioned.[112]

Jackie's idea was to create a guidebook, the sales of which would be used to fund the renovations. Clifford thought the idea for the guidebook was a good one and, with his law partner, Carson Glass, created a legal entity that could realize the First Lady's dream. With the assistance of Deputy Attorney General Nicholas Katzenbach, a bill was drafted and passed that made the White House a part of the National Park Service. Once that was completed, Clifford and Glass incorporated the Fine Arts Commission for the White House. At that point, they were open for business. Jackie was ecstatic. "At last the guidebook is a reality!—and I can never thank you enough for all you did to make it possible," she wrote to Clifford.[113]

Clifford continued to provide legal advice and serve on the board for the White House Historical Association. Clifford and Jackie Kennedy developed a close relationship as a result of their involvement in the White House renovations, and there were rumors that the relationship was more than platonic. According to Truman Capote, Jackie was never unfaithful to Jack, but she did carry on an affair of the imagination with Clifford, among others. There is no evidence that Clifford had an affair with Jackie, but it is mildly intriguing that Clifford destroyed much of her correspondence. As Carson Glass recalled, "She also used to write verbose instructions to Clark Clifford, full of items on which she wanted his advice, but he destroyed all of these. I could have killed him. The historical content alone would have been invaluable, but he didn't want to keep the letters because they discussed friends."[114]

Much has been written about the myriad of tragedies that befell the Kennedy family over the years. In August 1963, the Kennedys suffered the death of their baby, Patrick Bouvier Kennedy, who had been born prematurely. The Kennedys mourned, and the nation mourned along with them. "You have been much in my thoughts lately," Clifford wrote to the president. "I just wish it could have happened to me instead of to you."[115]

A few months later the Kennedy family, and the nation, would suffer an even more devastating loss. An assassin's bullet took the life of the young president on November 22, 1963. Clifford was at the White House chairing a meeting of the Foreign Intelligence Advisory Board that day, and was in the cafeteria eating lunch when the news came in.

Initially reports indicated that Kennedy had been wounded, and not seriously. That first erroneous report was soon corrected, leaving all assembled in a state of shock. Clifford wrote that he lived through the events of the next few days, including the funeral services, in a state of numbness. He received a personal sympathy note from his friend Benjamin Bradlee, the Washington bureau chief for *Newsweek*. "He admired you so, Clark," he wrote. "I can remember a recent night, when he suddenly asked me: 'You know who's the greatest advocate I ever knew? Clark Clifford.'"[116]

Clifford felt the loss personally. Months later he was still holding on to the memory of the president. In April 1964 he wrote a letter to Evelyn Lincoln, Kennedy's secretary, asking for a list of the president's favorite books. "I thought I would start in and read all of them over the next few months," he wrote in reply to the list she provided. Clifford's request was sincere: he wrote several letters to booksellers trying to track down items on the list, not all of which were readily available. "I miss him greatly," he confided to Lincoln.[117] But the truth was that in the months since the assassination Clifford had little time to devote to grief. Just days after Kennedy's funeral a call came in from the White House. The new president wanted to see him.

# 9

# This Could Be a Quagmire

It was not a foregone conclusion that one of the first persons President Johnson would seek out was Clifford. The two had known each other for years, back to the days when Johnson was an occasional participant in Truman's poker games. While Clifford served Truman his relationship with Johnson was cordial, but not especially close; once Johnson became Senate minority leader, however, he began to call on Clifford with greater frequency. First and foremost Johnson was a legislator. He was drawn to Clifford's White House experience, political instincts, and Washington contacts, especially Senator Robert Kerr of Oklahoma. The correspondence between Clifford and Johnson is typical of the type of relationship nurturing that Clifford was adept at, as, for example, an August 1958 letter to Johnson, in which Clifford writes: "Dear Lyndon, I'm bursting with pride over the magnificent job you did in this Congress. When I contemplate what would have happened up there without you it makes me believe that a beneficent God has an interest in our destiny." Clifford recalled his relationship with Johnson as the typical Washington friendship: they saw each other socially, with spouses, a few times a year, but it never developed into anything close.[1]

In 1963, however, just days after he took the oath of office, Johnson called Clifford and asked him to come over to the White House. During a wide-ranging discussion that lasted more than four hours Clifford offered his insights regarding how Johnson should make the transition from the Kennedy administration to his own. The only other person in attendance at this meeting was Supreme Court Justice Abe Fortas, who was perhaps Johnson's closest confidant. In what would become a pattern throughout his administration, Johnson frequently brought Fortas and Clifford together when he had a difficult decision to make. Johnson relied on Clifford to such a great degree that he called him five to ten times a day and would often ask if Clifford could join him in the Oval

Office. Of course Clifford never declined a request from the president; if he was meeting with an important client, he would apologize and excuse himself with the announcement that the president was calling.[2] For someone who relied on influence to the extent that Clifford did, it is likely that these interruptions were welcome, rather than a burden. In fact, these interruptions probably helped, rather than hindered, his law business.

During Johnson's first year as president Clifford helped him navigate two very sensitive personnel matters. The first was what to do with Bobby Kennedy. Tensions between the two had been present since the 1960 Democratic convention and Johnson's politically expedient selection as vice president. Bobby had strenuously opposed the choice, and Johnson, a proud man, had never gotten over this initial rejection. Bobby's emotional response to his brother's assassination and his inability to accept Johnson as president only compounded the difficulties. "It seemed to irritate Bobby Kennedy when he saw President Johnson as President," Clifford recalled. "His attitude was almost—and I think to a certain extent the attitude of the Kennedy family—was that President Johnson was an interloper of some kind."[3] Johnson also feared the younger Kennedy, at least in the sense that he feared that Bobby would succeed him as president and that he would forever be overlooked as a caretaker, sandwiched between the two Kennedys.

As the 1964 Democratic convention approached Johnson obsessed over how to dismiss the Kennedy issue, especially given that a newspaper editorial campaign was under way urging Johnson to select Bobby as his running mate. While discussing the matter with Clifford the two of them decided on a strategy for eliminating Kennedy from consideration, hopefully without antagonizing his supporters: Johnson would announce that it would be best not to select any member of the Cabinet as his running mate. As it turned out, no one was fooled by this strategy—although, as Clifford pointed out, there had been stories in the newspapers suggesting that Secretary of Defense Robert McNamara and Secretary of Agriculture Orville Freeman, in addition to Kennedy, were possible candidates for the vice presidency.

The other personnel matter concerned longtime Johnson aide Walter Jenkins. Jenkins had been Johnson's closest and most loyal adviser for twenty-five years, but he kept a secret from his boss—a secret that came out at a most inopportune time for the president. Jenkins was a homosexual at a time when homosexuals were forced to hide their sexual orientation. Weeks before the 1964 election Clifford received a call from Fortas asking for his help with an urgent problem, which he refused to discuss over the phone. They agreed to meet, at which point Fortas explained the situation. Jenkins had been arrested a week earlier at a known gathering place for homosexuals in Washington (homosexuality was at the time illegal in Washington). Clifford and Fortas sprang into damage control mode and made the rounds of the local newspapers, trying to contain the story, to no avail. Jenkins was quickly checked into a hospital for psychiatric help and thus partially shielded from press scrutiny, but the damage was done. In addition to homosexual activity being a virtual taboo and a crime, homosexuals were also perceived as a national security risk, on the assumption that they were susceptible to blackmail. Johnson conferred by telephone several times with Clifford and Fortas on the problem, and Clifford recommended that the White House release a statement for the morning papers announcing Jenkins's resignation, without elaborating on the reasons why. Johnson suggested that the White House explain, off the record, that "every family has some problem and we regret it very much but we don't think we can add anything to it." Clifford thought this would be a grave mistake. "No. . . . Every family has problems, but don't happen to have *this* kind. And I believe it would not be wise to attempt to deprecate it. I think that might play into their hands. I think that this is clean and clear-cut, and I believe, by God, it's about all that can be said." With only weeks until the election, Johnson took the difficult step necessary to minimize the political fallout and requested Jenkins's resignation. After that, Johnson never spoke of him again. "It was just as though the book was closed on it," Clifford recalled.[4]

The tragedy of Lyndon Johnson was that despite his many legislative accomplishments in civil rights, health care, and antipoverty programs, his administration is best known for the quagmire that was Vietnam. Yet it was in this arena, both as an informal adviser to Johnson and ultimately as secretary of defense, where Clifford distinguished himself. With but one exception, Clifford was the lone voice in the Johnson administration speaking out against the war.

In March 1965 the first combat troops were dispatched to Vietnam: two battalions, or about 6,000 men. The troops were sent to protect the air bases from which U.S. forces were unleashing the bombing campaign known as Rolling Thunder. General William C. Westmoreland, commander of the U.S. forces, requested that the president provide him with ground forces with which to pursue the enemy. Clifford was one of the few opponents of escalation who had any access to the president. On May 17 he sent Johnson a letter in which he argued against committing ground troops:

> I believe our ground forces in South Vietnam should be kept to a minimum, consistent with the protection of our installations and property in that country. My concern is that a substantial buildup of U.S. ground troops would be construed by the Communists, and by the world, as a determination on our part to win the war on the ground.
>
> This could be a quagmire. It could turn into an open ended commitment on our part that would take more and more ground troops, without a realistic hope of ultimate victory.[5]

Johnson never replied, which would suggest that he dismissed Clifford's warning, yet a few months later he called on him again. Although it wasn't yet the quagmire that Clifford predicted, the commitment became more open ended after the initial two battalions were dispatched. McNamara returned from a visit to Vietnam with a request from Westmoreland for an additional 100,000 men. On July 21 Johnson convened his foreign policy team to discuss the request, and while the meeting was in progress asked for Clifford to come over. One hundred thousand men, or thirty-two battalions, was a substantial troop request, but Westmoreland was also asking for more men for the following year, 1966, as well as permission to expand the bombing of North Vietnam. When Clifford arrived at the meeting and quietly observed the proceedings, he found that virtually everyone in the room was inclined to support the request for additional forces and the implicit change in policy. The lone dissenter was Undersecretary of State George Ball. Ball strenuously argued that Vietnam would become a "protracted war with large casualties." Whereas McNamara, Secretary of State Dean Rusk, National Security Advisor McGeorge Bundy, and others framed Vietnam as a Cold War test of American resolve, Ball turned the argument on its head and predicted that neither the Russians nor the Chinese would tolerate a U.S. victory within their sphere of influence. He also cautioned that U.S. troops were not adequately trained in jungle combat. Echoing Clifford's argument from May, Ball warned that an increase in troops would inevitably result in a long-term commitment. Instead of agreeing to additional troops, Ball advocated planning to withdraw completely.[6]

The meeting resumed the next day, and again Clifford was asked to attend at the president's request. Uncertain of his role, and perhaps mindful that the president had not responded to his May memorandum, Clifford opted to continue as a silent observer. He did, however, pose a question to General Earle Wheeler, the chairman of the Joint Chiefs of Staff: "If the military plan is carried out, what is the ultimate result if it is successful?" Wheeler replied with the formulaic answer that the objective was a sovereign South Vietnam and that he expected that the United States would be able to withdraw most, but not all, of its troops.[7] No doubt convinced that he had an ally in the room, Ball asked to speak with Clifford privately after the meeting adjourned. "You have said the only sensible thing I have heard said by anybody in that group for a very, very long time," Ball said to Clifford. "I can only tell you that you and I are in total agreement on this, and I think that your influence with the President is tremendously important." Ball asked Clifford to read a recent series of memoranda he had sent the president, assuming that Clifford had the appropriate security clearance. Clifford replied that he did indeed have the requisite security clearance as a member of the President's Foreign Intelligence Advisory Board (PFIAB) and promised to safeguard the documents.[8]

Before Clifford could leave the White House he was summoned to see the president in the Oval Office. Johnson, who was with Bundy, wanted Clifford's impressions of the meeting. Clifford indicated that he needed time to reflect on what he had heard, and perhaps read Ball's memoranda; however, he was clearly troubled with a military commitment to a war that seemed unwinnable. Clifford studied the memoranda until two o'clock in the morning and found Ball's arguments "impressive and persuasive." Ball's analysis confirmed Clifford's suspicions, and he became more determined to do all that he could to convince Johnson not to head down a path he believed was fraught with danger.[9]

Johnson asked Clifford to come out to Camp David for the weekend, along with McNamara, for one final meeting before the president made his decision. Thus the stage was set for a showdown with McNamara, eerily similar to Clifford's showdown with George Marshall over Israel seventeen years earlier. Back in 1948, however, Clifford knew that Truman was sympathetic to his position. This time he believed that Johnson had all but made up his mind to approve the troops. Nonetheless, Clifford immersed himself in preparation for the meeting, knowing full well that his powers of persuasion were the last thing standing in the way of a dramatic military escalation in Vietnam.

The group that flew out to Camp David with Johnson included Clifford, McNamara, Senator Birch Bayh, White House staffers Jack Valenti and Horace Busby, and Arthur Goldberg, the Supreme Court justice and soon to be U.N. ambassador. The guests and their wives enjoyed a relaxing Saturday afternoon and dinner that evening. The next day, at 5:00 P.M., Johnson began his meeting with Clifford and McNamara by asking for Clifford's opinion of a proposal to bring the Vietnam issue to the United Nations. Clifford quickly dispensed with the suggestion and moved on to his presentation. It was a mistake, he argued, to substitute the South Vietnamese army with the U.S. army, as it would inevitably lead to a long-term commitment of troops. Next, Clifford contrasted the blatant aggression of the Korean War with the far more ambiguous circumstances in Vietnam. Although the two wars were quite different, Clifford warned that China was likely to intervene, as it had done in Korea, to prevent a U.S. military victory. For good measure, he also predicted that Russia would provide aid and assistance to their Asian proxy.[10]

Recognizing Johnson's proclivity to personalize everything, Clifford suggested that it was no one's fault that the current policy in Vietnam had failed. The bombing of North Vietnam might have worked, he said, but it didn't. Clifford also addressed Johnson's concern that a failure to confront communism in Vietnam would weaken U.S. credibility elsewhere. In fact, he argued, investing America's prestige in a lost cause would be far more damaging to U.S. credibility. Attempting to frame Vietnam within the larger struggle against communism, Clifford cautioned Johnson that he would need to pick and choose his battles. "This is not the last inning in the struggle with communism," he warned. Clifford also attempted to make Johnson consider the outcome of a protracted war in Vietnam. He questioned whether a victory would be worth the cost. "If we win—what have we won?" he asked rhetorically. Far more tragic, Clifford added, would be the possibility that the United States might actually lose.[11] With uncanny prescience, Clifford proffered what must have seemed to Johnson like a nightmare scenario, but one that turned out to be frighteningly accurate. "If we send in 100,000 more, the N VN [North Vietnamese] will meet us. If the N VN run out of men, the Chinese will send in volunteers. Russia and China don't intend for us to win the war. If we don't win, it is a catastrophe. If we lose 50,000+ it will ruin us. Five years, billions of dollars, 50,000 men, it is not for us."[12]

The U.S. eventually retreated from Vietnam in 1973 after suffering more than 58,000 casualties.

After Clifford finished, McNamara made his case, at which point Johnson abruptly brought the meeting to a close. Then the president spent some time alone, no doubt pondering all that he had heard over the past few days.

The meetings resumed the next day, a Monday, back in Washington, with the full foreign policy team, and again Clifford had an opportunity to present his case. "We cannot win the war in S VN [South Vietnam]," he warned. "China and Russia don't intend for us to win the war. They will match us in manpower. No matter how many men we send, they will match us." He also warned that the political outcome would be disastrous. "This war is going to destroy this administration. If things go on as they're going now, and we keep escalating this thing, the American people aren't going to accept it." Clifford recommended that the monsoon season provided an opportunity to curtail the hostilities and seek out a resolution. "I don't believe we will suffer prestige if we can't sustain," he suggested.[13]

Clifford believed that Johnson had already made up his mind and that he was given an opportunity to speak merely so that the president could say he had listened to both sides. The fact that no one engaged in the argument, which Ball considered an "embarrassment," suggests that Clifford assessed the situation correctly.[14] After he was done speaking Ball slipped him a note. "Clark, I'm glad to have such an eloquent and persuasive comrade bleeding on the same barricade. I thought your statement was great," he wrote.[15]

Clifford and Ball's lonely stand at the barricade was not enough, however, and Johnson approved the troop request, initiating a major change in policy and setting the stage for the biggest military failure in U.S. history.

Despite his opposition to the war Clifford publicly supported the president after the decision had been made, and most observers classified him as a hawk. Clifford explained in his memoirs that "once the President had committed us in Vietnam, I would generally support actions that I hoped would shorten the war or minimize American losses." He also provided two other reasons why he abandoned his initial opposition to the war. He questioned his intuitive opposition to the war in contrast to the foreign policy experts in the administration, who had far more knowledge of the situation in Vietnam, and who supported the policy. He also claimed that as a member of the PFIAB and Johnson's inner circle, he was privy to and duped by the overly optimistic reports from the military.[16]

Another possible explanation for his subsequent support for the war—one that Clifford did not admit—was his desire to remain in Johnson's good graces. Clifford relished his access to the president, and while he was never someone who could have been labeled a "yes-man," he also did not want to jeopardize his relationship with Johnson. Clifford was well aware of Johnson's insecurities and volatile temper, especially toward his subordinates, and he must have understood that Johnson would stop calling if he continued to criticize the president's policy.

A few months later Clifford was asked to make a trip to Vietnam to evaluate firsthand the effects of the bombing and military campaign. While meeting with U.S. military officials there, Clifford stressed the president's need for accurate information concerning the attitude of the Vietcong and their willingness to continue fighting, the impact of the bombing on both the North Vietnamese leadership and the general public, and the reaction and intentions of the Chinese with respect to Vietnam. "In addition, I had an excellent opportunity to get a much better 'feel' of the entire situation," he wrote.[17] Unfortunately for Clifford, a story that ran in the *Los Angeles Times* shortly after he returned reported that then–Harvard political scientist Henry Kissinger and Clifford were dismayed by the attitude of South Vietnam's political leadership. Clifford denied the story, as did the White House, which released a statement claiming that Clifford had not been sent to Vietnam by Johnson.[18] Johnson, who despised leaks, was furious and took Clifford to task, but Clifford continued to deny that he had anything to do with the story.

The American forces won their first major victory in November 1965 at Ia Dreng, near the border of Laos. The battle seemed to affirm Westmoreland's search-and-destroy strategy, and the general confidently went on the aggressive. In order to pursue his strategy he would need more men, a staggering increase to 400,000 troops by December 1966 and an additional 200,000 the following year. This total—600,000 troops—represented a level of escalation that almost made the July argument for the first 100,000 seem beside the point. McNamara began to have his first doubts about Vietnam, doubts that would fully form over the next two years. In particular, he was concerned that 600,000 troops would invite Chinese intervention. Before agreeing to a level of escalation of that magnitude, McNamara believed that an attempt at diplomacy should first be made. Accordingly, he suggested a bombing pause of about three to four weeks to probe North Vietnam's intentions.[19]

Clifford met with a group including Rusk and McNamara on

December 6, 1965, to discuss Westmoreland's request. When he first heard about the troop request he was incredulous. "Where the Hell [are we] going?" he asked, then offered his own pessimistic answer. "Further [and] further in with no prospect of a return." This is the type of war Mao would have us fight, warned Clifford, and he pleaded for a military strategy that played to America's strengths. "Can't we use air power," he asked, and instead use combat troops for defensive purposes.[20]

As far as the Christmas bombing pause, as it came to be known, Clifford was basically opposed to it. His stance in opposition to this pause in bombing was perhaps the single biggest reason why he was long considered a hawk on Vietnam. Clifford maintained that once the decision was made to go to war he was determined to do anything that would bring the war to a successful conclusion as soon as possible, and that was why he was against the idea of a pause.

Johnson's first meeting on the subject took place on December 18, 1965, with Clifford and Fortas in attendance. When it was Clifford's turn to speak, he expressed his opposition:

> The arguments of the pause are well presented. Even if I accepted them, I still feel deep concern over this move.
>
> One, I have tried to figure out the circumstances under which Hanoi would talk. It is only their belief that they are not going to win the war in the South. I don't believe they are at that stage now. I think they believe they are *not* losing. They are sending large numbers of men down. They have the example of the French before them. They believe that ultimately the U.S. will tire of this and go home and the North will prevail. Until they know they are not going to win, they will not talk and the Russians cannot convince them.
>
> Two, I believe the president and the government have talked enough about peace. I don't believe any more talk will do any good. Any objective citizen knows the government position. Talk of peace is interpreted in Hanoi as a sign of weakness. This pause will encourage North Vietnam. They will take this to be a step backward, in response to U.S. protest opinion and world opinion. Anything that hinders the North from figuring they can't win, hinders the close of the war.[21]

Clifford also opposed the pause because he believed it would make it difficult to resume the bombing. In addition, given the proximity to the holidays, he believed the pause would be perceived as a gimmick. He discounted the possibility that the Vietnam War was going to be settled diplomatically, but instead would be resolved only when North Vietnam believed that continued fighting was counterproductive. On that assumption, a public declaration of a pause in bombing would not bring about a resolution of the conflict. Nor would it push the Soviets to seek peace, he argued. If the Soviets were interested in peace they could make a positive overture regardless of the status of the bombing. Finally, Clifford argued that a bombing pause should be saved until there was a chance that it would be successful.[22]

As with the July troop deployment decision Clifford's argument did not carry the day. The bombing pause began just before Christmas and held until into the new year. Near the end of January Johnson convened his advisers, including Clifford, to evaluate the efficacy of the pause. Although he believed that the pause in bombing had been effective with the domestic and international audience, as it demonstrated a desire to find a peaceful settlement, it had failed to modify North Vietnam's behavior. Nonetheless, Clifford counseled caution in resuming the bombing, believing that the experience of the French in Indochina was instructive. He believed that an indiscriminate resumption of bombing would convince Hanoi, and the international audience, that the United States was no different from the French.[23]

Despite these misgivings, Clifford also argued that a demonstration of U.S. military superiority, especially in the air, was essential. The "only way to get out of Vietnam is to persuade Hanoi we are too brave to be frightened and too strong to be defeated. We must persuade them we cannot lose—and they will never talk until they are so convinced," he said. The "U.S. attitude is misunderstood in Hanoi. They hear Senators and protests and they are convinced we are losing the support of our people. [The] war must be made more costly to Vietnam." According to Clifford, sufficient military pressure just might convince North Vietnam that the benefits of waging the war were not worth the painful losses inflicted by U.S. airpower. Clifford also argued that the bombing campaign could serve as a deterrent to China. Yet it was important for the bombing to resume quickly, he cautioned, because a delay might induce Hanoi to make a phony peace overture. If that happened, then the United States would be handcuffed and the North would use the opportunity to rebuild.[24]

Johnson ordered the bombing to resume on January 31, 1966. In this case Clifford, as he later admitted, badly misread North Vietnam's intentions.[25] Although he cited the experience of the French, he did not take away the lesson of that earlier war. The Vietnamese had demonstrated their tenacity against the French, but it would take a little more than two years for Clifford to become convinced that their willpower was more than the United States' commitment to a limited war.

In October 1966, Johnson asked Clifford to accompany him to the Philippines to attend a conference of nations that had joined the United States in committing troops to Vietnam. The meetings accomplished little of substance, except for the formal declaration that the U.S. and its allies were in Vietnam at the request of that country's government for the purpose of fighting aggression, and that they would remain until North Vietnam abandoned its war efforts. Following the summit meeting Johnson made an unannounced side trip under heavy security to visit the troops in Vietnam. The trip was historic, as it was only the second time a president had visited troops in a foreign war zone, the first being Franklin Roosevelt's trip to Casablanca in 1943. The only other comparable occasion was when president-elect Eisenhower had visited Korea in late 1952. Johnson's brief visit of two and a half hours provided him with an opportunity to meet and greet the troops, present medals, and praise the men for their service.[26] The trip became famous for Johnson's unscripted exhortation to a group of officers to "go out there and nail that coonskin to the wall."

Shortly after they returned from the trip to the Philippines and Vietnam, Johnson had surgery to remove a throat polyp and Clifford paid him a visit in the hospital. Johnson shrewdly used the opportunity of his convalescence to ask Clifford to join his administration as attorney general. Johnson had earlier offered Clifford the post of attorney general as well as UN ambassador, national security advisor, director of Central Intelligence, and undersecretary of state. Each time Clifford had turned him down, offering a variety of reasons that all suggested he was quite content with his current arrangement. And why not? He was close to the president and yet independent of him, and his law business was thriving. Although Clifford was candid in stating his preference for continuing his private law practice, he was also somewhat disingenuous with his other reasons for refusing Johnson's job offers. He told Johnson that he did not want to be attorney general because his interest was foreign policy and national security, yet he refused the positions of national security advisor and undersecretary of state.[27]

Hoping to avoid another rejection, Johnson asked Clifford again about the attorney general position while in the hospital. Perhaps taken by surprise, or perhaps not wishing to anger the president, Clifford this time asked for some time to think it over. The next day he returned and told Johnson, to the president's disappointment, that he would not accept the assignment. Johnson, unable to speak because of his surgery, scrawled on a legal pad, asking Clifford whom he should select. Clifford indicated that he was favorably impressed with Ramsey Clark.

Johnson's decision to appoint Ramsey Clark as attorney general was the first part of a complicated plan to eventually nominate Thurgood Marshall as the first African American on the Supreme Court. Ramsey Clark was the son of Tom Clark, who had been attorney general under Truman. Once the younger Clark was named attorney general his father, then a Supreme Court Justice, would have to recuse himself from the high court, thus creating a vacancy on the court. Marshall had distinguished himself by having successfully argued the case *Brown v. Board of Education,* which outlawed segregation in schools, and Johnson believed that he was the best-qualified African American candidate. Clifford, however, opposed the idea, believing that Marshall was not a sufficiently qualified candidate. "I believe that Thurgood does not have the ability or standing to succeed him," Clifford argued. "You can do much better and I do not think it should be a negro."[28] Clifford did not elaborate on his reasons for opposing a black Supreme Court nominee, but it is worth noting that he opposed black Supreme Court nominations on two separate occasions.

More than thirty years have elapsed since the end of U.S. military involvement in Vietnam, but the war still provokes arguments from those who believe that the military was betrayed by the antiwar movement and a lack of fortitude on the part of the political leadership. Others argue that a military victory in Vietnam was an impossible goal and that the United States had no business intervening in an anticolonial civil war. The beginnings of this debate could be seen in 1967.

In an effort to maintain political support for the war Johnson asked Westmoreland to make an address to the Congress. It would be the first time a military commander had ever given a speech to Congress during wartime. In a rousing speech on April 28, 1967, frequently interrupted by applause, Westmoreland pledged that American forces "backed at home by resolve, confidence, patience, determination and continued support would prevail in Vietnam over the Communist aggressor." Sitting in the front seats, and certainly an important target audience, were Senators William Fulbright, Robert Kennedy, and George McGovern, all critics of the war. Addressing these critics in a passage that elicited the most enthusiastic applause, Westmoreland assured his audience that the communists could not succeed militarily in Vietnam.[29]

Westmoreland's confidence was not uniformly shared among the soldiers or, more importantly, among his officers. Writing for the *New York Times* in July—on the Fourth of July, no less—Neil Sheehan reported that "the military situation there has developed into a virtual stalemate." According to the officers cited in the article, the gradual buildup of American forces over the previous two years had afforded the North Vietnamese the time to build up their forces as well, through intensive recruitment and infiltration. A few days after the *Times* article, McNamara made a visit to the war zone and was met with a request by Westmoreland for an additional 100,000 troops, thus implicitly bolstering the Sheehan article's claims of a stalemate. But Westmoreland was having none of it. "The war is not a stalemate," he said. "We are winning slowly but steadily. North Vietnam is paying a tremendous price with nothing to show for it in return."[30] McNamara concurred with Westmoreland's assessment. "There is not a military stalemate," he asserted during a July 12 meeting. "Reports on the scene are better than press reports at home." He accused the press of being in a "very bad mood" and believing the "war isn't worth the price we are incurring."[31]

Always sensitive to public opinion, Clifford pointed out that the public was concerned that Vietnam might be "the war that can't be won," and asked McNamara for his opinion. McNamara replied that U.S. forces would continue to destroy the enemy's forces and that there was a limit to the forces the enemy could send into the South. McNamara's confidence contradicted the officers who had spoken to Sheehan. They had argued that the North was able to keep pace with the American troop levels. Clifford, however, did not press McNamara on this point. McNamara was confident. He felt that the current strategy would yield a victory and end the fighting. He also suggested that the North Vietnamese were testing the unity and patience of the American people. Johnson agreed and said he would support an increase in troop levels, but urged his advisers to "shave it the best we can."[32]

Johnson was willing to increase the number of U.S. troops, but he believed that in order to ensure public support for the idea, other nations, especially those most affected by the situation in Vietnam, needed to contribute more troops. With that in mind he announced that Clifford would accompany General Maxwell Taylor, a special military assistant to the president, on a mission to the allied nations. The stated purpose of the trip was to consult with the allies, but Ferdinand Marcos, the Philippine president, did not want to engage in any discussions about contributing troops and even tried to disinvite the Americans from coming. Marcos's unwillingness to commit troops, given his nation's proximity to Vietnam, annoyed Clifford, but he understood the political risks that Marcos would face if he acceded to the U.S. requests.[33]

The first stop on Clifford and Taylor's August 1967 trip was Vietnam, where they met with Nguyen Van Thieu and Nguyen Cao Ky, the leaders of the military government. The partnership between the two men was unstable at best, and Clifford observed that while there seemed to be a truce between them, he was uncertain how long it would last. During the meeting Clifford delivered the message to Ky and Thieu that the upcoming elections must be perceived by the international community as fair and honest, and based upon their response he was comfortable that they would be. Clifford was skeptical of the two Vietnamese leaders, however, and believed that they were paying the Americans lip service. "They know all the right answers," he told Johnson. "They know what we want them to say and often will say it before they are asked." They also promised another 65,000 troops.[34]

The remainder of the trip was more of a challenge. Every step along the way Clifford and Taylor were met with a reluctance to commit more troops to Vietnam. In each case the head of state publicly declared that there would be no immediate decision regarding troops and made a point of demonstrating he was not "on the tail of the kite of the United States." Clifford complained that the difficulty of their task was compounded by newspaper reports that they were asking the allies for more troops, reports that he and Taylor continuously denied. In presenting his case Clifford argued that because of the war there was a deficit in the U.S. budget of $20 billion, necessitating an increase in taxes. Clifford explained that the United States would be reluctant to fund the war absent a greater commitment by like-minded nations. The obvious question U.S. citizens would ask is: "If we have to put this much money in the war, what are our allies going to do?" Clifford feared that without an infusion of allied troops the United States would be forced to continue the same level of ground warfare and bombing and would be no closer to victory. "A year from now we again will be taking stock," he warned. "We may be no closer a year from now than we are now."[35]

Clifford believed that the United States was hampering the effectiveness of the war effort by limiting the targets attacked by air and on the ground. "As long as the supplies continue to reach the troops in the South coming in from Laos, over the Northeast Railroad, through Haiphong Harbor, and down from Cambodia we can't get the war over," he argued. "As long as the faucets are on, we cannot reach our objective." Clifford also reported that the allied nations believed there was little chance that either the Chinese or the Soviets would enter the war. Therefore, Clifford felt that Johnson was free to order bombing of targets closer to the Chinese border.[36]

As the summer faded away into fall some limited movements toward peace were made. Ironically, this movement toward peace came in the form of an attempt to rouse public support for the war. On September 29 Johnson gave a major speech in San Antonio, Texas, in which he declared that America had the will to outlast the North Vietnamese. "Why, in the face of military and political progress in the South, and the burden of our bombing in the North, do they insist and persist with the war?" he asked. The North had ignored all previous attempts at dialogue, he answered, because they were convinced that the American people were not committed to fight the war to the finish. He then proposed what came to be known as the San Antonio formula:

> As we have told Hanoi time and again, the heart of the matter is really this: The United States is willing to stop all aerial and naval bombardment of North Vietnam when this will lead promptly to productive discussions. We, of course, assume that while discussions proceed, North Vietnam will not take advantage of the bombing cessation or limitation.[37]

Around the same time as he made this pronouncement, however, Johnson attempted to open a back channel to dialogue with the North Vietnamese. In August Henry Kissinger had made contact with two European college professors who had long-standing relationships with the North Vietnamese leader, Ho Chi Minh. Johnson asked Kissinger to return to Paris to continue the dialog with his contacts, Hebert Marcovich and Raymond Aubrac, and in a meeting on October 18 the president gave Kissinger his instructions. Also attending the meeting was a skeptical Clifford, who argued that the North Vietnamese would not use a back channel if they were serious about negotiations. He doubted they were engaging in substantive diplomacy. "It looks like they are saying the same thing they have said before," he said. He reasoned that if the North was serious about diplomacy they would approach the United States through the appropriate channels. On the subject of the bombing, he was adamant that there must be no cessation because the North would use the opportunity to resupply their troops. Instead, he argued, continuation of the bombing would demonstrate resolve and might lead to productive discussions.[38] Although he had initially opposed the war, Clifford again demonstrated his willingness to see it through until the end. McNamara, however, was moving in the opposite direction.

The doubts that had first crept into McNamara's mind during the debate over the Christmas bombing pause of 1965 had become more pronounced over the following two years. During a September 1967 conversation with Averell Harriman, then an ambassador at large, McNamara voiced his concerns. When Harriman asked about the mood of the president, McNamara replied that he was not quite sure. He said that Johnson was surrounded by hawks, such as National Security Advisor Walt Whitman Rostow and Clifford, who seemed to think that victory was just around the corner. (Given that Clifford had argued the case against the war so passionately during their Camp David showdown, it is interesting that McNamara singled him out.) McNamara confided to Harriman that he doubted the prospects for a quick victory, and he suggested that Johnson felt the same way. He speculated that the president might have been "horse trading" with the hawks in the Senate, particularly Richard Russell of Georgia and Everett Dirksen of Illinois. By taking a hard line now, McNamara reasoned, Johnson might be able to make a case for peace if the military strategy failed.[39]

On October 31, during the president's weekly Tuesday lunch meeting with his foreign policy advisers, McNamara finally gave voice to his concerns. Continuation of the present course in Vietnam, he declared, "would be dangerous, costly in lives, and unsatisfactory to the American people." The next day he laid bare his change of heart in a private memorandum to the president. "Continuing our present course will not bring us by the end of 1968 enough closer to success, in the eyes of the American public, to prevent the continued erosion of popular support for our involvement in Vietnam," he wrote. He suggested a change of course that would entail stabilization of the current troop levels and no further escalation in North Vietnam. The objective would be to demonstrate that America was making a long-term commitment to Vietnam while shifting more of the burden to the South Vietnamese and reducing U.S. casualties. Years later, McNamara recounted that the memorandum "raised the tension between two men who loved and respected each other—Lyndon Johnson and me—to the breaking point." According to McNamara, Johnson was not ready to accept the course of action he was recommending. "It was becoming clear to both of us that I would not change my judgment, nor would he change his. Something had to give." And something did give, although McNamara was not sure what actually transpired. "I do not know to this day whether I quit or was fired," he wrote. "Maybe it was both."[40]

McNamara's sudden change of heart, for sudden it must have appeared to Johnson, might have given the president reason to doubt the strategy in Vietnam. McNamara wielded tremendous influence with Johnson, and his determination that the existing strategy had failed could very well have raised some doubts in the president's mind. Counteracting McNamara's doubts, however, was the consensus of a group that came to be known as the Wise Men. In an effort to expand his circle of foreign policy advisers, Johnson asked Clifford and Rostow to assemble a group of senior government officials.[41] The group included Clifford, George Ball, McGeorge Bundy, Maxwell Taylor, former chairman of the Joint Chiefs of Staff General Omar Bradley, former undersecretary of state Robert Murphy, former ambassador to Vietnam and 1960 Republican vice presidential nominee Henry Cabot Lodge, Dean Acheson, Abe Fortas, Korean War negotiator Arthur Dean, and former treasury secretary Douglas Dillon. They met for the first time during the evening of November 1, without the president, and then with the president the next day.[42]

Typical of the discussion was Acheson's encouragement that "we certainly should not get out of Vietnam" and his reminder that there was a great outcry to withdraw from Korea following the intervention of the Chinese in November 1950. Part of the problem, Acheson noted, was the opposition Johnson was receiving from the "lousy" Senate Foreign Relations committee, and the dilettante fool who was its chairman, Senator Fulbright. Bundy said, "Getting out of Vietnam is as impossible as it is undesirable." Much of the conversation revolved around how to restore public support for the war. Dillon suggested that younger college professors and their students were a major source of opposition to the war and that a series of briefings directed at college presidents might help counteract the criticism. It was important to demonstrate to the American people that there was "light at the end of the tunnel," said Dillon. Bradley said the administration needed to arouse patriotism through the use of patriotic slogans. "An effort must be made to explain and to educate the American people," Clifford suggested.[43] But he also cautioned that support, and opposition, to any war was a fleeting thing:

> The thing to keep in mind however is that no matter what this accomplishes, this will not be a popular war. No wars have been popular. In the Revolutionary War there was an enormous body who felt this was a tragic mistake. The same was true in the Civil War where President Lincoln was beleaguered day after day with people who thought he should get out. The First World War was enormously unpopular with many of the American people. In the Korean War, it was popular in 1950, and in 1951 more than 60% thought we were wrong.[44]

Clifford weighed in on the McNamara memorandum a few days after the meeting of the Wise Men, although by his account he was unaware of its authorship.[45] "I disagree with the recommendations presented in the memorandum of November 1, 1967," he wrote. "I believe that the course of action suggested therein will retard the possibility of concluding the conflict rather than accelerating it." He echoed both the content and phrasing of Johnson's San Antonio speech when he suggested that the North Vietnamese continued to prosecute a war they could not win in the belief that the United States lacked the will to carry on the war. "It is my opinion that Hanoi will never seek a cessation of the conflict if they think our determination is lessening," he argued. "On the other hand, if our pressure is unremitting and their losses continue to grow, and hope fades for any sign of weakening on our part, then some day they will conclude that the game is not worth the candle." He also opposed McNamara's recommendation to suspend the bombing. "I am at a loss to understand this logic. Would the unconditional suspension of the bombing, without any effort to extract a quid pro quo persuade Hanoi that we were firm and unyielding in our conviction to force them to desist from their aggressive designs?" he asked. "The answer is a loud and resounding 'no.'" Repeating the argument he made two years earlier, he suggested that the North would use a bombing suspension to rebuild their infrastructure and war-making potential, and that a subsequent resumption of bombing "would create a storm of protest."[46]

Clifford also delivered the sort of rousing defense of the war that Johnson surely was looking for, in stark contrast to the change of course McNamara was now advocating. "Can there be any doubt as to the North Vietnamese reaction to such an announcement?" Clifford provocatively asked. "The chortles of unholy glee issuing from Hanoi would be audible in every capital of the world." He argued that McNamara's change of course would demonstrate a lack of resolve, which in Clifford's mind was absolutely essential to reaching a diplomatic settlement. "Is this evidence of our zeal and courage to stay the course? Of course not! It would be interpreted to be exactly what it is. A resigned and discouraged effort to find a way out of a conflict for which we had lost our will and dedication."[47]

If McNamara planted any doubts in the mind of the president, the combination of the strong endorsement from the Wise Men and Clifford, along with the continued support of the war within his own administration, convinced Johnson that the policy was correct. However, he would need a new secretary of defense to carry it out. A few days after receiving McNamara's memo Johnson announced that McNamara would assume the presidency of the World Bank. The logical choice to succeed McNamara was Clifford, yet the president waited until January 18, right after the 1968 State of the Union address, to pose the question, if indeed it was a question. "In the past you've said your interest was foreign policy and national security," he said to Clifford. "Now I've got exactly the right place for you— Secretary of Defense. It will suit you and you cannot possibly have an objection to it."[48] Clifford accepted, telling the press, "When the President of the United States looks you in the eye and says, 'As President I must ask you as a citizen to assume this burden,' I don't think anyone can refuse a request when expressed in that manner."[49]

Predictably, press coverage of the announcement revolved around the question of whether Clifford was a hawk or a dove, with the general conclusion being that he was a hawk. Writing in the *New York Times* Patrick Anderson described him "as the most influential advocate within the President's inner circle of a hard-line hawk policy on Vietnam." According to Anderson, Clifford viewed the war in Vietnam "as a test of national will" and believed that the United States had to take a stand against communism in Vietnam or risk having to fight it elsewhere.[50] A *New York Times* editorial indicates that Clifford had been described as more of a hawk than Rusk and was one who believed that Johnson's position on Vietnam was correct and would be "so judged by history."[51] For his part, Clifford was not particularly forthcoming, saying wryly that he was "not conscious of falling under any of those ornithological divisions."[52] As he later observed, he was a hawk at the time of his appointment, and would have been obligated to decline the position if he could not support the president's policy.[53] Speaking to the press after the announcement Clifford declared, "I will have but one client from now on, if confirmed, and that client will be the United States."[54]

Clifford had been out of the government for almost two decades, and while he had been frequently close to the center of power as an outside adviser, his policy-making influence was limited. Now, in addition to his own formidable intellect and powers of persuasion, he would have the Pentagon bureaucracy and Cabinet stature behind him. And he would need all the help he could get, as 1968 would prove to be, until the BCCI debacle, the most difficult year of his life.

If Clifford hoped to ease into his new assignment, he was to be disappointed. He had yet to face his confirmation hearings and McNamara was scheduled to stay on as secretary of defense until the end of February, but Clifford was the designated successor and the problems would be his. Within days of his nomination the North Koreans seized a U.S. naval intelligence vessel, the USS *Pueblo,* and had taken the ship and its crew to a port in the communist country. The North Koreans justified the action by claiming the ship was engaged in a spying mission in their waters and refused to release the sailors. Upon hearing the report concerning the *Pueblo,* Clifford defused some of the tension in the room by turning to Johnson and asking, "Mr. President, may I leave now?"[55] By the end of January the North Vietnamese launched the Tet Offensive, which dramatically changed the course of the war, particularly from a political perspective.

With the nation at war Clifford expected a relatively smooth path to confirmation, and for the most part he was spared harsh questioning. Although it would only become clear in hindsight, Clifford's confirmation hearings were notable for what they presaged about the change of course he would soon pursue with respect to the war. In response to a question regarding the meaning of the San Antonio formula, Clifford offered a lawyerly (as he described it) clarification. Johnson was vague when he proposed the conditions for negotiations, saying only that he expected the North Vietnamese would not take advantage of any halt in the bombing. When asked whether he believed the North Vietnamese needed to cease all military activity as a condition of a bombing cessation, Clifford responded no, and then offered a far more liberal interpretation of the San Antonio formula: "Their military activity will continue in South Vietnam, I assume, until there is a cease-fire agreed upon. I assume that they will continue to transport the normal amount of goods, munitions, and men to South

Vietnam. I assume that we will continue to maintain our forces and support our forces during that period. So what I am suggesting is, in the language of the President, that he would insist that they not take advantage of the suspension of the bombing."[56]

Clifford's interpretation relaxed the standards for compliance with the San Antonio formula because it specifically allowed the North to move men, munitions, and supplies into the South during a bombing halt. For Clifford, the operative word was "normal" and the implication was that the North could continue to supply the normal amount of food, ammunition, and materials to the troops already in the South, but not increase the flow.[57] In a conventional war the distinction might not have been so profound, but Vietnam was, at least until Tet, a guerrilla war in which the North Vietnamese and their allies in the South, the National Liberation Front (NLF), or Vietcong, infiltrated the South and minimized direct engagement with the enemy. Clifford's interpretation, therefore, lowered the standards for compliance and opened the door a bit more to a negotiated settlement. According to Clifford, he approached the question as a lawyer and "simply offered what I considered the most reasonable interpretation of the San Antonio formula."[58] Maybe so, but during the October discussions regarding the Kissinger channel he had specifically opposed a bombing halt as it would allow the North to resupply their troops. Just a few months later he was willing to allow what he had adamantly opposed—hardly the demonstration of resolve he had so boisterously argued for in response to the McNamara memorandum.

Clifford was unanimously confirmed by the Senate on January 30, 1968, as he was participating in the president's weekly lunch with his foreign policy advisers, none of whom were yet aware that the Tet Offensive had begun. Johnson and his military advisers, including Westmoreland, were convinced that a major battle was about to begin, but they were far off in their estimates of the location. They were focused on Khe Sanh, just south of the Demilitarized Zone (DMZ) that divided the country. In preparation for the battle they were certain was coming, as opposed to the massive offensive that was then in progress, General Wheeler asked permission for Westmoreland's plan of a diversionary amphibious landing north of the DMZ, in order to reduce pressure on Khe Sanh. The plan also entailed leaking the feigned assault to the South Vietnamese, with the expectation that North Vietnamese spies who were infiltrating the South would learn of the plan and divert their forces from Khe Sanh. The assumption was that the U.S. public would not know about the plan, and even if it broke publicly, there would be no actual attack anyway. Clifford, however, was concerned with the public reaction, and thought that the plan in general was a mistake. But he treaded lightly because McNamara, who supported the idea, was still technically secretary of defense. "Here is my uninformed reaction," he said. "If we go ahead and plan on this and it should become known, people would say we used this as an excuse for the real thing." Johnson approved Westmoreland's plan despite the opposition of his new secretary of defense.

While the meeting was still in progress Rostow received notice of an urgent call and returned a few minutes later with a dramatic announcement. "We have just been informed we are being heavily mortared in Saigon. The Presidential Palace, our B O Q's [Base Officer's Quarters], the Embassy and the city itself have been hit. This flash was just received from the N M C C [National Military Intelligence Coordination Center]." The Tet Offensive had begun. "This could be very bad," said a shocked Johnson.[59]

It turned out to be very bad indeed; in fact, it was the turning point in the war. The scope of the attack was immense. In addition to the attacks in the capital of Saigon, the North Vietnamese also attacked six of the largest cities in South Vietnam, 36 of 44 provincial capitals, and 64 of 242 district centers.[60] The shock of the Tet Offensive finally soured Clifford on the optimistic battlefield reports coming from Vietnam. "Now my faith in our ability to achieve our objectives within an acceptable period of time was shaken and began to erode," he recalled.[61] "Tet had had a very substantial impact on me as it had on others," he said. The meeting with the Wise Men back in November had been optimistic with talk of seeing the light at the end of the tunnel. "Well, Tet changed all that," said Clifford. "After Tet, I assure you, there was no suggestion that we could see any light at the end of the tunnel, nor was there any thought of sending any American boys home."[62]

Amidst the first few chaotic days of the Tet Offensive Johnson met with his foreign policy advisers, including the confirmed but still secretary-designate Clifford, to discuss how to handle the crisis. Clifford advised caution. "The situation is so fluid in Vietnam and Korea now I don't feel it advisable for the President to have any public comment," he said.[63] "Any statement now will just augment public concern." Johnson, however, disagreed, arguing that the administration needed to make the case that the Tet Offensive had not been a great defeat. Whereas only a few weeks before Clifford had argued for a more expansive interpretation of the San Antonio formula, now he was making the case that the North Vietnamese had already rejected it. "I am inclined to move in the direction that their action over the past two weeks shows a dramatic answer to the San Antonio Formula and to the request for talks," he said. He also concurred with the Pentagon's recommendation to resume bombing in the North.[64]

During the first few days of the Tet Offensive, of which Clifford had been unexpectedly thrown into the middle, Johnson passed along a quote from English philosopher John Stuart Mill, perhaps in preparation for the difficult days ahead:

War is an ugly thing, but not the ugliest thing: the decayed and degraded state of moral and patriotic feeling which thinks nothing worth a war is worse. . . . A man who has nothing which he cares about more than his personal safety is a miserable creature who has no chance of being free, unless made and kept so by the exertions of better men than himself.[65]

The next day, during a meeting with the Joint Chiefs of Staff, Wheeler presented a request from Westmoreland for reinforcements, another 40,000 men, prompting a challenge from a skeptical Johnson. "All last week I asked two questions," he said. "The first was 'Did Westmoreland have what he needed?' (You answered yes.) The second question was, 'Can Westmoreland take care of the situation with what he has there now?' The answer was yes. Tell me what has happened to change the situation between then and now." Wheeler responded that the latest intelligence suggested that there were more North Vietnamese troops in the South than had been previously estimated. Wheeler, Rusk, McNamara, and Johnson then discussed the current military situation. Rusk was skeptical that the North Vietnamese could launch another attack, but McNamara, while acknowledging that the communists had suffered losses, argued that they could.[66]

Ever mindful of public perception, Clifford argued that an increase in troops would send the wrong message, especially since the president himself had said the Tet Offensive had been a failure:

There is a very strange contradiction in what we are saying and doing. On one hand, we are saying that we have known of this build up. We now know the North Vietnamese and Viet Cong launched this type of effort in the cities. We have publicly told the American people that the communist offensive was: (a) not a victory, (b) produced no uprising among the

Vietnamese in support of the enemy, and (c) cost the enemy between 20,000 and 25,000 of his combat troops.

Now our reaction to all of that is to say that the situation is more dangerous today than it was before all of this. We are saying that we need more troops, that we need more ammunition and that we need to call up the reserves.

I think we should give some very serious thought to how we explain saying on one hand the enemy did not take a victory and yet we are in need of many more troops and possibly an emergency call up.[67]

Clifford had not yet transformed from hawk to dove, but his skepticism was evident. Alone among the participants in the meeting, he was the one to point out that the battle couldn't simultaneously be both a victory and a defeat. In Clifford's mind it was essential for the government to present a clear message; otherwise, critics of the war might feast on the contradiction.

One such critic, Senator William Fulbright, had requested that Rusk appear before the Senate Foreign Relations Committee. With the situation in Vietnam spiraling out of control, Rusk would have been subject to harsh questioning, a situation Clifford wanted to avoid. He strongly advised against allowing Rusk to testify, but also suggested that it was equally important to avoid a confrontation with Congress. "The times are too serious and the public too concerned for a public feud between the Senate Foreign Relations Committee and the Secretary of State," he said. "I think the people are hopeful that we would be working together at times like these. I think it unwise to write a formal letter turning this down. . . . We should quiet the whole matter down. The Committee wants either a Roman Holiday with Dean Rusk or a confrontation with the President." Clifford thought that Johnson should handle the situation personally, perhaps by meeting privately with Fulbright over dinner.[68]

Dealing with Fulbright was the least of the administration's problems, of course. Instead the group focused on the continuous reports of bad news from Vietnam. This was complicated by the persistent suspicion that Tet was merely a prelude to something else. Even as late as February 10, Westmoreland still believed that the Tet Offensive was a diversionary tactic and that Khe Sanh was the real target, a theory shared by Johnson. Clifford thought otherwise. "All we have heard is about the preparation the North Vietnamese have made for the attack at Khesanh," he said. "I have a feeling that the North Vietnamese are going to do something different. I believe our people were surprised by the 24 attacks on the cities last week. God knows the South Vietnamese were surprised with half of their men on holiday. There may be a feint and a surprise coming up for us."[69]

Two days later the group was still discussing Westmoreland's request for "reinforcements," which in the initial days of the Tet Offensive he had ambiguously worded. As the situation worsened Westmoreland stopped being coy and explicitly requested more troops. The skepticism Clifford had revealed a few days earlier was back, and he peppered Wheeler with questions: "What change in strategy has the enemy made?" "In his cable, General Westmoreland also points out that it is national policy to keep the enemy from seizing and holding the two northern provinces. Hasn't that been the situation all along?" "Westmoreland says in his cable that he cannot hold without reinforcements. What change has taken place to keep him from holding?" "General Westmoreland also says that we are now in a new ballgame with the enemy mobilized to achieve quick victory. Is that something new?" Clifford also noted that Westmoreland's latest request was far more urgent than his prior ones. Wheeler responded that the changed circumstances required greater candor.[70]

In his memoirs, Clifford wrote that he remained silent when Johnson asked if there were any objections to the increase in troops. The reason for his silence, Clifford explained, was that McNamara was still the secretary of defense and Clifford thought it best to express his views in private until he was sworn in.[71] Yet Clifford was not remaining completely silent; he was asking some pointed questions. This did not yet constitute opposition to the current policy, but at the very least it meant that he was starting to have reservations and would not let Wheeler's and Westmoreland's statements go unchallenged. Johnson approved of Clifford's approach and was perhaps becoming somewhat skeptical himself. "I want to ask all the questions that I possibly can now so that we get answers to them before a situation develops and we didn't have them," the president said. "I hope all of you see what has happened during the last two weeks. Westy said he *could* use troops one day last week. Today he comes in with an urgent request for them."[72]

On February 13 Townsend Hoopes, the undersecretary of the Air Force, sent Clifford a long letter expressing his reservations about the war. The letter was marked "personal" and was sent to Clifford at his law firm, thus avoiding official Pentagon channels. Hoopes took this step "with more candor than discretion" because he believed it was important for Clifford to receive a point of view contrary to the consensus of the rest of the Pentagon, and because "candor and clarity are needed at this juncture of our affairs." Hoopes argued that the "idea of a U.S. military victory in Vietnam is a dangerous illusion." He believed that the Chinese and the Soviets would never allow the United States to win in Vietnam and would intervene, either with supplies or troops, to prevent a U.S. victory. Contrary to Clifford, who had recommended negotiation from a position of strength, Hoopes suggested that "definitive de-escalation is a prerequisite" to a negotiated settlement, as was cessation of the bombing in the North.[73]

In spite of the fact that he was a representative of the Air Force, Hoopes believed the bombing had been a failure. He told Clifford that when he first became undersecretary of the Air Force the previous October, one of the first things he asked for was a current assessment of the effectiveness of the bombing. Inexplicably, there was no current assessment of effectiveness, only technical analyses regarding such things as bombing accuracy. Since then Hoopes had learned that while the bombing had caused extensive damage, it had not inhibited the ability of the North Vietnamese to infiltrate men and materiel into the South. In Hoopes's opinion the bombing campaign had "diminishing relevance to the struggle in the South," but it did serve another purpose. "We seem to have in the bombing campaign an instrument of some modest, but indeterminate, value which plays an essentially psychological role in the struggle and whose most useful service to us may be as a counter to be traded away in a serious bargaining," he wrote. Since the bombing was "making only a marginal military contribution," Hoopes advocated a cessation under the auspices of the Clifford interpretation of the San Antonio formula. He also recommended curtailing ground operations in order to reduce U.S. casualties. Hoopes argued that the high level of casualties was the result of the current war of attrition and that an increase in casualties would not necessarily follow a cessation of the bombing. Although he believed that there was no link between U.S. casualties and a bombing halt, he acknowledged that "it exists as a political fact." Accordingly, a halt in ground operations would need to coincide with a bombing halt.[74]

The same day Clifford received the Hoopes memo recommending a curtailment in the bombing, Johnson and his senior advisers discussed bombing targets in Hanoi during their Tuesday lunch meeting. Rusk was in favor, saying, "I am ready to hit almost anything." McNamara disagreed; he believed that the military value was small and the risk too high. Clifford said it was "very reasonable and, in fact, well justified to increase the level of pressure in North Vietnam. I would favor a step up in the military pressure."[75]

Clifford and Rusk were not the only voices advocating an increase in military pressure. At the end of February Wheeler returned from a brief trip to Vietnam. He brought with him a pessimistic assessment of the situation. "There is no doubt that the enemy launched a major powerful nation-wide assault against the Government of South Vietnam and its Armed Forces," Wheeler wrote. "This offensive has by no means run its course." He also warned that there might be additional North Vietnamese troops in the South that U.S. intelligence had not been able to detect. He reported that military commanders in the field believed that 1968 would be the critical year, and while they were uncertain whether the war would last past 1968, they were certain the situation would never return to a pre-Tet state. In order to meet this challenge, Wheeler reported that Westmoreland was requesting an additional 205,179 American troops.[76] It was a staggering number. Westmoreland's request would come to dominate policy discussions over the next month and lead Clifford to reassess his support for the war.

The same day, Clifford discussed the request with Rusk, Rostow, McNamara, Undersecretary of State Nicholas Katzenbach, Assistant Secretary of State for East Asian and Pacific Affairs Bill Bundy (brother of McGeorge), and White House aides Harry McPherson and Joseph Califano. McPherson was shocked. "This is unbelievable and futile," he lamented. Perhaps taking the position of devil's advocate, Clifford offered, without endorsing, an increase of 500,000 to one million men—a figure that, McNamara acerbically noted, had the virtue of clarity. Rusk and Rostow, who would remain hawks until the end, were optimistic and believed the North Vietnamese had taken a beating during Tet. Westmoreland should be reinforced now, Rostow recommended, until the weather improved. "What then?" an overwrought McNamara countered. "Let's not delude ourselves into thinking he cannot maintain pressure after good weather comes." Rostow corrected McNamara, saying that he was referring to air attacks. At that point McNamara lost his composure and blurted out, "The goddamned Air Force, they're dropping more on North Vietnam than we dropped on Germany in the last year of World War II, and it's not doing anything!" Then he turned and pleaded to Clifford, "We simply have to end this thing. I just hope you can get hold of it. It is out of control."[77]

Everyone in the room was embarrassed for McNamara, and Clifford broke the uncomfortable silence. Without challenging them by name, he explained that Rostow and Rusk did not understand the full impact of the Tet Offensive. As he had previously pointed out, Clifford argued that the military significance of the Tet Offensive was secondary to the political. "Look at [the] situation from [the] point of view of [the] American public and Vietnamese," he said. "Despite optimistic reports, our people (and world opinion) believe we have suffered a major setback." The administration's problem was one of credibility, but a reassessment of the policy was also in order. "How do we gain support for [a] major program, defense and economic, if we have told people things are going well?" he asked. "How do we avoid creating the feeling that we are pounding troops down [a] rathole? What is our purpose? What is achievable? Before any decision is made, we must re-evaluate our entire posture in S VN [South Vietnam]."[78]

The next day Johnson convened his advisers to discuss Westmoreland's troop request. Wheeler again warned that 1968 would be the critical year for the war and expressed his support for Westmoreland's request for 205,179. The magnitude, and the implications, of the request made the president uncomfortable. "What are the alternatives?" he asked. "What about those 65,000 troops the A R VN [Army of the Republic of South Vietnam] was supposed to provide?" Rather than offer alternatives Wheeler suggested that without the additional troops the South Vietnamese army would collapse and the United States would forfeit the two northernmost provinces of South Vietnam. Johnson asked McNamara for his opinion. The outgoing secretary responded that the additional 205,179 troops would not make a difference. The decisive factor would be the performance of the South Vietnamese army, a tenuous proposition given that they had been not been able to match the enemies' determination and fighting abilities. Johnson ended the meeting without approving the troop request. Instead, he announced that Clifford would conduct a full review, as Clifford himself had suggested the day before.[79]

McNamara's outburst revealed the tremendous strain he had been under, and the timeliness of his departure. Following a public ceremony at which the president awarded him the Medal of Freedom and a formal farewell at the Pentagon on February 29, McNamara passed the baton to Clifford. Clifford was officially sworn in on March 1 and immediately went to work on the president's request for a full review of Vietnam policy. Clifford's team at the Pentagon included Paul Nitze, the author of NSC-68, as deputy secretary of defense;

Phil Goulding, assistant secretary of defense for public affairs; Paul Warnke, the assistant secretary of defense for international security affairs; Air Force colonel Robert Pursley, who served as a military assistant; and George Elsey, Clifford's aide from his days as Truman's special counsel. Elsey had been out of government and was working for the Pullman Company when Clifford asked him to come work at the Pentagon.

The Clifford task force that would review Vietnam policy included Rusk, Katzenbach, Bill Bundy, Wheeler, Nitze, Warnke, Goulding, Taylor, Director of Central Intelligence Richard Helms, and Secretary of the Treasury Henry Fowler. The group met for the first time on March 2, with Clifford conducting a lawyerly cross-examination of the military's request for an additional 205,179 troops. "Will 200,000 more men do the job?" he asked. There was no assurance that they would. "If not, how many more might be needed—and when?" Again, there was no way of knowing. "Can the enemy respond with a buildup of his own?" he asked. They could and would. Clifford asked for an estimated cost of the request and the projected impact on the economy. The reply: $10 to $12 billion in the next fiscal year. "Can bombing stop the war?" he asked. Not by itself. The bombing was inflicting heavy losses, but bombing by itself would not stop the war. "Will stepping up the bombing decrease American casualties?" Very little, if at all, was the response. U.S. casualties were primarily the result of ground fighting in the South. When Clifford asked for a presentation of the military's plan for achieving victory, he was told that there was no plan in the traditional sense due to political restrictions imposed by Johnson.[80]

The absence of a plan for victory was most disquieting for Clifford because to him that meant that the Joint Chiefs were resigned to continuing a war of attrition. Ultimately the U.S. military believed that a continued war of attrition would become intolerable to the enemy and they would be forced to sue for peace—in hindsight, a disastrously implausible assumption. When Clifford asked for a time line they replied, "We don't know." Clifford, unsatisfied with their answer, pressed them. "Six months?" he asked. "Oh, no, it can't be done in that period," they replied. So Clifford tried again. "A year?" he asked. "Well, no," they replied. "Two years?" Clifford countered. "Well, we'll have made a good deal of progress in two years," was the noncommittal reply. Feeling that he finally had an answer he asked, "Well, is that the date that we're aiming for?" Again, the answer was no, so Clifford tried again. "Well, how much longer than two?" he asked. "Well, nobody knows," they replied. By now Clifford was frustrated. "Three years, four years?" he begged. Still, no one was willing to commit. "Well, here's this kind of bottomless pit," Clifford later recalled. "We could just be there year after year after year sacrificing tens of thousands of American boys a year, and it just didn't add up."[81]

It had taken Clifford only a few weeks to change his position on Vietnam. The Westmoreland request for troops, he believed, afforded an excellent opportunity to pursue a change in strategy. Another opportunity was a major presidential speech that Johnson was planning as a report on the status of the war, especially in the aftermath of the Tet Offensive. Together, the speech and the response to the troop request created a window of opportunity for a change of course. With Clifford centralizing the control and most of the content editing in the Pentagon,[82] the task force completed a draft memorandum for the president on March 4, recommending that only a fraction of the requested 205,179 additional troops be approved and placing strict conditions on further increases. The conditions, which Clifford later claimed was his concealed objective,[83] stipulated that further troop increases would be contingent upon:

a. Reexamination on a week-by-week basis of the desirability of further deployments as the situation develops;
b. Improved political performance by the G S V [Government of South Vietnam] and increased contribution in effective military action by the ARVN;
c. The results of a study in depth, to be initiated immediately, of possible new political and strategic guidance for the conduct of U.S. operations in South Vietnam, and of our Vietnamese policy in the context of our world-wide politico-military strategy.

The conditions, which were inserted at Clifford's behest, were designed to contain further troop increases. A supplement revealed the extent of his pessimism over the direction of the war. "It should be recognized that General Westmoreland's proposal does not purport to provide any really satisfactory answer to the problem in Vietnam. There can be no assurance that this very substantial additional deployment would leave us a year from today in any more favorable military position." Furthermore, the memo argued, the drastic change in strategy, as demonstrated by the Tet Offensive, "shows that there can be no prospect of a quick military solution to the aggression in South Vietnam."[84]

In an addendum to the draft memorandum Goulding pointed out probable difficulties with respect to public opinion, echoing comments Clifford had already made. If the troop increase were granted, the authorized troop level of 525,000 would be shattered, leaving a "bottomless pit" to deal with. Another concern, again already raised by Clifford, was the contradictory message that a troop increase would send. The American people had been told that Tet was a military victory and the enemy had suffered devastating losses; therefore, there was no military emergency to justify such a massive troop increase.[85]

Johnson and his senior advisers met the same day to discuss the contents of the draft memorandum, and Clifford presented the case for approving an increase of 22,000 troops, not the 205,179 Westmoreland had requested. "There is a concern that if we say, yes, and step up with the addition of 205,179 more men that we might continue down the road as we have been without accomplishing our purpose—which is for a viable South Vietnam which can live in peace," he said. "We are not convinced that our present policy will bring us to that objective." Clifford informed Johnson that Westmoreland's request brought him to a "watershed," a decision equally as grave, in Clifford's mind, as the one the president had confronted at Camp David three years earlier. "Do you continue to go down that same road of 'more troops, more guns, more planes, more ships'?" Clifford rhetorically asked. "Do you go on killing more Viet Cong and more North Vietnamese and killing more Vietcong and more North Vietnamese?"[86]

Clifford argued that the Tet Offensive demonstrated that the North Vietnamese were far stronger than the United States had believed and that they would be able to match the proposed troop increase, thus leading to a continued stalemate, but with even greater casualties. He warned that the Westmoreland troop request was not the final word on force levels, predicting that the general would be back in a year requesting another 200,000 to 300,000 troops, "with no end in sight." The 22,000 troops that Clifford was requesting were what would be required within the next three to four months, which Clifford believed would be the crucial period. "This is as far as we are willing to go," he said. As a compromise, however, he also recommended a call-up of 262,000 reserves to meet future contingencies in Vietnam or anywhere else.[87]

He stressed that a comprehensive study of military strategy was necessary. This might entail a focus on the cities and major population centers of South Vietnam at the expense of the countryside. The current seek-and-destroy strategy was not working, Clifford argued, and an additional 205,179 troops absent a change in policy would not result in a conventional military victory. Clifford warned Johnson that the most likely outcome of a dramatic increase in troops would be a significant increase in casualties. Instead of the current strategy, Clifford suggested that American troops could be used as a "shield" to protect the South Vietnamese government and army, with the expectation that they would eventually stand on their own. Instead of fostering independence, the current policy only fostered a greater reliance on the United States. "Under the present situation, there is a good deal of talk about what the ARVN 'will do' but when the crunch is on, when the crunch comes, they look to us for more," Clifford explained. "When they got into the Tet Offensive, Thieu's statement wasn't what more they could do but that 'it is time for more U.S. troops.' There is no easy answer to this." He also offered the dire warning—prescient, as it turned out—that "if we continue with our present policy of adding more troops and increasing our commitment, this policy may lead us into Laos and Cambodia."[88]

"I see more and more fighting with more and more casualties on the U.S. side and no end in sight to the action," Clifford warned. He emphasized that the task force was unanimous that the current strategy was not working and that a comprehensive analysis was necessary. But Clifford understood that while the group was unanimous, Johnson might be inclined to defer to his military commander, and therefore Clifford questioned Westmoreland's credibility and judgment.

> We can no longer rely just on the field commander. He can want troops and want troops and want troops. We must look at the overall impact on us, including the situation here in the United States. We must look at our economic stability, our other problems in the world, our other problems at home; we must consider whether or not this thing is tieing us down so that we cannot do some of the other things we should be doing; and finally, we must consider the effects of our actions on the rest of the world—are we setting an example in Vietnam through which other nations would rather not go if they are faced with a similar threat?[89]

Although most of the meeting was occupied with discussion of the troop increase, the possibility of negotiations with the North Vietnamese, a prospect Rusk considered bleak, was also discussed. But

Nitze was unwilling to concede the difficulty of negotiations, and thought that a bombing cessation was a prerequisite to serious discussions. "We must make up our own minds when we want to cease the bombings and see what happens," he said. "We have to look at what we can do to get into negotiations. We must choose our own time. We should do this no later than May or June."[90] To Clifford's great surprise, Rusk seemed amenable to the suggestion.[91] "We could stop the bombing during the rainy period in the North," Rusk offered. Perhaps looking for a way out, Johnson urged Rusk to "get on your horses" to make that happen.[92]

The following day Johnson asked Rusk for his ideas relative to a bombing halt, and the secretary of state read from a proposed statement announcing a relatively low-risk strategy. In Rusk's formulation the United States would limit bombing to what was needed to protect the troops, with a stipulation that it was up to the North Vietnamese to determine whether this step would lead to peace. But Rusk seemed only slightly committed to the idea, suggesting that a bombing pause would likely last about three days and would be called off if the cities or Khe Sahn was attacked. As he had indicated the previous day, the primary driver of the bombing pause was the weather, and the bombing could be resumed when the weather improved. Rusk may not have been fully committed to the idea of a bombing pause, but whether it was a serious recommendation or not, there was no further discussion of the plan.[93]

Instead of consideration of a bombing pause, the bulk of the meeting was devoted to discussion of the military and budgetary implications of the limited troop increases and the anticipated reactions from Congress. Johnson observed that they were embarking on a change of policy that would require the South Vietnamese army to assume much more of the burden of fighting, and that he would not approve any future troop commitments unless they "get with it." Johnson asked if the administration should inform Congress of the change of policy, and Clifford, perhaps nudging him to make a decision, said, "That depends on the President's attitude toward the recommendations." Johnson replied that he was in favor of the recommendations, but wanted to consult with Russell, Dirksen, and others in the Senate before making an announcement, and instructed Clifford and Wheeler to go up to the Hill.

Clifford and Wheeler met with Senators Richard Russell, Stuart Symington, Henry "Scoop" Jackson of Washington, and John Stennis of Mississippi. The senators told the two flat out that they would not support additional troops or a call-up of reserves. Jackson and Stennis told Clifford that they had given up on Vietnam, that it was hopeless. Russell also threatened to introduce a resolution repealing the Gulf of Tonkin resolution, the 1964 congressional authorization for the president to use military force in Southeast Asia. On hearing this news from his emissaries, Johnson realized that unless he was able to convince the senators to change their minds, his hands would be tied. Wheeler cabled Westmoreland, "I feel I must tell you frankly that there is strong resistance from all quarters to putting more ground force units in South Vietnam."[94]

At the same time, Clifford moved to rein in Westmoreland, whose anonymous, optimistic assessments of the situation in Vietnam had, in Clifford's opinion, damaged the Johnson administration's credibility. Clifford spoke to Wheeler, who conveyed the message to the recalcitrant general:

> I had a most interesting and informative conversation today with our new Secretary of Defense, Mr. Clifford. He is a very astute, intelligent and able man who is closely in touch with Congressional leaders, the business community, and the heads of the news media agencies. As you no doubt know, he has been the trusted advisor to four Presidents. In my judgment, apart from his important official position, he is a man of stature and achievement, one whose views must be accorded weight.
>
> The Tet offensive mounted by the enemy came as a great shock to the American public. He believes that this shock was the greater because of the euphoria engendered by optimistic statements in past days by various spokesmen supporting administration policy in South Vietnam.

Wheeler explained that Clifford was concerned that additional attacks, perhaps comparable to Tet, "could create a credibility gap with the American public and the news media which would be virtually unbridgeable."[95]

Two days later the Johnson administration, and the war effort, suffered a major setback in the form of a disastrous leak to the *New York Times*. The Sunday edition of the *Times* led with a major headline reporting that Westmoreland had requested 206,000 troops and that it had provoked a debate within the administration: "The scope and depth of the internal debate within the Government reflect the wrenching uncertainty and doubt in this capital about every facet of the war left by the enemy's dramatic wave of attacks at Tet."[96] Johnson, of course, was furious over the leak. He tried to contain the damage, but to no avail.

Johnson suffered further political damage two days later in the New Hampshire primary. Although he was not a declared candidate, a strong write-in campaign was underway, and as a sitting president, he should have won the vote handily. His opponent, Senator Eugene McCarthy of Minnesota, was running on an antiwar platform. The results were a political embarrassment: Johnson could garner no more than 49 percent of the vote. Clearly McCarthy's antiwar message had won a good deal of support, and the results presaged a divided Democratic Party in a presidential election year.

Sensing an opportunity, Robert Kennedy considered entering the presidential race, also on an antiwar platform. The strategy that Kennedy and Theodore Sorensen developed entailed their approaching Clifford with a proposal that President Johnson appoint a commission to study the Vietnam War and have that commission make a recommendation to the president. Assuming the guise of the reluctant candidate, Kennedy said that if Johnson appointed such a commission Kennedy would have met his obligation to the country and would be able to tell his supporters that Johnson had taken the appropriate steps toward peace in Vietnam. Clifford thanked Kennedy and Sorensen for coming to see him and promised to take their proposal to the president, but before seeing Johnson Clifford was fairly certain that he would reject it. "I was never in any doubt that what it was an ultimatum," Clifford recalled. "It just seemed as clear to me as it could be." The obvious implication was that if Johnson refused, Kennedy would be under pressure to enter the race. The other problem with the proposal, as Clifford saw it, was that the outcome was preordained. Rather than just proposing the idea of a commission, Kennedy and Sorenson presented Johnson with a handpicked list of members, all of whom were opponents of the war. Johnson's animosity toward Kennedy knew no bounds and he most likely would have dismissed the idea anyway, but he also objected to the proposal because it would have entailed an abdication of his responsibility as president to conduct foreign policy.[97] Clifford, for his part, was concerned about what Kennedy would do whether Johnson acted on the idea or not. For one, he was nervous that Kennedy would seek to shape the debate by planting stories in the press. He also had some doubt over whether Kennedy would stay out of the race. Johnson feared that the commission would be perceived as a deal, and the political repercussions for both Kennedy and Johnson would be negative.[98] After discussing the matter with Johnson at some length, Clifford reported back to Kennedy that Johnson had refused his proposal. Two days later, Kennedy announced his candidacy for president of the United States.

Election-year concerns, even on the subject of Vietnam, were a partial distraction from Clifford's focus on the conduct of the war. While Clifford worked the Hill to approve the limited troop increase, Senator Fulbright asked him to testify before the Foreign Relations Committee, another distraction Clifford wanted to avoid. Since he had a personal relationship with Fulbright, he asked the senator for a reprieve, insisting that he was "still learning." Fulbright agreed and asked Clifford to send Nitze in his place, but Nitze refused and threatened to resign if ordered to testify. Clifford convinced him to drop the threat to resign, and Nitze sent a memo to Johnson asking to be excused, saying that he was did not feel he was in "a position properly to defend the Executive Branch in a debate before the Foreign Relations Committee."[99]

While the Clifford task force was deliberating, Hoopes weighed in with a follow-up to his February 13 memorandum, provocatively entitled "The Infeasibility of Military Victory in Vietnam." In it he wrote, "The idea of military victory in Vietnam is a dangerous illusion, at any price that would be compatible with U.S. interest, the interests of the people of South Vietnam, or the cause of world peace." He proposed a change in policy in favor of a negotiated settlement, cessation of the bombing, negotiations with the NLF, and a coalition government. Zbigniew Brzezinski, then a member of the Policy Planning Council of the State Department and later Jimmy Carter's national security advisor, sent Clifford a confidential memorandum in which he wrote, "It is time to recognize that every additional U.S. soldier is politically counter-productive and militarily useless." Furthermore, he argued, continued involvement risked changing the nature of the conflict. "We face the real danger that additional U.S. ground forces will transform what so far has been a combination of civil war and aggression by the North into a national liberation struggle against the U.S."[100] Their recommendations served to reinforce Clifford's conviction that a change in policy was desperately needed.

The president's upcoming speech on Vietnam, finally scheduled for March 31, represented an opportunity for the administration to change the course of the war. The initial drafts, however, while not overly bellicose in tone, were nonetheless a rallying cry to win in Vietnam: "We shall not be moved; we shall not give up; we shall not be defeated by this latest outbreak of aggression and driven out of South Viet Nam. We shall put in the men who are necessary to stem the tide of this aggression."[101] If Clifford was to change the policy, he would need allies on his side. Fortunately for him, Dean Acheson, the respected former secretary of state, became the ally he needed.

Johnson had asked to meet with Acheson on February 27, and a meeting that was ostensibly a consultation with a foreign policy veteran degenerated into an emotional Lyndon Johnson rant about the war. Convinced that Johnson was looking to vent rather than consult, Acheson abruptly left. An incredulous Rostow tracked him down at his law office and asked why he left. "You tell the President—and you tell him in precisely these words—that he can take Vietnam and stick it up his ass," Acheson replied. This obviously got Johnson's attention, and he asked Acheson to come back, appealing to his sense of duty. When Acheson returned to the White House he told Johnson, "With all due respect, Mr. President, the Joint Chiefs of Staff don't know what they're talking about." When Johnson replied that he was shocked to hear Acheson say that, the former secretary of state said, "Then maybe you should be shocked." Acheson promised to help, but demanded access to all relevant information and individuals in order to form his own opinion. Johnson agreed, and Acheson immersed himself in the study of Vietnam. He did not like what he saw.[102]

Clifford, who had his finger perpetually on the pulse of Washington, was aware that Acheson had come around to his view on Vietnam. Clifford met Acheson privately at his home and confided to him his growing opposition to the war. "I told him of my agony, in detail, so he might get the feel of it," Clifford recalled. Acheson shared his doubts.[103] At the Tuesday lunch meeting on March 19, Clifford suggested that perhaps Johnson should reconvene the Wise Men. "You have your committee of senior advisers," he said. "They met prior to the Tet offensive. . . . You had unanimous expression for carrying on as you were in Vietnam. A lot has taken place. I wonder if it would be of value, if in the last three to four months—if you were to find that the same men either affirmed their attitude or reached a change of attitude. It would be of considerable help to you." This was a shrewd move on Clifford's part because the casual manner in which he suggested it belied the strategizing that was involved. Clifford compiled a list of the expected participants and circled the names of those who favored a policy of de-escalation. He wanted Johnson to see that there had been a substantial shift in opinion among the group. (Curi-

ously, Clifford did not circle his own name.) He recommended that
Johnson meet with the group confidentially, because otherwise Kennedy would be convinced that he had forced the president's hand and
would take credit for it. Johnson agreed, and asked Clifford to make
the arrangements.[104]

The next morning Clifford called Johnson and told him that he
had spoken to McGeorge Bundy, who indicated that he was not receptive to Kennedy entering the presidential race and who offered his services in drafting the March 31 speech. Johnson accepted Bundy's offer
and then proceeded to discuss political strategy, lamenting that both
McCarthy and Kennedy had defined him as the war candidate. Using
a boxing metaphor to describe the current Vietnam policy, Johnson
said that the right hand was the war hand and the left hand was the
peace hand, but that they had been fighting with one hand, the left
hand, tied behind their back. Johnson said he had to become the peace
candidate in addition to the war candidate, in order to counter the
appeal of McCarthy and Kennedy. Clifford agreed, and proposed to
rephrase the president's message: "we are not out to win the war—we
are out to win the peace." Using similar phrasing to that later utilized
by Richard Nixon, Clifford told Johnson their slogan should be "win
the peace with honor." Johnson replied that they needed to add something new and fresh to the message that the United States would win
the war.[105]

This was the opening Clifford was looking for, and he seized the
opportunity to try to reshape the direction of the March 31 speech.
"But we have to be very careful of what it is we say that we are going
to win," Clifford said. "I think we would frighten the people if we
just said we are going to win. They would think, 'Well, hell, that just
means we are going to keep pouring men in until we win militarily,'
and that isn't what we are after really." Johnson wasn't quite ready to
go that far. He was more concerned with securing the support of the
hawks, believing that he would never be able to appease the doves.
The best he could hope for was to neutralize them. But Clifford was
not deterred, and he reiterated the point, being careful to emphasize
the political implications to the president:

We have a posture now in which Kennedy and McCarthy are
the peace candidates and President Johnson is the war candidate. Now we must veer away from that and we can do it.
What we need is a policy now that is a consistent far-ranging
policy, but which we don't have. I think we need a policy of

the kind that—say a five-step policy, Mr. President, that we will continue to exert the military pressure. That I know we have to do. We'll never get anything from them if we don't do that. So, as you say, with our right hand we continue to exert the military pressure, then I think we have to have a well thought-out program that we try with our left hand. Step number one. Then that might be some kind of mutual de-escalation that really doesn't hurt us. If it isn't successful, we might move to step number two. Now at some stage in this matter, if nothing else works, then I think we have to keep in mind that before the [Democratic National] Convention, then if not before the Convention, before the election, I think we have to work out some kind of arrangement where we start some kind of negotiation.[106]

That same morning Clifford met with Bui Diem, the South Vietnamese ambassador to the United States. Abandoning the usual diplomatic tone, Clifford informed him that the American people were "sick and tired of this war, and our support is limited." Clifford asked Diem to convey the message to Thieu and Ky so that they would understand that they could no longer rely on the United States to fight North Vietnam on their behalf.[107]

Late that afternoon Johnson convened a meeting to discuss the speech, and he seemed to have been influenced by his conversation with Clifford that morning. "I asked all of you here to help me prepare a well thought out, well-balanced statement," he said. "Let's explore ways to strengthen our ways militarily and diplomatically; let's find new ways to strengthen our society and our nation. . . . Let's look at every suggestion. Let's see what we could do we haven't done better. Let's see how we can improve ourselves." When it was his turn to speak, Clifford laid out what he believed to be the important points to make in the March 31 address. The primary objective, he suggested, should be to reiterate to the American people the importance of Vietnam. Clifford paired that thought with the need to emphasize the domino theory, the risk to all of Southeast Asia if Vietnam fell to the communists. Clifford also thought it was important to explain the reasoning behind the request for additional troops, emphasizing that the next three to four months would be the critical period. Clifford stressed that the speech needed to address the allegation that the war had become an American war and that the South Vietnamese army was content to let the Americans fight for them.[108]

Having outlined the military imperatives of the speech, the boxer's right hand, Clifford stressed the need for a proposal for the boxer's left hand. With that in mind he suggested a gradual de-escalation of the war, starting with a halt to all bombing north of the 20th parallel, subject to a cease-fire in the demilitarized zone. From a military standpoint, Clifford believed this would be an acceptable trade-off, and from an international relations standpoint it would be perceived as a reasonable step. Politically, it would establish Johnson as the peace candidate, as they had discussed that morning. The president was hesitant to curtail the bombing, believing that it was protecting U.S. troops. Clifford disagreed and suggested that thus far airpower had not been very effective in Vietnam. Abe Fortas, who had consistently been a hawk, disagreed with Clifford's approach. He thought the focus of the speech should be to explain the reasons for, and the budgetary impact of, the troop increase and call-up of reserves. "This is [the] time when we must be firm and courageous," Fortas said, and argued that the timing was not right for a peace initiative. "It will be seen as [a] sign of weakness," he said. Clifford disagreed. A "continued application of strength and power does not show us the road to ultimate success," he countered, though he conceded he had some doubt that the North Vietnamese would respond to de-escalation.[109]

Johnson heard the respective arguments and decided to keep any peace overtures out of the speech, yet he didn't abandon the concept entirely. "Let's work up an agenda on possibilities. See which are worth pursuing," he said. His instructions to McPherson, who was drafting the speech, were only to say that the United States was willing to talk. In an indication of how conflicted the president was, he then immediately shifted back to a militaristic posture. "Situation at [the] moment is [a] very serious one. We must support the men we have there."[110]

Clifford had other ideas, however, and called McPherson after the meeting to speak to him privately. Clifford asked for McPherson's views, and when McPherson shared his doubts and concerns about the war, Clifford realized he had another ally. "Old boy, we have a lot of work to do together," Clifford said. "And I think we're going to pre-vail [sic]. Let me tell you what I've been doing." He told McPherson that he believed that the war could not be won without an escalation and since that was inconceivable, the war would only be prolonged. Therefore, they needed to find a way to "wind it down." "Now you must tell me what you hear over there," he cautioned, "and I will keep you advised of my activities. We must be careful for any sign that the war is to be wound up again, and not down. That would be tragic—for the country, and for the man himself. Keep in constant touch."[111]

Johnson's hard-line tone had been evident in two speeches he had given in the preceding days. "We must meet our commitments in the world and in Vietnam," he said in a March 16 speech to the National Alliance of Businessmen. "We shall and we are going to win."[112] Two days later, in a speech to the National Farmers Union Convention in Minneapolis, he declared that the North Vietnamese were unwilling to make peace and a complete military victory was the only viable option.

> We hope to achieve an honorable peace and a just peace at the negotiating table. But wanting peace, praying for peace, and desiring peace, as Chamberlain found out, doesn't always give you peace. If the enemy continues to insist, as he does now— when he refuses to sit down and accept the fair proposition we made, that we would stop our bombing if he would sit down and talk promptly and productively—if he continues to insist, as he does now, that the outcome must be determined on the battlefield, then we will win our peace on the battlefield by supporting our men who are doing that job there now.[113]

Johnson also appealed to the public—almost begged them—to support the war effort. "But I point out to you the time has come when we ought to unite, when we ought to stand up and be counted, when we ought to support our leaders, our Government, our men, and our allies until aggression is stopped, wherever it has occurred," he said.[114]

The president reconvened with his advisers on March 22 to review the latest draft of the March 31 speech, which was still quite hawkish in tone. Johnson and Rusk briefly left the room to deal with another matter, and while they were gone McGeorge Bundy, whose help Johnson had accepted, said that "extreme care" had to be taken with the president's public remarks. Clifford agreed and said that the speech to the National Alliance of Businessmen "had caused concern among thoughtful people because the President seemed to be saying that he was going to win the war no matter what the cost in American lives." After Johnson returned and the discussion of the speech resumed, Clifford tried to shift the tone by noting the rising level of discomfort with the course of the war among the general public. Reiterating comments

he had made a few weeks earlier, Clifford said the public was pessimistic that a military victory was achievable, and he said the military
did not have a plan for victory. Support for the war was waning, he
warned, as "more men go in and are chewed up in a bottomless pit."
Clifford reintroduced the suggestion of a bombing halt north of the
20th parallel. This was met with opposition from Rostow and Fortas,
and tepid support from Rusk and McGeorge Bundy.[115]

The second gathering of the Wise Men convened at the State
Department on the afternoon of March 25. The group had the same
membership as it had in November, with two additions: former deputy secretary of defense Cyrus Vance and General Matthew Ridgway,
who led the American and UN forces in Korea after Douglas MacArthur was relieved of command. Walter Isaacson and Evan Thomas,
authors of *The Wise Men: Six Friends and the World They Made*,
described the meeting as the "most distinguished dinner party of the
American Establishment ever held," calling it the "high water mark of
U.S. hegemony."[116] After dinner the group sat through a series of briefings by Philip Habib, the deputy assistant secretary of state for East
Asian affairs; Major General William E. DePuy; and George Carver,
the CIA's lead analyst for Vietnam.

"Do you think a military victory can be won?" Clifford asked,
no doubt certain of the answer. "Not under present circumstances,"
Habib replied. "What would you do?" asked Clifford. "Stop bombing and negotiate," replied Habib. In perhaps the most memorable
exchange of the evening, UN ambassador Arthur Goldberg challenged
DePuy's assertion that 80,000 North Vietnamese and Vietcong troops
had been killed during the Tet Offensive. "What is the normal ratio
of wounded to killed?" he asked. DePuy answered that a conservative
estimate was three to one, wounded to killed. Goldberg then asked
how many enemy troops were in the field. "Two hundred thirty thousand," replied DePuy. Goldberg did not need to be a math genius to
determine that the army's figures did not add up. 80,000 dead and
a three-to-one ratio of wounded to killed totaled 320,000 casualties, which would mean that all the enemy troops were either dead or
incapacitated. "Then who the hell are we fighting?" Goldberg asked,
incredulous. Dillon remarked that it looked like it might take five to
ten years to win the war, whereas back in November they had been
told that it would take a year. The American people would not stand
for it, he remarked. "We had to find a way out," recalled Vance.[117]

The meeting broke up at 11 P.M. George Ball was "absolutely
delighted" with the briefings, believing they were the first truthful

reports he had heard about Vietnam.[118] Rostow, however, was disgusted. "I smelled a rat," he recalled. "It was a put up job."[119]

The following morning the group reconvened to discuss what they had heard the night before. Relative to their meeting a few months back, the turnaround was dramatic. Ball thought to himself, "There's been a mistake in the invitation list; these can't be the same men I saw here last November."[120] While the Wise Men discussed the events of the prior evening, Johnson was meeting with Wheeler and General Creighton Abrams, who had been named to succeed Westmoreland as commander in Vietnam. They gave the president an optimistic briefing, which Johnson asked them to repeat for the Wise Men. For the Wise Men, the contrast between the pessimistic briefings of the night before and the optimistic assessment from Wheeler and Abrams was striking. In fact, it was so striking that it seemed to Rostow that the Wise Men were not even listening.[121]

That afternoon Johnson asked to speak with the Wise Men alone, anxious to hear their candid observations. McGeorge Bundy spoke for the group. "There is a very significant shift in our position," he began. "When we last met we saw reasons for hope. We hoped then there would be slow but steady progress. Last night and today the picture is not so hopeful, particularly in the countryside." Acheson spoke for the majority: "We can no longer do the job we set out to do in the time we have left and we must begin to take steps to disengage." Johnson solicited the opinions of everyone in the room. Arthur Dean said, "All of us got the impression that there is no military conclusion in sight. We felt time is running out." Acheson remarked that with support for the war on the wane, time was too limited to achieve the goal of a viable, independent South Vietnam, and that they would have to settle for something less. Vance, George Ball, and C. Douglas Dillon indicated that they were in agreement with Acheson and Bundy. In an indication of how profoundly the situation had changed, Bundy remarked, "I must tell you what I thought I would never say— that I now agree with George Ball." Omar Bradley, Maxwell Taylor, and Robert Murphy dissented from the majority, as did Fortas, who remained hawkish. Acheson was the most outspoken, and he clashed with both Fortas and Wheeler, whom Johnson had asked to join the group to take questions. Wheeler disputed Acheson's criticism that the military was "bent on military victory" and said he recognized that a "classic military victory" was not achievable. This was too much for Acheson, who snapped, "Then what in the name of God do we have five hundred thousand troops out there for? Chasing girls?"[122]

Johnson became angry over the turn of events, perhaps feeling that he had been betrayed. Before the meeting concluded, he asked to speak with Rusk and Clifford privately. "Who poisoned the well with these guys? I want to hear those briefings myself." The president complained to Ball, of all people, saying, "Your whole group must have been brainwashed and I'm going to find out what Habib and the others told you."[123]

Johnson's anger over the outcome of the meeting of the Wise Men played out in the hard-line tone he requested for the latest draft of the March 31 speech. With only a few days remaining, Clifford suggested that he and McPherson work on the speech together. They met Thursday morning, March 28, in Rusk's office, along with Bill Bundy and Rostow. Clifford was distraught over the direction of the speech and spoke in very emotional terms, unusual for him, about the war. McPherson, who recalled the meeting as the best he had ever attended, was struck by the unique perspective Clifford brought to the discussion as someone intimately aware of what members of the business and legal establishment were thinking. "These guys who have been with us and who have sustained us so far as we are sustained are no longer with us," Clifford lamented. He was very concerned that public support was waning, and he spoke with great passion. "This Speech as it is presently written, is wrong," he said. "The speech is more of the same. The American people are fed up with more of the same, and they're not going to—. Because more of the same means no win, and only a continual long drag on American resources."[124] His performance was masterful. Townsend Hoopes described it well: "The Clifford manner is deliberate, sonorous, eloquent and quite uninterruptible. It gathers momentum as it proceeds, and soon achieves a certain mesmerizing effect; the perfection of the grammar is uncanny. During the course of several hours, speaking slowly, his fingertips pressed together, and glancing occasionally at an envelope on which he had scribbled a couple of points, Clifford mustered every available argument in the powerful arsenal of reasons why it was not in the United States' interest to go on pouring military resources into South Vietnam."[125]

Clifford argued that a different type of speech was required, something drastically different than a call to arms. Instead, he recommended a strategy of de-escalation, reciprocal steps to be taken by both the United States and North Vietnam to drastically reduce the level of hostilities. The burden would then shift to the South Vietnamese to defend their own country. The president, said Clifford, needed to send a clear message that the United States would not continue to pour troops into the country. To that end Clifford recommended a halt to the bombing north of the 20th parallel. Surprisingly, neither Rusk nor Rostow voiced opposition to this approach, and while their position was not quite support it was the opening Clifford needed. Rather than abandoning the hard-line speech, the group decided to prepare a second draft embracing Clifford's position and leave it to the president to decide which of the two to work with.[126]

The next morning McPherson met with the president to go over his changes to the speech, and as he reviewed the draft for the changes the president wanted to make he realized, to his great surprise and relief, that Johnson was working from the alternate speech. As soon as he returned to his office, he rushed to the telephone and called Clifford. "We've won," he exclaimed. "The President is working from our draft!"[127]

On March 31 President Johnson spoke to the nation in a televised address. "Tonight I want to speak to you of peace in Vietnam and Southeast Asia," he began. The substantive part of the speech reads as follows:

> We are prepared to move immediately toward peace through negotiations. So, tonight, in the hope that this action will lead to early talks, I am taking the first step to de-escalate the conflict. We are reducing—substantially reducing—the present level of hostilities. And we are doing so unilaterally, and at once. Tonight, I have ordered our aircraft and naval vessels to make no attacks on North Vietnam, except in the area north of the demilitarized zone where the continuing enemy buildup directly threatens allied forward positions and where the movements of their troops and supplies are clearly related to that threat. . . . Whether a complete bombing halt becomes possible in the future will be determined by events.

Then, at the end of the speech, Johnson delivered an announcement that stunned the nation.

> With America's sons in the fields far away, with America's future under challenge right here at home, with our hopes and the world's hopes for peace in the balance every day, I do not believe that I should devote an hour or a day of my time to any personal partisan causes or to any duties other than the

awesome duties of this office—the Presidency of your country. Accordingly, I shall not seek, and I will not accept, the nomination of my party for another term as your President.[128]

The mood in the White House that evening was somber, much like a wake, Clifford recalled.[129] Clifford lamented in his memoirs that Johnson had not shared with him the decision to step down. Had he known that Johnson was not going to run, the tone of the speech would have been different, and Clifford would have argued strenuously for the president to call a full halt to the bombing. A full halt, he surmised, might have led to more substantive and serious negotiations. Instead, the March 31 speech had been drafted for an "embattled candidate, not a man ready to sacrifice his career, in his own eyes, in the pursuit of peace."[130] Clifford was determined that Johnson's sacrifice not be in vain.

The president's March 31 speech was not the final word on the Vietnam War, however, and a struggle continued between the hawks and doves in Johnson's administration. Initially, Clifford and his allies enjoyed the advantage conferred by the president's speech.[131] Yet his foes, Rusk and Rostow, were formidable adversaries and continued to view Vietnam as a critical bulwark against communist expansion. Clifford, by contrast, was convinced that his mission was to extricate the United States from Vietnam by the end of the year. With decisive leadership from the president this internal struggle could have been resolved, yet despite his March 31 speech Johnson continued to send mixed messages and even shifted toward the Rusk camp. His vacillating raised legitimate questions, both at the time and years later, about the meaning of his March 31 speech. Throughout the rest of 1968, until just before Nixon's inauguration in January 1969, Clifford battled with his adversaries in the administration, and with Johnson himself, to ensure that the president lived up to the words he spoke on March 31: "But let men everywhere know, however, that a strong, a confident, and a vigilant America stands ready tonight to seek an honorable peace—and stands ready tonight to defend an honored cause— whatever the price, whatever the burden, whatever the sacrifice that duty may require."[132]

Writing in 1969, Townsend Hoopes gave Clifford high praise for turning the president around on Vietnam.

Without question, Clifford played a pre-eminent—I believe the decisive—role. He was the single most powerful and effective catalyst of change, bringing each day to the stale air of the inner circle a fresh perception of the national interest, unfettered by connection with the fateful decisions of 1965. He rallied and gave authoritative voice to the informed and restless opposition within the government, pressing the case for change with intellectual daring, high moral courage, inspired ingenuity and sheer stubborn persistence. It was one of the great individual performances in American history, and achieved in the remarkably taut time span of thirty days.[133]

Three years earlier Clifford had warned Johnson of a quagmire in Vietnam. Widely regarded as a hawk following Johnson's decision to commit significant ground troops, he had come full circle in his first exhausting month as secretary of defense. Summoning all of his powers of persuasion, as well as an influential collection of allies, he had, if only temporarily, convinced Johnson to draw down American troop levels and seek peace. In the remaining ten months of Johnson's term he would continuously fight to regain the ground he held at the end of March, battling with hawks in the administration, the military, and the president himself. The road ahead would not get any easier, but Clifford had fundamentally altered the trajectory of the war. Instead of a call to arms, the president was talking about peace.

# 10

# I Search for Why I Find Myself Constantly Alone

"Tonight I want to speak to you of peace in Vietnam and Southeast Asia," President Johnson had declared on March 31, 1968; yet peace would prove to be elusive. Although he had publicly proclaimed his desire for peace during a primetime television address, and had sacrificed his political ambitions in the process, Johnson did not move decisively to bring the war to an end. The president's vacillation, emotional outbursts, and unpredictable behavior were an endless source of frustration for Clifford, who could never be certain that he had the president's support. In sending mixed messages Johnson also exacerbated the rivalry between Clifford and hawks Dean Rusk and Walt Rostow, who continued to argue that America's prestige and security were at stake in Southeast Asia. At times the bureaucratic infighting was vicious, as Clifford's adversaries sought to discredit him in front of the president and disregarded his authority over the military. Although he had allies in the Pentagon and White House, among Johnson's senior foreign policy advisers Clifford was very much alone.

Having made the offer to seek peace with North Vietnam it was now up to Johnson to take the necessary steps to prove that he truly meant what he said. Almost immediately that situation was made more complicated. On April 1, the day after the president's speech, U.S. warplanes bombed a military target in Thanh Hoa, just south of the 20th parallel. This immediately caused a political problem for Johnson, especially with Senator William Fulbright, because the president had been vague, promising that he would cease bombing north of the DMZ without specifying that the line had actually been drawn, as Clifford had suggested, at the 20th parallel. Although it was below the 20th parallel, Thanh Hoa was two hundred miles north of the DMZ. Johnson and his advisers met the next day and discussed whether to revise the orders and restrict bombing below the 20th parallel. Somewhat contradicting his position in favor of de-escalation, Clifford argued that they should continue to bomb up to the 20th parallel. "If we limit ourselves below 20th they will take advantage of it," he said. He also indicated that he doubted that the enemy would be willing to engage in peace talks, thus raising questions regarding Clifford's own intentions. "Odds are 100 to 1 Hanoi will turn us down," he said. "Best thing we can do is to show a continuing effort." He assured Johnson that the 20th parallel was the appropriate boundary because it left three-fourths of the land and 90 percent of the population of North Vietnam off limits while still inhibiting the North's ability to move men and materiel into South Vietnam. He also observed that 90 percent of the sorties were within sixty miles of the DMZ, while only 2.3 percent were against targets in the Thanh Hoa area.[1]

The following day the North Vietnamese broadcast a statement over Hanoi radio responding to Johnson's peace initiative. Initially it appeared that they had rejected Johnson's offer, describing it as a "defeat and at the same time a shrewd trick." However, the statement then veered from belligerency to accommodation: "However, for its part, the Government of the Democratic Republic of Vietnam declares its readiness to appoint its representative to contact the U.S. representative with a view to determining with the American side the unconditional cessation of the U.S. bombing raids and all other acts of war against the Democratic Republic of Vietnam so that talks may start."[2]

In the afternoon Johnson met with his Cabinet to discuss the North Vietnamese response. Abandoning his tone of pessimism from the previous day Clifford suggested that the North Vietnamese were willing to seek peace. "This appears to be a departure from [their] previous position about unconditional cessation of bombing," he said, and recommended "that we construe this as a reciprocal step on the part of Hanoi and now proceed to the second part of the program that the President had in mind."[3]

On April 4 the news reached Washington of a national tragedy, the first of two horrific losses for the country, the assassination of Martin Luther King. In the aftermath of the King assassination, Johnson canceled a previously scheduled trip to Vietnam to confer with Westmoreland, who would soon step down as U.S. commander in Vietnam. Instead, Westmoreland flew to Washington, providing Clifford with an opportunity to question the outgoing commander as well. During a lengthy meeting with Johnson and his foreign policy advisers, Westmoreland confidently predicted victory. Adopting the position that had so infuriated the Wise Men, Westmoreland declared that the Tet Offensive was a "colossal military defeat" for the enemy, who had suffered 60,000 dead. "I say to [negotiations leader] Ambassador Harriman he will be negotiating from [a] position of strength," Westmoreland proudly declared. "Under what condition would a cease-fire be acceptable?" Clifford asked. "I do not see the acceptability of that," Westmoreland replied. In response to a follow-up question the general said, somewhat ingenuously, "We would like for the North Vietnamese to go home and turn in their weapons."[4]

During the meeting Clifford got into a dispute with Abe Fortas over the immediate objective of the president's speech, which in Clifford's mind was a lessening of hostilities. No doubt trying to minimize the impact of the president's offer of peace, Fortas suggested that they needed to understate calls for a cease-fire. "We must have a different term from cease-fire," he offered. But Clifford adamantly disagreed. "One of the great goals on the minds of Americans is for a 'cease-fire,'" he responded.[5]

Two days later Johnson met with Clifford, Rusk, Rostow, and Press Secretary George Christian to decide on a site for the negotiations with the North Vietnamese. The North Vietnamese had sent a message proposing that negotiations begin in the capital of Cambodia, Phnom Penh. Rusk indicated that the South Vietnamese favored New Delhi, while the president said that he favored Rangoon, the capital of Burma, or Jakarta. Rusk suggested that the United States offer a list of four cities. Clifford felt that these suggestions ran counter to Johnson's offer of a week earlier to meet anytime, anywhere.[6]

The next day Ellsworth Bunker, the ambassador to Vietnam, arrived in Washington to consult with the president. Westmoreland had by then returned to Vietnam, but he might as well have been at the meeting, for it seemed that Bunker and the general were of the same mind as to the current conditions in Vietnam in the aftermath of the Tet Offensive. "In going into negotiations," Bunker said, "let's keep in mind we are strong and not weak." He suggested that the true impact of Tet was psychological, consistent with the Westmoreland argument that Tet had been a spectacular defeat for the enemy. Bunker also said he believed that the South Vietnamese government was not yet ready for negotiations. "In three or four months they'll be stronger," he said. Clifford disagreed and challenged Bunker on the facts. "If they are getting stronger, etc.," he said, "why do they feel such a concern for the NLF?" Bunker responded that the South Vietnamese feared them politically, not militarily.[7]

In response to a question from the president, General Earle Wheeler indicated that the military would prefer to have the authority to bomb up to the 20th parallel. Clifford, however, looked to avoid the kind of misunderstanding caused by the bombing of Thanh Hoa and overruled him, stating that the 19th parallel was the boundary. Johnson asked if the North Vietnamese were sincere about negotiations or whether it was a ploy. Rusk, Bill Bundy, Bunker, and Rostow suspected that it was. Clifford hoped that was not the case, but conceded that the bombing restrictions would have to be lifted if it was. "If they play us for fools," he said, "Buzz [Wheeler] and I have some choice targets we want to recognize." Johnson closed the meeting by asking if everyone present concurred with the negotiating instructions given to Averell Harriman, who along with Cyrus Vance would represent the United States at the peace talks. Harriman observed that Bunker was unaware that public support for the war was declining and as a result seemed uncommitted to negotiations. Cognizant of that, Clifford intervened in the preparation of the negotiating instructions and recommended that Bunker's instructions be provided to the negotiators only as guidance. "There is no doubt that Clifford's initiative saved the instructions from mutilation," Harriman wrote.[8]

Clifford gave his first press conference as secretary of defense on April 11, and his announcement of a troop ceiling of 549,500 troops was the major story of the day. In conjunction with the announced troop ceiling he also indicated that the United States had adopted a policy of gradually transferring responsibility for the war over to the South Vietnamese. Clifford was careful to leave a loophole to future troop increases, however, using the qualifying phrase "at this time."[9] Nonetheless, the clear message was that the U.S. commitment of troops was not open-ended, at least not in the sense of the number of troops. Johnson was at his ranch in Texas at the time, but Rostow reported what he and Clifford had discussed:

> In the course of the conversation, Clark underlined a thought which he suggested I pass along to you. One of the purposes of his press conference was to begin to suggest to the American people that we have a long-range plan leading to our disengagement as the South Vietnamese expanded their armed forces and their capabilities for dealing with the military prob-

lem. He feels that it is particularly important now for us quietly to introduce this theme because it is not certain that the
negotiations will be productive. If they are, they may take a
long time. If they break down, we must have a concept for
continuing our commitment in Vietnam for the long pull but
on a basis which has some light at the end of the tunnel. Therefore, he is inclined to believe we should play the negotiations
in low key without excessive optimism and keep part of the
public attention focused on the idea we have come to a ceiling
in our forces and are looking to slow but ultimate disengagement. He believes the President might pick up this theme from
time to time. I suggested Thieu also might occasionally speak
in this vein.[10]

Clifford's press conference demonstrated that he was no longer
the hawk he had been believed to be, but also that he had become the
spokesman for the administration. Rostow's memo to Johnson, along
with the fact that Johnson did not overrule him, demonstrated that
Clifford had drastically changed the administration's policy on Vietnam in the short time he had been secretary. Reporter and Vietnam
War critic Neil Sheehan wrote that "to the surprise of Washington
. . . Clifford has emerged as a new voice with a different approach."
But Sheehan also qualified his observations (which Clifford neglected
to mention in his memoirs) by suggesting two possible motives for
the change in policy. The first interpretation was that Clifford was
"engaged in a public-relations exercise, with his actions motivated
by domestic political factors. This view holds that he and the Administration's Vietnam policy have changed more in appearance than in
reality." The second interpretation was that the Tet Offensive had a
dramatic impact on him and motivated him to reassess the situation
in Vietnam. "Clark is a very clear-headed man," Sheehan quoted a
friend of Clifford's as saying. "He has the ability to see things as they
are and not as he would like them to be."[11]
    Clifford was a political animal, but he was clearly alarmed by a
war that no longer seemed in America's best interests. Privately he
confided to his old friend David Lilienthal his disgust with the South
Vietnamese. The war had become too much of a drain, and if it was
to continue it would have to become "their war." "They've been put
on notice that all of them, all the Asians that have been depending on
Uncle Sam to fight for them, have got to get off their big fat Asian ass
and defend themselves."[12]

For the next several weeks the United States and the North Vietnamese sparred over a location for the peace talks, finally agreeing in early May to hold them in Paris. However, once a location was finally chosen, the lead hawks, Rostow and Rusk, seemed to become pessimistic about the negotiations. Clifford lamented during his 8:30 staff meeting that Rusk and Rostow were no longer as supportive of a negotiated settlement as they had been at the end of March. Confident that the United States had gained the military advantage, their position seemed to Clifford to be "no settlement—just beat the Hell out of them."[13]

That afternoon Clifford met with the president, his foreign policy advisers, and the Vietnam negotiators, and the tone of the meeting was decidedly pessimistic. Clifford was frustrated by the group's unwillingness to accept that the North Vietnamese would demand a total halt to the bombing. "Suppose they say they want [an] agreement on stopping [the] bombing, [and they will] do nothing else till that is done. Let's face that very real problem." Clifford emphasized that Johnson had taken the first step and that the North Vietnamese had responded in kind. Therefore, prior conditions, such as the San Antonio formula, were no longer relevant.[14]

The next day the conversation resumed, but Rusk had dug in his heels and insisted on a hard negotiating posture. "We should not pull our punches," Rusk said. "We should not understate our own case." Anything less than that, which he dismissively labeled the "Clifford formula," would never work. Johnson agreed, and he instructed Rusk and Clifford to meet with Vance and Harriman to make sure that they would be tough negotiators. "Let's not put our minimum condition on the table first," he said.[15]

The following day Johnson and his foreign policy advisers met with Vance and Harriman for the last time before they were to leave for Paris. Clifford gave them a little pep talk:

> Only one guarantee—the discussion will be lengthy and difficult. It took a month to get a site. It will take a long time. At present, there is a certain euphoria. I do not know why Hanoi has chosen to negotiate. It is possible they want us to relax our military posture. Hanoi will try to divide the United States during this time. They will attempt to divide the American people. We all want war to stop—but on a decent and honorable basis. We need to present an appearance of unity during these talks.[16]

A week later at the Tuesday lunch meeting Clifford and Rusk clashed over whether air strikes should resume north of the 19th parallel. Rusk argued that the North Vietnamese had not reciprocated the suspension and that he was inclined to extend the bombing midway between the 19th and 20th parallel to establish a buffer zone. Clifford said, "Psychologically, it would be a bad time to expand our bombings. It would be difficult to ask them to phase down. The targets are not worth the political and psychological problems created. The product of our bombing will not be that important." Rusk replied, "I also am concerned that Hanoi thinks it can mobilize public opinion such that they can do anything and we must stop all our efforts. They must learn you did not withdraw in order to bend to their wishes. I would not oppose strikes between 19th and 20th." Clifford and Rusk also had a tense exchange over Clifford's upcoming appearance before the Senate Foreign Affairs Committee, with Rusk condescendingly recommending that Clifford "memorize the March 31 speech and not go beyond it."[17] The atmosphere in the room was so tense that Johnson wondered aloud if he should have even made the March 31 speech.[18]

A couple of days later, Clifford vented his frustrations to George Elsey, Paul Warnke, and Robert Pursley during a Saturday session of their 8:30 staff meeting. Clifford believed he had made a strong case for curtailing the bombing between the 19th and 20th parallels. However, he suspected that the next time the subject came up it would be in the context of a policy, rather then a tactical, discussion and that Rusk, Rostow, and Wheeler would take a very hard position. Again, Clifford felt, they would say that we must stay in Vietnam until the United States succeed militarily and that Johnson would agree because it would appeal to his "nail the coonskin to the wall" mentality. Clifford felt that it was difficult for the president to side with him against Rusk, Rostow, and Wheeler. Eventually, said Clifford, they were all going to have to air out their differences. He sympathized with Johnson, who had inherited the problem from Kennedy, but he felt that the war had gone on far too long. The problem was that Johnson was too heavily invested in the war, in terms of lives and dollars, to simply pull out. Clifford felt that eventually he would need to confront Johnson, either alone or with Fortas, and convince him to withdraw from Vietnam. The only way to do that, he surmised, was to prepare his most persuasive and logical presentation, but allow Johnson to reach the conclusion on his own. Clifford knew the president well enough to know that he was too proud to be told what to do; he would have to make his own decision.[19]

Vietnam presented a unique challenge relative to conventional warfare, Clifford explained. The terrain was difficult, there was no "field of battle," and enemy retreated into neighboring Laos or Cambodia when pursued. In a guerrilla war such as in Vietnam, the enemy chooses the strategy, takes the initiative, and determines the level of casualties it is willing to absorb. With respect to casualties Clifford lamented that Rusk, Rostow, and Wheeler had convinced Johnson that the North Vietnamese were depleting their manpower. "I don't believe it!" he exclaimed. All of these factors, so obvious to Clifford but otherwise ignored by the administration, severely diminished the chances of achieving a conventional military victory. "I've sat in on ten meetings at the White House when McNamara was Secretary of Defense," he said. "But we never came to grips with the fundamental issues of the war!"[20]

Clifford reflected for a moment, and then said, "I think I should see him alone, privately." He thought it worked to his advantage that he was still relatively new to the Pentagon. "I have no previous posture, no previous position, no public record to defend," he imagined himself telling Johnson. "Let me tell you what I found. . . . Here is the story. Here are the facts. Here are my conclusions." But then he lapsed briefly into despair. "If he thinks he must stick to a military victory, then I guess there is no end to it." Yet Clifford felt that they had made some progress in the last couple of months, which he described with a baseball metaphor. "We made it around second base on March 31," he said. Rusk and Rostow were formidable adversaries, however, and they challenged him every step of the way. "It's a constant struggle," he lamented. "I have to keep struggling or I lose again." In contrast to Johnson's preference for a tough negotiating posture at Paris, Clifford believed that the circumstances in Vietnam necessitated a flexible approach. "I want to impress on LBJ that our posture is so basically impossible that we've got to find some way out."[21]

Warnke seemed surprised that Clifford's position on the war had progressed so much. "Do you want a way out?" he asked. Clifford replied yes and indicated it was a question of timing as to when he would broach the subject to the president. Again Clifford emphasized the importance of allowing Johnson to reach his own conclusion—the final 5 percent of the equation, as he described it. It would be up to Clifford and his core group at the Department of Defense to assemble the other 95 percent so that it was absolutely persuasive. "We should end up with a memo that makes the case for disengagement on our part a matter of transcendent importance from the standpoint of this country." Clifford closed by stressing that what they discussed needed to remain confidential.[22]

The peace talks in Paris had barely begun, but already Rusk was convinced that they were going nowhere and that the North Vietnamese were not negotiating in good faith. Accordingly, he recommended during the lunch meeting on Tuesday, May 21, that bombing should resume between the 19th and 20th parallels. Clifford disagreed, saying that he thought they had a good week at Paris and he did not want to sabotage any momentum that was developing. Most important, the United States had demonstrated that it was seeking peace, whereas the enemy was being inflexible and was interested in nothing more than propaganda. To Clifford, this was important to the domestic audience weary with the war, but also to the way the United States was perceived on the international stage. He also thought that the North Vietnamese had hurt themselves with the incredible claim that they did not have troops in South Vietnam. Clifford believed that the San Antonio formula was no longer relevant, and that the United States was in a much stronger position having curtailed the bombing. Were the United States to resume bombing between the 19th and 20th parallels, he argued, the North Vietnamese would likely demand a total cessation of bombing in order to resume negotiations. "We got North Vietnam to the bargaining table by the President's offer of moderate restraint," he said.[23]

Rusk disagreed. "We should not have rigid limits on the 19th," he said. Johnson agreed. Clifford did not back down, however, arguing that they were achieving results at the bargaining table, and that was only possible because of their restraint with the bombing. He argued that it would be counterproductive to lift the bombing restrictions. "We are waiting for them to de-escalate," he said. "The heat is on them. If we go back in, we remove some of this heat." Johnson was not convinced and instead believed that bombing between the 19th and 20th parallels was working to the Americans' military advantage, a point on which he and Wheeler agreed. "You're just carrying me along week-to-week," the president said to Clifford.[24] Clifford conceded the point, but countered that the marginal advantage was not worth the risk. Johnson was concerned that the longer they refrained from bombing between the 19th and 20th parallels, the more problematic it would be to resume. Clifford disagreed, but Rusk sided with the president.[25]

Clifford then tried a different tactic, arguing that the peace talks represented the best chance of a favorable result in Vietnam. "If we escalate, it will diminish the chance of success," he said. "We have to make Paris a success—it will be catastrophic if Paris breaks up and we have to go back to pure military action." "Why is that so bad?" asked Johnson. It would be bad because "more boys would be lost than ever before," Clifford warned. He argued that the restrictions Johnson placed on the military, including a refusal to invade the North or mine its harbors, precluded the possibility of a military victory. The "enemy controls the situation in the South," he said. "They can hit and run, they can attack cities, they can control casualties. We can hope only for success in Paris. We are in a war we can't win." Essentially, the war had become a stalemate. The North Vietnamese had made a major gamble during Tet, and having failed to achieve a military victory, their best chance was at the bargaining table. "They can't win [the] war militarily," he said. "We can't win the war militarily."[26]

Johnson disagreed, as did Rusk, who noted that the United States had prevented the North from overrunning South Vietnam. But Clifford countered that the absence of a win by North Vietnam did not constitute a victory for America. "Hanoi cannot win the war militarily," he argued. "They know that. That doesn't mean we have won it. I do not believe they are going to give up that effort unless we reach some agreement in Paris." He argued that the United States could not sustain the war effort indefinitely and that the high level of casualties had led to an erosion of popular support. The North Vietnamese, by contrast, had the will to absorb a much greater level of casualties.[27] Clifford then asked a tough question. "Can anybody here tell me what our plan is to bring the war to an end if the Paris talks fail? If Paris fails, we have no alternative but to turn back to the military and I need to know what is to be done to bring it to an end."[28]

Rusk argued passionately that the peace talks would fail unless the United States proved that the North Vietnamese could not win in the South. He said that their primary reason for attending the peace talks was to gain a reprieve from the bombing. This was the fundamental difference: Clifford believed that the peace talks were the only solution to a military stalemate and that the North was willing to negotiate, whereas Rusk believed the peace talks would fail absent a U.S. military victory. Johnson finally intervened and announced that, against his better judgment, he would put off expansion of the bombing for another week.[29]

After the meeting Rusk called Clifford and suggested that they meet privately to try to iron out their differences. But when they met three days later they could not come to an agreement. Rostow sided with Rusk and, in a memo to the president, suggested that failure in Paris could lead to setbacks on the battlefield, a scenario he believed that Clifford ignored. But Clifford took action to protect his flank by asking the Joint Chiefs to develop contingency plans in the event that the negotiations were unsuccessful.[30]

Clifford's biggest challenge during 1968 was the vacillation of the president, whom Clifford described as a weathervane. At the May 21 luncheon meeting Johnson disagreed with Clifford regarding the notion that the war had become a stalemate and indicated that he was losing patience with the bombing restrictions; however, a week later he seemed to change his mind. At a breakfast meeting at the White House the president asked Clifford for his assessment of the chances for success in Paris. Clifford began by pointing out that the president's September 1967 peace feeler, the San Antonio formula, was rejected, whereas his March 31 offer was accepted. "Why?" he asked rhetorically. The reason, he explained, was the Tet Offensive. Clifford believed that the North Vietnamese had reached the conclusion at the end of 1967 that their guerrilla strategy was not effective, so they changed tactics and launched a massive assault on the cities—Tet—which they believed would bring about a dramatic conclusion to the war. After suffering tremendous losses and not achieving their objectives, they then concluded that they could not win and opted to pursue a negotiated settlement. It may be too optimistic to expect success in Paris, Clifford conceded, but he honestly believed the chances were good. It was a persuasive presentation, and Johnson was so pleased he called Clifford at home to thank him. Clifford was encouraged and believed that Johnson's support increased the chances of success in Paris, and strengthened his hand.[31]

As if it were not difficult enough managing Johnson, Clifford ran into a problem with the new commander in Vietnam, General Creighton Abrams. Abrams, who had replaced Westmoreland, was angry over a report issued by the U.S. embassy documenting abuses inflicted upon the local population. The report, which reached the president, was embarrassing for the military and provoked an angry and somewhat insubordinate reaction from Abrams. Abrams's reaction led Clifford to question his fitness to take over command in Vietnam. After discussing the matter with Johnson, Clifford reprimanded the general in a letter addressed to Wheeler. "I would be less than candid if I did not inform you that General Abrams' message has caused me real uneasiness," he wrote. "Am I to conclude that the submission of a relevant question on the conduct of the war, a question of great concern to the Commander-in-Chief and to the Secretary of Defense, constitutes placing a field commander 'constantly on the rebuttal'?"[32] Abrams apologized the next day, and Clifford never had another problem with him.

June 5 saw a breakthrough in the peace process in the form of a letter from Soviet Premier Alexei Kosygin. In the letter Kosygin requested that the United States halt the bombing of North Vietnam, but what was particularly intriguing was the phrasing: "I and my colleagues believe—and we have grounds for this"—that a cessation of the bombing could lead to a breakthrough in the peace talks. The language was subtle but the implication was obvious, and Clifford was encouraged that the message could facilitate a peace settlement. Rusk and Rostow were unconvinced, however, and Clifford was concerned about a draft reply from State that was hawkish in tone.[33] On June 9 Johnson and his foreign policy advisers met to discuss the letter, with Rusk taking the position that Kosygin could not be trusted and therefore the letter should be dismissed. Clifford, however, made the case that this represented an opportunity they must seize. "We have a great opportunity here," he said. "We should take serious advantage of it. . . . We won't end the war by negotiations with the North Vietnamese. They control the level of the war. They can go on indefinitely from the manpower aspect. . . . What will stop it is an arrangement with the Soviets so they can use their leverage—which we don't have—to bring the Soviets to force Hanoi to stop it." Clifford believed that the United States could rely on Kosygin's assurances and that it was a prudent risk to halt the bombing in the interest of peace.[34]

What was most striking about this exchange, as Harriman observed, was that Rusk seemed to have deliberately undermined Clifford. Prior to their heading over to the White House, in a preliminary meeting Clifford explained his views to Rusk. Rusk asked some questions, but did not oppose him, nor did he warn that he would present a counterargument to the president. "I have never participated in any discussion in the White House where there was such a clear attempt made on the part of one member of the President's Cabinet to destroy the position of another before the second man had a chance to present it," Harriman wrote. When Harriman later asked Rusk for an explanation, the secretary of state replied, "The trouble with Clark is he has lost his nerve since he has been over in the Pentagon." Harriman concluded that Rusk had been using comparable language with the president in order to undermine Clifford and impugn his character. "To me, this kind of attack on a colleague is contemptible," Harriman wrote.[35]

Johnson disagreed with Clifford's interpretation of the Kosygin letter and sided with Rusk. "I am not willing to take their assurance and rely on it on face value," he said. "We have softened. They have done nothing." He also challenged Clifford's assessment of the military situation in Vietnam. "I think we may have them beaten now," he said. "Only thing that will stop us from making a peace is ourselves. I think Clark is unrealistic about [the] attitude of how our men will react to this." Rostow took the position, to paraphrase one of the more memorable quotes from the Vietnam War era, that it might be necessary to break up the peace talks in order to save them. He wrote to the president, "I believe they are laughing at us and playing us for suckers on the diplomatic-military front, in the short run." He also dismissed an argument that Clifford had made that Vice President Hubert Humphrey, the probable Democratic nominee, would be politically wounded if the peace talks failed. Accordingly, he recommended that the president reject the veiled overture from the Soviets. Johnson sided with Rostow and authorized only a vague response to Kosygin. "I search for why I find myself constantly alone," Clifford lamented.[36]

Less than two weeks earlier Clifford had been encouraged by Johnson's attitude toward the peace talks, but now the president had shifted back to being a hawk again. A visit with some wounded soldiers at Walter Reed Hospital had affected him and intensified his resolve to fight on in Vietnam. He claimed that the administration was not doing enough to sell the war to the American people and instructed Clifford and Rusk to begin a public relations effort to build up support. Johnson fumed and complained that he felt "hornswaggled on the bombing" and was determined to "knock Hanoi and Haiphong off the map." An exasperated Clifford rhetorically asked his staff how he could convince Johnson that a World War II type of public relations effort would be futile with respect to Vietnam.[37]

Clifford gave a press conference on June 20 and, in deference to Johnson's request, gave an upbeat report on the war. Quoting figures that indicated that North Vietnamese casualties were ten times the rate of U.S. casualties, Clifford suggested that there was "a very real question as to how long they would choose to submit their military force to this extreme degree of attrition." Despite his defense of the status of the war, however, the headlines centered on his comment that he detected "bits and straws" of progress toward a peace agreement.[38] Taking their disagreement public, Rusk contradicted Clifford at a press conference the following day. "I won't quarrel with 'bits and straws' in the wind," he said, "but we have not yet, I think, taken giant strides. It would be a mistake to go beyond 'straws in the wind.'"[39] Discussing the matter with his staff the following Monday Clifford confided that there was a real policy difference between the departments of State and Defense. As Clifford saw it, State had been taking a hard line for years, but McNamara, Clifford's predecessor in Defense, always deferred to Rusk, thus minimizing the public and private impact of the dispute. This presented Clifford with a quandary: should he defer to Rusk or speak up about what he believed, and if he spoke out, should it be done in public or private? Rusk was "terribly upset" about Clifford's press conference, and Clifford believed that Rusk had harbored those feelings since his reinterpretation of the San Antonio formula during his confirmation hearings. Clifford believed that he was in a battle with Maxwell Taylor, Rusk, and Rostow, all of whom were constantly undermining the Paris peace talks. Venting his frustration, Clifford exclaimed, "I think 'they' are wrong! They aren't conceiving of what would happen to LBJ and the nation if we went back to the pre-March 31 erosion of trust and confidence" in the administration.[40]

Clark Clifford had, since his time in the Truman administration, a reputation as a political fixer, and Johnson turned to him for political advice frequently before naming him secretary of defense. Once sworn in, however, Clifford focused primarily on the Vietnam War and other defense matters. Johnson's ill-fated attempt to install Abe Fortas as chief justice of the Supreme Court was a notable exception to that rule. In June 1968 Johnson asked Clifford to assist with his effort to elevate Fortas to chief justice, a move Clifford supported. However, in a major tactical error Johnson also planned to name Homer Thornberry, an appeals court judge, fellow Texan, and long-time friend of the president, for the vacant justice seat held by Fortas. Clifford thought the Thornberry nomination would be opposed by Senate Republicans and urged the president to nominate a prominent, respected Republican lawyer instead. He warned Johnson that he would be charged with an attempt to pack the court with friends and political allies and that the Republicans would stall both appointments until after the election. Johnson was defiant, however. "Well, I don't intend to put some damned Republican on the Court," he said. He instructed Clifford to meet with key Republican senators in an effort to convince them not to filibuster the nomination. Over the next couple of months Clifford worked on the nomination, but he was unable to persuade opponents in the Senate to support it, especially in light of the accusations that Fortas had violated the separation of powers between the executive and judicial branches by advising Johnson and assisting with the drafting of the 1966 State of the Union address. In October, in the aftermath of a failed cloture vote in the Senate, Fortas withdrew his nomination. Clifford had been right, and Johnson would have been wise to heed his counsel.[41]

In mid-July Clifford made his first visit to Vietnam as secretary of defense. Clifford had been hoping that the South Vietnamese Army would be soon be ready to assume primary responsibility for the war, lessening the burden on the Americans. His trip, however, convinced him that they were not ready for the task, and would not be for some time absent a major commitment by the South Vietnamese government. "Despite all the talk over the years, they still are badly in need of better leadership, better training, additional equipment and an improvement of living conditions for themselves and their families," he wrote. "Present plans for equipping the South Vietnamese forces are, in my opinion, inadequate to enable them to assume as rapidly as possible the amount of the total burden which they should be carrying." Contributing to his sense that the war was dragging on indefinitely was President Thieu's warning that the North Vietnamese might choose to resume their guerrilla tactics, knowing that they had the will to wait out the Americans.[42]

While he was in Saigon, Clifford met with Ambassador Ellsworth Bunker, Deputy Ambassador Samuel Berger, and Bill Bundy. Clifford tried to convince Bunker and Berger that there should be a concerted effort to resolve the war through diplomatic means over the remaining six months of Johnson's term. "You don't know what you'll have after November," he suggested. "Every candidate is moving fast away from the war." Entrenched as they were in Saigon, neither Bunker nor Berger was receptive to Clifford's argument, and the meeting became quite contentious. "We had a head-long, head-on fight," Clifford recalled, and for the rest of his visit Bunker maintained a diplomatically formal, but otherwise cold demeanor toward Clifford.[43]

Following his visit to Vietnam, Clifford flew to Honolulu to take part in a summit meeting between President Thieu and Johnson, a meeting that contributed to Clifford's pessimism. Bunker briefed Rusk on his meeting with Clifford, and the two of them were unified in their opposition to him at the conference. Nonetheless, Clifford was not deterred from making his case, and he requested a meeting with the president, Rusk, and Rostow. There Clifford made three points, the first of which was to reiterate his opinion that the war could not be won given the existing restrictions. He pointed out that the United States was fighting a defensive war in Vietnam, not exactly a recipe for victory. Furthermore, he argued, as a guerrilla army the North Vietnamese and Vietcong could always retreat to their sanctuaries in North Vietnam, Laos, or Cambodia to await a change in conditions more favorable to them. Second, the South Vietnamese government had no interest in ending the war. "I'm absolutely certain of it now," he stated passionately. Clifford explained that there was no incentive for the government of South Vietnam to end the war because it would mean forgoing the protection afforded by 540,000 U.S. troops and the "golden flow of money." Finally, Clifford reiterated the point he had made to Bunker and Berger: that all of the presidential candidates were moving away from the war, and that this provided the administration with the leverage necessary to force Thieu to reach an agreement at the bargaining table. Only such a threat would provide the sense of urgency necessary to force the South Vietnamese to make concessions. Otherwise, he warned, "they'll let it drag on forever."[44]

Following their meeting Johnson pulled Clifford aside. He said he was impressed with Clifford's arguments and promised to present them to Thieu. That afternoon Clifford and Wheeler briefed the president on the military situation in Vietnam and reported that although there was a lull in the fighting, there was no evidence that the enemy was matching the de-escalation that the United States had undertaken since March 31. Rather, the military's assessment was that the North Vietnamese were rebuilding their forces for future attacks. During the conference Presidents Johnson and Thieu agreed that there had been no substantive progress in the Paris negotiations, and this fact, in conjunction with the expectation of heavy fighting in the near future, precluded any discussion of U.S. troop withdrawals. Instead, they issued a joint statement that largely reflected Rusk's views and read, "As North Viet Nam takes its men home and ends its aggression against South Viet Nam, U.S. forces will be withdrawn."[45]

Clifford returned from Honolulu and Vietnam more determined than ever to find a way to end the war. "If I needed any proof we should get out, this trip did it," he told his staff. "I wonder how in the name of God we ever got in!" Assessing the situation analytically Clifford suggested that he and his staff faced three challenges. The first was to convince Johnson that, one way or another, he had to pull the troops out of Vietnam. Second, they had to convince Vance and Harriman to be flexible during the peace talks. Third, they had to convince Bunker and the rest of the diplomatic staff at the embassy that they were viewing the situation from the perspective of the South Vietnamese, rather than from the U.S., point of view.[46]

Of the three challenges that Clifford laid out, the first would be the most difficult to achieve, and a July 17 memorandum from Maxwell Taylor to the president augured the possibility of an increase in the fighting. Taylor's memo, provocatively titled "The Stalemate in Paris," deliberately adopted the language that Clifford had recently used at his press conference. "In spite of occasional 'straws in the wind,' there is very little of substance to show for more than two months of negotiations in Paris," he wrote. Taylor argued that nothing had been accomplished during the first two months of the peace negotiations, a situation that favored the enemy. He suggested a couple of courses of action to break the stalemate, but favored lifting the bombing restrictions and suggested linking bombing in the North to the level of hostilities in the South.[47] Understandably, Clifford decided that the Taylor memorandum could not go unchallenged. While meeting with his staff he explained that the fallacy of the memo was that it was based on the assumption that America had an absolute obligation to be in Vietnam. However, if one assumed that the United States did not have an obligation to be in Vietnam, one would reach a totally different conclusion. "Taylor's basic premise is wrong," he stated.[48]

The Taylor memo only reinforced Clifford's perception that the Honolulu conference had been a disaster, and the hard-line statement seemed to foreclose the possibility of negotiations. Clifford rejected the premise that there was a stalemate and felt that Taylor had reached that conclusion because he dismissed the importance of the Paris peace talks. On the contrary, "They're of signal importance," Clifford stressed, "because how hideous was the alternative—to go back to pre March 31." Taylor had completely misread the situation, Clifford reasoned, because he assumed that the Paris peace talks were an obstacle on the road to victory, whereas Clifford believed that the United States had not been on the road to victory.[49]

A little more than a week later Taylor sent another memorandum to the president in which he reprised an argument he had made in his "stalemate" memo. This July 30 memo was written in response to an editorial in the New York Times the day before that took the administration to task for not acting in the spirit of the president's March 31 speech by matching the apparent de-escalation by the North Vietnamese. Taylor suggested three alternatives: stop the bombing completely, continue the current policy, or link the level of bombing to the level of enemy violence in South Vietnam. Taylor favored the final option, which he believed addressed the concerns of the administration's critics and also "would achieve a kind of automatic reciprocity independent of Hanoi's veto." Taylor also recommended a lifting of the bombing restrictions north of the 19th parallel.[50]

Johnson, perhaps influenced by Taylor, had taken a hard line recently, and he reacted angrily to a proposal he received from Harriman and Vance, who had been representing the United States in the Paris peace talks. They proposed a modification of the San Antonio formula, in which the United States would unilaterally impose a cease-fire in North Vietnamese territory in return for immediate, substantive negotiations in Paris.[51] Johnson was furious, and sounding paranoid, bitterly complained about an "overall conspiracy" to influence him. The enemy was using as "dupes" his own people, which Clifford interpreted as himself, Harriman, and Vance. The president at this time also indicated a willingness to resume bombing up to the 20th parallel.[52]

Clifford summoned Taylor to the Pentagon, where he upbraided him point by point over the July 30 memo. "I think I shook Max Taylor to his vitals," Clifford told his staff. Yet Taylor posed a challenge because he was, as Clifford described him, an "unreconstructed hard man" with respect to Vietnam. He also wielded a fair amount of influence and could act independently, since he was not technically a member of the administration—ironically for Clifford, who had formerly enjoyed such freedom himself. Taylor "plays on the President like a harp," Clifford complained. But Clifford did not shrink from the challenge, especially since Johnson asked him for his views. "This lays it on the line," he concluded.[53]

Clifford instructed his staff to direct their "unlimited attention" to crafting a response. "This may be our only chance," he warned, feeling that the situation now was similar to the one that had existed just before the March 31 speech. "We are at a watershed." After three and a half years of war Clifford believed that the United States was no closer to achieving its objectives. "It was all so hopeless," he lamented. "On March 31 we got him around. Now we are in danger of losing it all." The resulting memorandum from Clifford to the president on August 1 describes Taylor's plan as "unworkable and unproductive." Clifford argued that past experience had proven that bombing in the North had no impact upon the level of enemy violence in the South. "There is no reason to believe, and no evidence to suggest," he wrote, "that renewal of a bombing campaign against any and all military targets in the north would accomplish now what it has never been able to accomplish before." He also made the case that the level of bombing should be based solely on what was necessary to protect U.S. troops. Linking the bombing to the level of violence in the South "could lead to intensification rather than diminution of the overall level of hostilities and would, in my opinion, end all chances of bringing the war to an acceptable conclusion during your term in office."[54]

Johnson was about to leave Washington to spend the weekend down at his ranch, and Lady Bird asked Clifford and Marny to join them, not knowing how strained her husband's relationship with his secretary of defense had become.[55] It was not until Sunday that Clifford finally had a chance to speak to the president privately about Vietnam, and he started by pointing out their successes. Clifford argued that the United States had done everything it was obligated to do in Vietnam, defining that obligation in less absolute terms than hawks such as Taylor had. U.S. intervention in Vietnam had prevented subjugation of the South by the North, had reversed military gains by the enemy, and had contributed to the development of the government of South Vietnam, Clifford said. Having accomplished all of that, he stressed, it was time to reach a settlement in Paris, and he warned that the North had the will to continue fighting whereas the United States, because of domestic considerations, did not. The hard-line statement of the Honolulu conference was the wrong approach, and Clifford argued for an even more relaxed interpretation of the San Antonio formula.

With that in mind, he recommended that the president give a televised speech a week after the Republican convention promising to cease all bombing within a week, provided that substantive talks began, the DMZ was respected, and the North did not take advantage of the bombing cessation. If Hanoi rejected the proposal, he suggested, the United States would be free to resume bombing and the whole world would know that the United States went the last mile for peace.[56] Johnson replied that he did not agree with anything that Clifford had just said, although he did say that it was "interesting." He then lectured Clifford on firmness, vowing that he would rather leave office with a "fine military solution" than be craven.[57]

As the president, it was Johnson's prerogative to lecture a subordinate with whom he disagreed, but in this case he was also exacting some form of retribution for Clifford's abandoning his support for the war. Harry McPherson thought that Johnson's bouts of anger and impatience with Clifford were completely understandable, if not well founded. As he later told biographer Merle Miller:

Johnson's reaction to Clifford's doubting was terrible. He did mind it—of course he did. I would have minded it. When you've spent as much time laboring with this thing as he had, when so much that was in you was invested in this, when it had seemed the only decision to make, and when the judgment of history on his administration was riding on this, as it clearly was, no matter what else he did—on whether it had been right to escalate in Vietnam—having a young English-major law-yer sitting back sniping from the sidelines is an uncomfortable and unwanted thing.[58]

Johnson's shift back to a hard-line stance percolated down through his administration. A few days after he returned from the ranch Clifford met with Rusk and Vance, who was back from Paris. Clifford understood that the agenda was to discuss "new avenues" in Vietnam, so he was surprised when Rusk categorically rejected every idea Clifford proposed on "grounds that any new approach by us would be an indication of weakness." Rusk took the position that the bombing would continue until the North Vietnamese made some firm commitments at the bargaining table—in other words, a "total impasse," as Clifford saw it. Clifford reminded Rusk that men were dying in Vietnam while the two sides jockeyed for position, but Rusk was unmoved. "You never can tell when they'll break and give in," he replied. A frustrated Clifford lamented that Rusk was "just following LBJ's line."[59]

Johnson's unexplained shifting of positions had Clifford com-pletely baffled. "I have been mystified by the change in LBJ's attitude from the time Wheeler and I saw him just before we left for Saigon until we got to Honolulu," he said. "I was astounded and then deeply disturbed by the substantial hardening which was reflected in the Honolulu communiqué." Clifford recounted to his staff how the pres-ident had taken a hard line with Rusk, demanding that he insist on strict conditions before ordering a halt to the bombing. "All through this period, including last Sunday at the Ranch, I've been baffled," he said.[60]

Vietnam had, to a large degree, consumed and ruined Johnson's presidency, and his moodiness and shifting of positions made it dif-ficult to work for him. Perhaps out of desperation Johnson came up with an idea for possibly saving his presidency with one dramatic ges-ture. In late July Soviet Premier Kosygin had invited Johnson to a summit meeting in Moscow. The problem was that the summit would take place during the same time as the Democratic Party convention, ordinarily a command performance for a lame-duck president to improve the chances of extending his party's control of the presidency. Johnson, however, wanted to open arms-control negotiations with the Soviets and believed that a dramatic success in Moscow might not only salvage his presidency, but also make the Democrats draft him to run for another term. Clifford was horrified at this idea, believing that it would be perceived as either a "grand slam bid to get re-nominated" or a reflection of the president's disenchantment with the Democratic candidates. He also thought this was typical of Johnson's flamboyance and "desire to dramatize everything in the last few months" of his presidency. As for the Republican convention, Johnson thought he might upstage it with a White House ceremony honoring five Medal of Honor recipients. This Clifford flatly thought "stupid," adding disgustedly, "He thinks he is so cute and it just catches up with him."[61]

Johnson floated the summit idea to Clifford and Rusk that evening, and Clifford laid out all the reasons why he thought it was a bad idea, using such words as "calamity" and "disaster." He pointed out that Johnson risked undermining the Democratic nominee, presumably Hubert Humphrey. He also warned Johnson that the administration could become engulfed in a news story that would spiral out of control. Johnson was disappointed to hear Clifford's reaction, but in this case he decided to follow Clifford's counsel and postpone the summit until after the convention.[62] Rusk was charged with making the arrangements for the meeting with the Soviets, and on August 20 the two sides agreed that the summit would take place during the first week of October. Circumstances, however, conspired to deny Johnson the reprieve he had been seeking. The Prague Spring reformist movement in Czechoslovakia had been gathering momentum, and the Soviets decided to crack down on what they saw as a challenge to their authority. That evening Soviet and Warsaw Pact troops invaded Czechoslovakia and violently put down the uprising. A devastated Lyndon Johnson canceled the summit before he could even announce it.

Johnson's willingness to upstage Humphrey by considering a summit meeting during the Democratic convention raised questions about his support for the party's anticipated presidential candidate. In fact, Johnson considered Humphrey weak on Vietnam and believed that Richard Nixon, the Republican candidate, was more in line with his position. Privately, Clifford confided to Harriman that he believed Johnson wanted to see Humphrey defeated.[63] On July 24 the president told his foreign policy advisers that he wanted to meet with Nixon, whom he thought might be more "responsible" on Vietnam than the Democratic nominee.[64] Johnson and Nixon met at Johnson's ranch on August 10, at which time Nixon agreed that he would not criticize the administration as long as they did not "soften" their position on Vietnam. Clifford thought this arrangement favored Nixon. "If I were Nixon, the one development that would worry me would be the announcement that real Paris progress was being made, that bombing was stopping, and substantive talks starting," he explained. Clifford believed that Nixon benefited from "disenchantment" with the war— in other words, maintenance of the status quo. Nixon had outmaneuvered Johnson, Clifford believed, because by publicly supporting, or at least not opposing, the president, Nixon made him seem inflexible. Meanwhile, Humphrey's hands were tied because he would not risk incurring the president's wrath by publicly taking a different position. "I think the President has been so anxious to take a hard inflexible line that he thinks he's actually made a gain by getting Nixon to go along," Clifford reasoned. "Whereas actually, Nixon is playing LBJ for a dupe. Nixon has made LBJ dig in deeper and now Nixon has got the war hanging around the Democrats' neck so tightly it can't be loosened."[65]

Later that same day, Elsey met with Charles Murphy, who had years earlier succeeded Clifford as Truman's special counsel and was now serving as a liaison to the Humphrey campaign. Murphy confided to Elsey that Johnson had told him a few days earlier that he would vote for Nixon if Eugene McCarthy won the Democratic nomination and that "it would be better for the country" if Nixon won because Humphrey was not willing to hold the line on Vietnam. This confirmed what Clifford and his staff had been worrying about that very morning.[66] The next day Johnson was speaking to Clifford about the upcoming U.S.-Soviet summit, which was then in the planning stage, and he alluded to how he might transition the arms control negotiations to his successor. "Maybe we should just start it and then turn it all over to Nixon," he suggested.[67]

Leading up to the Democratic convention, supporters of McCarthy, Senator George McGovern, and the late Robert Kennedy, who had been assassinated in June, clamored for language in the convention platform calling for an end to the bombing and the establishment of a coalition government in Vietnam. Humphrey, unwilling to repudiate the administration in which he was serving, was conflicted about what should be included in the platform or what position he should take during the campaign. Unfortunately for Clifford, he was brought into the debate. In an August 19 editorial the *New York Times* opined that a halt in the bombing would not adversely affect the safety of U.S. troops in Vietnam, and the editors cited Clifford to prove their point. "I do not attach any real relationship between the restrictions in the bombing and the increased number of infiltrees into South Vietnam," he was quoted as saying. The newspaper then challenged Johnson to resolve Humphrey's problem—and the nation's—by imposing a bombing freeze and embracing a negotiated settlement.[68]

Clifford knew this would not help him with Johnson; and, while his words were public knowledge, the way they were used in the article, he knew, would be problematic for him. "Over at the White House, they're obsessed with bombing; their judgment is wholly distorted on all matters regarding the bombing," he said.[69] Obsessed or not, Rostow disputed Clifford's assessment of the impact of the bombing and argued that the bombing was a constraint that limited the capabilities of the enemy and that it logically followed that reducing that constraint would increase the enemy's capabilities.[70] Johnson, of course, was incensed at the *Times*'s use of Clifford's press conference, mostly because he did not approve of a public airing of differences among members of his administration. "Every day I read that there is a sharp difference between you and Rusk, and I want it stopped!" he chastised Clifford. No doubt thinking that he had been unfairly criticized, Clifford had his staff parse the entire press conference, or as Elsey described it, "psychoanalyzing it all."[71]

In an effort to prevent the inclusion of language in the party platform repudiating the bombing, Rostow sent a list of questions regarding the efficacy of the bombing to General Abrams through a back channel intended to bypass Clifford. Mindful of their previous altercation Abrams dutifully copied Clifford on the response, thus blowing Rostow's cover. Clifford thought it was outrageous that Rostow had gone behind his back, but there was little he could do, as Rostow had been following the president's orders.[72] Nonetheless, Clifford pressed the case that it was totally inappropriate to enlist the military in what was essentially a political dispute.[73] In his response to Rostow, Abrams predicted that the enemy's military capabilities in the DMZ area would be increased fivefold if the bombing were suspended.[74] Congressman Hale Boggs of Louisiana, chairman of the platform committee, cited Abrams's analysis in making the case for a platform supportive of the Johnson administration's policies in Vietnam. In the vote that followed, the pro-administration platform defeated the opposing platform, which called for an unconditional end to the bombing.[75] The ensuing violent demonstrations surrounding the convention, which exposed a major fissure in the Democratic Party to the nation and contributed to Nixon's victory in November, were prompted by the dispute over the Vietnam language in the Democratic party platform.

The violence at the Democratic convention was disastrous for the party. Clifford had earlier argued, over the strenuous objections of Attorney General Ramsey Clark, for the prepositioning of army troops in order to quell such demonstrations. Johnson agreed, and the troops were moved into place.[76] Chicago Mayor Richard Daley, however, opted to use the local police to contain the demonstrations, a move that Clifford argued contributed to the unrest. Clifford believed that Army troops would have done a more effective job at countering the demonstrations.[77]

Following the convention Johnson seemed to mellow a bit, perhaps from the week he spent down at the ranch. On September 2 he spoke to Clifford on the telephone and asked him to come up with some ideas for resolving the impasse in Vietnam. Johnson good-naturedly needled Clifford for making what he considered to be the naïve assertion that the bombing could be suspended and then subsequently renewed if conditions warranted. Johnson also explained away his recent intransigence by noting that he did not want to make any policy changes before or during the convention because it would be seen as politically motivated. Now that the convention was over, he said, "I want new proposals, any damn kind, I'll pay a reward for them." Johnson asked Clifford, whom he flattered "as the best pleader I ever heard," to formulate his arguments for a debate with Rusk and Rostow. They should try to reach an agreement, Johnson said, "that (a) will give us some hope of success, that (b) will at least be treating the American people fair, and (c) that we'll damn sure look good before an investigating committee in February when they say what in the hell did you do." Clifford was pleased with Johnson's new willingness to discuss peace, which he predicted would be "the crowning glory of your administration."[78] Clifford's optimism was misplaced, however, as this debate never took place.

Humphrey gave a speech in Philadelphia on September 9 and stated that some American troops could be brought home from Vietnam later in the year or in early 1969. The next day Johnson contradicted his vice president, saying that the troops would stay in Vietnam until they had brought "an honorable, stable peace to Southeast Asia" and that nothing less was worthy of the sacrifices of those who had died in Vietnam. Humphrey called Clifford at 2:30 A.M. the next morning, desperately worried about whether he had misspoken. Clifford corrected him and explained that it was Thieu who had predicted that U.S. troops would be coming home, and explained to Humphrey that he had misspoken when he claimed that a Marine unit was coming home; in fact, it was being rotated. During a meeting the next day Johnson asked about the call. Clifford pointed out that Humphrey had misspoken regarding the claims that troops were being withdrawn and that a Marine unit was coming home. He also said that Humphrey would run on the minority platform from the Democratic convention, which favored an immediate end to the bombing, thus contradicting the administration. Looking to protect the president, Clifford recommended that Johnson assign a trusted adviser to shadow Humphrey and make sure he did not make any more misstatements regarding Vietnam during the rest of the campaign. Clifford knew, however, that if Humphrey continued to adhere to the administration's policy on Vietnam he risked alienating the antiwar segment of the Democratic Party. Johnson understood that the administration's policy on Vietnam was a threat to Humphrey's campaign, and so felt compelled to assert his support for the vice president. "I want the Vice President to win," he said. "I want the Democratic Party to win." Rusk recommended that they speak with Humphrey and suggested that he might want to create a little space between himself and the administration. Johnson believed the opposite to be true, however; he thought that in his heart Humphrey actually sided with the administration and his antiwar leanings were merely political calculation.[79] Clifford disagreed.[80]

Clifford joined the president that weekend at Camp David. The meetings he had there with the president—an hour and a half on Saturday night and another two hours on Sunday—were, in Clifford's opinion, the most productive conversations he had had on Vietnam since he became secretary of defense. During the Saturday night conversation Clifford suggested that the United States had little to show for five months' worth of negotiations and that they needed to get something from the North Vietnamese in return for stopping the bombing. Johnson was surprised to hear this, and reassured because he had thought that Clifford wanted to curtail the bombing without any concessions. The following day they received welcome news: Harriman was reporting some progress in the Paris negotiations with the North Vietnamese. "It proves the North Vietnamese are there, meaning business," Clifford said.[81]

Johnson and Clifford agreed that if the situation in Czechoslovakia remained calm for another week, Johnson should reach out to Kosygin with an offer to revive their canceled summit meeting and an offer to halt the bombing if the Soviets provided certain assurances. Paul Nitze exploded at that suggestion. "It's asinine—it's pissing away an advantage we have! It'll undo the North Atlantic alliance if LBJ gets into bed with Kosygin," he argued. Clifford was shocked because Nitze earlier had wanted to enlist the Soviets' help, but Nitze said that their violent suppression of the Prague Spring demonstrations had completely changed the equation. Elsey and Warnke protested that there was not sufficient time to get the Russians involved before the November elections. "I'm for anything that will get the President to stop the bombing!" an irritated Clifford replied. "No, I'm not!" argued Nitze. "Not if it means doing things contrary to our national interest. Wrecking NATO by playing footsie with Kosygin would do so." Clifford scolded them. "All of you are trying to think logically," he argued. "You don't realize LBJ's mood. It's: 'I'm Goddamned if I'll stop the bombing without something from the other side.'" The meeting was breaking up, but Clifford made his case one last time. "Do not deprecate the concept of finding the means of persuading the President to stop the bombing in the North," he pleaded. "Until we get it stopped we can't get anyplace. I'm ready to take risks elsewhere, anywhere."[82]

The following day Clifford met with Harriman, who was back from Paris to attend his mother-in-law's funeral. Harriman reported that he was optimistic regarding the prospects for peace, but Clifford tried to temper his enthusiasm and prepare him for the harsh questions that Johnson would ask. As he and Harriman talked, Clifford became convinced that the negotiations were still at an impasse, with the North Vietnamese demanding a cessation of the bombing as a condition for substantive talks and Johnson demanding concessions prior to stopping the bombing. Clifford suggested instead that they try for incremental progress, a reduction in the hostilities, which might be easier for Johnson to accept. Illustrative of the challenges Clifford faced when confronting the hawks in the administration was a recent article in *U.S. News and World Report*, which reported that the Paris talks were a fiasco. Clifford was certain that this piece would infuriate the president. "This is the kind of story Rostow feeds to LBJ all the time," Clifford grumbled. He also suggested that Johnson might not be truly committed to the peace talks and might be stalling until Nixon took over, assuming he won the election. Harriman replied that if that were the case he would quit.[83]

After meeting with the president, Harriman was glad that Clifford had briefed him beforehand; otherwise, he would have been "knocked for a loop." During their meeting Harriman realized that Johnson's desire for a summit meeting with Kosygin might be the key to progress in Vietnam. Sensing an opening, Harriman suggested that Johnson would have to stop the bombing within two weeks if he wanted to meet with Kosygin during his remaining months in office. The potential summit with Kosygin was the "big carrot" to get Johnson to move on Vietnam, explained Harriman.[84] Johnson believed that if there were no progress in Paris, he could reach an agreement with Kosygin to resolve the impasse. Clifford thought this idea was preposterous.[85] He suspected that Johnson's interest in the summit was due to a desire for a "blaze of publicity." Clifford thought the idea of a summit was beside the point. The time to talk with the Soviets, he maintained, was when Kosygin had sent the letter indicating that he had reason to believe that the North Vietnamese would be willing to negotiate. Had Johnson took Kosygin up on his offer then, he argued, they would have stopped the bombing, avoided the fiasco in Chicago, made more progress in Paris, and perhaps even have avoided the Soviet invasion of Czechoslovakia.[86]

Clifford and Marny had dinner with the president and first lady on September 24, and before that dinner Clifford mused with his staff over which direction Johnson was headed. On the one hand, it appeared that Johnson had now convinced himself that stopping the bombing would put U.S. troops in jeopardy, which in Clifford's mind was a rationalization that let Johnson completely off the hook. On the other hand, Clifford thought Johnson had changed his tone. "He's gotten more friendly," he said. "I hope it means he'll listen. . . . We're running out of time."[87] As it turned out, he had reason for optimism. The day after the dinner, Clifford told his staff that he'd had his "best talk in five years" with the president. Clifford and Marny arrived at the White House at 7:30, and the president and Clifford spent an hour swimming in the pool and talking. After dinner they talked for another three hours. Clifford would make his points, Johnson would argue back, and then Clifford would rebut the president's comments, but what was striking about this meeting was that Johnson was less emotional than he was in any other discussion on Vietnam in which Clifford had taken part. "He heard me out completely," Clifford reported. They discussed the bombing alone for forty-five minutes. Clifford made the case that only 5 percent of U.S. military capability in Vietnam was dedicated toward bombing between the 17th and

19th parallels. In order to get some movement in Paris, Clifford said, they could easily forgo that 5 percent while still engaging the other 95 percent. This argument seemed to resonate with the president.[88]

Clifford pleaded with the president to drop his conditions for halting the bombing, pointing out that he had not attached conditions during his San Antonio speech. Johnson quibbled over that point, but Clifford argued that the current situation was much different than what it was a year ago. Rather than attaching conditions, Clifford implored Johnson to proceed on the assumption that the North Vietnamese would not take advantage of a halt in bombing. "The risk is minimal," he said. "Nonsense," Johnson countered. "Abrams says our men are in danger." Clifford replied that the troops would only be in danger if the North Vietnamese took advantage of the halt in bombing, and he assured the president that would not happen. If they did take advantage, however, no one would blame the president for resuming the bombing. "It's your responsibility to stop bombing," he pleaded. Johnson said he did not agree, but Clifford was nonetheless encouraged that the president at least had listened. Clifford closed by suggesting that Johnson consider his legacy and not allow Nixon to be the one to take credit for ending the war.[89]

The following day, during the meeting of the National Security Council, Clifford was asked to repeat his presentation from the night before. "We preserve 95% of our forces," he said. "We gamble with 5%. I think it will be successful." George Ball, then the ambassador to the United Nations, strongly endorsed Clifford's position. Wheeler argued against stopping the bombing, and even disputed Clifford on the validity of the 5 percent figure. Clifford discounted Wheeler's views, however, believing that he had been primed by the president. Rusk warned that there would be no way to counter infiltration through the DMZ or protect the cities of South Vietnam if the bombing were halted. At the conclusion of the meeting there was a vote on Clifford's proposal. Johnson opposed the idea, as did Rusk and Wheeler. Although he had not convinced the president, Clifford had been given a chance to present his views, and he considered that progress. "Rusk and Rostow until now have kept this as their private little war and not allowed others to get into it," he said.[90] Not only did Clifford believe that Rusk and Rostow wanted to keep Clifford out of their sandbox, he also believed that they did not play fair. He complained about the way they "hammered" at Johnson, distorted cables, and interpreted information as it suited their interests. He particularly resented Rostow for cabling General

Abrams through CIA back channels and even suspected that Rostow told Abrams how to answer.[91]

Humphrey finally tired of playing by Johnson's rules, and in an act of independence necessary to salvage his presidential campaign publicly broke with the administration. In a September 30 speech in Salt Lake City, Humphrey said, "As President, I would stop the bombing of the North as an acceptable risk for peace because I believe it could lead to success in the negotiations and thereby shorten the war."[92] George Ball, who believed Nixon was a liar and a crook, felt that he had to do his part to help Humphrey win, so he resigned from his position in the administration and joined the Humphrey campaign. Clifford believed that Humphrey's shift was an act of desperation.[93]

Humphrey had finally broken from the administration, and Clifford seemed to conclude that it was time to be more decisive himself. He told his staff that he had reached the point where he had "to step up and slug it on the nose." "We've tried conciliation and persuasion," he said. "Ever since Honolulu, LBJ has hardened more and more." He defended Humphrey when the president asked whether the Salt Lake speech contained a condition for stopping the bombing. Johnson thought that Humphrey had implied that he would halt the bombing without conditions, but Clifford disagreed.[94]

Contrasting with Clifford's determination to be more decisive was his feeling of despair that nothing was going to change in the remaining months of Johnson's presidency. He resigned himself to the fact that there was no progress in Paris, which he considered "criminal." During another late-night meeting with the president, Clifford encouraged him to avoid making any "last ditch desperation measures" in response to what Clifford considered to be some "screwball" ideas on Johnson's part to garner headlines. The odds of any major breakthroughs were ten to one, Clifford said, and instead of desperate measures now was the time to keep one's cool.[95]

A couple of days later, however, the odds seemed to change. North Vietnamese negotiators Le Duc Tho and Xuan Thuy met secretly with Harriman and Vance at a location just outside of Paris. The North Vietnamese proposed to accept the participation of the South Vietnamese government at the Paris peace talks in return for a commitment to end the bombing. Up to then the North Vietnamese considered the South Vietnamese government to be illegitimate and refused to negotiate with them. Closing their meeting, the North Vietnamese indicated that "they believed that rapid progress could be made if we were really determined to move toward peace."[96]

On October 14 Johnson convened his advisers to discuss the proposal. "The major equation is elementary," Clifford explained, "taking Hanoi at its word and seeing if it really means what it says." He said the United States had been insisting on three conditions at the peace talks: participation of the government of South Vietnam, no attacks on the cities, and respect for the DMZ. The first had been a condition precedent to substantive negotiations, while the other two were conditions subsequent. As Clifford saw it, the North Vietnamese had changed their position on the condition precedent, and therefore the United States was obligated to enter into serious negotiations. If the subsequent conditions were not adhered to, he argued, the United States would be entitled to resume the bombing. Looking to pin him down, Johnson asked, "Would you favor resumption of bombing if they violate any of these three?" "Yes, Sir, I would," Clifford replied. "I recommend the President proceed on this," he said. "As soon as possible. There is more benefit than detriment. It will leave not a single stone unturned in your quest for peace." Maxwell Taylor recommended caution, suggesting that there was time to ensure the North Vietnamese complied. "I do not have the same sense of urgency," he said. Clifford disagreed. "There comes a time in the tide of men's affairs that it is a time to move," he argued. "It is away (three weeks) from the election. It will receive [the] commendation of the world and the country. I consider it a very real point to get the job done now."[97]

With respect to the election, the president was concerned that if he accepted the North Vietnamese offer he would be charged with playing politics; yet he hinted that he was willing to try, but not optimistic of success. Clifford responded that the president was not trying to influence the election, but was merely reacting to an overture from the other side. "The decision to move at this time is not based on our initiative," he said. "It is based on Hanoi's initiative." He also indicated that he doubted that the peace overtures would have any effect on the election. "The people have made up their minds on the election already," he said. "I can understand how Mr. Nixon feels. He doesn't want anything that could possibly rock the boat. He likes the shape that it is in now and any little new development might rock the boat, so he would be opposed to it. But what's the matter with rocking the boat? Remember what Mark Twain once said that occasionally is relevant. He said, 'When in doubt, do right.'" After confirming that everyone in the group, including Rusk, was on board, Johnson approved a cable to Saigon announcing the decision, although with some trepidation. "I do not want to be the one to have it said about that one man died tomorrow who could have been saved because of this plan," he said. "I do not think it will happen, but there is a chance. We'll try it. We'll be scared, but let's try it."[98]

After many setbacks and false starts, it appeared that Clifford had finally won over Johnson's mind and persuaded the president to make a concerted effort to seek a peaceful resolution to the war in his remaining days in office. After presenting his case over a long seven months he had finally worn down both Johnson and Rusk, and convinced them, albeit reluctantly, to come to the bargaining table. Unfortunately for Clifford, his wariness and distrust of America's South Vietnamese allies was well founded, and they would find every reason imaginable to stall on their way to the Paris peace talks. As Clifford would soon learn, someone was whispering in their ear, and that person had their attention.

# 11

# October Surprise

With the clock ticking down on the Johnson administration, Clifford had convinced Johnson to make one last concerted effort to bring the war to a close. "When in doubt, do right," Clifford had argued, and with some trepidation, Johnson had agreed. Even steadfast hawks Dean Rusk and Maxwell Taylor would soon come around. It had been an almost impossible task for Clifford to impose his will on Johnson, but through sheer perseverance he had carried the day. Unfortunately for Clifford, the South Vietnamese could not be persuaded to come to the bargaining table, and without two willing partners a peace settlement remained agonizingly out of reach. Clifford had been right when he warned that Vietnam would become a quagmire.

While on the one hand there was progress, on the other there were setbacks. The North Vietnamese were displeased with a new condition that they seat an NLF delegation in Paris within twenty-four hours of a bombing halt, the United States having agreed to allow the NLF to participate in four-party negotiations: the governments of North and South Vietnam, the United States, and the NLF. The North Vietnamese wanted the talks to commence no later than a week after the bombing stopped, but the Americans considered a week too long, fearing that such a delay would undermine the morale of the South Vietnamese. The other problem, and the one with greater implications, was that inclusion of the NLF at the negotiating table conferred legitimacy to the group and was seen as an embarrassment to the South Vietnamese government. A few days later the South Vietnamese ambassador to the United States, Bui Diem, warned Walt Rostow that his government might not participate in peace talks if the NLF were in attendance. Further complicating the matter, the North Vietnamese wanted a joint communiqué announcing the bombing halt and the commencement of four-party talks. The American delegation rejected the request, preferring to characterize the peace talks as "our side–your side."[1] The differences, while technical, nonetheless represented obstacles that had to be resolved before substantive negotiations could begin.

Discussing the status of the talks during a meeting with Johnson and his senior foreign policy advisers, Clifford voiced his frustration over the newly erected roadblocks. "There is a missing factor here," he said. "I don't know what happened since last week. . . . When I left here Monday, I thought we had a deal. On Tuesday, I learned we didn't have a deal since the Paris delegation had to go back to Hanoi." The misunderstandings regarding the peace talks over the previous week had been a "debacle," he told the president. During the president's weekly Tuesday lunch meeting the participants continued the discussion of the inclusion of the NLF at the peace talks. "Nixon will ask me if this isn't like putting a fox in the chicken coop," said Johnson. Rostow wondered whether the South Vietnamese government would even participate if the NLF was present, as Bui Diem had warned him. Clifford, however, believed that participating in the talks actually conferred legitimacy on the South Vietnamese government and that the participation of the NLF was more of a benefit than a detriment.[2]

Later in the day Johnson telephoned Clifford to discuss again the political ramifications of the bombing pause and peace talks, and Clifford reassured the president that it was the North Vietnamese who chose the timing. Clifford also reiterated his familiar argument that a bombing pause, even if unsuccessful, was necessary to demonstrate that the president did everything possible to secure a peaceful resolution to the conflict.[3]

October 27 brought news of a breakthrough in the negotiations when Cyrus Vance called to inform the White House that the North Vietnamese had dropped their last condition and agreed to commence the discussions on November 2, three days after the proposed bombing halt.[4] Rusk detected the influence of the Soviets. "I smell vodka and caviar in it," he said. The president, however, was unconvinced. "Why do we have to yield?" he asked. "They have made the major step," Rusk replied. "If ten steps separated us," Clifford added, "they have taken eight and we have taken two." Rusk, unexpectedly, thought it was even better. "I would say it is nine to one," he said. Johnson, however, remained unconvinced. "I still think this is a political move to affect this election," he said. "Even if it were so," Rusk replied, "it is in our interest to do this." Even the consistently hawkish Maxwell Taylor was in agreement. "I have been a hard-nosed man,

Mr. President, but I am for this," he said. "They are hurting." Despite the concurrence of his senior advisers, Johnson remained stubbornly unconvinced. "I think we are being herded into this under pressure," he said. His opposition was based upon two concerns: (1) the enemy would exploit the bombing halt and violate the DMZ and attack the cities, and (2) November 2 was too close to the elections and he would be accused of trying to swing the election to Humphrey.[5]

The solution, the president concluded, was to bring General Creighton Abrams back to the United States for consultations, or at least a photo opportunity, with the president, thus lending the field commanders' support to the initiative. Clifford, however, believed this to be unnecessary and a waste of valuable time relative to the election, and argued that Earle Wheeler should serve as the stand-in for Abrams. "I disagree," Johnson replied. "He has [the] color of [a] military commander who is in [the] field." Then the president really dug in his heels. "All of you are playing with this like you have been living in another world—with a bunch of doves," he charged. Clifford tried again. "You have a good story to tell," he said to the president. "For five months we have told Hanoi we couldn't go ahead without the G VN [Government of Vietnam] present. Finally, they changed their position. They chose the time—not us." Johnson, however, remained stubbornly convinced that the United States was conceding too much and that the tradeoff of the Government of Vietnam for the NLF was unfair. "What we wanted was to get to substantive discussions," Clifford argued. "They have capitulated. Since San Antonio, we have said we would stop the bombing and proceed on certain assumptions." Unfortunately for Clifford, Johnson still was not persuaded.[6]

Johnson ordered Abrams to return to Washington for consultations, and when the general arrived in the wee hours of October 29 he headed straight to the White House for a meeting that began at 2:30 in the morning. Abrams told the president that a halt to the bombing would not result in greater American casualties, a stark contrast from his position during the Democratic convention. Under intense questioning by the president, Abrams indicated that he was confident that the North Vietnamese would not violate the DMZ, although he was wary about the possibility of attacks on the cities. Most notably, he opined that he believed the enemy had "shifted tactics from the battlefield to the conference table." Finally, Johnson asked if Abrams would order the bombing halt if he were president, and the general indicated that he would. "I have no reservations about doing it," Abrams answered. "I do think it is the right thing to do." Satisfied with Abrams's answer, Johnson asked Rusk and Clifford to weigh in, with Rusk offering a cautious endorsement. "This is a culmination of events begun with the San Antonio speech," Clifford replied. "It has taken a year of setbacks and losses before they will sit down and negotiate. . . . I recommend this without reservations."[7]

While the president was meeting with Abrams and his advisers, Ambassador Ellsworth Bunker was meeting with President Thieu to finalize his agreement to the four-party peace talks. At 5:00 A.M. Johnson asked if there was any word from Bunker; after hearing that there was not, he left for the residence. An hour later Rusk called with the devastating news that Thieu was stalling. Johnson immediately sensed that behind Thieu's dissembling was the handiwork of Richard Nixon. "That's the old Nixon," Johnson lamented.[8]

When Clifford had suggested a few days earlier that there was "a missing factor," he was closer to the truth than he realized. The FBI had recently provided the president with information that the Nixon campaign had opened a clandestine back channel with which to communicate to President Thieu. Anna Chennault, the widow of famed World War II "Flying Tiger" General Claire Chennault, was an important figure in the China Lobby, a virulently anticommunist interest group. Chennault, also known as the "Little Flower," served as an intermediary between the Nixon campaign and Saigon. John Mitchell, Nixon's campaign manager, instructed her to communicate to Saigon via Ambassador Bui Diem the message that Thieu should avoid the peace table until after the election, promising better terms under a Republican administration.[9]

At 6:15 A.M. Johnson and his exhausted senior foreign policy advisers reassembled to discuss the latest developments. In addition to the breakdown in the Paris negotiations, Johnson struggled with the decision over whether or not to go public with the information so close to the election. It "would rock the world if it were said he was conniving with Republicans," the president said in reference to Thieu. "Can you imagine what people would say if this were to be known; that we have all these conditions met and then Nixon's conniving with them kept us from getting it. If we go public—and they object—we have a real problem on our hands." "It seems to me they are playing extraordinary games," Clifford said, dismissing Thieu's excuse that three days was not enough time to get a South Vietnamese delegation to Paris. Clifford also worried that if the United States did not handle the situation properly it could lead to the downfall of the South Vietnamese government they had invested so much effort cultivating.

"Their situation could become so grave under President Johnson's term in office that it would be untenable," he said. "We need to take [a] hard look at this," he added, referring to South Vietnam's delaying tactics. "It seems reprehensible and utterly without merit." Clifford suggested that there were two possible courses of action: postpone the bombing pause and wait to hear what Thieu had to say, or simply inform him that the United States was going ahead with the bombing pause anyway. He added that the second option could be justified by noting that it was the will of the president and the American people and that it was too late to turn back anyway.[10]

At the weekly Tuesday lunch meeting that afternoon the discussion continued. Clifford reiterated his argument that Thieu's excuse was not credible, and instead offered the obvious, if distasteful, explanation. "They are trying to decide what is best—a Johnson Administration or a Nixon Administration to go on with." He also suggested that Ambassador Bunker might not be exerting sufficient pressure on the South Vietnamese. Rusk defended Thieu, noting that the South Vietnamese might have concluded that Nixon would win and might be afraid of antagonizing him. Clifford dismissed that argument. "They have a moral obligation to go along with us," he said. "I think they have left us in an almost impossible position—Saigon throws a wrench in the wheel just as we are about to go on this." Johnson, like Rusk, was sympathetic to the South Vietnamese position and speculated that they might be afraid of what course Humphrey might pursue if elected. Nonetheless, he was ready to proceed without them. "I think we have to go through with it," he said, "making every effort to take them with us." He also indicated that the timing with respect to the election was less important than the prospect of serious peace negotiations. "It is not of world-shaking importance whether it's November 2, 4, 6 or 8," he said. That said, Johnson thought Thieu had backed the wrong horse. "Nixon will double-cross them after November 5," he predicted. Nevertheless, Johnson indicated that he was ready to order the bombing halt, with or without the cooperation of the South Vietnamese. "I was ready to go. I was 80% ready before General Abrams came here," he said. "Now I am ready to go."[11]

Johnson reconvened the group at 6:30 that evening, and Clifford was determined not to let the chance for peace slip away. "Although sometimes doing nothing is better," he said, "this is not the time. I feel it is inappropriate for us, after bearing these burdens for so many years, to turn this over to Thieu and his people and a new Administration. We know this is a decent, honorable deal. All your advisers can live with it." But unfortunately, the president could not, and he opted not to go it alone, as Clifford had advocated. Johnson decided to give the South Vietnamese more time, and sympathized with their willingness to trust Nixon and their concerns about Humphrey. "Thieu doesn't realize what he is doing to himself," the president said, but he agreed to postpone the start of the peace talks to November 4. For Clifford, it was a demoralizing end to two emotionally and physically exhausting days.[12]

But the roller-coaster ride was not over. The president called Clifford the next morning, no doubt rethinking his decision from the prior evening. "Let's start all over again," he said, "and see if a different approach will give us a result." He asked Clifford to come over to the White House immediately. But this latest meeting was more of the same, and the normally unflappable Clifford finally vented his rage. "We have known before how Thieu would react," he said. "Now they have been asked would you rather have three months of Johnson or four years of Nixon. Their whole approach is delay. This message is 'horseshit.' This message is thoroughly insulting." Perhaps Johnson was influenced by Clifford's emotional outburst, because he then made up his mind. "Tell Bunker we are ready to go tonight," he said. The first meeting in Paris would be November 6, the day after the elections, and Thieu would have 168 hours, as Johnson put it, to get his people to Paris.[13]

"We've been on a roller-coaster for days," Clifford told his staff the next morning as he recounted the previous day's drama. He confided to them that it was the third time he thought the decision on the bombing halt had been settled, but he still feared that Johnson would reverse himself again. He was most suspicious of Bunker, who he felt was representing the interests of the South Vietnamese instead of his own country. In fact, Clifford was so suspicious of Bunker that he predicted that Thieu would beg for more time and that Bunker would plead his case. Yet despite his concerns, he remained guardedly optimistic that the bombing halt would come to pass. "I think LBJ will stick with his decision—if Thieu does ask for delay, I think LBJ will go ahead anyway," he said. At 10:30 A.M. Ben Read, from the State Department, called Clifford with news that confirmed Clifford's fears about Thieu, who was "acting very badly." Half an hour later a report came in over the news wire. "Saigon does not agree with U.S. terms," Thieu said in a statement to the press. As Clifford read aloud Thieu's statement he moaned in disgust. "Thieu is playing a very dangerous game," he said. Thieu's obstinacy worried Clifford for a variety of reasons, not the least of which was the fear that without Saigon's backing the decision to halt the bombing would backfire politically. Maybe Johnson should wait to announce the bombing halt until after the election, Clifford mused, and thus avoid the charge that the decision was driven solely by political calculation.[14]

Despite Thieu's stonewalling, Johnson decided to go ahead with the bombing halt anyway. He planned to announce the decision on television that evening, but he scheduled a conference call with the presidential candidates to inform them first. In light of the Nixon campaign's back-channel dealings with the South Vietnamese, Johnson could not resist getting in a little dig at the Republican. Now I know that "some of the old China lobbyists, they are going around and implying to some of the embassies and some of the others that they might get a better deal out of somebody that was not involved in this," he said gravely. "Now that's made it difficult and it's held up things a little bit. And I know that none of you candidates are aware of it or responsible for it . . ."[15]

Speaking on television that evening the president announced that he had ordered a complete halt of all bombardment of North Vietnam. "I have reached this decision on the basis of the developments in the Paris talks," he said, "and I have reached it in the belief that this action can lead to progress toward a peaceful settlement of the Vietnamese war."[16]

The day after the announcement Clifford sent the president a personal letter commending him for the decision:

> Mr. President, there have been times without number in the past 5 years when I have admired you for your fortitude and determination and very unique effectiveness. As of this moment, however, I feel it more deeply than ever before. Your performance on the Vietnam cessation has been magnificent. It was handled with courage, with rare distinction, and the most admirable statesmanship. I was aware of the myriad difficulties that confronted you and I drew comfort and inspiration from the masterful manner in which you met and overcame all of them. I have a profound sense of pride in your performance and in your success.[17]

Clifford's sense of relief and satisfaction over the bombing halt was comparable to the despair he felt the next day, after he had completely digested Thieu's obstructive attitude toward the peace talks.

Paul Nitze tried in vain to convince him that the actions of the South Vietnamese were consistent with their self-interest, but Clifford was having none of it. He laid the blame on Rusk, Rostow, and Taylor, who had so much at stake in their pursuit of a "beautiful democracy" in Southeast Asia that they were unwilling to admit that the South Vietnamese government could not deliver. Lapsing into self-pity, Clifford bitterly complained about the debacle in Vietnam. "I do not believe we ought to be in Vietnam," he said. "I think our being there is a mistake," he added. "I'm disgusted with it all."[18]

With just days before the election Johnson struggled with the decision of whether to expose Nixon's perfidy with respect to the peace negotiations. Clifford suggested that the president discuss the matter with Senator Everett Dirksen, who was on friendly terms with both Nixon and Johnson. The president placed a call to Dirksen that evening. "We're skirting on dangerous ground," he said, "and I thought I ought to give you the facts and you ought to pass them on if you choose. If you don't, why then I will a little later." Johnson explained that Thieu had initially supported the idea of a bombing halt followed by peace negotiations, but because of interference from the "old China crowd" he suddenly backed out. Johnson instructed Dirksen to deliver a cease-and-desist order to the Nixon campaign; otherwise, he would be forced to go public. "I don't want this to get in the campaign," he said. "And they oughtn't to be doing this. This is treason."[19] Dirksen promptly alerted Nixon, who realized that if Johnson broke the story it could sabotage his campaign. Nixon assured Johnson that he had nothing to do with the back-channel maneuvering and would never do anything to undermine the peace negotiations.[20]

As late as the day before the election, Johnson still had not decided if he should go public. However, a reporter from the *Christian Science Monitor* was working on the story and asked Rostow if he could confirm anything. Johnson told Rostow not to say anything, and then placed a call from the ranch to Clifford, Rusk, and Rostow. Rusk recommended restraint, as did Clifford. "I think that some elements of the story are so shocking in their nature that I'm wondering whether it would be good for the country to disclose the story, and then possibly to have a certain individual elected," he argued. "It could cast his whole administration under such doubts that I would think it would be inimical to our country's interests." Johnson was concerned that the story would break anyway, and then they would be accused of trying to bury it. Clifford was unconcerned about that. "I don't believe that would bother me," he said. "I think that the amount of information that we have—that we don't think we should publicize—it has to do with the sensitivity of the sources, it has to do with the absences of absolute proof. So, I don't believe we have the kind of story that we'd be justified in putting out."[21] Johnson decided to remain silent.

The next day Nixon defeated Humphrey in a close election. Had Humphrey won the presidency, he would have appointed Clifford secretary of state,[22] allowing Clifford the opportunity to bring the war to a negotiated settlement. Instead he was a lame-duck secretary of defense with less than three months left in office.

On November 11 the president-elect met with Johnson and his foreign policy advisers. Nixon indicated that he would do nothing with respect to Vietnam, unless there was something he could do that would be helpful to the president. Johnson replied that it would be best to allow the Paris talks to continue without interference, but added that Nixon should appoint a representative to sit in on the administration's Vietnam meetings during the transition. "I think it is a practical necessity to have a man here," Clifford agreed. Knowing full well of Nixon's back-channel dealings with Thieu, Clifford could not resist dropping a facetious comment. "You can be very helpful in [the] next 65 days—I know you want to wind this up as soon as we," he said.[23]

At the time there were rumors circulating that Nixon would ask Clifford to stay on as secretary of defense. Given how he felt about Nixon, Clifford knew that he could not serve under him, and he tried to quash the rumors. "Kill it—step on it—tell everybody there's nothing to it!" he told his staff.[24] Of course rumors are slow to die in Washington, and this one lingered until Nixon named Clifford's successor.

Three days later Clifford called a press conference to address accusations from the South Vietnamese that the Johnson administration had enacted a bombing halt without the agreement of the South Vietnamese government. Clifford was furious, and he used the press conference as a forum to lash out at Thieu and his compatriots. The president had labored over the prior five and a half months to reach a peaceful settlement, Clifford explained, "and then in the last out of the ninth inning, why, suddenly they say, 'No, we can't go along.'" Red-faced, and pounding the podium for emphasis, he said, "I believe the President was absolutely right in not giving Saigon a veto on the plan."[25] Irrespective of what the South Vietnamese decided to do, the president "has the constitutional responsibility of proceeding with the talks." Reaction within the administration was mixed. Rostow thought that Clifford had "overstated the case" that Thieu was privy to Johnson's deliberations regarding the bombing halt. Harriman, however, thought that Clifford was simply telling the truth.[26] Elsey agreed, believing that Clifford was the only one in the administration with the credibility and will to expose the South Vietnamese as obstacles to peace.[27]

Thieu, of course, was angry about Clifford's remarks, but suspected that the secretary of defense was merely speaking as a surrogate for the president, and thus he transferred his anger to the administration in general.[28] Partially to punish Johnson, but primarily because he believed that he would obtain a more favorable deal with Nixon, Thieu was determined to stall until after Johnson left office. The infamous debate over table shapes was tangible evidence of the South Vietnamese strategy of delaying until Nixon was inaugurated.

As the tumultuous year of 1968 came to an end the South Vietnamese continued to stall, yet Clifford still held out some hope that there could be some progress in the waning days of the Johnson administration. But he was also realistic; he knew that the odds were long. Referring to the South Vietnamese he complained, "'They' want Lodge and Nixon and so they'll not move at all before [January] 20th." Assessing his state of mind at the time, Elsey concluded that Clifford was so driven by his anti-Saigon views that it was hard for him to recognize that he was essentially waging a one-man war against the South Vietnamese government. Privately wrestling with increasing feelings of powerlessness and frustration, Clifford despondently wondered what his position should be. Should I "just sit back and do nothing between now and [January] 20th," he rhetorically asked. "Continue to let Saigon make all decisions?" Yet despite his frustration, he was determined to try. "By tomorrow, it'll be my last chance to do anything."[29]

That last chance came at the Tuesday luncheon of January 7. Clifford argued that it was wrong to allow Saigon to have a veto over U.S. policy and that while they were "sitting supinely by" American soldiers were dying. An angry Johnson agreed, demanding that Rusk see to it that the talks got started before the inauguration, "even if we have to admit Clark has been right."[30] Unfortunately, it did not matter whether or not Clifford was right, and, in fact, Saigon did have a veto, which they exercised. The peace talks did not begin until January 25.

What Clifford overestimated—and what Nixon and Henry Kissinger overestimated over the next four years—was the willingness of the North Vietnamese to accept a negotiated settlement. Despite the intensification and expansion of the war, Hanoi proved to be a reluctant negotiating partner, and even after the Paris accords were signed in 1973 they continued to press for a military advantage. The North Vietnamese understood that the United States, like the French before them, did not have the political will to wage an all-out, protracted war, and that time was on their side. Given the continuation of the war for the next four years it is fairly certain that an enduring peace was impossible in 1968; but neither was victory. Clifford may have been naïve in thinking that a peace deal was possible, but he was realistic enough to understand that a military victory against a committed adversary was far less probable.

With the South Vietnamese looking to run out the clock on the Johnson administration, and the North Vietnamese stalling as well, there was nothing realistic that Clifford could accomplish, other than to satisfy himself that he had exposed an unworthy partner in democracy and brief his designated successor, Representative Melvin Laird of Wisconsin. The last month in office was, as is typical, a time for valedictories. On New Year's Eve McGeorge Bundy sent a personal letter to Clifford praising him for his dedication and commitment during a difficult year, suggesting that he should be named "Man of the Year." "You more than any other man have been brave and right at the right time and in the right place," he wrote. "You have been the President's best and most tenaciously honest counselor, and you have got the damned thing turned around." In addition to the praise Bundy also suggested that they discuss how Clifford might continue in public service, and hinted at a run for elected office. "And then I hope we can talk not only about this great service and how you did it—but also about some things that are ahead of all of us where you will be needed more than ever," he wrote. "Honest men who care and don't need anything are the most precious stones of the Republic."[31]

Johnson expressed similar sentiments in a birthday letter to Clifford. "I am convinced that it was no coincidence that you were born on Christmas Day," the president wrote. "For somewhere in your stars, it must have been written that your full and fruitful lifetime would be spent in selfless pursuit of peace and goodwill among all men."[32] Yet the tone of Johnson's note belied the strain to their relationship as a result of a tumultuous year of arguing about Vietnam. In thanking Bundy for his letter Clifford expressed regret that he and Johnson had a falling out. "It has been an incredible period," he wrote. "The road has been tortuous and painful and, at times, unbelievably lonely. The account that I had in the LBJ bank stood me in good stead for awhile but it became dangerously low these last few months, and recently I have been tiptoeing on the brink of bankruptcy." Years later, he lamented, "Our long friendship would never be the same again."[33]

Johnson's lingering animosity toward Clifford raises the obvious question of what his expectations for Clifford were when he selected him as secretary of defense. Assuming that the president had lost faith in Robert McNamara when he could no longer support the war, then it logically follows that he would look for someone whose support and commitment to the war was unwavering. Given that, his selection of Clifford was curious because although Clifford had come to be considered a hawk, his initial—and vociferous—opposition to the war could not be easily dismissed. Ultimately the decisive factor that would determine how Clifford would perform as wartime secretary of defense would be his commitment to that war; and the undeniable fact was that fundamentally he believed it was a mistake. Psychoanalyzing any historical figure is a risky proposition, and even more so with as notoriously volatile a figure as was Lyndon Johnson; yet it is not out of the realm of possibility that Johnson might have been, on some level, looking for a way out. Joseph Califano suspected as much, believing that Johnson selected Clifford because Clifford's warnings from 1965 had been so prescient, and that Clifford therefore was uniquely positioned to reevaluate the administration's policy.[34] The notion that Johnson hoped Clifford could help bring about an end to the war is all the more plausible for the simple reason that the president did not fire him once his opposition became apparent. After all, Johnson had fired McNamara because he could not support the president's policy, so he could have fired Clifford as well. The short-term political consequences would have been an acceptable price to pay in order to have someone truly committed to the endeavor. Johnson may have been unable to dedicate himself completely to ending the war, but he was willing to take steps in that direction, even if he had to be shoved from time to time. Only Clifford had earned the respect necessary to convince the stubborn president to change course.

Clifford's motives should be scrutinized as well. By his account he had opposed the war at the very beginning, but once the decision was made to send in troops he supported the president, and also supported any decision that would bring the war to a successful conclusion as soon as possible. Yet only a few weeks after assuming the office of secretary of defense he turned against the war and devoted himself to extricating America from the quagmire in Southeast Asia. Clifford's conversion from dove to hawk and then back to dove again could be explained in a couple of different ways. One option would be to take Clifford at his word. The other possibility is that he was secretly a dove all along who waited until he was installed in the Pentagon to reveal and act on his beliefs. The notion that he was a secret dove is not plausible, however, because it is inconsistent with Clifford's respect for the office of the president and his belief that Cabinet officers and members of the administration were to serve the president. Clifford looked after his own interests, but always with the understanding that he served at the pleasure of the president. Clifford had access to President Johnson long before he officially joined the administration. He knew that his unofficial status afforded him the opportunity to speak frankly, and he also knew that he would sacrifice that independence once he joined the Cabinet. It is also possible, as suggested earlier, that Clifford did not speak frankly in order to maintain access to the president. He agreed to join the administration only when the right offer came along, and he supported the president's policy until it was untenable. The fact that he shifted positions so soon after becoming secretary of defense is hard to explain unless the circumstances of the war changed dramatically during that time. In fact, the circumstances did change, and quite dramatically. The shock of the Tet Offensive convinced Clifford that the war was unwinnable and that he was duty bound to bring Johnson around to that view.

The role of Clifford during the Vietnam War is especially significant because of the insight it sheds on the influence of domestic politics on foreign policy. In July 1965 Clifford warned Johnson that the war would become a quagmire and that it would destroy his administration. He understood that the American people would determine that the price of an elusive victory in Southeast Asia was too dear and that the country could not sustain the political will necessary to fight a guerrilla war on the other side of the world. This judgment was based primarily on his instinctive understanding of U.S. electoral politics rather than broad expertise in international relations or Asia. Clifford presented his case to Johnson in stark political terms, warning him that Vietnam could cost him his presidency and, implicitly, the thing Johnson valued most, the Great Society.

Clifford's efforts to end U.S. involvement in Vietnam, both in 1965 and in 1968, were the high-water mark of his long and distinguished Washington career. Both times he took a strong opinion in opposition to the consensus in the administration and to the president himself. For a man that cherished close relationships with powerful men, and whose career depended on it, Clifford courageously took a position that jeopardized and strained his relationship with Lyndon Johnson. Clifford looked back at his battles with Johnson with regret over the strain they put on his relationship with the president, but with confidence that he had done the right thing. As he said later:

> I believe that as the year '68 went on, I think I was conscious of some erosion of our relationship. I felt very strongly about Viet Nam, and I think I was something of an irritant to him in '68 with reference to Viet Nam. I did it with a clear conscience because I thought it was not only in the country's interest, but I think it was in his interest. And I'm greatly comforted by some of the decisions that he did make, the cutting back of the bombing in March, and the decision not to send more troops; and finally on October 31, the cessation of the bombing completely. . . . But I believe because I did push hard through that year, I think I felt our relationship lessening some.[35]

In many respects Clifford's tenure as secretary of defense signified his emergence as his own man, as David Halberstam observed:

> Clifford was the prototype of the rich man's Washington lobbyist, the supersmooth, urbane lawyer who knows where every body is buried, the former high official who works for government just long enough to know where the weak spots are. But Clifford was proving to be a new kind of high official for Johnson; whatever else he was not the corporate man. Instead he had a great sense of his own value, and did not believe that anyone hired Clifford except to gain the full benefit of his services. A great lawyer is paid for telling a rich and powerful client the truth, no matter how unpalatable.[36]

Even without the wisdom of four decades of hindsight it is clear that Johnson should have heeded Clifford's words in 1965. The war in Vietnam brought an end to his presidency and has remained a black mark on Johnson's legacy. Despite his formidable accomplishments, he is best remembered as the president who led America into a quagmire, and as the first president to lose a foreign war.

# 12

# The Wise Man

As secretary of defense Clifford had achieved a position of enormous prestige and had served with honor and great personal courage. Once out of power Clifford joined the community of Washington elder statesmen, like the group he had assembled to reassess the Vietnam War in March 1968. He continued to crusade for an end to the war, and because of his stature his words commanded significant attention, as well as the enmity of the Nixon administration. In the aftermath of the Watergate scandal the Democrats regained the White House, and he would be called upon again, although with far less frequency, to advise another president. As a result of his age, experience, and status as a former Cabinet secretary, Clifford was now more than simply a Washington power broker. He was now one of the wise men.

When Richard Nixon took the oath of office, Clifford was forced to the sidelines. There had been pressure on Nixon to retain Clifford as secretary of defense, but the new president believed that it would be a mistake to retain someone who supported the policies that Nixon had criticized during the campaign.[1] Clifford's efforts to extricate the United States from the quagmire of Vietnam had been for naught. He believed, however, that it was only a matter of time before Nixon pulled out the American troops. The circumstances were reminiscent of 1953 when Eisenhower took office, with Nixon as his vice president, and ended U.S. involvement in another unpopular war. "Surely," Clifford thought, "we will be out within the year."[2] With that thought in mind, he refrained from publicly criticizing the new administration. By the summer of 1969, however, it was clear to him that Nixon was not moving toward a withdrawal; and, while he could not directly influence U.S. foreign policy, as a former secretary of defense his words carried weight.

Accordingly, Clifford published an article entitled "A Viet Nam

Reappraisal: The Personal History of One Man's View and How It Evolved" in the Summer 1969 issue of the influential journal *Foreign Affairs*. Given the title, the article was, to an extent, an apologia. Curiously, however, Clifford made no mention of his initial opposition to escalation. "When decisions were made in 1965 to increase, in very substantial fashion, the American commitment in Vietnam, I accepted the judgment that such actions were necessary," he wrote. No doubt Clifford wanted to avoid offending Johnson, but the article certainly provided him with the opportunity to set the record straight and go on record as having opposed the war in the first place. Instead, he wrote: "At the time of our original involvement in Vietnam, I considered it to be based upon unassailable premises, thoroughly consistent with our self-interest and our responsibilities."[3]

Clifford recounted that by March 1968 he was convinced that continued U.S. involvement in the war would be counterproductive. "A further substantial increase in American forces could only increase the devastation and the Americanization of the war, and thus leave us even further from our goal of a peace that would permit the people of South Vietnam to fashion their own political and economic institutions," he wrote. But in addition to arguing that it was time to withdraw, he also noted that the United States had already achieved its objectives. The United States had entered the war with limited objectives, he argued in language reminiscent of the Truman Doctrine. The objective in Vietnam was to "prevent its subjugation by the North and to enable the people of South Vietnam to determine their own future." Clifford asserted that the United States was not obligated to undertake a nation-building exercise in Vietnam, nor was it obligated to ensure a complete victory by South Vietnam over the North. Invoking the doctrine of limited war, Clifford argued that the American commitment was well out of proportion to the objectives and that the material and human costs were no longer justified. Continued involvement would only "continue to devastate the countryside and to prolong the suffering of the Vietnamese people."[4]

Accordingly, Clifford stated that it was time to reduce the U.S. military commitment and withdraw all combat troops by the end of 1970. He suggested an aggressive schedule of withdrawal and firm deadlines to force the government of President Nguyen Van Thieu to assume primary responsibility for waging the war. Clifford's plan entailed a reduction of 100,000 American combat troops by the end of 1969 and the remaining 100,000 to 150,000 combat troops by the end of 1970, leaving about 300,000 troops behind to provide logistic and air support for the South Vietnamese forces. Clifford argued that the removal of U.S. combat troops would actually put pressure on the North because it would confront them with a "prolonged and substantial presence of American air and logistics personnel in support of South Viet Nam's combat troops." By withdrawing U.S. combat troops, casualties would be substantially reduced, leading to a corresponding reduction in political pressure by the antiwar movement. In effect, Clifford argued that a withdrawal strategy would be an effective countermeasure to the North's Tet Offensive strategy, which was intended to force a precipitous withdrawal by inflicting an unacceptable level of casualties.[5]

James Reston considered Clifford's strategy to be plausible but not heroic, and as good a compromise as anyone else had put forward. He also admired Clifford's uncanny ability to come forward at the "moment of decision."

> It is interesting that Clifford should have emerged once more in this role. He seems to have a genius for emerging at the critical moment. He is not a far-sighted man. Nobody could have been more loyal to Presidents Truman, Kennedy or Johnson as a confidential adviser, but once he took the oath of office as Secretary of Defense and put his mind to his responsibilities in that office, he challenged not only the established policies but even his own preconceived opinions—and switched. As a symbol of how to serve one's own private interests and also the public interest, his career is a classic.[6]

Unbeknownst to Clifford, who had written his article in early May, Nixon had been formulating plans to withdraw 25,000 troops from Vietnam and announced his plans only days before Clifford's article appeared in *Foreign Affairs*. The article was not critical of the president, and Nixon could have used it to demonstrate that there was bipartisan support for his plan. But that was not Nixon's style. He perceived Clifford's article as a partisan attack and responded in kind. When asked during a press conference if he thought Clifford's timetable was realistic, Nixon responded:

> Well, I noted Mr. Clifford's comments in the magazine *Foreign Affairs,* and, naturally, I respect his judgment as a former Secretary of Defense. I would point out, however, that for five years in the Administration in which he was Secretary of

Defense in the last part, we had a continued escalation of the war: we had 500,000 Americans in Vietnam; we had 35,000 killed; we had over 200,000 injured. And, in addition to that, we found that in the year, the full year, in which he was Secretary of Defense, our casualties were the highest of the whole five-year period and, as far as negotiations were concerned, all that had been accomplished, as I indicated earlier, was that we had agreed on the shape of the table. This is not to say that Mr. Clifford's present judgment is not to be considered because of the past record. It does indicate, however, that he did have a chance in this particular respect, and did not move on it then. I believe that we have changed that policy. We have started to withdraw forces. We will withdraw more. . . . As far as how many will be withdrawn by the end of this year, I would hope that we could beat Mr. Clifford's timetable, just as I think we have done a little better than he did when he was in charge of our national defense.[7]

Patrick Anderson, writing in the *New York Times,* described the outburst as a "classic Nixonism—the pious disclaimer followed by the distortion and innuendo—the sort of petty outburst that always hurts Nixon more than the people he is attacking."[8]

H. R. Haldeman, Nixon's chief of staff, was startled by Nixon's comments and thought that Nixon had let his anger at Clifford get the better of him. National Security Advisor Henry Kissinger was distraught and thought that a withdrawal of U.S. troops would lead to the collapse of the Thieu regime in the near future. Furthermore, Kissinger believed that Nixon's comments were a calculated shift in policy. Haldeman disagreed, but he believed that, in his zeal to lash back at Clifford, Nixon had encumbered the administration's policy in Vietnam.[9]

By the spring of 1970 Clifford was discouraged by the slow pace of withdrawal in Vietnam, believing that Nixon was not living up to his earlier pledge. But it was the dramatic announcement that U.S. troops would move into Cambodia that prompted Clifford to take further action. In May 1970 he published an article in *Life* magazine entitled "Set a Date in Vietnam. Stick to It. Get Out." Although he had avoided attacking Nixon in the *Foreign Affairs* article, he was less measured in his criticism this time. "I cannot remain silent in the face of his reckless decision to send troops to Cambodia, continuing a course of action which I believe to be dangerous to the welfare of our nation," he wrote. "It is my opinion that President Nixon is taking our nation down a road that is leading us more deeply into Vietnam rather than taking us out."[10]

Clifford wrote that he had learned three lessons from his experience with the war in Vietnam. Expanding upon his argument from a year earlier, Clifford first argued that U.S. national security was no longer at stake in Vietnam, and he ridiculed Nixon's belief in the "domino theory" of communist expansion. "I cannot remain silent when President Nixon acts as though he believes that a certain political result in a small underdeveloped country of 18 million persons in Southeast Asia is somehow crucial to 'the future of peace and freedom in America and in the world.'" Second, he argued that a military victory in South Vietnam was out of the question. Political constraints precluded a full-scale assault in North Vietnam, and this condition compelled U.S. forces to fight a guerrilla war for which it was poorly equipped against an enemy willing to accept a great number of casualties. "Our problem in Vietnam is due not only to our inability to attain the military goals, despite our great effort, but to the fact that the struggle is basically a political one. The enemy continues to symbolize the forces of nationalism. The regime which we support is a narrowly based military dictatorship," he pointed out. Finally, Clifford warned that the domestic repercussions of the war were causing irreparable harm and dividing the country. In addition to the bitter debate between those in favor and those opposed to the war, Clifford argued that the war adversely affected a rash of domestic problems including poverty, crime, education, and the economy.[11]

Clifford believed that Nixon failed to understand any of these three lessons, as evidenced by his decision to send troops into Cambodia. "Any military gains will be temporary and inconsequential," he predicted. In a particularly revealing passage Clifford lamented the futile loss of life, especially in the pursuit of temporarily held territory. "A perfect illustration is Hamburger Hill. We drove the enemy off Hamburger Hill at great loss of life to our troops, and then later on withdrew. As soon as we pulled out, the enemy reoccupied Hamburger Hill and we went back and repeated the process. I do not know who holds the hill today. I am certain it doesn't matter."[12]

Clifford's solution went further than the one he proposed in *Foreign Affairs* a year earlier. Now he argued for an immediate and complete withdrawal of all U.S. forces from Vietnam, not just ground forces. A complete withdrawal would "Vietnamese the peace rather than prolong the war," and to that end Clifford made three recommendations.

First, he argued that all combat troops should be withdrawn by the end of the year and all support military personnel removed by the end of 1971. Second, he recommended that all offensive actions, including bombing attacks and search-and-destroy missions, be immediately suspended except as necessary to protect the departing troops. Finally, he suggested that the United States could advance the peace process by promising an even faster withdrawal if accompanied by either a cease-fire or a guarantee that the North Vietnamese would not attack the departing American troops.

The Nixon administration prepared an immediate response. Presidential speechwriter, and later political pundit and presidential candidate, Patrick Buchanan wrote a tough speech blasting Clifford and other foes of the administration. The speech was written for Vice President Spiro Agnew to deliver on Thursday, May 28, but Nixon wanted to wait because he planned to give a nationally televised address regarding the military operation in Cambodia.[13] Agnew finally gave the speech on June 21 at a Republican Party fund-raiser. "The President is not listening to the counsel of defeatists, who blame every deadlock at the conference table and every impasse in negotiation on the United States," he charged. "Mr. Clifford's current writings seem to emanate from a deep desire to convince his friends that he was an early convert and not a late-blooming opportunist who clambered aboard the rolling bandwagon of the doves when the flak really started to fly."[14]

No doubt troubled over the way he was being characterized by the Nixon administration, Clifford reached out to an old ally from the 1965 troop escalation debate, George Ball. "Not a week goes by but that I don't recall the soundness and accuracy of your views with reference to Vietnam," he wrote. "Would that you prevailed."[15]

Clifford continued to apply pressure on Nixon to pull out of Vietnam. In June 1971 he proposed a modified version of the plan in *Life*, but this time he stated that U.S. withdrawal from Vietnam should be contingent upon the release of all prisoners of war. He also claimed he was convinced, based upon consultations with individuals, "some of them American and some of them not," that the North Vietnamese would agree to this offer. Clifford did not reveal his sources, although there was speculation that he had spoken to the North Vietnamese. The White House disputed Clifford's contention that the North was ready to negotiate and release prisoners. "We have no indication directly from them that they are prepared to do anything more than discuss the release of our prisoners," said Ronald Ziegler, Nixon's press secretary. Ziegler also charged that Clifford was carelessly raising false hopes of a prisoner release "for domestic political purposes."[16]

Despite Nixon's denials, the North Vietnamese offered a peace plan shortly thereafter that was almost identical to the one Clifford predicted they would accept. Clifford believed that Nixon had dismissed his proposal because he was unwilling to accept defeat in Vietnam and instead believed the American people would accept a long-term military commitment there, provided that casualties were kept to a minimum. "I have analyzed everything President Nixon has said about Vietnam, going back to the early nineteen-fifties," he said. "I keep a file on every word he utters. I read about it, I underline it, and I think about it. I now believe I understand what his policy is. What worries me is that his plan is not going to bring him out where he thinks it is."[17]

Six months after the *Life* article Clifford turned up the heat on Nixon, this time in response to a recent speech in which the president, in Clifford's opinion, undermined the chances of a peace agreement by stipulating that a cease-fire must precede a settlement, a condition the North had repeatedly rejected. "Last Tuesday, the day of President Nixon's speech on Vietnam," Clifford said, "proved to be a sad day for our country. If one took the time to pierce the rhetoric, he found there a record of two and a half years of completely unproductive negotiations in Paris. The collapse of our negotiating effort was compounded by President Nixon's decision to publicize the results of secret meetings so as practically to insure major difficulty in resuming effective off-the-record discussions."[18]

Clifford's peace plans and his criticism of Nixon earned him the enmity of the White House. William Safire, a White House speechwriter, recalled a spirited, yet civil debate over Vietnam that he had with Clifford at a dinner party. However, when he told Haldeman about his conversation with Clifford the chief of staff flew into a rage:

> I recounted the episode to Haldeman the next day and the mention of Clifford's name was like waving a red bull in front of an angry flag [*sic*]. Clifford was the very personification of "them": he had helped mire the United States in Vietnam, and now that Nixon was extricating the nation from the result of the folly of men like Clifford, he had the gall to tell us that the only way out was abject surrender. Beyond that, he was a certified Nixon-hater, a new hero of the Movement, and a fre-

quent writer in the best of the worst media. Any form of association with the likes of Clifford—even in argument—was, in Haldeman's view, only a way of encouraging him to clobber us.[19]

The Nixon administration did more than engage in a public debate with Clifford. It was later determined, based upon information obtained from FBI wiretaps, that Nixon knew about the *Life* article before it was published and Haldeman and domestic adviser John Ehrlichman had discussed how "to combat" Clifford's criticism.[20] Nixon had even ordered the Internal Revenue Service to pore over Clifford's tax records.[21] But Clifford was unfazed when the financial surveillance was revealed during the 1973 Watergate hearings. "They can plow through those returns by the hour and they won't find a dollar," he said. "My instruction twenty-three years ago when I left the Truman administration was: 'If there is a serious question about an item, pay it.' I have followed that policy ever since."[22] In addition to the IRS scrutiny Clifford also had the distinction of making the infamous Nixon enemies list, although his name was misspelled "Gifford."[23] Clifford was also investigated as a possible source of the leak of the Pentagon Papers.[24]

Even after a peace agreement had been reached, the White House still directed its fire at Clifford. Special counsel to the president Charles Colson argued that rather than promoting peace, Clifford's peace proposals and criticisms of Nixon had both undermined the war effort and needlessly prolonged the war. According to Colson, bipartisan support for Nixon's policies would have expedited the peace process. Clifford was "representative, really, of a group of people who would have compromised this country's position in Vietnam." Critics such as Clifford, said Colson, were advocating a "dishonorable peace."[25]

Thoroughly unconvinced of Nixon's commitment to achieving an honorable peace, Clifford's first choice for the Democratic presidential nomination in 1972 was Senator Edmund Muskie of Maine, and he was an active contributor to Muskie's campaign. By the end of April 1972, however, Muskie was far behind in the delegate count, and he met with a group of core advisers, including Clifford, and opted to withdraw from the race.[26] Senator George McGovern of South Dakota secured the nomination. He chose to run as a Washington outsider, a curious decision for someone who had served in the House and Senate since 1957. Clifford served on a panel of national security advisors for McGovern that recommended sweeping reform of the armed services, a subject dear to Clifford's heart. Two days before the election McGovern conferred with Clifford and in a speech that evening charged that the war was "intensifying" and that Nixon had deliberately misled the public into believing that peace was near.[27] The voters were not swayed, however, and Nixon won reelection in a landslide.

Nixon's landslide victory over McGovern was a stinging defeat for the Democrats, and within a few months of the 1972 election Clifford absorbed two personal losses, which exacerbated his sense of despair. The day after Clifford's sixty-sixth birthday he received the news that former president Harry Truman had died. Clifford was one of a small group of guests who attended the service. A month later Lyndon Johnson died, and while Johnson to the end harbored resentment at Clifford for his turnaround over the Vietnam War, Clifford still felt the loss personally.

Early 1973 was not a happy time for devotees of the Democratic Party, due to the stinging defeat of 1972 and the consecutive deaths of two of their last three former presidents. But shortly thereafter the Watergate scandal broke, which ultimately led to the downfall of Richard Nixon, who had long tormented the Democrats. In the summer of 1973 Clifford wrote an editorial in which he presented a plan for a government of national unity, its aim being to restore confidence in government (with Nixon no longer leading it, of course). He took a tone of high-minded statesmanship: "As each new chapter in the Watergate tragedy unfolds, I have an increasing sense of grim foreboding as I look at the future. The extent of the damage already sustained, and the worsening of the Administration's posture as further revelations occur, emphasize the fact that this is no time for partisanship. This is the time for Americans to work together to save this country."[28] In private, however, Clifford made no pretense of bipartisanship and gloated at Nixon's self-inflicted troubles. Ben Bradlee, then the editor of the *Washington Post,* the paper that broke the Watergate story, recounted a phone call from Clifford in January 1973. He said to Bradlee, "This morning I got up and put on my robe and walked to the door and opened the door. It was a beautiful day and I picked up my newspaper and looked at it and I looked up and said, 'Thank God for the *Washington Post.*'"[29] Clifford's plan for a government of national unity called for the resignations of both Nixon and Agnew under the auspices of the Twenty-fifth Amendment, with Nixon selecting a new vice president from a list of three qualified individuals, and the new vice president then assuming the presidency.[30]

Clifford must have known that his proposal would never be taken seriously. Supporters of Nixon were outraged, and one *New York Times* reader wrote that the Clifford article was "one of the most insidious as well as treasonable utterances" directed against "a man who is without question the most honest and loyally oriented President this country has had since Theodore Roosevelt." Critics of the president, while perhaps supportive of Clifford's idea, considered it impractical, believing that it was totally unrealistic to expect either Nixon or Agnew to resign. One observer noted that the idea was contrary to the most basic principle of the Constitution, the right of the people to choose the president through the electoral process.[31] Not surprisingly, Nixon did not implement Clifford's plan; instead, he tried to contain the damage. In August 1973 he made a televised defense of his conduct during the Watergate scandal, but Clifford dismissed the speech as insignificant relative to Nixon's infamous "Checkers" speech of 1952, sarcastically claiming that he slept through it.[32]

Clifford's idea in fact was not a purely partisan proposal for Nixon's demise; it reflected his belief in the need to reform parts of the Constitution. In 1970 he told C. L. Sulzberger of the *New York Times* that the federal government had become archaic: "It had been adequate for thirteen small agricultural communities called states and even then was the result of a good deal of compromise among our Founding Fathers. For example, one original concept was that in a Presidential election the candidate obtaining the largest vote would be President and the one with the next largest vote would be Vice President. The party concept simply didn't exist. This really illustrates how unmodern and unrealistic the Founding Fathers were." Clifford did not advocate for a parliamentary system, as in Britain, where the opposition leader would become Prime Minister following a vote of no confidence. "We don't need a Prime Minister," he argued. "We have a Vice President. But the office is not being properly used."[33]

As it happened, both Nixon and Agnew did ultimately resign, although under circumstances different than Clifford envisioned in his plan for a government of national unity. But, as Clifford had suggested, the solution to the Watergate scandal was to invoke both sections of the Twenty-fifth Amendment.

One of the many outcomes of the Watergate scandal was an assertive Congress, then controlled by Democrats, insisting on greater oversight of the executive branch. The most notable example of that increased oversight was the Church Committee, named after Senator Frank Church of Idaho. The Church Committee investigated allegations of abuse of law and power by the U.S. intelligence agencies, including accusations of assassination attempts against foreign leaders in Cuba, Vietnam, Congo, and the Dominican Republic. As a former secretary of defense Clifford was called to testify, and he told the committee that during his service to Truman and Johnson he was never aware of any plots to assassinate foreign leaders. He noted that many of the types of abuses unearthed by the Church Committee were never contemplated by the drafters of the 1947 National Security Act, and recommended that Congress pass legislation providing for greater oversight.[34]

During follow-up testimony in December 1975 Clifford acknowledged that covert operations "have gotten out-of-hand." He explained, "There were too many cases where the agency [the CIA] was given the authority to start with A and go to B, and when it got to B it seemed logical to go to C on its own authority, and so on to D and beyond." Yet, despite his misgivings, Clifford did not advocate abolishing covert activities. Instead, he reiterated his earlier recommendation that greater congressional oversight was required, along with other reforms. Clifford suggested that covert activities should be authorized only under circumstances in which there was "a profound impact on the continued existence of this country." He also argued that certain methods, notably political assassinations, should always be prohibited. In addition, in order to ensure accountability Clifford recommended that covert activities should not be untaken without presidential authorization. Clifford contradicted his own testimony, however, when he explained that he had advised Kennedy to resist congressional efforts to investigate the CIA. Clifford explained that at the time he was trying to keep the Bay of Pigs fiasco out of the "political arena."[35]

The Watergate scandal presented Democrats with a unique opportunity to retake the White House, and the candidate that emerged with the nomination was Jimmy Carter, the governor of Georgia. Carter campaigned as a Washington outsider and, after winning the election, attempted to govern as one. Carter's disdain for business as usual in Washington ensured that Clifford's role in the new administration would be limited. It was a difficult adjustment for Clifford, who had enjoyed access to and influence with the past three Democratic presidents. Carter consulted Clifford regarding the defense budget, CIA reform, and debate preparation; but, as Clifford himself acknowledged, he played only a minor role in the campaign.[36] One Beltway insider complained that Carter was "treating Washington like a leper colony."[37]

Carter met with Clifford during the transition, but their meeting could best be described as a courtesy call. According to Clifford, despite Carter's profession of admiration for Harry Truman, the president-elect had no questions about either Truman or his administration. Clifford did, however, make the bland announcement that Carter was interested "in the way past Democratic Administrations had met problems."[38]

During the Carter administration Clifford did not enjoy the level of access to the White House that he had in previous administrations, but Carter did give him a couple of assignments. Shortly after taking office the new president asked Clifford to serve as his envoy to Cyprus, the site of a bitter dispute between its majority ethnic Greek community and the ethnic Turkish minority. In 1974 Turkey invaded the island and established the Turkish Republic of Northern Cyprus, a state recognized only by Turkey, while the internationally recognized Republic of Cyprus controlled the remainder of the island. The ongoing dispute over the island represented a manifestation of the historic rivalry between Greece and Turkey, which were both members of NATO. The tense relations between the countries were a concern for the United States and other NATO countries because it threatened the stability of the southeastern region of the alliance.

Clifford's first stop was Athens, Greece, where he met with Prime Minister Constantine Karmanlis, and from there he flew to Ankara, Turkey. After two days of meetings with Turkish officials, Clifford announced that he was pleased with the progress. "At one stage we considered two separate statements, but because our views were so close we decided to issue one statement representing the views of both sides," he reported. Clifford also hinted at his support for ending the U.S. arms embargo to Turkey, which the U.S. had imposed after the 1974 invasion of Cyprus. "In the operations of NATO, it is necessary that nations have arms agreements and understandings so that the full strength of NATO can be maintained," he said.[39] From Turkey Clifford flew to Cyprus to meet with Archbishop Makarios, the president of Cyprus, and Rauf Denktash, leader of the Turkish state in Cyprus. As with the White House reporters of the Truman era, Clifford impressed the Greeks, Turks, and Cypriots with his physical presence. They were particularly struck by the contrast of his height with his soft-spoken voice.[40]

As a result of his talks, Clifford was extremely optimistic about the prospects for peace in the region. "Real progress has been made," he told the press just before returning to America, "and I leave with a sense of optimism that progress can be maintained." In testimony to Congress, Clifford said that "with good faith on both sides, a settlement is possible before the end of this year."[41] Carter was pleased with the results and sent Clifford a handwritten note thanking him for his efforts, which he hoped would "pay rich dividends for world peace."[42]

Both Clifford and Carter were overly optimistic of the chances for peace, as it turned out, and the prospects for peace dimmed considerably with the death of Archbishop Makarios in August. Clifford attended the funeral as part of the official American delegation. Despite the death of Makarios, Clifford still expressed confidence that a solution to the problem in Cyprus was within reach, even if it took months or years to achieve. Yet his tone was less optimistic when he confided to Carter his concern that the road to peace "will be a tortuous one, and the journey long and arduous, but that just increases the challenge." Nonetheless, Clifford promised that he would remain Carter's envoy for the duration.[43] Despite Clifford's efforts over the next two years, however, reconciliation between the Greeks and Turks proved elusive.

Clifford served ably and capably as Carter's envoy to the Eastern Mediterranean, but still he sought a more active role in the administration. Carter, however, intended to govern by relying primarily on his core of Georgia advisers while minimizing the influence of experienced Beltway figures such as Clifford. Despite these intentions, when confronted with the first scandal of his administration Carter turned to Clifford for help. Writing for *Esquire* magazine Aaron Latham observed that "the moment the Washington legal community knew that everything was going to be all right was when the Carter White House turned to Clark Clifford to defend Bert Lance. Washington was going to run the way it always had, oiled by the charm of Washington lawyers."[44]

As the first president elected in the wake of the Watergate scandal, and as a candidate who promised never to lie to the American people, Jimmy Carter would be held to a higher standard of ethics than his predecessors. Bert Lance would be the victim of that higher set of standards. He was the director of the Office of Management and Budget and a close adviser to Carter from his years as governor of Georgia. Lance's problems were the result of a promise he made during his confirmation hearings to divest himself of stock in the National Bank of Georgia, of which he had been president. Exhibiting a political naiveté that would be a recurring problem for the Carter administration, Lance later asked for permission to defer the sale for six months because the stock had declined in value. Carter argued that Lance should be granted a dispensation from the normal conflict-of-interest standards because the mere announcement that he would sell the shares had caused the stock to decline, and it would be unfair to force him to suffer the financial penalty. In an article that would earn him a Pulitzer Prize, William Safire, then a columnist for the *New York Times,* charged that the real reason the stock declined was Lance's mismanagement of the bank. According to Safire, Lance allowed the company to carry bad loans on the books when prudent accounting practices would dictate that the bad loans should be written off. After Lance left the bank, his successor took the necessary write-offs and suspended dividend payoffs, hence the reason for the stock to decline. In short, Safire charged, Lance's mismanagement had artificially inflated the stock price. Safire also accused Lance of a number of sweetheart deals in which he leveraged his relationship with then-Governor Carter.[45] As a result of these accusations, the Senate Governmental Affairs Committee decided to reexamine Lance's banking activities.

On September 4, 1977, Lance called Clifford and asked him to be his attorney, and the Washington legal community, as Aaron Latham observed, breathed a collective sigh of relief. Although he publicly supported Lance, Carter wanted him to resign. Clifford, however, advised Lance not to resign, but instead mount an aggressive defense. Clifford asked the Senate committee for a one-week delay to prepare his defense, and the hearings were rescheduled to September 15. "On the Sunday before Labor Day, Lance called me," Clifford said. "That gave us eight or nine days to get ready. We should have had eight or nine weeks. We became absolutely exhausted. We worked every night until midnight. One night we worked until ten minutes till four in the morning."[46]

Clifford told Lance when he agreed to represent him that it would be Lance's interests that came first, even if they were inconsistent with Carter's interests.[47] Accordingly, Clifford decided that the best defense was to go on offense against his accusers in the Senate. "Defense strategy in a criminal case is often to try to get the trial away from trying your client," Clifford explained. "The idea is to get the trial directed toward trying someone else. Turn the case into a trial of the main prosecution witness."[48] Clifford's strategy was to accuse the Senate and media of mistreating Lance and to counterattack against each and every accusation. In order to maximize the impact, Clifford did not release a copy of Lance's opening statement in advance, but relied on Lance's delivery for dramatic effect.[49]

Lance's statement, which ran forty-nine pages, was greeted with applause in the Senate chamber and succeeded in putting his accusers on the defensive. Lance charged the Senate with threatening his human rights and said he considered the American people to be the primary arbiter of his guilt or innocence. "I am secure and comfortable knowing that my conscience is clear and that the people's verdict will be a fair and just one," he said. Attacking one of his accusers, Lance characterized as a "savage charge" Senator Charles Percy's suggestion that he had backdated checks in order to improperly take income-tax deductions. Lance's presentation was so effective that the committee appeared to be disorganized and made scarcely a dent in the defense. In fact, Clifford's defense of Lance was so effective that it elicited a statement of regret from Senator Abraham Ribicoff of Connecticut that some of the newspaper accounts contained "lies," and Percy apologized for accusing Lance of backdating checks.[50]

The Lance hearings, more than the diplomatic mission to the Mediterranean, reestablished Clifford as a Washington power broker. The New York Times pointed out the irony that Clifford, Lance's defender, was part of the very Washington establishment that Carter had so effectively run against. "The outlanders came in," said a former aide in the Kennedy administration. "They thought they had all the answers. They ran against Washington. But when the water comes up to their knees, they call for Clark Clifford." Columnist Russell Baker wrote that "when you have a bad problem, a really bad problem, you go to Clifford," whom he described as "the human Washington Monument." In a Man in the News profile, the New York Times described Clifford as "one of the most elegant figures on the Washington scene," still "tall and handsome at age 70." Esquire magazine observed that even at ten minutes to four in the morning, the impeccably dressed Clifford was still wearing his coat, cuff links, vest, and tie tight around his neck. "One has the impression he bathes with his vest on," the magazine wryly noted.[51]

Despite Clifford's spirited defense, however—or perhaps because of it—Lance's position in the Carter administration could not be saved. James Reston commented that "in politics there are some battles you can't afford to win" and that by attacking his accusers Lance had chosen to save himself, but not his job. "Nobody knows better than Mr. Lance's lawyer, Clark Clifford," Reston wrote, "that you can defy the Senate or live with the Senate, but you can't do both for long."[52] Just a few days after his dramatic testimony, Lance resigned.

Shortly after Lance's resignation Clifford suffered a minor heart attack, which temporarily reduced his work schedule and thus limited his involvement with the Carter administration. But requests for help did come in from time to time, especially pertaining to foreign policy. In preparation for a presidential trip to France and India, National Security Advisor Zbigniew Brzezinski asked Clifford for help with Carter's speeches. First of all, Clifford advised against suggesting any new initiatives. "It is risky when enunciated abroad and is not worth the chance," he advised. "The major consideration to keep in mind is the reaction to the speech in the United States." With respect to India Clifford recommended that Carter refrain from attacking Marxism, which he felt would unnecessarily antagonize China and the Soviet Union. Clifford advised against speaking about nuclear proliferation while in France, believing that it was too controversial and would overshadow all the other items on Carter's agenda. Instead, Clifford advised Carter to talk about American values and reiterate a determination to advance the cause of world peace. It is worth noting that Clifford's advice focused on the domestic implications of Carter's trip, suggesting that, for Clifford at least, foreign policy was secondary to politics.[53]

A year later Clifford offered his perspective on the Persian Gulf in another memo to Brzezinski. Clifford was correct in noting that the Shah of Iran was barely clinging to power and that his continued presence in the country would only lead to chaos and anarchy. He argued that the shah had no choice but to abdicate his throne; he believed that the people of Iran would accept nothing else. However, Clifford was way off the mark when he predicted that religious leaders would be unable to run the country in the long run. He also failed to recognize the significance of the Islamist movement in Iran, believing it was a front for communist subversion. "The political groups are not easily distinguishable because Communists are operating under the banner of religious leaders," he wrote. Clifford emphasized the importance of Pakistan, which he believed to be the linchpin to the region. "As far as we are concerned, Pakistan is just not another country," he wrote. "It could be the bomb, which, if detonated, could cause an explosion that would have the most serious implications for the United States and the West."[54]

Brzezinski's correspondence with Clifford was indicative of an emerging trend in the Carter administration. Whereas they had initially eschewed the advice of seasoned Washington hands, the administration learned that the success of their agenda depended in part on cooperation and consultation with Democratic establishment figures such as Clifford. Accordingly Carter, through his recently appointed assistant for political coordination, Anne Wexler, sought out Clifford's help in advocating his administration's agenda.[55]

Passage of the second Strategic Arms Limitation Treaty, SALT II, was one item on Carter's agenda that called for Clifford's assistance. The Carter administration was criticized for its relatively lukewarm efforts to generate support for the treaty, especially in contrast to the organized and vocal opposition. In order to counter that perception, Carter asked Clifford to form a group called Americans for SALT. The group, which also included former undersecretary of the Air Force Townsend Hoopes, Henry Cabot Lodge, and the Reverend Theodore M. Hesburgh, president of Notre Dame, committed to spend about $200,000 to promote the treaty.[56] A few months later the U.S.-Soviet SALT II negotiations were complete, and Carter invited Clifford to attend a White House reception in support of the treaty. Enunciating the talking points in favor of the treaty, Carter emphasized that while SALT II called for significant reductions in nuclear arms it was not a substitute for a strong defense and would not end political competition between the United States and the Soviet Union.[57] Carter continued his personal lobbying campaign with a letter to Clifford soliciting his views on the treaty and, perhaps more important, his thoughts on how it should be presented to the Senate for ratification.[58] Continuing the effort, Clifford agreed to stand in for Brzezinski and Secretary of State Cyrus Vance and deliver a pro-SALT II speech to the annual convention of the American Political Science Association.[59] The prospects for formal passage of the treaty dimmed, however, following the "discovery" of a Soviet military brigade in Cuba and the Soviet invasion of Afghanistan. Nonetheless, both sides informally abided by the terms until President Reagan, citing Soviet transgressions, withdrew the United States in 1986.

When Congress took up the subject of intelligence reform again in the spring of 1978 Clifford was the first person called to testify. He urged the Senate Select Committee on Intelligence to delete language from the draft bill prohibiting political assassination, torture, germ warfare, and the violent overthrow of a democratic government. In Clifford's opinion such language was "demeaning," and it was unnecessary if covert operations had been properly authorized. Here his argument was slightly different than his testimony three years earlier, at which time he indicated that certain activities, such as political assassinations, should always be prohibited. This time he implied that it was redundant to prohibit these activities because properly authorized operations would not utilize such questionable techniques. "Of course the U.S. will not engage in such activities, but is it necessary, whatever the historical record, to enshrine this principle in legislation?" Clifford asked. "It offends my regard for my country and it doesn't do any good."[60]

Once he recovered from his heart attack, Clifford's law business thrived, especially with a Democrat back in the White House. In August 1978 Firestone hired Clifford to fight the recall of an estimated 13 million steel-belted radial tires. Blowouts of Firestone 500 radial tires had been implicated in thousands of accidents and had caused at least thirty-four fatalities. One accident, which led to the amputation of a seven-year-old girl's leg, had been a public-relations disaster for Firestone. After the National Highway Traffic Safety Administration issued a preliminary finding that the tires had a safety defect, the company hired Clifford, hoping the Washington lawyer could negotiate a settlement that contained the damage. The final settlement included the recall of 7.5 million tires at a cost of $344 million. According to Joan Claybrook, the administrator of the highway safety agency, Clifford stipulated the upper limit of the settlement, declaring that the company could not afford to pay out more than $300 million, irrespective of the number of tires recalled.[61]

IBM hired Clifford & Warnke, as the firm was then named, along with former deputy attorney general Nicholas Katzenbach, to help negotiate a settlement of its ten-year-old antitrust suit with the federal government. Eastern Airlines hired Clifford to represent its position in support of the merger of Pan American World Airways and National Airlines. Eastern took the unusual position of supporting the merger of two rivals because the Civil Aeronautics Board (CAB) recommended approval of the merger on the condition that National's lucrative Miami–London route be transferred to another carrier, such as Eastern. In a letter to Joseph Onek, deputy counsel to the president, Clifford endorsed the CAB's decision. Wary of Clifford's tactic of appealing directly to the White House, Onek passed the memo to the Department of Transportation. Clifford's influence even extended to foreign governments, with the Algerian government paying his firm a reputed $150,000 per year to represent its interests.[62]

Clifford's law business may have been thriving, but Carter's presidency was on the decline. Some of the problems were Carter's own doing, including his tendency to micromanage his administration, persistent bickering between Vance and Brzezinski, and the relative lack of Washington experience in his administration. The highlight of his presidency was the peace treaty between Israel and Egypt, the result of an intensive diplomatic commitment on the part of the president. Following that, however, things took a turn for the worse, and the administration never recovered its footing. A series of misfortunes, some beyond the president's control, rendered the remaining two years of Carter's presidency a failure. The Arab oil embargo, the improbable combination of rising inflation and high unemployment, the Soviet invasion of Afghanistan, and the hostage crisis in Iran were the biggest crises that confronted the beleaguered Carter. In an effort to regain control of his presidency, in the summer of 1979 Carter summoned a succession of governors, congressional representatives, private citizens, oil-company executives, and energy experts to Camp David for a series of meetings over a ten-day period. Unfortunately for Carter, the effort backfired and instead solidified the perception that he had lost the confidence of the people. Clifford did not help matters by quoting the president as saying that "he had the feeling that the country was in a mood of widespread national malaise."[63] Although Carter did not use the phrase outside the confines of Camp David, the term was picked up and became the shorthand term that described his presidency.

Clifford also assisted in damage control for an intelligence fiasco that made the Carter administration appear to be amateurish. Carter asked Clifford to lead a group of outside advisers, including McGeorge Bundy, John McCloy, former and future national security advisor Brent Scowcroft, and former CIA director John McCone, to investigate a "lost" Soviet brigade in Cuba. Because of an intelligence blunder, the CIA had failed to monitor a Soviet combat brigade that had been based in Cuba since the Cuban missile crisis. When the intelligence community became aware of the Soviet brigade sixteen years later, it was incorrectly believed to be an indication of aggressive intentions. Clifford's group, whose membership eventually expanded to sixteen and was referred to as the "Wise Men" by the White House, investigated the matter and confirmed what Soviet Foreign Minister Andrei Gromyko had been saying, that there was no crisis and that the brigade had been in Cuba the entire time. Unfortunately, Carter mishandled the situation, declaring in a nationally televised speech that "the presence of a Soviet combat unit in Cuba is a matter of serious concern to us." The overreaction, especially by Brzezinski, contributed to the growing impression that the United States had become militarily weakened in relation to the Soviets, and further weakened an already diminished presidency.[64]

Reprising the diplomatic role he had played earlier in the Mediter-ranean, Clifford was also dispatched to India to meet with Prime Min-ister Indira Gandhi. Carter believed that it was important to foster the U.S.-India relationship, which suffered as a result of the friendly rela-tions that the U.S. had fostered with India's enemy, Pakistan. Rela-tions with India had also been strained by the American response to the Soviet invasion of Afghanistan. During a press conference following his meeting with Gandhi, Clifford noted that the United States regarded the Soviet invasion of Afghanistan as a serious matter and that it rep-resented a disproportionate response in the absence of an actual threat to Russian security. Rather than its being a defensive exercise, Clifford viewed the invasion as a calculated attempt on the part of the Soviets to assert their power in the Persian Gulf, and he warned that the United States would view further incursions as a threat to national security. "If they move towards the Persian Gulf, that means war," he said. Accord-ing to Clifford, he was merely repeating a policy that Carter had enun-ciated eight days before, during the State of the Union address, a policy that declared that the United States would regard any attempt by an outside force to gain control of the Persian Gulf as a threat to national security. Vance was concerned that Clifford had gone too far, however, and the White House retreated from his remarks. Press Secretary Jody Powell said that while Clifford was told to carry that message with him, "he wasn't sent out to say those exact words."[65]

As Carter struggled through the last year of his administration, Clifford offered words of encouragement, perhaps in an effort to curry favor or gain greater access. When Carter gave a press conference on his brother Billy's alleged ties to the Libyan government, Clifford was effusive in his praise. "Your press conference with reference to your brother was not only the best press conference *you* have had, but it was the best press conference *any* President has had," he gushed.[66]

Even the best press conference was not enough for Carter, how-ever, and he lost his reelection bid to Ronald Reagan, ushering in twelve years of Republican control of the White House. Clifford memorably characterized Reagan as "an amiable dunce" during a political dinner that he mistakenly believed was off the record. His words were often quoted, much to Clifford's dismay. But even apart from the "dunce" remark, Clifford's influence had declined with the Republicans back in power.

Clifford had reached the pinnacle of his prestige and influence as secre-tary of defense under Lyndon Johnson, and after leaving the Pentagon he settled into the role of senior statesman. While Nixon was president he utilized his stature as former secretary of defense to continue to advocate for an end to the Vietnam War. Because of his reputation it was inevitable that Jimmy Carter would seek out his counsel, yet Carter had campaigned, and was determined to govern, as a Washington outsider, which circumscribed Clifford's influence. With a Republican elected as president four years later, especially someone as conservative as Reagan, Clifford realized that he was now the outsider. Not content to fade away, however, Clifford decided he wanted a new challenge; and, as someone who had mastered almost everything he had undertaken, his prospects still seemed promising, even though he was in his seventies. As someone who had known Clifford for years observed, "Everything he's ever done, he's done with great style. But the important thing about Clifford is that he has endured in this town. He's never really gotten into trouble."[67] Unfortunately for Clifford, that long and successful run was about to come to an end.

# 13

# BCCI

It should have been the triumphant coda of a long and distinguished Washington career. On May 22, 1991, a long line of limousines pulled up in front of the Georgetown home of Pamela Harriman. Harriman, the socialite second wife of Averell Harriman and a prominent Democratic fund-raiser, was hosting a book party in honor of Clark Clifford, who had recently published his memoirs, *Counsel to the President.* More than four hundred people were in attendance, including such Democratic Party luminaries as Virginia governor Douglas Wilder; Speaker of the House Tom Foley; Democratic National Committee Chairman Ron Brown; Senators Ted Kennedy, Alan Cranston, Claiborne Pell, Paul Simon, Chris Dodd, Howard Metzenbaum, Sam Nunn, and Frank Lautenberg; and Representatives John Dingell, Jack Brooks, Steny Hoyer, and Patricia Schroeder. Other guests included Tim Russert of NBC, former Nixon speechwriter and *New York Times* columnist William Safire, former White House counsel Lloyd Cutler, and *Washington Post* publisher Katharine Graham. Several of the guests described the evening as "upbeat," a curious choice of words to describe an event that was supposed to be the Washington political establishment's equivalent of a lifetime achievement award.[1] In fact, the evening could only be euphemistically described as "upbeat" because it was hardly a celebration at all. The subplot of the entire evening, a veritable elephant in the room, was the fact that the guest of honor was in trouble—a lot of trouble.

Clark Clifford had spent the better part of a lifetime cultivating and living off his reputation, and he had become one of the most powerful and respected men in Washington. Unfortunately for Clifford, a reputation is a fragile thing in Washington, especially when tarnished by scandal. In Clifford's case the scandal would cost him his reputation, a fair amount of his fortune, and his beloved law firm, and it turned him into fodder for those who rejoice in watching how the mighty have fallen. The scandal was known simply as BCCI.

BCCI, otherwise known as the Bank of Credit and Commerce International, was founded in 1972 by a Pakistani named Agha Hasan Abedi. The bank, headquartered in Luxembourg and operated out of London, catered mostly to the wealthy rulers of the Arab states in the Persian Gulf. Abedi, however, was not content simply to serve the oil-rich Arab states; he wanted to expand into the United States. Unfortunately for Abedi, his initial attempts to acquire a U.S. bank were blocked by New York State regulators, so he enlisted the help of an influential ally. In 1977 Bert Lance, who had recently resigned from the Carter White House, was introduced to Abedi and was hired by the Pakistani to identify another acquisition target. As a gesture of goodwill Abedi arranged for a Saudi businessman to purchase Lance's interest in the National Bank of Georgia, yielding Lance a substantial profit. Lance reciprocated and identified a suitable target, Financial General Bankshares of Washington. The bank, however, was unwilling to be acquired and filed suit against Lance, Abedi, BCCI, and a group of Arab investors for violating U.S. securities laws by failing to disclose that they had been operating as a group in their attempt to gain a controlling interest in Financial General. In February 1978, Lance asked Clifford to defend them in the lawsuit.[2]

The next month the Securities and Exchange Commission (SEC) also filed suit against the group, but Clifford worked out a settlement favorable to his clients. As a consequence of the settlement the group of investors was allowed another opportunity to acquire Financial General, provided they first sought approval from federal bank regulators. Another stipulation was that BCCI be excluded from any future effort to acquire Financial General, other than serving as an investment adviser.[3] Ultimately it was this condition that would prove to be Clifford's downfall.

Following the SEC agreement Abedi and the other investors met with Clifford again to discuss the acquisition of Financial General. Also in attendance was one of Clifford's law partners, Robert Altman, who would become a central character in the BCCI saga. Altman had joined the firm as an associate in 1971, but distinguished himself, in Clifford's estimation, during the Bert Lance case. Only thirty-one years old at the time of the Lance case, Altman impressed Clifford with his work ethic and dedication, and he soon leapfrogged over the other partners and associates in the firm's pecking order.[4]

Initially Altman expressed reservations that the investors were too closely associated with BCCI, but Clifford dismissed his concerns. Clifford had checked with the State Department and learned that Abedi had an excellent reputation in the Persian Gulf, and that was all that Clifford needed to know. For his part, Clifford conferred upon Abedi and the investors' group his reputation and stamp of approval. For Clifford, this would prove to be a mistake with tragic consequences.[5]

The Arab investors remained determined to acquire Financial General, which continued to oppose the transaction, charging that the investors' group was merely a front for BCCI. In order to counteract those charges, BCCI set up a holding company called Credit and Commerce American Holdings, or CCAH. The structure of CCAH was designed to disguise its relationship to BCCI; CCAH was crafted to appear to be a company formed by the investor group and independent of BCCI. Despite how carefully BCCI had hidden its tracks, however, Financial General and the federal banking regulators still viewed CCAH with suspicion, and Clifford would be central to helping it pass muster. Knowing that he would be unable to convince the board of Financial General to accede to the acquisition on its merits, Clifford decided that he needed to change the composition of the board to one that would be more amenable to the takeover. To that end, Clifford assembled a group of three men who would seek election to Financial General's board at the annual shareholders' meeting in April 1980. The group was designed to put an American face on the takeover effort, and included Clifford's old friend Stuart Symington, who was then retired from the Senate, and retired Air Force lieutenant general Elwood R. Quesada. Through his business connections Clifford knew one of the existing board members, Armand Hammer, the chairman of Occidental Petroleum. Following a meeting with Clifford, Hammer agreed to support CCAH, thus clearing the way for the board to approve the acquisition.[6]

In November 1980, with Financial General's board behind them, CCAH filed an application with the Federal Reserve to acquire Financial General.[7] Clifford lobbied on behalf of CCAH, assuring the Federal Reserve regulators that CCAH and its Arab investors would be passive and would rely upon Americans to run the bank. "There is no function of any kind on the part of BCCI," Clifford assured the regulators. "I know of no present relationship. I know of no planned future relationship that exists." He also gave his personal assurances of the merits of the deal. "I am comforted," he said, "that I know that it's good for our country." In August 1981 the Fed unanimously approved the acquisition, in no small part due to Clifford's personal assurances.[8]

Clifford's involvement with CCAH, BCCI, and Financial General did not end there, and he did not just represent the bank and the investors in a legal and regulatory capacity. Abedi and the Arab investor group were so pleased with Clifford's performance during the three-year effort to acquire Financial General (and had committed to remain passive investors) that it made sense to ask Clifford to become chairman of the bank.

Clifford accepted the offer for a number of reasons. The first was that his law firm was not as vibrant as it once was, with a Republican in the White House and Clifford's age approaching seventy-five. The second reason was that the bank represented a new challenge. For most of his career Clifford was either the sole or the senior partner in his law firm, and thus he had no experience running a large company. As secretary of defense he oversaw a massive federal bureaucracy, which was certainly a management and organizational challenge, but quite different from managing a business in the competitive free market. Finally, and perhaps most significant, running a bank provided another outlet for the workaholic Clifford.

At his age and with the opposition party in power, the early 1980s would have been an opportune time for him to retire, write his memoirs, and receive the accolades and acknowledgment that he had earned—and craved. But Clifford did not know anything other than work. Indeed, work was his life. The thought of retiring was completely foreign to him, and he was uninterested in most of the activities that people use to fill their leisure time. As an example, Clifford's wife, Marny, spent her summers on Nantucket and went on long cruises during the winter, but always without her husband, who was not interested in traveling. In fact, for years he would only take a week's vacation every year for a stag golf trip down in Florida. But even that did not appeal to him, he said, and "about the second or third or fourth day I would have had enough." Marny concurred. "He doesn't like vacations," she said. "Hates them."[9]

The opportunity and challenge of running the bank was far more appealing to what he considered his alternatives at that stage of his life, as he remarked in an interview:

> "I think, at the time, without considering, I was looking at other contemporaries who were 75, looking to see what they did. Some of them would go with their wives each morning to

the market and help with the marketing, help pushing those carts and all. Well, I didn't find that very appealing. Another was to go down to the post office every morning and get the mail. That wasn't anything that excited me much. A lot of them go to Florida and disappear. Some of them just sit on the front porch and rock and wait to die." He infuses the syllable with drama, then adds the dryly comic punctuation: "That didn't appeal to me either."[10]

So Clifford immersed himself in the running of the bank, which had been renamed First American Bankshares. He had always exhibited a strong work ethic, but his devotion to this new endeavor was remarkable even for him. In fact, unlike so many of his peers in or out of government, he was no longer interested in power lunches, preferring to grab a quick sandwich at the lunch counter of the neighborhood drugstore. His efforts paid off, as Clifford, with Altman at his side as president of the holding company, led First American Bankshares to greater profitability. By the mid-1980s the bank had become the largest financial institution in Washington.[11]

Clifford relished his role as chairman of the bank, and it seemed to invigorate and sustain him. He found his new role to be quite different from his position at his law firm, where the client came first. "Practicing law is fun, but you are always doing something for somebody else," he said. "Here was an opportunity to do it yourself." Running the bank also bestowed upon Clifford a sense of power that he had never experienced while serving presidents or corporate clients. "Bob, two billion dollars," he said to Truman biographer Robert Donovan, referencing the bank's assets and the power that went along with it. "Two billion dollars." Clifford also appreciated the increased stature and publicity that came with the job. His picture was featured prominently in the bank's annual reports, and he even appeared in a commercial. When his friend and fellow Washington power lawyer Edwin Bennett Williams was dying of cancer, Clifford offered to show him around the bank before he became too ill, and Clifford, Williams, and fellow lawyer Bob Strauss ate their lunch under the formal gaze of an oil painting of Clifford himself. "It was almost like a father showing off accomplishments to his son," said Strauss.[12]

Clifford and Altman did not run the bank by themselves, but rather consulted frequently with Abedi on matters large and small. Abedi and the other BCCI officials exercised the most control over the New York branch of the bank, which they ran somewhat independently of the other banks. Otherwise, Clifford and Altman were technically in charge. But irrespective of how much control Abedi and BCCI wielded, Clifford believed that he was in charge, and he took great pride in the bank. "You are working for a quality bank, a bank you can be proud of," he told a group of trainees. "You'll never read about us in a newspaper. You do your job and you'll be proud to work here."[13]

Things were not quite so rosy at BCCI, however, and that institution began to appear in the paper all too frequently. In October 1988, following a two-year undercover operation, the bank was indicted on charges of laundering millions of dollars in illegal drug money on behalf of clients such as the Medellin drug cartel of Colombia and Panamanian dictator Manuel Noriega.[14] As if the money-laundering charges were not enough, BCCI was also linked to Palestinian terrorist Abu Nidal. Robert Gates, then the deputy director of the CIA, privately referred to the bank as "the Bank of Crooks and Criminals."[15]

Around the same time Clifford and Altman were the beneficiaries of a suspicious stock transaction that would land them on the front pages of all the major newspapers three years later. The transaction, which resulted in a combined profit of $9.8 million, was financed by BCCI and entailed no risk on the part of Clifford and Altman. BCCI loaned the men $18 million, which was used to purchase 8,168 shares of First American Bankshares stock in 1986 and 1987, with nothing but the shares pledged as collateral. In 1988 they sold about 60 percent of the shares to a BCCI shareholder for $32 million, which generated a $9.8 million profit after repaying the loan and all interest. The shares were sold at three times the price Clifford and Altman had paid for them eighteen months earlier, and they were left holding the remaining shares free and clear.[16]

In January 1990 BCCI pleaded guilty to the money-laundering charges in order to avoid a lengthy and embarrassing trial. One person who thought the bank got off lightly was Senator John Kerry of Massachusetts. Kerry was chairman of a Senate Foreign Relations subcommittee that had been investigating BCCI's ties to Noriega, and he believed that BCCI should thenceforth be barred from conducting business in the United States. In an effort to dissuade Kerry, Clifford tried both the hard and the soft approach, first calling Kerry's office to ask if the senator would sign a letter commending Clifford's management of First American Bankshares. Such a letter would discredit Kerry if he ever linked Clifford to BCCI, and it is likely that was Clifford's intent. Frances Zwenig, Kerry's assistant, believed that Clifford was attempting to intimidate the senator. "He was very polite. It was subtle. But it was intimidation. I didn't realize it at the time, but he was trying to compromise John Kerry. He didn't miss a trick." Using the soft approach, Clifford, Altman, and others at the law firm contributed $1,000 each to Kerry's reelection campaign. Shifting tactics again, Altman enlisted the help of a friend, Senator Orrin Hatch of Utah, in defending the BCCI plea bargain and thus implicitly attacking Kerry.[17]

The storm gathering around First American Bankshares and Clifford would strike soon, but Clifford had one last opportunity to bask in the Washington spotlight. In March 1990 he was extended the courtesy of addressing a joint session of Congress, marking the centennial of the birth of President Eisenhower.

On February 3, 1991, the *Washington Post,* following a nine-month investigation, published a lengthy article suggesting that BCCI controlled First American Bankshares, and cited an investigation into the matter by the New York district attorney's office. Clifford categorically denied the charges. "There has been no participation, directly or indirectly, by BCCI," he said. Clifford claimed that BCCI had served as First American's investment adviser, and in that capacity he periodically briefed BCCI officials about First American's performance. The arms-length relationship between BCCI and First American Bankshares he described was consistent with the testimony he had given ten years earlier. "The representation we made was that BCCI would not manage or control First American," Clifford said. "At no time did we say that we would not have some contact with" BCCI. He also fell back on his reputation as sufficient evidence that the relationship between the two banks was completely above board. "I value the reputation I have for honesty and character," he said. "I have not dissembled in any way. Others, who are enemies of BCCI, who perhaps do not wish First American well, have attempted to assemble circumstantial evidence to disprove what I have told you."[18]

Clifford's assurances were not enough this time, and on March 4 the Federal Reserve ordered BCCI to sell its hidden interest in the parent company of First American. New York District Attorney Robert Morgenthau also warned that he might file charges in the matter because "false representations, false filings were made to the Superintendent of Banks in New York."[19] The worst was yet to come.

On Sunday, May 5, the *Washington Post* reported the stock transaction, thoroughly undermining Clifford's assurances that First American was independent of BCCI. The stock deal, with its $9.8 million profit, was "the first public indication that Clifford and Altman profited personally through their private dealings with BCCI," the *Post* reported. The obvious implication was that the stock deal was not only a reward for running the bank on behalf of BCCI, but also for keeping the true nature of the relationship secret for so long.[20]

Intimately familiar with the ways of Washington, Clifford professed his innocence and made a subtle appeal for sympathy. "All I can say to you is it has been the most dif-fi-cult pe-ri-od in my life," he told the *Post,* which attempted to capture his laborious, yet theatrical, speaking style in the quotations. "This is the first time that an-y cloud has ever been associated with my name or my reputation." The BCCI story was extremely damaging to Clifford, no matter what the outcome or what people believed, because it threatened his reputation for both probity and wisdom. The worst scenario, as the *Post* observed, was that he knowingly misrepresented the BCCI relationship to regulators and continued to lie about it for ten years. Alternatively, the best case was that he was duped by the unscrupulous investors at BCCI. However, Clifford's entire career was based on his track record for providing sage advice to presidents and business clients, and to suggest that he could be duped that easily would call his judgment into question. "I have a choice of either seeming stupid or venal," he memorably observed.[21]

Despite the personal risks, Clifford staunchly maintained that he knew nothing about BCCI's secret ownership of First American. "When people say, 'Oh, Clifford must have known,' the fact is, I would have been the last one to know," said Clifford. "I would have been the last one [BCCI] would have told. . . . Because maybe they did use my good name at the beginning. Maybe they did depend to some extent upon my reputation. All right, if that's an asset then it's an asset. But they wouldn't tell me what was going on, because the day they would have told me was the day that I would have left them." Clifford also staunchly defended the propriety of the stock transaction, which seemed the most damning part of the story. "At the time, under the conditions that existed, it all seemed perfectly appropriate," he said. "Let me add that there's nothing illegal in any way with the deal regarding the purchase of the stocks."[22]

In addition to pleading his innocence, Clifford also attempted to make the case that the BCCI affair was much ado about nothing, asserting that it was at worst, a "victimless crime." At worst, he suggested, the BCCI case was a technical violation of a law that prevents an outside interest from controlling more than 25 percent of an American bank. The intent of the law, he argued, was to prevent an outside interest from controlling a bank, and in the case of First American, he asserted that they did not exercise any control. He firmly maintained that he was in charge of the bank and that therefore the spirit of the law had not been violated.[23]

In a cruel twist of fate, Clifford's memoirs were published around the same time as the BCCI story broke. In a futile effort to minimize the impact of the scandal, Clifford in his book relegated his involvement with BCCI to a single lengthy footnote. The juxtaposition of the two depictions of Clifford—on the one hand, the wise man of Washington gracing the cover of *Counsel to the President,* and on the other the beneficiary of a sleazy, insider stock transaction funded by a rogue bank—was reminiscent of a Greek tragedy. Predictably, as with any scandal in Washington, the story was major news. Just days after the story broke the *Washington Post* published a two-part series entitled "Clark M. Clifford and His Threatened Reputation." With respect to his memoirs the *Post* observed, "What was to be his triumphant act of self-definition threatens instead to be an ironic comment on the evanescence of image." A friend of Clifford, who requested anonymity, remarked, "It is one of the grand falls."[24]

The supposedly "upbeat" book party at Pamela Harriman's was indicative of just how much Clifford had become damaged goods. The evening was described as a "flat, subdued affair: no happy buzz, no easy chatter, no slaps on the back. It was, as one guest put it, 'a purposeful occasion.'" Clifford did have many people who supported him throughout the BCCI ordeal. Jacqueline Kennedy, by then Jacqueline Kennedy Onassis, invited him to lunch, and Lady Bird Johnson called or visited frequently. Lloyd Cutler and onetime Johnson aide Jack Valenti were also staunch supporters.[25]

The rest of Washington was not as forgiving. Clifford was not asked to speak at a celebration honoring the centenary of Averell Harriman's birth, a notable omission, but the scene at the dinner afterward was more telling. One guest observed that "one of the most unforgettable sights" she ever witnessed was Clifford making his way through the crowd to his table without being acknowledged by any of the guests. "People did not know how to deal with him," the guest observed. "I've become a social pariah in the town," Clifford lamented.[26] Years later George Elsey reflected on the havoc the BCCI scandal wrought on Clifford's life and reputation. "You may be moved to tears when you consider his final years," he wrote. "They were indeed sad . . . but to me the tragic aspect was that he was deserted by younger men for whom he had done so much."[27]

A case in point was Clifford's junior law partners, who looked for a way to distance themselves from Clifford & Warnke. One of the partners, John Kovin, informed Clifford that a Newark, New Jersey, law firm wanted to hire the partners en masse and set them up as that firm's Washington office. However, there was no provision for either Clifford or Altman, and without Clifford's blessing, the deal fell through.[28] The rest of the partners joined another Washington firm, Howrey & Simon, and took many of their clients with them. Clifford was merely informed of that fact; the time for consultation had passed. It was a stunning reversal for a man who was both the founder and marquee attorney of the firm, and who had run the organization virtually unchallenged. "The parting was not unfriendly," Clifford recalled. "It was just cold. They could have handled it in a way as a kind of 'merger of firms' or something and taken some of the stigma out of it. But they didn't. It was: Get away from Clifford & Warnke, because it's doomed. By that time I could see that as far as my practicing law was concerned, it was over."[29]

To the extent that Clifford was still practicing law, his primary client was himself, although both he and Altman both retained defense counsel in anticipation of an indictment. Robert Fiske, a former U.S. attorney, was hired to represent Clifford and Altman in New York, and Robert Bennett, later famous for representing President Bill Clinton during his impeachment proceedings, was hired in Washington.

In September 1991 Clifford had the opportunity to present his defense during a hearing before the House Banking Committee, an appearance Marjorie Williams of the *Washington Post* described as the "performance of a lifetime":

> He was the elderly trial lawyer, bringing all his skills to the summation of his last, most important case. He was a ventriloquist, playing straight man to a partner assigned the riskier lines. He was Grampy, telling the kids about how he built the homestead in aught-four—a statesman reminding a roomful of aspirants that he was present at the creation of their universe. He was everything he had to be if he hoped to persuade the committee—and the vastly more important television audience beyond—that he was, in a word he stressed, mystified to find himself at the helm of an institution secretly owned by an outlaw foreign bank.

"Now, I recognize as I listen to you gentlemen we have a formidable task in persuading many of you of our innocence in this," Clifford said in an hour-and-a-half-long opening statement. "But I approach it willingly. I approach it with a desire to have this hearing." Clifford argued that he had been unjustly accused and that the coverage of the story had been completely one-sided. "The whole atmosphere of the public, all the proceedings that have taken place, all would be against us. And yet, we appear here so that you can hear our side. And I suggest to you that it is my deep conviction that when you have heard us, you will at least in some way have a different attitude." Despite the grave damage done to his reputation, Clifford was still convinced that his word should be sufficient, and on that account he asserted, "our consciences are clear." Using the familiar defense of someone proclaiming their innocence, he declared that he was "mystified" by what had transpired. "My judgment is questionable," he said with regret. "I guess I should have learned [of BCCI's ownership] some way. . . . I'd give a lot if somebody had told me, back in 1984, that this operation was the kind that it was. I would have given anything if I could have avoided what I've gone through this past year."[30]

"Mr. Clifford is most impressive," said the ranking Republican on the committee, Chalmers P. Wylie of Ohio. "Mr. Clifford could sell hams in a synagogue." Others, such as New York representative Charles Schumer of New York, were not convinced. "Mr. Altman and Mr. Clifford are asking us to believe that when their house was on fire, they didn't smell the smoke, feel the heat or hear the alarms."[31]

The hearing took on the feel of a Hollywood media circus due to the presence of Altman's wife, actress and former *Wonder Woman* star Lynda Carter. Their arrival and departure—and Carter's theatrical kiss of support—were recorded in detail by the paparazzi. Clifford and Marny received far less attention.[32]

A month later Clifford and Altman appeared before the Senate Foreign Relations Committee's Subcommittee on Terrorism, Narcotics and International Operations, where they repeated their testimony delivered to the House Banking Committee a month earlier. Unlike the packed hearing room in September, the subcommittee hearing was only sparsely attended. John Kerry, who chaired the subcommittee, had compiled an extensive collection of documents that suggested a connection between Clifford, Altman, and BCCI, yet there was no definitive proof, and Clifford and Altman explained away each piece of evidence. They also went a step farther in their defense than before, asserting that BCCI may have had a secret plan to acquire First American Bankshares without their knowledge. Altman also made the case that the evidence of blatant improprieties typical of other BCCI operations was missing from the First American case and that this constituted proof that BCCI did not own the bank. During a break in the proceedings, frustrated members of Kerry's staff suggested that the senator, a former prosecutor, was not pressing Clifford hard enough to recall specific names and dates. "He's an old man," Kerry fired back. "He couldn't remember. I'm not going to humiliate an old man."[33]

Clifford had done a laudable job defending himself and may have scored some points in the realm of public opinion, but he would soon have to account for himself in a court, or courts, of law. By the middle of 1992 it was clear that an indictment was coming. Morgenthau had been building a case in New York, and there was a chance that Clifford would also be indicted in federal court. As Morgenthau was building his case he tried to persuade Clifford to turn against Altman, but Clifford refused to sacrifice his partner and protégé, whom the evidence suggested was more intimately involved.[34] Clifford also refused to accept a plea bargain, and with it the acknowledgment of guilt. He was determined to clear his name. On July 29 separate indictments were announced in New York and federal court.

The arraignment was, for Clifford, the most humiliating part of the entire ordeal. "You stand up there before the court," he recalled. "The judge says, 'Guilty or not guilty?' And you say, 'Not guilty.' Then two or three big fat bailiffs take you in charge. You're led out with a guard on either side of you holding your arm, with the press right in front, walking backwards and taking pictures. A *felon,* you see. It's really pretty rough." Clifford also found the taking of mug shots and fingerprints particularly demeaning. The indictment also changed the story from suggestions of impropriety to something more damning. "Overnight that changes," he said. "You are *charged.*" Once he was indicted Clifford knew what people were thinking and saying when they saw him. "God, there's *Clifford,* and he's under *indictment!* My God, do you think there's some possibility that he's going to *prison?*" In the final indignity, all of his personal accounts, credit cards, and law firm accounts were frozen, perhaps in an attempt to intimidate him to accept a plea.[35]

Clifford would not plea, and two days after the indictments were announced he appeared before the press under far more favorable circumstances. Clifford was determined to get his good name back before he died, and he launched into a forty-five-minute account of his side of the story. "We did not know," he began, speaking virtually without notes. "I'd give almost anything I have today if we had known because it would have spared me and my family from the most painful period that one can imagine these past years." Clifford attacked the prosecutors for their overzealousness, charging that they had "not one scintilla of direct evidence." "As long as I have the strength and the health to do it," he promised, "I will fight each day. I am spending the rest of my life to get my good name restored to me."[36]

Unfortunately for Clifford, he had neither the health nor the strength to continue to defend his name. He had been on medication for his heart for years, but now his doctors informed him that three of his four arteries were 90 percent blocked, and the other was 70 percent blocked. Without an immediate bypass operation he would die, and there was a 20 percent chance he would not even survive the operation. But because he was expecting the trial to begin soon, Clifford refused. In October Clifford was hospitalized for hemorrhages and other heart-related complications, but was soon released. Clifford's attorneys tried to get Morgenthau to agree to allow the federal trial in Washington to go first, but Morgenthau refused. Clifford's attorneys argued that he would not survive living in a hotel throughout the New York trial, and five doctors appointed by the court concurred. Clifford was severed from the New York case and on March 22, 1993, underwent the grueling quadruple-bypass surgery. Clifford's fate, by association, would be decided by the outcome of Altman's trial.[37]

From the outset the trial did not go well for the prosecution. The complexity of the case was too difficult for the jury to follow, especially compared to the concise and coherent defense. The absence of a "smoking gun" piece of evidence also made it difficult for the prosecutors to prove their case, whereas the defense merely had to demonstrate reasonable doubt.

As the trial in New York proceeded, Clifford was recovering from his surgery back in Washington. He suffered a setback when one of the bypasses failed and he suffered a major heart attack. In his weakened state there was no chance that he would be able to travel to New York to testify, which he found extremely frustrating. "I've got to go there and defend my reputation," he told his daughter Joyce. "This is so frustrating. There has never been a cloud against my name and now I must defend myself." But as far as the trial was concerned, Clifford's testimony was not needed. The judge threw out the two most important charges, bribery and conspiracy, because he believed the prosecution had not produced sufficient evidence. For Clifford, things seemed to be looking up.[38]

In a move indicative of the weakness of the prosecution's case, Altman's defense opted to forgo a formal defense and proceeded immediately to closing arguments. Clifford was so confident of the outcome that he ventured out of the house for the first time in months, taking Richard Holbrooke, with whom he had written his memoirs, out to lunch at the Metropolitan Club. "He wanted to show everyone he was alive and well," Holbrooke recalled. Several people stopped at the table to wish him well. On Saturday, August 14, Altman telephoned with the good news. "Marny, they've freed me," he exclaimed. Altman had been acquitted and, by association, so had Clifford. At three or four o'clock the next morning Clifford woke up, as he had many times throughout the trial. Only this time he was not trying the case in his own mind, but instead savored the victory and sense of relief. "I just lay there and glowed," he said.[39]

The *Washington Post* described the acquittal as a "vindication" for Clifford. "You caught Clark Clifford at a very happy moment," he said, speaking in the third person. "It is deeply gratifying. It's more than the end of a trial. It's the end of a two-and-one-half-year nightmare." The biggest weakness of the prosecution's case, according to the jurors, was the reliance of testimony from former BCCI individuals who were themselves under indictment. Jurors simply discounted their testimony. Barbara Conley, the jury's forewoman, said she felt "insulted" by the prosecution.[40]

If there was a silver lining to the BCCI scandal it was that it brought Clifford closer to his family. He had always been closest to his middle daughter, Joyce, who spent a good deal of time with him during his darkest hours. Whereas Clifford had always been an authoritative figure by dint of his position and reputation in Washington, the fallout of the BCCI affair seemed to bring him back down to earth. Joyce felt that, for the first time, she and her father could communicate as equals. Clifford also drew closer to his wife, whom he came to depend on for the first time in their long marriage.[41]

The fallout from the BCCI scandal was obvious even after the acquittal. Clifford had been vindicated, but not totally. The taint of scandal remained, and Clifford was never able to restore his life to the way it was before BCCI became a household word. Clifford died on October 10, 1998, at age ninety-one, remembered as both the elegant counsel to the president as well as the Washington establishment figure forever linked to a rogue bank that financed drug dealers and terrorists.

The New York verdict settled the question legally, and the federal charges were never prosecuted. The verdict, however, did not provide a satisfactory answer in the court of public opinion. Could a man as smart and savvy as Clifford actually have been duped by Abedi and the BCCI investors, as he claimed? Alternatively, did Clifford knowingly break the law? The first scenario strains the bounds of credibility: Clifford knew that BCCI coveted First American, and he was aware of BCCI's desire to exercise influence in the management of the bank. Even if Clifford did not know that BCCI owned First American, the fact that BCCI funded the stock deal should have made it abundantly apparent. However, it is similarly implausible to believe that Clifford willingly conspired to shield First American's ownership from the regulators because he had no credible motive for doing so. Clifford's detractors point to the stock deal as sufficient financial incentive to induce him to break the law, but the fact is that Clifford did not need the money. He was already a very wealthy man. Moreover, he did not have an opulent lifestyle. Clifford was not interested in possessions; he did not travel; and his home, which occupied valuable land, also exhibited what one observer called the "confident negligence of the upper class."[42]

The most plausible explanation is that Clifford simply chose to believe what he wanted to believe: that he knew nothing about BCCI's ownership of First American, that he was in sole control of the bank, and that he was deceived by unscrupulous individuals. At a time in his life when most men would have been content to retire, write their memoirs, and bask in the glow of their accomplishments, Clifford still needed to work because work was the only thing that gave his life purpose. At a time when he was long past his prime and with the opposition in power, Clifford needed something to make him feel important again, and the bank restored some of the sense of stature that he craved. As much as BCCI and its investors needed Clifford to confer respectability to their bank and business dealings, Clifford needed the bank to keep him active. Despite the scandal and loss of face, Clifford said he never regretted his decision to take on the chairmanship of the bank. "I actually think it has kept me alive," he said.[43]

What is particularly striking about the entire BCCI episode was the fact that all along an escape hatch was readily available, but Clifford never took it. The obvious way out was for Clifford to blame it all on Altman and claim that Altman deceived him. The young, brash attorney had neither the stature nor the temperament of his courtly mentor, and the press, public, and prosecution were predisposed to believe that Altman was the more culpable party. The opportunity to make Altman the scapegoat and save himself was always available, yet Clifford chose to be loyal rather than protect his own interests.

Clifford's critics, especially in the press, delighted at his downfall and considered the BCCI case an encapsulation of his entire career. Historian Warren I. Cohen, in an article that appeared in *The Nation,* wrote, "When the BCCI scandal broke and Clifford's travails began, there was little reason for me to be surprised. The story had all the elements of the Clifford I had observed for several decades."[44] But another theme, overlooked by the press, was Clifford's sense of loyalty. As much as Clifford was an ambitious self-promoter, he was also loyal to the presidents and clients he served and to those with whom he worked. In the end he chose to defend Altman when it would have been easier to make him the scapegoat, and in defending Altman Clifford sacrificed what was most important to him: his reputation.

# Conclusion

Clark Clifford arrived in Washington in 1945 as a young naval officer serving in a largely ceremonial role. During the years that followed he rose to the highest ranks of the Truman administration and then parlayed his government experience into a lucrative law career, a prototype of the many well-connected lawyer-lobbyists who followed him. As a result of his carefully cultivated reputation, Clifford was sought out by Democratic presidents for the next twenty years. During that time he served his country in an official capacity for only one year, but he served with distinction. Late in his life he was disgraced by a scandal that cast a permanent black mark on his reputation—a scandal that ironically coincided with the release of his memoirs.

Clifford possessed an array of talents that contributed to his success inside the Beltway. First of all, he filled the suit. If a Hollywood producer was looking to cast someone in the role of an influential presidential adviser they could have picked no one better than Clifford. He was tall, handsome, and always impeccably dressed. He commanded authority from his mere presence. He exuded self-confidence and spoke in an authoritative manner, which conferred a sense of self-evident truth upon the words he spoke. Second, Clifford had an ability to take the words and ideas of others and present them in a coherent and persuasive fashion to the presidents he served. Third, he was a relentless self-promoter who carefully developed and nurtured his reputation. Finally, this penchant for self-promotion allowed Clifford to appropriate the work and ideas of others as his own and accept accolades that properly belonged to someone else. It may thus be said that in many respects Clifford's reputation was built upon a myth.

Stephen Spingarn, who worked under Clifford in the Truman White House, had this to say about the Clifford myth: "This is the mythology that has been established, and mythologies tend to be self-perpetuating.

I think it developed for two reasons I would say—two main reasons; one, Clark Clifford is impressive in appearance and personality; he impresses; he looks the way a top presidential staff man should look, and his personality is extroverted and impressive; his impact is considerable on everyone he meets. He is a big, handsome, distinguished looking man and with a fine personality."[1]

Robert Allen and William Shannon, authors of the *Truman Merry-Go-Round,* wrote of Clifford in 1950: "Glamorous Clark Clifford is one of those people who is too good to be true. . . . His face is too handsome, his blond hair too evenly waved, his smile too dazzling, his voice too resonant, his manner too patently sincere, his family background, childhood, college record, romantic courtship, and legal career are all too storybookish to be real. Somewhere there must be a flaw, a glaring weakness, an idiosyncrasy. But so far Washington hasn't discovered it."[2]

Irwin Ross, author of *The Loneliest Campaign: The Truman Victory of 1948,* wrote that Clifford "was tall, leanly built, with the wavy blond hair and precision ground good looks of a movie actor. He had a silken voice, a dazzling smile, and the courtly manners of a less hurried time; nothing ever seemed to ruffle him."[3] Jack Valenti, a White House adviser to Lyndon Johnson, perhaps best captured the essence of Clark Clifford:

In a town filled with legends, Clifford held his own. He was tall, still strikingly handsome, with a face cast by some skilled sculptor. He wore—no matter what the fashion or fad—the same carefully, expensively tailored double-breasted suits with wide lapels and wide, boxed shoulders. No matter how passionate the discussion or how crucial the issue, Clifford always spoke slowly, as if each word was being minted specially for that occasion. His voice was sepulchral, his words unhurried, precise. One had the feeling that one was listening to dogma sprung from a prophet's deeds, and even the most confident foes hesitated a second or two, before taking on Clifford. He *had* to be right, because he *sounded* so right. He had a habit or holding his hands in front of him, palms facing, fingertips pressed against each other, the two graceful hands forming a billowing tent. I never failed to be impressed with Clark, for I was sure that behind the carefully architectured words there was also some master builder at work in that mind of his, measuring, making sure that what was being constructed was stout and accurate. In all my contacts with Clifford I never saw him once ruffled or confused. In almost any crisis, Clifford, brow unfurrowed, would carefully dissect the action alternatives with neither haste nor anxiety.[4]

A 1989 article in the *Washington Post* Sunday magazine also describes Clifford's presence and sheds light on his style and manner. The aura of wisdom he commanded as an elder statesman in 1989 was not in his repertoire in his younger years in the late 1940s and early 1950s, but his flair for presentation and the conviction it conveyed certainly was. Sidney Blumenthal wrote:

Clifford's voice is a melodious instrument. His brisk expositions are interrupted by grave, knowing pauses. He draws out syllables, leans over and speaks in a stage whisper and often ends a statement with a loud, triumphant coda followed by a large smile, making his point seem irrefutable. His long, thin fingers occasionally form a steeple, which he raises before his face, his words rapidly marching through like drilled troops. Sometimes, he closes his eyes, briefly touching his fingers to his forehead, séance-like. When he does this, he seems to be in communion with great events of the past, conjuring up the presidents and their retinues.[5]

The *Post* article captures the sense of drama Clifford infused into his presentations. Truman biographer Robert Donovan seemed to agree, observing that "Clifford had studied drama. He was on stage all the time. Appearances were much with Clark."[6]

When making presentations or arguing a position in front of the president, Clifford was often presenting other people's ideas. As Leon Keyserling observed, Clifford was a "synthesizer and operator," not an "idea man."[7] Spingarn said, "He's a master salesman. He's a very effective guy in selling other people's ideas. He is a tactician, a good political tactician, but he is not an idea man, he gets the ideas from other sources."[8] Kennedy speechwriter and adviser Ted Sorensen once remarked that "Clark has the ability to listen to what you just said and then give it back to you, but make it sound much more powerful."[9] *Time* magazine, in 1948, concluded that "one of the chief reasons for Clifford's rise has been his methodical practice of meticulously copying down the thoughts of the various men around the President, carefully sorting them out and then presenting them in a manner which suits Harry Truman to a T."[10]

Much of Clifford's success, therefore, was based upon his ability to paraphrase the arguments and ideas of others on the White House staff rather than come up with ideas on his own. This, however, should not obscure the fact that Clifford had a remarkable ability both to simplify complex ideas and to keep relatively simple ideas from becoming overly complicated. Hugh Sidey, a political journalist with *Time,* said, "There is nothing clever or brilliant in what Clifford said. But I soon came to realize that this was his genius: he didn't try to do anything that fancy, he just provided commonsense advice. There was always a stark logic to his expositions."[11] Clifford's critics were less willing to acknowledge that his talent for synthesizing ideas was indicative of an intelligent mind. *The New Republic* wrote that "those who have worked closely with Clifford report that he has a sharp but somewhat superficial mind," thus lending further credence to the notion that Clifford was at his best as an advocate arguing someone else's points rather than presenting original ideas.[12]

In a town of oversized egos and unremitting ambition, Clifford stood out among his Washington peers for his capacity for self-promotion. In the day-to-day operations of the Truman White House this manifested itself in Clifford's ongoing struggle with his main adversary, John Steelman. Clifford jealously guarded his private access to the president and made sure that he was the last person to have Truman's ear at the end of the day. His care and feeding of the press resulted in an unusual amount of media coverage, certainly more than typical for a White House aide in the 1940s. While not all of it was favorable, the news accounts inflated his image and turned him into a media personality. This fact troubled Truman, who once lamented in his diary that "Clifford has gone prima donna on me."[13]

Clifford's courting of reporters ensured that he received favorable coverage in the press, even though they were otherwise critical of what they perceived to be the mediocrity of the Truman administration. The "Missouri Gang" of White House staff was the frequent target of criticism by a press corps that held the eastern Establishment New Dealers of the Roosevelt administration in high esteem. As part of that group, Clifford was considered the most talented out of a weak bunch. Allen and Shannon best captured the prevailing wisdom regarding Clifford and his colleagues in the administration: "Alone of all the Truman entourage, Clifford has the brains, the personal *élan,* and the *savoir faire* requisite for a big-leaguer. He is really of White House class. None of the others are, or ever can be."[14] Cabell Phillips, journalist and author of a 1966 history of the Truman presi-

dency, opined that "the Truman team was generally lacking in lus-
ter—competent but pedestrian, conscientious but unimaginative. The
striking exception was Clark Clifford." In particular, Phillips singled
out White House rival Steelman for criticism. "John R. Steelman, who
acquired in time the resounding and unique title '*The* Assistant to the
President,' never quite measured up to it in either performance or personal relationship," he wrote.[15]

Clifford's contemporaries did not appreciate the characterization
of him as the only person of stature in a weak administration. In particular, Spingarn was incensed over Clifford's flattering treatment at
the expense of the rest of the staff. During his Truman Library oral
history interviews Spingarn was quite critical of Clifford, and while
a bit of jealousy may have prompted some of his remarks, his candor
and insights are worthy of note. In particular, Spingarn accused Clifford of inflating his own importance and accomplishments by influencing how the history of the Truman administration was ultimately
written. Spingarn astutely pointed out the numerous accolades Phillips paid to Clifford for assistance with Phillips's book. According to
Spingarn, this explains the basis for the book's praise of Clifford at
the expense of everyone else.[16] Given Phillips's criticism of Clifford's
primary rival, Steelman, Spingarn's assessment seems to have been on
the mark. In Spingarn's opinion, Clifford's contribution to the Phillips
book was indicative of his propensity for self-promotion: "Clifford
. . . has a keen sense of his own place in history as a major figure in the
Truman administration, and he has made himself unstintingly available to people who were going to do important writing in this field.
It is obvious that he devoted an enormous amount of time to Cabell
Phillips' book. You can tell that by reading the credits in the chapter
notes, you see, as well as in the foreword."[17]

Spingarn may have had an axe to grind, but there is no questioning the validity of his observations. He said, "I looked at the book. I
read the foreword—voluminous thanks to Clark Clifford. I read the
chapter notes, practically every one began with lavish thanks to Clark
Clifford for having contributed so much to that chapter. I looked at
the index and I found that Clark Clifford was indexed twenty-five or
thirty times, and Charlie Murphy, who had held the same job longer
than Clifford had . . . was only indexed four times."[18]

Given Clifford's extensive involvement and interest in the book,
and Phillips's obvious debt to him for his invaluable assistance, it is
reasonable to assume that the book would be somewhat biased in
favor of Clifford. And Phillips did not disappoint: "Clifford's gifts, it

soon developed, were many and varied. He was urbane, gracious, and socially talented. He had a mind of extraordinary scope and analytical capacity, and he expressed himself with easy, unpretentious clarity. He brought to his job of Presidential aide an intelligence and creativity that sensed the loopholes and detours by which the obstacles to Presidential initiative could be surmounted. For a Chief Executive geared to action rather than deliberation, such as Truman was, Clifford came close to being the ideal No. 2 man, the how-to-do-it man."[19]

It is often said that history is written by the victors, and in this case Clifford was proudly standing in the winner's circle. Although Phillips was the author, Clifford obviously influenced some of Phillips's observations and conclusions. Despite the modesty expressed in his memoirs, Clifford was proud of his accomplishments and his place in history, and often recounted the stories of his greatest triumphs to friends, acquaintances, clients, and writers. White House staffer Ken Hechler recalled that Clifford would meet other members of the Truman White House at the Cosmos Club to reminisce. "Clifford is a great storyteller," Hechler said.[20] Over the years Clifford told these stories so many times he began to have trouble distinguishing between his embellishments and occasional fabrications, and the truth. In the case of his greatest triumph, the 1948 election, it was only after George Elsey convinced him that James Rowe's authorship of the campaign memorandum was widely known that Clifford gave Rowe some of the credit in his widely publicized memoirs.

The final factor that contributed to Clifford's success in the Truman White House was his capacity for taking credit for other people's work. His three most significant accomplishments—the 1948 campaign memorandum, the Clifford-Elsey report, and the recognition of Israel—were primarily the intellectual property of James Rowe, George Elsey, and Max Lowenthal, respectively. Elsey's modesty and loyalty to Clifford precluded him from challenging Clifford's assertions of ownership, but Rowe did try to set the record straight regarding the campaign memorandum. Other members of the White House staff, such as Spingarn, believed that Clifford too often got credit that properly belonged to others.[21] Assistant Press Secretary Eben Ayers, whose diary provides a firsthand account of the Truman White House, was incredulous at the press attention Clifford was beginning to receive in late 1946:

Newspaper and magazine writers and columnists are beginning to devote attention to Clark Clifford. . . . It is interesting to watch how the newspapers and writers trail actual developments, and how little even the reporters who cover the White House from day to day actually know of personalities and what goes on. . . . . Likewise they know almost nothing of what individuals like Clifford do from day to day. Suddenly they discover that someone has had a part in advising the president, though he may have been performing similar work for months, and they immediately see him as the primary influence in all decisions by the president.[22]

In June 1948, Ayers again lamented that "Clifford is credited with writing the speeches and has had a large part in many of them, if not most of those recently, but much of the work has been done by others."[23] Clifford's willingness to accept recognition for the intellectual property of others was crucial to his success and, with his talented yet self-effacing and loyal aide Elsey, Clifford accomplished much in the Truman White House.

Combining a keen mind with a commanding physical presence, a voice and speaking style that exuded authority, and relentless ambition, Clifford had all the tools necessary for a successful career in Washington. Yet the crucial determinant of his success was his capacity for self-promotion. He was at his best when presenting the arguments and ideas of others and, as the spokesman, he was often able to claim credit for the ideas themselves. After leaving the White House Clifford continued to exaggerate his contributions to the Truman Doctrine and the 1948 campaign, and his legend grew. He had a talent for getting his name in the papers and used the press to build and solidify his reputation. Reporters knew they could rely on Clifford for leaks so they seldom criticized him, thereby inflating his image. Truman was often annoyed with Clifford's "prima donna" tendencies, but he may have tolerated them because flattering accounts of one his closest advisers conferred a level of competence upon the rest of his administration.[24]

Clifford's personal charm and penchant for flattery were no less crucial to his success. He carefully nurtured his relationship with Truman and even adopted the president's interests and colloquialisms. Clients, congressmen, government officials, and reporters were enthralled by Clifford's courtly manners and magnetic personality. Richard Cohen, a reporter for the *Washington Post*, vividly recounted a typical charm offensive from Clifford: "He was smiling. He continued to talk. He was on his feet. So was I. He led me to the door. We shook hands. . . . The elevator arrived. The questions were still in my pocket. I should check to see if I still had my watch."[25]

Clark Clifford's many talents were undeniable, but they were also exaggerated. He was not the political mastermind of the 1948 campaign, although he did play an important role in Truman's stunning victory. He did not craft foreign policy so much as he helped Truman articulate the policies that arrived fully formed from the State Department. His most important contribution to the Clifford-Elsey report was the cover note he attached to it before handing the report to Truman. He was a gifted and influential adviser, yet writers such as Cabell Phillips overstated his importance and achievements. Clifford also exaggerated his own achievements, and over time the line between embellishment and fabrication became increasingly hazy. Ultimately the myth of Clark Clifford and his accomplishments in the Truman White House were more impressive than the reality.

Fortunately for Clifford, he would have an opportunity to prove that he could live up to the myth, and he seized that opportunity.

After setting up his law practice Clifford capitalized on his reputation, even if his actual accomplishments were somewhat exaggerated. As a Washington lawyer he was in an elite class of wealthy and influential power brokers. For the remainder of his career, with the exception of a single year, Clifford was a private attorney; yet his practice and his passion for politics always kept him close to senior figures in government. Despite his association with, and advocacy for, corporate interests, Clifford remained a lifelong Democrat. When the Democrats reclaimed the White House in 1961 Clifford's influence and stature correspondingly increased. President Kennedy called on Clifford from time to time, but not nearly as much as did his successor.

As a confidant and informal adviser to Lyndon Johnson, Clifford had the opportunity to provide his insights on the most important decision of Johnson's presidency. As early as 1965 Clifford foresaw that further U.S. involvement in the Vietnamese war would be a disaster for the country, and he passionately presented his case to Johnson. As with the decision to recognize Israel, he opposed a figure of towering stature, yet he did not shrink from the challenge. Unfortunately, Johnson did not heed his warning, and Clifford's dire predictions came to pass. A few years later, after Johnson had lost faith in McNamara, he asked Clifford to oversee the Department of Defense and the war that Clifford had so vociferously opposed at the beginning. Shortly after he was sworn in, Clifford began a concerted effort to extricate the country from Vietnam. At virtually every step of the way he ran into a wall of opposition from the president's senior advisers, and often from the president himself. But Clifford never gave up. He continued to press his case, certain that what he was doing was in the best interests of the country and the president he served. Because of Johnson's hesitation, the intransigence of the South Vietnamese allies, and partisan sabotage from the Nixon campaign, Clifford ultimately failed. The war dragged on for another five years, unleashing social upheaval, leaving scars on the American psyche that are evident to this day, and resulting in the deaths of more than 58,000 American soldiers, much as Clifford had predicted.

When given the chance to prove that he was worthy of the myth that surrounded him, Clifford more than rose to the challenge. It would have been far easier to conform to the consensus within the highest levels of the Johnson administration and the military that victory in Vietnam was inevitable and essential. Yet Clifford continued to battle for the heart and soul of the president until the final days of the administration. Clifford's foreign policy credentials during the Truman administration may have been exaggerated, but his admonition to avoid becoming entangled in the Vietnam War in the first place and his heroic effort to get the country out later have not received sufficient notice. A notable exception was a 2002 HBO movie, *Path to War*, which depicts Clifford as a sage presidential adviser who urges Johnson to get out of Vietnam, generally presenting him very favorably. Historians should take note.

Lyndon Johnson's adviser George Reedy best described the brilliance of Clifford's strategy:

> It was Clifford who finally found the way out—Clifford who knows more about presidents than any other living man simply because he sees them instinctively as the kings that they are. Where intellectuals and politicians have failed, this man succeeded because he combined a high order of intellect with the skill of a crafty palace guerrilla fighter. He knew what the others had not realized—that no president can be argued into changing his mind but that he can be persuaded to change it if he is led to believe that the change was his own idea.[26]

Late in his life, long after most of his contemporaries had either retired or passed away, a restless Clifford commenced an ill-fated association with BCCI. It was the biggest mistake he ever made, and he paid dearly for it. But the final verdict of history should not be based on a scandal late in Clifford's career. In any case, the evidence is inconclusive that Clifford intentionally broke the law; the more plausible explanation is that he chose to overlook what seemed obvious to the regulators and prosecutors. He demonstrated poor judgment in associating himself with the BCCI investors, who used his good name as a cloak of legitimacy. Certainly he failed to exercise the oversight necessary to make sure that his company was operating within the law. Perhaps it had become too easy for him. Clifford's good name had opened doors and solved problems in Washington for forty years. But in the case of BCCI, his reputation was the source of his undoing. In this final act of the Clifford drama, his critics celebrated his fall from grace, yet failed to see that it also demonstrated the full measure of his character. Clifford could have put the blame on Robert Altman and thus might have emerged with his reputation intact; yet he chose loyalty over his own interests. For a man who had worked for his entire life at cultivating his own reputation, such a sacrifice was, perhaps, unexpected.

Clark Clifford cast a long shadow over Washington during a career that spanned six decades. Once celebrated as Truman's "bright young man," later disgraced by scandal, he was a compelling figure. He rose to fame and power by a combination of good fortune, intelligence, tenacity, and a flair for self-promotion. Although his own accomplishments were embellished, he proved worthy of his reputation at one of the most critical moments of the Cold War. His heroic opposition to the war in Vietnam permanently damaged his relationship with Lyndon Johnson, but he accepted the consequences for the good of his country. Despite his shortcomings and the scandal that disgraced him, Clifford should be judged kindly by history for his efforts to extricate America from its disastrous involvement in Vietnam. It is futile for historians to ponder what might have been, yet there is no question that if Lyndon Johnson had heeded his warning in July 1965, 58,000 Americans need not have perished in the jungles of Southeast Asia.

# Notes

## INTRODUCTION

1. Clark Clifford with Richard Holbrooke, *Counsel to the President* (New York: Random House, 1991), 410–11; Clifford to Johnson, May 17, 1965, Lyndon Johnson Presidential Papers, National Security File, Vietnam Country File, Box 74.

2. Notes of meeting, July 25, 1965, U.S. Department of State, *Foreign Relations of the United States* [hereinafter *FRUS*], *1965,* vol. 3 (Pittsburgh, Pa.: U.S. Government Printing Office, 1996).

3. Samuel Kernell and Samuel L. Popkin, eds., *Chief of Staff: Twenty-Five Years of Managing the Presidency* (Berkeley: University of California Press, 1986), viii.

4. Ibid., 2.

5. Patrick Anderson, *The President's Men* (Garden City, N.Y.: Doubleday, 1968), 113.

6. Roosevelt quoted in Robert E. Sherwood, *Roosevelt and Hopkins: An Intimate History* (New York: Harper & Brothers, 1948), 1–3.

7. Patrick Anderson, "The New Defense Secretary Thinks Like the President," *New York Times,* January 28, 1968, sec. 6, p. 70.

8. Douglas Frantz and David McKean, *Friends in High Places: The Rise and Fall of Clark Clifford* (New York: Little, Brown and Co., 1995), 8–9.

9. Ernest Havemann, "Clark Clifford," *Life,* January 27, 1947, 45.

10. Anderson, "The New Defense Secretary Thinks Like the President," 20.

11. Cabell B. H. Phillips, *The Truman Presidency: The History of a Triumphant Succession* (New York: Macmillan, 1966), 135, 137.

12. Alonzo L. Hamby, *Man of the People: A Life of Harry S. Truman* (New York: Oxford University Press, 1995), 304.

## 1. SPECIAL COUNSEL

1. Tris Coffin, "Harry Truman's Bright Young Man," *The New Republic,* 6 January 1947, 14.

2. Early biographical information on Clifford comes from ibid., 14–17; Clifford with Holbrooke, *Counsel,* 26–37; Frantz and McKean, *Friends in High Places,* 14–35.

3. Coffin, "Harry Truman's Bright Young Man," 14.

4. Frantz and McKean, *Friends in High Places,* 34–39, Clifford with Holbrooke, *Counsel,* 45–46.

5. Clifford with Holbrooke, *Counsel,* 50.

6. Ibid., 51.

7. George McKee Elsey, *An Unplanned Life* (Columbia: University of Missouri Press, 2005), 1–17.

8. Clifford with Holbrooke, *Counsel,* 56–57.

9. Ibid., 64–66.

10. Rosenman Oral History, April 23, 1969, Harry S. Truman Library, Independence, Missouri (hereinafter HSTL).

11. Clifford with Holbrooke, *Counsel,* 74.

12. Elsey Oral History, February 10, 1964, HSTL.

13. News clipping, *St. Louis Post-Dispatch,* April 5, 1946, Clifford File, HSTL.

14. Clifford with Holbrooke, *Counsel,* 75.

15. Ibid., 88.

16. Truman quoted in Hamby, *Man of the People,* 378. John L. Lewis was president of the United Mine Workers union.

17. Clifford with Holbrooke, *Counsel,* 90.

18. Clifford quoted in David McCullough, *Truman* (New York: Simon & Schuster, 1992), 528; Clifford with Holbrooke, *Counsel,* 92–95; Frantz and McKean, *Friends in High Places,* 57–59; Robert J. Donovan, *Conflict and Crisis: The Presidency of Harry S. Truman, 1945–1948* (New York: Norton, 1977), 241; Hamby, *Man of the People,* 419; Robert Underhill, *The Truman Persuasions* (Ames: Iowa State University Press, 1981), 181.

19. Clifford with Holbrooke, *Counsel,* 92.

20. "Problems of President's Right-Hand Man," *U.S. News and World Report,* December 20, 1946, 60.

21. Clifford with Holbrooke, *Counsel,* 92–95; Frantz and McKean, *Friends in High Places,* 57–59.

22. News clippings, *St. Louis Star Times,* November 26, 1946; *St. Louis Post-Dispatch,* December 11, 1946, and October 31, 1946; Clifford Papers, Box 1, Manuscript Division, Library of Congress.

23. Ross quoted in Anderson, *The President's Men,* 124.

24. Donovan, *Conflict and Crisis,* 242.

25. Charles T. Lucey, "Clifford Is Quarterbacking Mr. T.'s Varsity Advisers," *Washington Daily News,* December 13, 1946, 20.

26. David Lilienthal, *The Journals of David Lilienthal,* vol. 2, *The Atomic Energy Years, 1945–1950* (New York: Harper & Row, 1964), 125.

27. Coffin, "Harry Truman's Bright Young Man," 14.

28. Havemann, "Clark Clifford," 53.

29. Clifford with Holbrooke, *Counsel,* 121.

30. Phone message, September 18, 1946, Clifford Papers, Box 19, HSTL.

31. Lilienthal, *Journals,* vol. 2, 88.

32. Clifford with Holbrooke, *Counsel,* 121.

33. "The President's relationships with an opposition Congress," December 1946; Clifford to Truman, December 16, 1946, Clifford Papers, Box 3, HSTL.

34. Ibid.

35. Hamby, *Man of the People,* 430; Clifford with Holbrooke, *Counsel,* 84–85.

36. Ewing Oral History, April 30, 1969, HSTL.

37. Clifford Oral History, May 10, 1971, HSTL.

38. Francis Heller, ed., *The Truman White House: The Administration of the Presidency, 1945–1953* (Lawrence: Regents Press of Kansas, 1980), 191.

39. The group continued to meet through the end of Truman's second term, although it lost much of its cohesiveness in 1950. Clifford with Holbrooke, *Counsel,* 86.

40. Keyserling Oral History, May 3, 1971, HSTL.

41. Ewing Oral History, April 30, 1969, HSTL.

42. Elsey, letter to author, January 1, 2003.

43. Hamby, *Man of the People,* 430.

44. Clifford with Holbrooke, *Counsel,* 77–80, 85.

45. Harold I. Gullan, *The Upset That Wasn't: Harry S. Truman and the Crucial Election of 1948* (Chicago: Ivan R. Dee, 1998), 62.

46. Hamby, *Man of the People,* 361–63.

47. Bell Oral History, August 20, 1968, HSTL.

48. Heller, *Truman White House,* 66.

49. Clifford with Holbrooke, *Counsel,* 122.

50. Lou Gordon, "White House Wonder," *St. Louis Globe-Democrat,* June 22, 1947, Magazine Section, pp. 21, 25.

51. Hamby, *Man of the People,* 430.

52. Underhill, *Truman Persuasions,* 182.

53. Elsey Oral History, July 17, 1969, HSTL.

54. Eric F. Goldman, *The Crucial Decade: America, 1945–1955* (Westport, Conn.: Greenwood Press, 1981), 64.

55. News clipping, Arthur Krock, "Capital Sees Increase in Truman's Prestige," *New York Times,* December 15, 1946, Week in Review, p. E3, Clifford Papers, Box 1, Manuscript Division, Library of Congress.

56. Underhill, *Truman Persuasions,* 183.

57. Ayers Oral History, August 15, 1969, HSTL.

58. Clifford Oral History, May 10, 1971, HSTL.

59. Quoted in Ray Tucker, "News behind the News," news clipping, Clifford Papers, Box 1, Manuscript Division, Library of Congress. The newspaper and date are unknown.

60. Coffin, "Harry Truman's Bright Young Man," 14.

61. Lucey, "Clifford Is Quarterbacking Mr. T.'s Varsity Advisers," 20.

62. Gordon, "White House Wonder," 25; Havemann, "Clark Clifford," 45.

63. Anderson, *The President's Men,* 124; Frantz and McKean, *Friends in High Places,* 61.

64. Frantz and McKean, *Friends in High Places,* 57.

65. George Elsey, interview by author, Washington, D.C., March 19, 2002.

66. Anderson quoted in Frantz and McKean, *Friends in High Places,* 175.

67. Ray Tucker, "News behind the News."

68. Michael Medved, *The Shadow Presidents: The Secret History of the Chief Executives and Their Top Aides* (New York: Times Books, 1979), 221; Clifford with Holbrooke, *Counsel,* 96.

69. Coffin, "Harry Truman's Bright Young Man," 14.

70. Clifford quoted in Bert Cochran, *Harry Truman and the Crisis Presidency* (New York: Funk & Wagnalls, 1973), 217.

71. Underhill, *Truman Persuasions,* 182.

72. Lester Markel, "Truman, as the Crucial Third Year Opens," *New York Times,* March 16, 1947, sec. 6, p. 9.

73. Vardaman quoted in Arthur Krock, *Memoirs: Sixty Years on the Firing Line* (New York: Funk & Wagnalls, 1968), 235.

74. Clifford with Holbrooke, *Counsel,* 71. The agreed-upon limit that a player could lose in these games was $900, a sizable sum considering that Clifford's annual salary as special counsel was $12,000. Ibid.

75. Quoted in Frantz and McKean, *Friends in High Places,* 62.

76. Gordon, "White House Wonder," 25.

77. Anderson, *The President's Men,* 116.

78. Medved, *Shadow Presidents,* 223.

79. Ayers Oral History, August 15, 1969, HSTL.

80. Clifford with Holbrooke, *Counsel,* 76.

81. Heller, *Truman White House,* 170.

82. Anderson, *The President's Men,* 91.

83. Clifford with Holbrooke, *Counsel,* 75.

84. Alan D. Harper, *The Politics of Loyalty: The White House and the Communist Issue, 1946–1952* (Westport, Conn.: Greenwood Publishing Corp., 1969), 245.

85. Robert H. Ferrell, ed., *Truman in the White House: The Diary of Eben Ayers* (Columbia: University of Missouri Press, 1991), 301.

86. Ayers Oral History, April 19, 1967, HSTL.

87. Keyserling Oral History, May 10, 1971, HSTL. Bell and Lloyd were members of the White House staff.

88. "Little Accident," *Time,* March 15, 1948, 28.

89. Neustadt quoted in Heller, *Truman White House,* 114.

90. Chapman Oral History, April 21, 1972, HSTL.

## 2. THE ELSEY REPORT

1. Frantz and McKean, *Friends in High Places,* 52.

2. Clifford with Holbrooke, *Counsel,* 136.

3. Clifford Oral History, April 13, 1971, HSTL.

4. Hamby, *Man of the People,* 339.

5. Clifford with Holbrooke, *Counsel,* 102. This statement contradicted an earlier assessment in which Clifford said he was not sure "that any particular significance was attached to it." Clifford Oral History, April 13, 1971, HSTL.

6. Quoted in Clifford with Holbrooke, *Counsel,* 105.

7. Elsey handwritten notes, July 12, 1946, Elsey Papers, Box 63, HSTL.

8. Clifford with Holbrooke, *Counsel,* 110.

9. This chapter is drawn largely from Elsey's notes, his oral history, and my own interviews and correspondence with Elsey. Elsey, however, was not present during the July 12, 1946, meeting; in addition, because he was a participant with potentially an agenda of his own, Elsey's account should be considered in the context of these caveats. On balance, however, Elsey's account appears to be quite accurate, for two reasons. The first is that Elsey made little effort to claim credit for the accomplishments cited by Clifford and did not evidence any grudges against him. He was candid in his recognition of Clifford's tendency to take credit for his,

and others', work, but always described him as a friend. The second reason is that Elsey was candid in admitting what he could and could not recall. For those reasons, I have concluded that his account is trustworthy.

10. George Elsey, interview by author, Washington, D.C., June 14, 2001.

11. Elsey Oral History, April 9, 1970. The July 12, 1946, meeting during which Truman asked for the report of Soviet violations of treaty agreements took place two months before the Wallace "fiasco."

12. Elsey, interview by author, Washington, D.C., June 14, 2001.

13. Clifford with Holbrooke, *Counsel,* 111; Elsey handwritten notes, July 16, 1946, Elsey Papers, Box 63, HSTL.

14. Elsey Oral History, April 9, 1970.

15. Elsey, interview by author, Washington, D.C., June 14, 2001.

16. Clifford with Holbrooke, *Counsel,* 111.

17. Elsey handwritten notes, July 17, 1946, Elsey Papers, Box 63, HSTL.

18. Ibid.

19. Elsey handwritten notes, July 19, 1946, Elsey Papers, Box 63, HSTL.

20. Elsey handwritten notes, July 18, 1946, Elsey Papers, Box 63, HSTL; Clifford with Holbrooke, *Counsel,* 111.

21. Elsey handwritten notes, July 24, 1946, Elsey Papers, Box 63, HSTL; Clifford with Holbrooke, *Counsel,* 111–13. Clifford's memoir indicates that the meeting with Byrnes took place on July 18, but Elsey's notes are dated July 24. When asked about the discrepancy Elsey confirmed that there was only one meeting and said he believed the date on his notes was accurate.

22. Elsey handwritten notes, August 8, 1946, Elsey Papers, Box 63, HSTL.

23. Clifford with Holbrooke, *Counsel,* 115.

24. Elsey handwritten notes, August 27, 1946, Elsey Papers, Box 63, HSTL.

25. Clifford with Holbrooke, *Counsel,* 115–16; Clifford Papers, Box 15, HSTL.

26. Elsey handwritten notes, undated, Elsey Papers, Box 63, HSTL. Emphasis in original.

27. Clifford with Holbrooke, *Counsel,* 123.

28. Ibid., 124.

29. Clifford Oral History, April 13, 1971.

30. Elsey letter to the author, January 10, 2003.

31. Frantz and McKean, *Friends in High Places,* 57.

32. Elsey, interview by author, Washington, D.C., June 14, 2001.

33. Frantz and McKean, *Friends in High Places,* 54.

34. Elsey, interview by author, Washington, D.C., March 19, 2002.

35. Clifford to Truman, September 24, 1946, Elsey Papers, Box 63, HSTL.

36. Underhill, *Truman Persuasions,* 193.

37. Clifford Oral History, March 16, 1972, and May 10, 1971, HSTL.

38. Ibid., March 23, 1971.

39. Elsey Oral History, April 9, 1970. Emphasis in original.

40. Clifford Oral History, March 23, 1971, and March 16, 1972, HSTL.

41. George Elsey, interview by author, Washington, D.C., June 14, 2001.

42. Krock, *Memoirs,* 425.

43. Ibid., 427.

44. Ibid., 468.

45. Ibid., 474–75.

46. Ibid., 476.

47. Ibid., 477.

48. Ibid.

49. Ibid., 478.

50. Ibid., 479.

51. Ibid., 482.

52. Clifford Oral History, April 13, 1971.

53. Melvyn P. Leffler, *A Preponderance of Power: National Security, the Truman Administration, and the Cold War* (Stanford, Calif.: Stanford University Press, 1992), 131.

54. Hamby, *Man of the People,* 353.

55. Clifford with Holbrooke, *Counsel,* 124.

56. Elsey Oral History, April 9, 1970. Emphasis in original.

57. Hamby, *Man of the People,* 360.

58. Ibid., 355.

59. Leffler, *Preponderance of Power,* 137–38.

60. Elsey, interview by author, Washington, D.C., June 14, 2001.

61. Clifford with Holbrooke, *Counsel,* 109.

62. Wallace delivered his Madison Square Garden speech on September 12.

63. McNaughton quoted in Hamby, *Man of the People,* 381.

64. Elsey, interview by author, Washington, D.C., June 14, 2001.

## 3. Cold Warrior

1. Clifford with Holbrooke, *Counsel,* 146.

2. Ibid., 149–50.

3. Ibid., 152.

4. Walter Millis, ed., *The Forrestal Diaries* (New York: Viking Press, 1951), 221; Clifford with Holbrooke, *Counsel,* 153.

5. Millis, ed., *Forrestal Diaries,* 298–99.

6. Elsey Oral History, February 10, 1964, HSTL.

7. Townsend Hoopes and Douglas Brinkley, *Driven Patriot: The Life and Times of James Forrestal* (New York: Knopf, 1992), 354; Clifford with Holbrooke, *Counsel,* 163–64.

8. George M. Elsey, "Some White House Recollections, 1942–53," *Diplomatic History* 12, no. 3 (Summer 1988): 364.

9. Thomas F. Troy, *Donovan and the CIA: A History of the Establishment of the Central Intelligence Agency* (Frederick, Md.: Aletheia Books, 1981), 339; Clifford with Holbrooke, *Counsel,* 166–67.

10. Troy, *Donovan and the CIA,* 370.

11. Clifford to Vandenberg, July 12, 1946, Clifford Papers, Box 11, HSTL.

12. Troy, *Donovan and the CIA,* 355; also see n. 8.

13. Ibid., 369–70; Clifford with Holbrooke, *Counsel,* 168.

14. Troy, *Donovan and the CIA,* 375, 380, 389, 390.

15. Clifford with Holbrooke, *Counsel,* 131.

16. Leffler, *Preponderance of Power,* 143.

17. Krock, *Memoirs,* 434.

18. Clifford with Holbrooke, *Counsel,* 131.

19. Vandenberg quoted in Leffler, *Preponderance of Power,* 145.

20. Vandenberg quoted in Walter Isaacson and Evan Thomas, *The Wise Men: Six Friends and the World They Made: Acheson, Bohlen, Harriman, Kennan, Lovett, McCloy* (New York: Simon & Schuster, 1986), 395.

21. Millis, ed., *Forrestal Diaries,* 248–49.

22. Hoopes and Brinkley, *Driven Patriot,* 302–3; Marx Leva Oral History, December 9, 1969, HSTL.

23. The memorandum can be found in Carl W. Borklund, *Men of the Pentagon: From Forrestal to McNamara* (New York: Frederick A. Praeger, 1966), 23–25.

24. George Elsey, interview by author, Washington, D.C., March 19, 2002.

25. Hoopes and Brinkley, *Driven Patriot,* 303.

26. Clifford with Holbrooke, *Counsel,* 134.

27. Elsey to Clifford, March 8, 1947, Elsey Papers, Box 17, HSTL.

28. Clifford with Holbrooke, *Counsel,* 133.

29. George Elsey, interview by author, Washington, D.C., June 14, 2001.

30. Elsey handwritten notes, March 9, 1947, Elsey papers, Box 17, HSTL; Clifford with Holbrooke, *Counsel,* 133.

31. Clifford with Holbrooke, *Counsel,* 134–35.

32. Undated handwritten notes, Clifford Papers, Box 27, HSTL.

33. Ferrell, ed., *Truman in the White House,* 170.

34. Elsey Oral History, April 9, 1970, HSTL.

35. Clifford with Holbrooke, *Counsel,* 135–37.

36. Dean Acheson, *Present at the Creation: My Years in the State Department* (New York: Norton, 1969), 221; Clifford with Holbrooke, *Counsel,* 137.

37. Charles Bohlen, *Witness to History, 1929–1969* (New York: Norton, 1973), 261.

38. Forrest C. Pogue, *George C. Marshall: Statesman, 1945–1959* (New York: Viking, 1987), 166.

39. Joseph Jones, *The Fifteen Weeks (February 21–June 4, 1947)* (New York: Viking, 1955), 157.

40. Acheson, *Present at the Creation,* 220–21.

41. Clifford with Holbrooke, *Counsel,* 679n5.

42. Elsey Oral History, April 9, 1970, HSTL.

43. Clifford Oral History, April 19, 1971, HSTL.

44. Clifford quoted in Howard Jones, *"A New Kind of War": America's Global Strategy and the Truman Doctrine in Greece* (New York: Oxford University Press, 1989), 55.

45. Clifford with Holbrooke, *Counsel,* 144.

46. Clifford Oral History, April 19, 1971, HSTL.

47. Hamby, *Man of the People,* 400.

48. Elsey to Clifford, September 22, 1947, Clifford Papers, Box 4, HSTL.

49. Clifford to Truman, September 22, 1947, ibid.

50. Clifford Oral History, April 19, 1971, HSTL.

51. Clifford to Truman, October 3, 1947, Clifford Papers, Box 4, HSTL.

52. Ferrell, ed., *Truman in the White House,* 206.

53. Ibid., 212.

54. Elsey Oral History, July 10, 1969, HSTL.

55. Elsey to Clifford, March 5, 1948, Elsey Papers, Box 21, HSTL.

56. Elsey handwritten notes, March 9, 1948, Elsey Papers, Box 21, HSTL.

57. Undated note slip attached to Lovett draft, ibid.

58. Elsey handwritten notes, March 11, 1947, ibid.

59. Elsey handwritten notes, March 13, 1947, ibid.

60. Clifford handwritten notes, undated, Clifford Papers, Box 31, HSTL.

61. Undated note slip attached to State Department draft of speech, Elsey Papers, Box 21, HSTL.

62. Clifford and Marshall quoted in Isaacson and Thomas, *The Wise Men,* 441.

63. Leffler, *Preponderance of Power,* 290; Isaacson and Thomas, *The Wise Men,* 441.

64. Telegram, Clifford to Truman, March 17, 1948, Clifford Papers, Box 1, Manuscript Division, Library of Congress.

65. William C. Spragens, ed., *Popular Images of American Presidents* (New York: Greenwood Press, 1988), 396–97.

66. Ferrell, ed., *Truman in the White House,* 206.

67. Batt to Clifford, March 18, 1948, Clifford Papers, and Elsey to Clifford, March 5, 1948, Elsey Papers, both in Box 21, HSTL.

68. Charles M. Dobbs, *The Unwanted Symbol: American Foreign Policy, the Cold War, and Korea, 1945–1950* (Kent, Ohio: Kent State University Press, 1981), 205.

69. Clifford to Truman, July 12, 1946, Clifford Papers, Box 15, HSTL.

70. Batt to Clifford, May 8, July 22, and August 9, 1948, ibid.

71. Ferrell, ed., *Truman in the White House,* 181; Humelsine to Clifford, September 24, 1947, ibid.

72. *FRUS, 1949,* vol. 5 (Pittsburgh, Pa.: U.S. Government Printing Office, 1976), 451, 459–60.

73. Jonathan Daniels interview with Clark Clifford for *Man of Independence,* October 26, 1949, Daniels Papers, Box 1, HSTL. The interview was conducted only months after the events in question.

74. Memorandum Concerning Draft of White Paper on China, July 5, 1949, Elsey Papers, Box 59, HSTL. Elsey's handwritten note at the bottom of the memo said, "CMC never read the White Paper Draft in question!"; Memorandum for the President Concerning Draft of White Paper on China, July 6, 1949, Clifford Papers, Box 2, HSTL; George Elsey, interview by author, Washington, D.C., June 14, 2001.

75. Memorandum Concerning Draft of White Paper on China, July 5, 1949, Elsey Papers, Box 59, HSTL.

76. Elsey handwritten notes, July 14, 1949, Elsey Papers, Box 59, HSTL.

77. Jessup to Clifford, August 2, 1949, Clifford Papers, Box 2, HSTL.

78. Donovan, *Conflict and Crisis,* 178.

79. Beal to Clifford, November 10, 1949, Clifford Papers, Box 2, HSTL.

80. Frantz and McKean, *Friends in High Places,* 115; David Welsh with David Horowitz, "Clark Clifford: Attorney at War," *Ramparts,* August 24, 1968, 47.

81. Clifford Oral History, March 23, 1971, HSTL.

82. Anderson, *The President's Men,* 121.

83. Clifford Oral History, March 23 and April 13, 1971, HSTL.

84. Clifford with Holbrooke, *Counsel,* 445.

85. Murphy quoted in Heller, *Truman White House,* 124.

86. Elsey Oral History, February 10, 1964, HSTL.

87. George Elsey, interview by author, Washington, D.C., June 14, 2001.

88. Elsey Oral History, July 7, 1970, HSTL.

89. George Elsey, interview by author, Washington, D.C., June 14, 2001.

90. Clifford quoted in Medved, *Shadow Presidents,* 223.

91. Clifford Oral History, October 4, 1973, HSTL.

92. Isaacson and Thomas, *The Wise Men,* 430.

93. George Elsey, interview by author, Washington, D.C., June 14, 2001.

94. Ibid.

95. Isaacson and Thomas, *The Wise Men,* 519.

96. George Elsey, interview by author, Washington, D.C., June 14, 2001; Elsey, "Some White House Recollections," 364.

97. Donovan, *Conflict and Crisis,* 410.

98. Lilienthal, *Journals,* vol. 2, 99.

99. Ibid., 143–44; Clifford with Holbrooke, *Counsel,* 179.

100. Hamby, *Man of the People,* 421, 430.

101. Lilienthal, *Journals,* vol. 2, 233–34, 336–37, 339, 341; Clifford to Truman, May 11, 1948, Clifford Papers, Box 1, Manuscript Division, Library of Congress.

102. Lilienthal to Clifford, August 1, 1948, Clifford Papers, Box 1, HSTL.

103. Clifford to Truman, December 29, 1948, Clifford Papers, Box 2, HSTL.

104. Anderson, *The President's Men,* 121.

## 4. The Recognition of Israel

1. Clifford with Holbrooke, *Counsel,* 4. Clifford's memoirs indicate that Acheson was among those opposed to a Jewish state, yet he was not serving in the State Department at the time.

2. Frantz and McKean, *Friends in High Places,* 75.

3. Hamby, *Man of the People,* 405–6.

4. Ibid., 407.

5. Ibid., 408, 409–10.

6. Krock, *Memoirs,* 434.

7. Clifford with Holbrooke, *Counsel,* 7.

8. Michael J. Cohen, *Truman and Israel* (Berkeley: University of California Press, 1990), 78.

9. Clifford with Holbrooke, *Counsel,* 5.

10. Loy Henderson Oral History, June 14, 1973, HSTL.

11. Ibid.

12. Truman quoted in ibid.

13. Ibid.

14. Cohen, *Truman and Israel,* 156.

15. Hoopes and Brinkley, *Driven Patriot,* 394.

16. Clifford quoted in Cohen, *Truman and Israel,* 169.

17. Forrestal quoted in Clifford with Holbrooke, *Counsel,* 4.

18. Hamby, *Man of the People,* 409.

19. Cohen, *Truman and Israel,* 91.

20. Ibid., 203–7.

21. Hamby, *Man of the People*, 411.

22. Cohen, *Truman and Israel*, 189; *FRUS, 1948*, vol. 5 (Pittsburgh, Pa.: U.S. Government Printing Office, 1975), 687, 690.

23. *FRUS, 1948*, vol. 5, 691–93.

24. Cohen, *Truman and Israel*, 180.

25. *FRUS, 1948*, vol. 5, 692.

26. Ibid., 694.

27. Ibid., 687–89.

28. Ibid., 696.

29. Ibid., 687–88.

30. Ibid., 690.

31. Ibid., 690–91, 693.

32. Elsey Oral History, July 7, 1970, HSTL.

33. *FRUS, 1948*, vol. 5, 639–40.

34. Truman quoted in Hamby, *Man of the People*, 411.

35. Ibid., 412.

36. Ibid., 413.

37. Michael Benson, *Harry S. Truman and the Founding of Israel* (Westport, Conn.: Praeger, 1997), 111.

38. Clifford quoted in Donovan, *Conflict and Crisis*, 377.

39. Clifford quoted in Cohen, *Truman and Israel*, 193.

40. Ibid., 214. Clifford meant March and was referring to the retreat on partition.

41. Donovan, *Conflict and Crisis*, 379.

42. Hamby, *Man of the People*, 413.

43. Memorandum of Conference on Palestine, March 24, 1948, Clifford Papers, Box 14, HSTL.

44. Cohen, *Truman and Israel*, 202.

45. Batt to Clifford, March 23, 1948, undated memorandum, Clifford Papers, Box 13, HSTL.

46. Thomas J. Schoenbaum, *Waging Peace and War: Dean Rusk in the Truman, Kennedy, and Johnson Years* (New York: Simon & Schuster, 1988), 169.

47. Henderson Oral History, June 24, 1973, HSTL.

48. Clifford to Truman, April 1, 1948, Clifford Papers, Box 1, Manuscript Division, Library of Congress.

49. Weizmann quoted in Hamby, *Man of the People*, 414.

50. Elsey handwritten notes, April 19, 1948, Elsey Papers, Box 60, HSTL.

51. *FRUS, 1948*, vol. 5, 906.

52. Clifford with Holbrooke, *Counsel*, 5–6.

53. Lowenthal to Clifford, May 7 and May 9, 1948, Clifford Papers, Box 13, HSTL.

54. Lowenthal to Clifford, May 9, 1948, ibid.

55. Lowenthal submitted a third memo on May 11. Lowenthal to Clifford, May 11, 1948, ibid.

56. *FRUS, 1948*, vol. 5, 746.

57. Clifford with Holbrooke, *Counsel*, 10.

58. Clifford quoted in Cohen, *Truman and Israel*, 213.

59. Clifford with Holbrooke, *Counsel,* 10–11.

60. Ibid., 11–12; Clifford Oral History, April 13, 1971, HSTL.

61. *FRUS, 1948,* vol. 5, 975.

62. Ibid.; Clifford with Holbrooke, *Counsel,* 13.

63. Clifford quoted in Benson, *Harry S. Truman and the Founding of Israel,* 157.

64. *FRUS, 1948,* vol. 5, 976.

65. John Snetsinger, *Truman, the Jewish Vote, and the Creation of Israel* (Stanford, Calif.: Hoover Institution Press, 1974), 107–8.

66. Clifford with Holbrooke, *Counsel,* 14.

67. Elsey handwritten notes, May 12, 1948, Elsey Papers, Box 60, HSTL.

68. Clifford with Holbrooke, *Counsel,* 13.

69. *FRUS, 1948,* vol. 5, 975.

70. Elsey handwritten notes, May 12, 1948, Elsey Papers, Box 60, HSTL.

71. *FRUS, 1948,* vol. 5, 976 (Elsey's notes; Clifford's notes are found on p. 906).

72. Pogue, *George C. Marshall,* 377.

73. Clifford with Holbrooke, *Counsel,* 15.

74. Ibid., 15; Clifford Oral History, April 13, 1971, HSTL.

75. Clifford with Holbrooke, *Counsel,* 17–18.

76. Ibid., 20.

77. Clifford quoted in Cohen, *Truman and Israel,* 216–17.

78. Clifford with Holbrooke, *Counsel,* 21–22.

79. Ayers Oral History, March 26, 1968, HSTL.

80. Clifford with Holbrooke, *Counsel,* 24.

81. *FRUS, 1948,* vol. 5, 105–7.

82. Clifford with Holbrooke, *Counsel,* 24.

83. Cohen, *Truman and Israel,* 223.

84. Clifford to Truman, October 23, 1948, Clifford Papers, Box 14, HSTL.

85. Snetsinger, *Truman, the Jewish Vote, and Israel,* 130.

86. Clifford to Truman, November 19, 1947, Clifford Papers, Box 22, HSTL.

87. Rowe to Truman, September 18, 1947, Kenneth Hechler Papers, Box 6, HSTL.

88. Krock, *Memoirs,* 434.

## 5. Mastermind of the 1948 Campaign?

1. Frantz and McKean, *Friends in High Places,* 73.

2. Ibid., 73.

3. Phillips, *The Truman Presidency,* 197–99.

4. Ibid., xii.

5. George Elsey, interview by author, Washington, D.C., May 7, 2004.

6. Patrick Anderson, "The New Defense Secretary Thinks Like the President," *New York Times,* January 28, 1968, sec. 6, p. 72.

7. Frantz and McKean, *Friends in High Places,* 224–25; Rowe to Clifford, February 24, 1968, James Rowe Papers, Box 87, Franklin D. Roosevelt Library, Hyde Park, New York. I was unable to locate the February 12 article by James Reston.

8. Rowe to Clifford, February 24, 1968, James Rowe Papers, Box 87, Franklin D. Roosevelt Library.

9. George Elsey, interview by author, Washington, D.C., March 19, 2002; Al Larkin, "The Campaign and the Presidency: An Interview with Richard Neustadt," *Boston Globe Magazine,* November 2, 1980, 13.

10. Rowe to Hechler, April 22, 1981, Hechler Papers, Box 6, HSTL.

11. Anderson, *The President's Men,* 119.

12. Clifford Oral History, May 10, 1971, HSTL.

13. Ibid.

14. George Elsey, interview by author, Washington, D.C., June 14, 2001.

15. Frantz and McKean, *Friends in High Places,* 73.

16. Sidney Blumenthal, "Clark Clifford: The Ultimate Insider and the Presidents He's Known," *Washington Post National Weekly Edition,* March 6–12, 1989, 9–11.

17. Kenneth Hechler, *Working with Truman* (New York: G. P. Putnam's Sons, 1982), 62–64.

18. Clifford with Holbrooke, *Counsel,* 189–91. George Elsey, interview by author, Washington, D.C., March 19, 2002.

19. Clifford to Truman, November 19, 1947, Clifford Papers, Box 22, HSTL; "The President's Relationships with an Opposition Congress," December 1946, Clifford Papers, Box 3, HSTL.

20. Hamby, *Man of the People,* 424.

21. Keyserling Oral History, May 10, 1971, HSTL.

22. Hamby, *Man of the People,* 441; Batt to McGrath and Jack Redding, June 21, 1948, Clifford Papers, Box 19, HSTL.

23. George Elsey, interview by author, Washington, D.C., March 19, 2002.

24. Batt Oral History, July 26, 1966, HSTL.

25. Clifford Oral History, May 10, 1971, HSTL.

26. Reston quoted in Clifford with Holbrooke, *Counsel,* 195–96.

27. Ibid., 197.

28. "Little Accident," *Time,* March 15, 1948, 26–27.

29. Clifford with Holbrooke, *Counsel,* 198.

30. Ibid., 198.

31. Ibid., 205.

32. Ibid., 207–8; Clifford Oral History, July 26, 1971, HSTL.

33. Clifford to Truman, November 19, 1947, Clifford Papers, Box 22, HSTL.

34. Hamby, *Man of the People,* 433–35.

35. Clifford to Truman, November 19, 1947, Clifford Papers, Box 22, HSTL.

36. Ibid.

37. David McCullough, *Truman* (New York: Simon & Schuster, 1992), 589–90.

38. Clifford with Holbrooke, *Counsel,* 204.

39. Ewing to Clifford, undated, Ewing Papers, Box 52, HSTL.

40. Batt to Sullivan, April 20, 1948, Clifford Papers, Box 21, HSTL.

41. Hamby, *Man of the People,* 435.

42. Clifford Oral History, July 26, 1971, HSTL.

43. Clifford with Holbrooke, *Counsel,* 218.

44. Clifford Oral History, July 26, 1971, HSTL.

45. George Elsey, interview by author, Washington, D.C., June 14, 2001.

46. Clifford Oral History, July 26, 1971, HSTL.

47. Clifford Oral History, May 10, 1971, HSTL.

48. Batt Oral History, July 26, 1966, HSTL.

49. Nash to Truman, November 6, 1948, Clifford Papers, Box 21, HSTL.

50. Clifford Oral History, July 26, 1971, HSTL; Clifford with Holbrooke, *Counsel*, 218.

51. Batt Oral History, HSTL; undated telegram, Elsey to Clifford, Clifford Papers, Box 21, HSTL.

52. Paul Taylor to Clifford, June 23, 1948, Clifford Papers, Box 21, HSTL.

53. Elsey to Murphy, August 26, 1948, Clifford Papers, Box 21, HSTL.

54. Unspecified author to unidentified recipient, June 29, 1948, Samuel Rosenman Papers, Box 9, HSTL.

55. Batt Oral History, July 26, 1966, HSTL.

56. Rosenman Oral History, October 15, 1968, HSTL.

57. Clifford Oral History, May 10, 1971, HSTL.

58. Keyserling Oral History, May 10, 1971, HSTL.

59. Ewing Oral History, May 2, 1969, HSTL.

60. Sean J. Savage, *Truman and the Democratic Party* (Lexington: University Press of Kentucky, 1997), 108.

61. Unspecified author to unidentified recipient, June 29, 1948, Rosenman Papers, Box 9, HSTL.

62. Elsey Oral History, February 17, 1964, HSTL; George Elsey, interview by author, Washington, D.C., March 19, 2002.

63. Clifford with Holbrooke, *Counsel*, 200.

64. Taft quoted in ibid., 202.

65. Clifford Oral History, July 26, 1971, HSTL; Elsey Oral History, February 17, 1964, HSTL.

66. Clifford to Truman, August 17, 1948, Clifford Papers, Box 22, HSTL.

67. Ibid.

68. Ibid.

69. George Elsey, interview by author, Washington, D.C., June 14, 2001.

70. Clifford to Truman, August 17, 1948, Clifford Papers, Box 22, HSTL.

71. Clifford with Holbrooke, *Counsel*, 200.

72. Clifford to Truman, August 17, 1948, Clifford Papers, Box 22, HSTL.

73. Elsey Oral History, February 17, 1964, HSTL.

74. Batt to Clifford, August 11, 1948, Clifford Papers, Box 22, HSTL.

75. Elsey to Clifford, August 13, 1948; Elsey to Clifford, undated, Clifford Papers, Box 22, HSTL.

76. Clifford with Holbrooke, *Counsel*, 226.

77. Batt to Clifford, May 8, 1948, Clifford Papers, Box 21, HSTL.

78. Batt to Clifford, March 18, 1948, ibid.

79. Batt to Clifford and Gael Sullivan, March 22, 1948, ibid.

80. Batt to Clifford, April 30, 1948, ibid.

81. Batt to Clifford, August 26, 1948, ibid.

82. Batt to Clifford, May 12, 1948, ibid.

83. Batt to Clifford, May 8, 1948, ibid.

84. Batt to Clifford, July 22, 1948, ibid.

85. Batt to Clifford, August 9, 1948, ibid.

86. Elsey handwritten notes, August 30, 1948, Elsey Papers, Box 33, HSTL.

87. McCullough, *Truman*, 631; Elsey Oral History, July 9, 1970, HSTL.

88. Elsey to Clifford, August 26, 1948, Elsey Papers, Box 33, HSTL.

89. Clifford to Truman, November 19, 1947, Clifford Papers, Box 22, HSTL.

90. Elsey to Clifford, June 6, 1947, Clifford Papers, Box 19, HSTL.

91. Americans for Democratic Action to the Democratic National Committee, undated, Clifford Papers, Box 21, HSTL.

92. Ferrell, ed., *Truman in the White House*, 257–58.

93. Batt to McGrath and Jack Redding, June 21, 1948, Clifford Papers, Box 19, HSTL.

94. Clifford with Holbrooke, *Counsel*, 232–33; Hamby, *Man of the People*, 460–61; Harper, *The Politics of Loyalty*, 81.

95. *Time* article quoted in Clifford with Holbrooke, *Counsel*, 234.

96. George Elsey, interview by author, Washington, D.C., June 14, 2001.

97. Clifford with Holbrooke, *Counsel*, 234–35.

98. Ibid., 234–35.

99. Clifford Oral History, July 26, 1971, HSTL; Clifford with Holbrooke, *Counsel*, 236.

100. Hamby, *Man of the People*, 459.

101. Clifford with Holbrooke, *Counsel*, 236.

102. Hamby, *Man of the People*, 459; Donovan, *Conflict and Crisis*, 425–26.

103. George Elsey, interview by author, Washington, D.C., March 19, 2002.

104. Clifford to Truman, November 2, 1948, Clifford Papers, Box 1, Manuscript Division, Library of Congress.

105. Clifford with Holbrooke, *Counsel*, 239.

106. Underhill, *Truman Persuasions*, 245.

107. George Elsey, interview by author, Washington, D.C., March 19, 2002.

## 6. ONE FOOT OUT THE DOOR

1. Clifford with Holbrooke, *Counsel*, 238.

2. Ibid., 245–46.

3. Clive Howard, "The Clark Cliffords," *Redbook*, June 1949, 83.

4. Elsey Oral History, July 10, 1969, HSTL.

5. Clifford with Holbrooke, *Counsel*, 249.

6. Ibid., 250.

7. Paul Nitze, *From Hiroshima to Glasnost: At the Center of Decision: A Memoir* (New York: Grove Weidenfeld, 1989), 68.

8. Elsey Oral History, July 10, 1969, HSTL.

9. Clifford Oral History, March 16, 1972, HSTL. Despite Acheson's known opposition to Point Four, Clifford told Jonathan Daniels that "Acheson went for it just like that," snapping his fingers for emphasis. Daniels interview with Clark Clifford for *Man of Independence*, November 12, 1949, Jonathan Daniels Papers, Box 1, HSTL.

10. Clifford with Holbrooke, *Counsel*, 252.

11. Clifford Oral History, October 4, 1973, March 16, 1972, HSTL.

12. Elsey to Clifford, January 9, 1950, and Elsey to Lloyd, January 9, 1950, Elsey Papers, Box 61, HSTL.

13. Elsey to Clifford, April 13, 1950, ibid.

14. George Elsey, interview by author, Washington, D.C., June 14, 2001.

15. Goldman, *The Crucial Decade,* 93.

16. Lilienthal, *Journals,* vol. 2, 448.

17. Acheson, *Present at the Creation,* 254.

18. Truman Inaugural Address draft, January 15, 1949, Clifford Papers, Box 37, HSTL.

19. Acheson to Clifford, January 17, 1949, ibid.

20. Clifford Oral History, March 16, 1972, HSTL.

21. Elsey Oral History, July 7, 1970, HSTL.

22. Isaacson and Thomas, *The Wise Men,* 463.

23. Acheson, *Present at the Creation,* 254.

24. Clifford Oral History, March 16, 1972, HSTL.

25. George Elsey, interview by author, Washington, D.C., June 14, 2001.

26. Ibid.

27. Frantz and McKean, *Friends in High Places,* 64; Krock, *Memoirs,* 474.

28. Clifford with Holbrooke, *Counsel,* 175–77.

29. Gary A. Donaldson, *Truman Defeats Dewey* (Lexington: University Press of Kentucky, 1999), 46–47.

30. Savage, *Truman and the Democratic Party,* 109.

31. The So-Called Spy Bills, January 25, 1949, Clifford Papers, Box 16, HSTL; Francis H. Thompson, *The Frustration of Politics: Truman, Congress, and the Loyalty Issue, 1945–1953* (Rutherford, N.J.: Fairleigh Dickinson University Press, 1979), 106.

32. Clifford to Truman, April 29, 1949, Clifford Papers, Box 16, HSTL.

33. Hamby, *Man of the People,* 550.

34. Clifford to Truman, April 29, 1949, Clifford Papers, Box 16, HSTL.

35. Clifford with Holbrooke, *Counsel,* 183–84.

36. Lilienthal to Clifford, May 25, 1949, Clifford Papers, Box 1, HSTL.

37. Lilienthal, *Journals,* vol. 2, 564.

38. Elsey to Clifford, September 26, 1949, Clifford Papers, Box 12, HSTL.

39. Clifford with Holbrooke, *Counsel,* 246.

40. Clifford Oral History, February 14, 1973, HSTL.

41. Clifford with Holbrooke, *Counsel,* 246.

42. Frantz and McKean, *Friends in High Places,* 46–47, 95–96.

43. Lilienthal, *Journals,* vol. 2, 433–35.

44. Ibid.

45. Frantz and McKean, *Friends in High Places,* 91; Isaacson and Thomas, *The Wise Men,* 397.

46. Spingarn Oral History, March 20, 1967, HSTL.

47. Clifford with Holbrooke, *Counsel,* 257.

48. News clipping, *St. Louis Globe-Democrat,* October 6, 1949, Clifford Papers, Box 1, Manuscript Division, Library of Congress.

49. Clifford with Holbrooke, *Counsel,* 259; Frantz and McKean, *Friends in High Places,* 100.

50. Clifford with Holbrooke, *Counsel,* 259.

51. Frantz and McKean, *Friends in High Places,* 102; Clifford with Holbrooke, *Counsel,* 260–61.

52. Clifford with Holbrooke, *Counsel,* 261.

53. *The New Republic* quoted in Anderson, *The President's Men,* 128.

54. Underhill, *The Truman Persuasions,* 185.

55. Goldman, *The Crucial Decade,* 131–32.

56. Anderson, *The President's Men,* 113.

## 7. WASHINGTON LAWYER

1. Clifford with Holbrooke, *Counsel,* 262.

2. Frantz and McKean, *Friends in High Places,* 101.

3. Tyler Abell, ed., *Drew Pearson Diaries: 1949–1959* (New York: Holt, Rinehart and Winston, 1974), 25.

4. News clipping, *The Commercial and Financial Chronicle,* date unknown, 11, 33–34, Clifford Papers, Box 64, Manuscript Division, Library of Congress.

5. Davidson to the Fiduciary Counsel's Forum, January 24, 1950, Clifford Papers, Box 65, Manuscript Division, Library of Congress.

6. Undated, handwritten note by George Elsey, Elsey Papers, Box 56, HSTL.

7. Clark Clifford, "Business and Government: Greater Teamwork to Expand U.S. Economy," *Vital Speeches of the Day* 16, no. 14 (May 1950): 426–30; "Plea to Business Made," *New York Times,* March 25, 1950, p. 7.

8. Clifford to Truman, March 27, 1950, Clifford Papers, Box 43, HSTL.

9. Notes for Speech by Clark M. Clifford at Meeting of the 50 Club of Cleveland, June 17, 1952, Clifford Papers, Box 65, Manuscript Division, Library of Congress.

10. Welsh and Horowitz, "Clark Clifford, Attorney at War," 47.

11. Clifford, "Business and Government," 426–30.

12. Clifford to Spivak, December 31, 1949; Telegram, Lonny Stagg to Clifford, February 4, 1950 (there was no punctuation in the telegram); John G. Scott to Clifford, February 6, 1950; Spivak to Clifford, February 6, 1950, Clifford Papers, Box 65, Manuscript Division, Library of Congress.

13. Elsey to Clifford, February 14, 1950, Elsey Papers, Box 56, HSTL.

14. Clinton Davidson Jr. to Clifford, February 7, 1950; Walter Lantz to Clifford, March 2, 1950, Clifford Papers, Box 65, Manuscript Division, Library of Congress.

15. Frantz and McKean, *Friends in High Places,* 104.

16. "Hughes Hires Clifford," *New York Times,* March 18, 1950, 10.

17. Clifford with Holbrooke, *Counsel,* 263–66; Frantz and McKean, *Friends in High Places,* 107–10.

18. Clifford with Holbrooke, *Counsel,* 264.

19. Clark Clifford, interview on *Meet the Press,* February 4, 1950, Recorded Sound Division, Library of Congress.

20. Frantz and McKean, *Friends in High Places,* 106.

21. Welsh and Horowitz, "Clark Clifford: Attorney at War," 48.

22. Clifford to Truman, August 25, 1950, Harry S. Truman Papers, President's Secretary's File, Box 117, HSTL; Clifford with Holbrooke, *Counsel,* 271–72. Clifford's memoirs are inconsistent with respect to the date of his meeting with Truman. On page 271 he says the meeting was on August 25, but on page 28 he indicates that it was August 24. Both of these dates appear to be incorrect. His thank-you note is dated August 25, a Friday, and refers to their meeting on Tuesday. Therefore, it is most likely that the meeting was on August 22.

23. Clifford to Truman, August 25, 1950, Harry S. Truman Papers, President's Secretary's File, Box 117, HSTL; Clifford with Holbrooke, *Counsel*, 271.

24. Clifford with Holbrooke, *Counsel*, 256–57, 280.

25. Clifford Oral History, February 14, 1973, HSTL.

26. Elsey handwritten notes, March 11, 1950, Elsey Papers, Box 56, HSTL.

27. Hamby, *Man of the People*, 502–6.

28. Elsey letter to the author, August 21, 2002.

29. Clifford to Truman, June 29, 1950, Clifford Papers, Box 43, HSTL.

30. Truman to Clifford, June 30, 1950, ibid.

31. Truman to Clifford, October 19, 1950, ibid.

32. Murphy to Clifford, January 5, 1951, Clifford Papers, Box 1, Manuscript Division, Library of Congress.

33. Donald McCoy, *The Presidency of Harry S. Truman* (Lawrence: University Press of Kansas, 1984), 291.

34. Clifford Oral History, February 14, 1973, HSTL.

35. Hamby, *Man of the People*, 596.

36. Ibid., 600.

37. Clifford with Holbrooke, *Counsel*, 283.

38. Ibid., 283.

39. Clifford to Truman, March 31, 1952, Truman Papers, President's Secretary's Files, Box 117, HSTL.

40. Frantz and McKean, *Friends in High Places*, 111–12.

41. Clifford with Holbrooke, *Counsel*, 276–78.

42. Hamby, *Man of the People*, 506–7.

43. Oscar Chapman Oral History, February 9, 1973, HSTL.

44. Clifford quoted in Frantz and McKean, *Friends in High Places*, 113.

45. Clifford to Kerr, January 4, 1952, Clifford Papers, Box 23, HSTL.

46. Malvina Stephenson, Press Secretary to Senator Kerr, notes from interview with Clifford, undated, Malvina Stephenson Papers, Box 6, Carl Albert Center, University of Oklahoma.

47. Frantz and McKean, *Friends in High Places*, 131; Malvina Stephenson, notes from interview with Clifford.

48. Kenneth Hechler Oral History, November 29, 1985, HSTL.

49. Clifford to Truman, March 15, 1952, Truman Papers, President's Secretary's Files, Box 117, HSTL. According to Frantz and McKean, *Friends in High Places*, 131, Clifford set up Kefauver as a "bogeyman."

50. Drew Pearson, "Cruel Blows Hit Veep, Harriman," *Washington Post*, July 25, 1952, Clifford Papers, Box 82, Manuscript Division, Library of Congress.

51. Frantz and McKean, *Friends in High Places*, 144.

52. Clifford quoted in Welsh and Horowitz, "Clark Clifford: Attorney at War," 48.

53. Frantz and McKean, *Friends in High Places*, 165.

54. Clifford Papers, Box 23, HSTL.

55. Ewing Oral History, May 2, 1969, HSTL.

56. Clifford to Ewing, July 29, 1952, Ewing Papers, Box 13, HSTL.

57. Elsey, Memorandum Concerning Mr. Clark Clifford's Wisconsin Speech, October 25, 1951, Elsey Papers, Box 56, HSTL.

58. Van Devander to Elsey, October 18, 1951, ibid.

59. Elsey, handwritten draft of speech, undated, ibid.

60. Truman to Clifford, October 21, 1951, Clifford Papers, Box 43, HSTL.

61. Elsey to Clifford, June 7, 1951, Elsey Papers, Box 56, HSTL.

62. Clifford with Holbrooke, *Counsel,* 291.

63. Harper, *The Politics of Loyalty,* 135–36.

64. Murphy to Clifford, August 3, 1950, Clifford Papers, Box 1, Manuscript Division, Library of Congress.

65. Hamby, *Man of the People,* 548–49; Spingarn to Clifford, April 19, 1949, Clifford Papers, Box 15, HSTL. The comparison was suggested by Stephen Spingarn a year earlier.

66. Thompson, *The Frustration of Politics,* 167.

67. Quoted in Harper, *The Politics of Loyalty,* 174.

68. McCullough, *Truman,* 861; John Hersey, *Aspects of the Presidency* (New York: Ticknor and Fields, 1980), 136–38.

69. Coffin, "Harry Truman's Bright Young Man," 14.

70. Elsey, handwritten draft of speech, undated, Elsey Papers, Box 56, HSTL.

71. Clifford with Holbrooke, *Counsel,* 292–94.

72. Ibid., 294.

73. Richard J. H. Johnson, "McCarthy Accuses Symington of 'Plot,'" *New York Times,* June 6, 1954, pp. 1, 13.

74. Clifford with Holbrooke, *Counsel,* 293.

75. Quoted in ibid., 298.

76. Clifford, text of undelivered statement, Clifford Papers, Box 1, HSTL.

77. Clifford with Holbrooke, *Counsel,* 299.

78. "Text of Stevens' Letter on Contact with Clifford," *New York Times,* June 18, 1954, p. 10.

79. Walter Trohan, "GOP Seeks Public Airing on Teapot Dome Reserves," news clipping, newspaper unknown, May 8, 1952, Clifford Papers, Box 82, Manuscript Division, Library of Congress.

80. Drew Pearson, "Unique Lobby Aids Railroads," *Washington Post,* May 14, 1952, ibid.

81. Drew Pearson, "Morison's Antitrust Role Recalled," *Washington Post,* June 19, 1952, ibid.

82. Luther A. Huston, "Fraud, Overpaying on War Contracts Put at $500,000,000," *New York Times,* June 7, 1952; Edward F. Ryan, "Clark Clifford Shared Law Firm's $25,000 Fee on Compromise Settlement of 'Fraud Case,'" *Washington Post,* June 7, 1952, Clifford Papers, Box 82, Manuscript Division, Library of Congress.

83. Huston, "Fraud, Overpaying"; Ryan, "Clark Clifford Shared Law Firm's $25,000 Fee."

84. Ryan, "Clark Clifford Shared Law Firm's $25,000 Fee."

85. Frantz and McKean, *Friends in High Places,* 12.

86. Clifford to Truman, June 9, 1952, Clifford Papers, Box 43, HSTL.

87. Truman to Clifford, June 10, 1952, ibid.

88. Elsey to Clifford, March 18, 1952, Elsey Papers, Box 56, HSTL.

89. W. John Kenny to Clifford, April 21, 1952, ibid.

90. Elsey notes, August 6, 1968, Elsey Papers, Box 1, Lyndon B. Johnson Library, Austin, Texas (hereinafter LBJL).

91. Memorandum for Connelly, December 15, 1952, Truman Papers, President's Personal File, Box 584, HSTL.

92. George Elsey, interview by author, Washington, D.C., June 14, 2001.

93. Frantz and McKean, *Friends in High Places,* 117.

94. Clifford with Holbrooke, *Counsel,* 278–79; Frantz and McKean, *Friends in High Places,* 142–43.

95. Truman Papers, President's Personal File, Box 584, HSTL.

96. Clifford to Kerr, December 29, 1952, Kerr Papers, Box 11, Carl Albert Center, University of Oklahoma.

97. Clifford to Kerr, September 28, 1953, ibid.

98. "Kerr-McGee Oil Pulls $15 Million Boner on Off-Shore Oil Tract," *Wall Street Journal,* October 18, 1954, 20.

99. Quoted in Frantz and McKean, *Friends in High Places,* 105.

100. Clifford with Holbrooke, *Counsel,* 269.

101. Frantz and McKean, *Friends in High Places,* 105.

102. Clifford's special counsel salary was raised to $20,000 in the fall of 1949.

103. David Lilienthal, *The Journals of David Lilienthal,* vol. 3, *The Venturesome Years, 1950–1955* (New York: Harper & Row, 1966), 136.

104. Clifford to Kennedy, November 12, 1952, Clifford Papers, Box 30, Manuscript Division, Library of Congress.

105. Clifford to Johnson, Symington, and Clements, February 19, 1954, Clifford Papers, Box 29, Manuscript Division, Library of Congress.

106. Clifford to Johnson, September 20 and 28, 1957, ibid.

107. Johnson to Clifford, November 8, 1958, ibid.

108. Drew Pearson and Jack Anderson, *The Case against Congress* (New York: Simon & Schuster, 1968), 305; Joseph C. Goulden, *The Superlawyers: The Small and Powerful World of the Great Washington Law Firms* (New York: Dell Publishing Co., 1972), 91.

109. Lilienthal, *Journals,* vol. 3, 136–37.

110. Ibid.

111. Welsh and Horowitz, "Clark Clifford: Attorney at War," 48.

112. Ibid.; Frantz and McKean, *Friends in High Places,* 181–82; "C. Clifford Is Retained by GE to Give Counsel on Antitrust Claims," *Wall Street Journal,* April 6, 1961, p. 27.

113. Quoted in Pearson and Anderson, *The Case against Congress,* 304.

114. Jack Anderson, "It Pays to Hire the Right Lawyer," *Washington Post,* February 16, 1963, Sec. D, p. 23.

115. Telephone message from Clifford, February 17, 1963, President's Office File, Box 29, John F. Kennedy Library, Boston, Massachusetts (hereafter JFKL). The probable expletive was redacted from the text of the message.

116. Clark Clifford, "Government and Business Today: Does the Reality Conform to the Myth?" President's Office Files, Box 29, JFKL.

117. Welsh and Horowitz, "Clark Clifford: Attorney at War," 45, 48; Frantz and McKean, *Friends in High Places,* 170.

118. Clifford to Kennedy, February 5, 1962, Clifford Papers, Box 2, Manuscript Division, Library of Congress.

119. Robert S. Allen and William V. Shannon, *The Truman Merry-Go-Round* (New York: Vanguard Press, 1950), 322–23.

120. Clifford with Holbrooke, *Counsel,* 652–53.

121. Ibid., 653.

122. Frantz and McKean, *Friends in High Places,* 12.

123. Medved, *Shadow Presidents,* 233.

## 8. Kennedy's Consigliere

1. C. David Heymann, *A Woman Named Jackie* (New York: Penguin Books, 1989), 175.

2. Abell, ed., *Drew Pearson Diaries,* 407.

3. Frantz and McKean, *Friends in High Places,* 149.

4. Clifford Oral History, p. 6, JFKL.

5. Text of ABC retraction statement, December 12, 1957, Clifford Papers, Box 2, JFKL.

6. Clifford handwritten notes, undated, Clifford Papers, Box 2, JKFL.

7. Hon. James M. Landis to Kennedy, December 18, 1957, Clifford Papers, Microfilm Roll 1, JFKL.

8. Abell, ed., *Drew Pearson Diaries,* 420.

9. News clipping, Drew Pearson column, February 16, 1958, Clifford Papers, Microfilm Roll 1, JFKL.

10. Clifford to Goldenson, February 18, 1958, ibid.

11. Clifford to Kennedy, February 19, 1958, ibid.

12. The watch was stolen four years later, and Clifford wrote to Cartier to ask for the serial number, hoping this would aid the police in finding it. Mary Weiler to Cartier, Inc., November 23, 1964, ibid.

13. Mike Wallace and Gary Paul Gates, *Close Encounters* (New York: William Morrow and Co., 1984), 67–68.

14. Kennedy to Clifford, April 7, 1959, Clifford Papers, Microfilm Roll 1, JFKL.

15. Clifford to Kennedy, April 10, 1959, ibid.

16. Robert Dallek, *An Unfinished Life: John F. Kennedy, 1917–1963* (New York: Little, Brown and Co., 2003), 199.

17. John Hellmann, *The Kennedy Obsession: The American Myth of JFK* (New York: Columbia University Press, 1997), 76.

18. Clifford with Holbrooke, *Counsel,* 310–11; Kennedy to Clifford, February 15, 1958, Clifford Papers, Box 30, Manuscript Division, Library of Congress; Kennedy to Clifford, January 12, 1956, Clifford Papers, Microfilm Roll 1, JFKL; Clifford to Kennedy, March 6, 1958, Clifford Papers, Microfilm Roll 1, JFKL.

19. Theodore White, *The Making of the President, 1960* (New York: Atheneum Publishers, 1961), 37.

20. James Reston, "Gov. Brown and 1960," *New York Times,* August 17, 1959, sec. 1, p. 15.

21. Ibid.

22. "Random Notes in Washington: The Senator Yields to Courtesy," *New York Times,* February 1, 1960, sec. 1, p. 21.

23. James Reston, "Democrats: Old-Timers vs. New-Timers," *New York Times,* April 15, 1960, sec. 1, p. 22.

24. David Halberstam, *The Unfinished Odyssey of Robert Kennedy* (New York: Random House, 1968), 76.

25. Clifford Oral History, p. 9, JFKL.

26. Frantz and McKean, *Friends in High Places,* 154; Clifford Oral History, p. 7, JFKL.

27. White, *Making of the President,* 39–42, 56.

28. Clifford handwritten notes, July 1, 1960, Clifford Papers, Microfilm Roll 1, JFKL; Clifford with Holbrooke, *Counsel,* 312–14; Frantz and McKean, *Friends in High Places,* 152–56.

29. Clifford Oral History, p. 8, JFKL.

30. Leo Egan, "Symington Heavy Favorite for Second Place on Ticket," *New York Times,* July 14, 1960, sec. 1, p. 1.

31. Arthur M. Schlesinger Jr., *A Thousand Days: John F. Kennedy in the White House* (Boston: Houghton Mifflin Co., 1965), 120–22.

32. Theodore C. Sorensen, *Kennedy* (New York: Harper & Row, 1965), 229; Kennedy quoted in Schlesinger, *A Thousand Days,* 123.

33. Clifford to Kennedy, July 19, 1960, Clifford Papers, Microfilm Roll 1, JFKL.

34. W. H. Lawrence, "Kennedy Calls on Truman," *New York Times,* August 21, 1960, sec. 1, p. 1.

35. Kennedy to Clifford, July 29, 1960, Clifford Papers, Microfilm Roll 1, JFKL.

36. According to Clifford the group met three times a week, but Fulbright recalled that the group met once or twice a week. Clifford with Holbrooke, *Counsel,* 324; Fulbright Oral History, p. 6, JFKL.

37. Gore Oral History, pp. 7–8, and Fulbright Oral History, p. 6, JFKL.

38. Khrushchev Visit Paper, undated, Clifford Papers, Microfilm Roll 1, JFKL.

39. Fulbright to Clifford, September 22, 1960, Clifford Papers, Microfilm Roll 1, JFKL.

40. Dutton to Clifford, September 23, 1960, ibid.

41. Clifford to Mike Feldman, October 12, 1960, ibid.

42. Clifford to Kennedy, September 27, 1960, ibid.

43. Dutton to Gore and Clifford, October 4, 1960, and Clifford to Dutton, undated, ibid.; "Transcript of the Second Nixon-Kennedy Debate on Nation-Wide TV," *New York Times,* October 8, 1960, sec. 1, p. 10.

44. Clifford to O'Brien, October 11, 1960, Clifford Papers, Microfilm Roll 1, JFKL.

45. Pete Kihss, "Kennedy Charges Nixon Risks War," *New York Times,* October 13, 1960, sec. 1, p. 1.

46. Discussion Points RE TV Debate Friday, October 21, 1960, and Clifford handwritten notes, undated, Clifford Papers, Microfilm Roll 1, JFKL.

47. Clifford with Holbrooke, *Counsel,* 326.

48. Clifford to Kennedy, November 9, 1960, Clifford Papers, Box 1, JFKL.

49. W. H. Lawrence, "Kennedy to Limit Assistant's Role at White House," *New York Times,* November 22, 1960, sec. 1, p. 1.

50. Clifford to Kennedy, November 9, 1960, Clifford Papers, Box 1, JFKL.

51. Ibid.

52. Ibid.

53. Schlesinger, *A Thousand Days,* 124.

54. Quoted in Dallek, *An Unfinished Life,* 306–7.

55. Kennedy staffer quoted in Sorensen, *Kennedy,* 230.

56. Clifford with Holbrooke, *Counsel*, 330; Clifford Oral History, p. 26, JFKL; Jack Raymond, "Unification Plan to Go to Kennedy," *New York Times*, November 13, 1960, sec. 1, p. 1; W. H. Lawrence, "Symington Panel Urges Revamping of the Pentagon," *New York Times*, December 6, 1960, sec. 1, p. 1.

57. Pearson and Anderson, *The Case against Congress*, 299.

58. "Back to the White House," *New York Times*, November 11, 1960, sec. 1, p. 20; James Reston, "President-Elect Kennedy and Stengel's Law," *New York Times*, November 11, 1960, sec. 1, p. 30.

59. Tom Wicker, "Transition Is Discussed by Clifford and Persons," *New York Times*, November 15, 1960, sec. 1, p. 1.

60. Peter Braestrup, "Transition Pace Gains in Capital," *New York Times*, November 19, 1960, sec. 1, p. 1.

61. Clifford Oral History, p. 28, JFKL; W. H. Lawrence, "Louisiana Group Demands Kennedy Give Rights View," *New York Times*, November 21, 1960, sec. 1, p. 1.

62. Quoted in Herbert S. Parmet, *The Presidency of John F. Kennedy* (Norwalk, Conn.: Easton Press, 1983), 65.

63. Clifford Oral History, p. 14, JFKL.

64. Clifford with Holbrooke, *Counsel*, 336–37.

65. Schlesinger, *A Thousand Days*, 129.

66. Isaacson and Thomas, *The Wise Men*, 592–93.

67. Clifford to Kennedy, December 22, 1960, President's Office Files, Box 29, JFKL.

68. Hugh Sidey, *John F. Kennedy, President* (New York: Atheneum, 1964), 17.

69. Felix Belair Jr., "Meeting Cordial," *New York Times*, December 7, 1960, sec. 1, p. 1.

70. Memorandum on Conference between President Eisenhower and President-Elect Kennedy, January 24, 1961, President's Office Files, Box 29a, JFKL.

71. Clifford with Holbrooke, *Counsel*, 347–48.

72. Clifford, Memorandum of Conversation with President Kennedy, January 24, 1961, Clifford Papers, Microfilm Roll 1, JFKL.

73. Clifford with Holbrooke, *Counsel*, 348.

74. Ibid., 337.

75. Clifford Oral History, p. 19, JFKL.

76. Clifford to Kennedy, July 24, 1961, Clifford Papers, Box 2, Manuscript Division, Library of Congress.

77. Clifford to Kennedy, July 26, 1961, ibid.

78. Clifford to Kennedy, April 3, 1962, Clifford Papers, Microfilm Roll 1, JFKL.

79. Clifford Oral History, p. 47, JFKL.

80. Clifford handwritten notes, March 20, 1962, Clifford Papers, Microfilm Roll 1, JFKL.

81. Ibid.; Dallek, *An Unfinished Life*, 494.

82. Short list for Supreme Court vacancy, March 21, 1962, President's Office File, Box 88A, JFKL.

83. Clifford Oral History, p. 48, JFKL.

84. Clifford to Kennedy, April 3, 1962, Clifford Papers, Microfilm Roll 1, JFKL.

85. Dallek, *An Unfinished Life*, 482–84.

86. Wallace Carroll, "Steel: A 72-Hour Drama with an All Star Cast," *New York Times,* April 23, 1962, sec. 1, p. 1.

87. "Transcript of Kennedy's News Conference on Domestic and Foreign Affairs," *New York Times,* April 12, 1962, sec. 1, p. 1.

88. Clifford with Holbrooke, *Counsel,* 376.

89. Goldberg Oral History, p. 189, JFKL.

90. Clifford with Holbrooke, *Counsel,* 377–78; Arthur Goldberg Oral History, p. 189, JFKL.

91. Clifford quoted in Richard Reeves, *President Kennedy: Profile of Power* (New York: Simon & Schuster, 1993), 301.

92. Robert F. Kennedy Oral History, p. 201, JFKL.

93. Anderson, "The New Defense Secretary Thinks Like the President," 70.

94. Wallace Carroll, "Steel: A 72-Hour Drama with an All Star Cast," *New York Times,* April 23, 1962, sec. 1, p. 1.

95. Clifford handwritten notes, undated, President's Office Files, Box 106, JFKL; *New York Times,* April 11, 1963, sec. 1, p. 1.

96. Clifford Oral History, pp. 39–40, JFKL. Graham committed suicide in August 1963.

97. Presidential Recordings, 10A.6, March 6, 1963, JFKL.

98. Kennedy quoted in Michael R. Beschloss, *The Crisis Years: Kennedy and Khrushchev, 1960–1963* (New York: HarperCollins, 1991), 143.

99. President's Foreign Intelligence Advisory Board—Memorandum of Conclusions and Recommendations Approved by the Board at its Meeting of July 18, 1961, President's Office File, Box 94, JFKL.

100. "Cloudy Intelligence," *New York Times,* April 29, 1963, sec. 1, p. 29.

101. J. R. Killian Jr., "Clark Clifford Endorsed," *New York Times,* May 12, 1963, sec. E, p. 10.

102. Bundy to Kennedy, March 25, 1963, President's Office File, Box 29, JFKL; Clifford Papers, Microfilm Roll 1, JFKL.

103. Clifford Oral History, p. 33, JFKL.

104. Ibid., pp. 41, 52; Clifford notes, July 25, 1963, Clifford Papers, Microfilm Roll 1, JFKL.

105. Robert F. Kennedy Oral History, p. 270, JFKL; Edwin O. Guthman and Jeffrey Shulman, eds., *Robert Kennedy: In His Own Words* (New York: Bantam Books, 1988), 372; "Korth Declares His Resignation Was Not Forced," *New York Times,* October 20, 1963, sec. 1, p. 1.

106. "Kennedy Rumor Held Unfounded," *New York Times,* September 18, 1962, sec. 1, p. 21; Clifford Oral History, pp. 45–46, JFKL.

107. Clifford with Holbrooke, *Counsel,* 362.

108. Clifford handwritten notes, Clifford papers, Microfilm Roll 2, JFKL.

109. Hand-drawn thank-you note from Jacqueline Kennedy, ibid. Newsclipping, *Washington Star,* November 5, 1962, Clifford Papers, Microfilm Roll 2, JFKL.

110. McIlwain to File, March 11, 1963, Clifford Papers, Microfilm Roll 2, JFKL.

111. Heymann, *A Woman Named Jackie,* 331–32.

112. Schlesinger, *A Thousand Days,* 670.

113. Heymann, *A Woman Named Jackie,* 332–33; Jacqueline Kennedy, handwritten note to Clifford, undated, Clifford Papers, Microfilm Roll 2, JFKL.

114. Heymann, *A Woman Named Jackie,* 333–34.
115. Clifford to John F. Kennedy, August 14, 1963, Clifford Papers, Microfilm Roll 1, JFKL.
116. Bradlee to Clifford, December 7, 1963, ibid.
117. Clifford to Lincoln, April 29, 1964, ibid.

## 9. This Could Be a Quagmire

1. Clark Clifford Oral History, March 17, 1969, LBJL; Clifford with Holbrooke, *Counsel,* 387.
2. Medved, *Shadow Presidents,* 231; Frantz and McKean, *Friends in High Places,* 204.
3. Clark Clifford Oral History, July 2, 1969, LBJL.
4. Ibid.; Michael Bechloss, ed., *Reaching for Glory: Lyndon Johnson's Secret White House Tapes, 1964–1965* (New York: Simon & Schuster, 2001), 74–75. Clifford's reference to "their hands" is to the Republicans.
5. Clifford to Johnson, May 17, 1965, Lyndon Johnson Presidential Papers, National Security File, Vietnam Country File, Box 74, LBJL.
6. Clifford handwritten notes, July 21, 1965, Clifford Papers, Box 1, LBJL.
7. Notes of Meeting, July 22, 1965, *FRUS, 1965,* vol. 3.
8. George Ball Oral History, July 9, 1971, LBJL; George W. Ball, *The Past Has Another Pattern* (New York: Norton, 1982), 402–3.
9. Clifford with Holbrooke, *Counsel,* 415–16; Ball, *The Past,* 402–3.
10. Clifford handwritten notes, July 23, 1965, Clifford Papers, Box 1, LBJL.
11. Ibid.
12. Notes of meeting, July 25, 1965, *FRUS, 1965,* vol. 3. Clifford's oral history, from July 1969, makes no mention of the Camp David meeting; instead, he claims that he played no part in the Vietnam decision of 1965. Clifford Oral History, July 2, 1969, LBJL. His 1969 and 1970 articles in *Foreign Affairs* and *Life* also omit any mention of the Vietnam meetings. It is possible that he did not disclose his early opposition to the war out of deference to Johnson.
13. Notes of meeting, July 26, 1965, *FRUS, 1965,* vol. 3, document 87; George Ball Oral History, July 9, 1971, LBJL.
14. Clifford with Holbrooke, *Counsel,* 421; George Ball Oral History, July 9, 1971, LBJL.
15. Ball handwritten note to Clifford, July 26, 1965, Clifford Papers, Box 1, LBJL.
16. Clifford with Holbrooke, *Counsel,* 422, 425–26.
17. Clifford to Johnson, November 1, 1965, Clifford Papers, Box 5, Manuscript Division, Library of Congress.
18. "Report Discounted on Saigon Dismay," *New York Times,* November 5, 1965, p. 6.
19. Lloyd C. Gardner, *Pay Any Price: Lyndon Johnson and the Wars for Vietnam* (Chicago: Ivan R. Dee, 1995), 269–71.
20. Personal Notes of Meeting, December 6, 1965, *FRUS, 1965,* vol. 3.
21. Clifford quoted in Jack Valenti, *A Very Human President* (New York: W. W. Norton, 1975), 236–37.
22. Clifford handwritten notes, December 18, 1965, Clifford Papers, Box 1, LBJL.

23. Bundy to Johnson, January 26, 1966, *FRUS, 1966,* vol. 4 (Pittsburgh, Pa.: U.S. Government Printing Office, 1998).

24. Notes of Meeting, January 28, 1966, ibid.; Clifford handwritten notes, January 28, 1966, Clifford Papers, Box 1, LBJL.

25. Clifford with Holbrooke, *Counsel,* 437.

26. Max Frankel, "President Visits G.I.'s in Vietnam in Surprise Trip," *New York Times,* October 27, 1966, p. 1.

27. Clifford with Holbrooke, *Counsel,* 438–40; Clifford Oral History, August 7, 1969, LBJL.

28. Clifford and Johnson handwritten notes, November 16, 1966, Clifford Papers, Box 1, LBJL.

29. Tom Wicker, "Westmoreland Tells Congress U.S. Will Prevail," *New York Times,* April 29, 1967, p. 1.

30. Neil Sheehan, "Military Frustration," *New York Times,* July 4, 1967, p. 3; R. W. Apple Jr., "Westmoreland Asks M'Namara for More Troops," *New York Times,* July 8, 1967, p. 1.

31. Notes of Meeting, July 12, 1967, *FRUS, 1967,* vol. 5 (Pittsburgh, Pa.: U.S. Government Printing Office, 2002).

32. Ibid.

33. Clifford Oral History, July 14, 1969, LBJL.

34. Notes of Meeting, August 5, 1967, *FRUS, 1967,* vol. 5.

35. Ibid.

36. Ibid.

37. Johnson quoted in Gardner, *Pay Any Price,* 389.

38. Notes of Meeting, October 18, 1967, *FRUS, 1967,* vol. 5.

39. Memorandum of Conversation between the Ambassador at Large (Harriman) and Secretary of Defense McNamara, September 19, 1967, *FRUS, 1967,* vol. 5.

40. Robert S. McNamara with Brian VanDeMark, *In Retrospect: The Tragedy and Lessons of Vietnam* (New York: Times Books, 1995), 311, 313.

41. Larry Berman, *Lyndon Johnson's War: The Road to Stalemate in Vietnam* (New York: Norton, 1989), 96.

42. Memorandum from the President's Assistant (Jones) to President Johnson, November 2, 1967, *FRUS, 1967,* vol. 5.

43. Ibid.

44. Ibid.

45. Clifford with Holbrooke, *Counsel,* 458.

46. Clifford to Johnson, November 7, 1967, *FRUS, 1967,* vol. 5.

47. Ibid.

48. Clifford with Holbrooke, *Counsel,* 462.

49. Max Frankel, "Johnson Names Clark Clifford to Head Defense," *New York Times,* January 20, 1968, p. 1.

50. Anderson, "The New Defense Secretary Thinks Like the President," 20. The article repeats verbatim the phrase "the game is not worth the candle" from the November 7, 1967, memorandum from Clifford to Johnson, suggesting that Clifford leaked it to Anderson.

51. "Pentagon: Clifford for McNamara," *New York Times,* January 21, 1968, p. E2.

52. Max Frankel, "Johnson Names Clark Clifford to Head Defense," *New York Times,* January 20, 1968, p. 1.

53. Clifford with Holbrooke, *Counsel,* 465.

54. Frankel, "Johnson Names Clark Clifford to Head Defense," p. 1.

55. Lyndon Johnson, *The Vantage Point: Perspectives of the Presidency, 1963–1969* (New York: Holt, Rinehart and Winston, 1971), 532. The negotiations for the crew's release lasted into December, although Clifford was not directly involved.

56. Editorial Note, January 25, 1968, *FRUS, January–August 1968,* vol. 6 (Pittsburgh, Pa.: U.S. Government Printing Office, 2002).

57. Clifford Oral History, July 14, 1969, LBJL.

58. Clifford with Holbrooke, *Counsel,* 471.

59. Notes of Meeting, January 30, 1968, *FRUS, January–August 1968,* vol. 6.

60. Editorial note, January 30, 1968, ibid.

61. Clifford with Holbrooke, *Counsel,* 475.

62. Clifford Oral History, July 14, 1969, LBJL.

63. Clifford's mention of Korea was a reference to the *Pueblo* incident.

64. Notes of Meeting, February 6, 1968, *FRUS, January–August 1968,* vol. 6.

65. Johnson to Clifford, February 8, 1968, Clifford Papers, Box 1, LBJL.

66. Notes of Meeting, February 9, 1968, *FRUS, January–August 1968,* vol. 6.

67. Ibid.

68. Notes of the President's Meeting with Senior Foreign Policy Advisers, February 9, 1968, ibid.

69. Notes of the President's Meeting with the Senior Foreign Affairs Advisory Council, February 10, 1968, ibid.

70. Notes of the President's Meeting with Senior Foreign Policy Advisors, February 12, 1968, ibid.

71. Clifford with Holbrooke, *Counsel,* 478.

72. Notes of the President's Meeting with Senior Foreign Policy Advisors, February 12, 1968, *FRUS, January–August 1968,* vol. 6.

73. Hoopes to Clifford, February 13, 1968, Clifford Papers, Box 1, LBJL.

74. Ibid.

75. Notes of the President's Luncheon Meeting, February 13, 1968, *FRUS, January–August 1968,* vol. 6.

76. Wheeler to Johnson, February 27, 1968, *FRUS, January–August 1968,* vol. 6.

77. Notes of Meeting, February 27, 1968, ibid.; Clifford with Holbrooke, *Counsel,* 485.

78. Notes of Meeting, February 27, 1968, *FRUS, January–August 1968,* vol. 6.

79. Notes of the President's meeting to discuss General Wheeler's trip to Vietnam, February 28, 1968, *FRUS, January–August 1968,* vol. 6.; Gardner, *Pay Any Price,* 437.

80. Clark Clifford, "A Viet Nam Reappraisal: The Personal History of One Man's View and How it Evolved, *Foreign Affairs* 47, no. 4 (July 1969): 610; Harry McPherson Oral History, March 24, 1969, LBJL. Notes of the meetings of the Clifford task force have not been found.

81. Clifford Oral History, July 2, 1969, LBJL.

82. Herbert Y. Schandler, *The Unmaking of a President: Lyndon Johnson and Vietnam* (Princeton: Princeton University Press, 1977), 143.

83. Clifford with Holbrooke, *Counsel,* 494–95.

84. Draft Memorandum for the President, March 4, 1968, Clifford Papers, Box 2, LBJL.

85. Ibid.

86. Notes of Meeting, March 4, 1968, *FRUS, January–August 1968,* vol. 6.

87. Ibid.

88. Ibid.

89. Ibid.

90. Ibid.

91. Clifford with Holbrooke, *Counsel,* 496.

92. Notes of Meeting, March 4, 1968, *FRUS, January–August 1968,* vol. 6.

93. Notes of Meeting, March 5, 1968, ibid.

94. Editorial Note and Telegram, Wheeler to Westmoreland, March 8, 1968, *FRUS, January–August 1968,* vol. 6; Isaacson and Thomas, *The Wise Men,* 690.

95. Telegram, Wheeler to Westmoreland, March 8, 1968, *FRUS, January–August 1968,* vol. 6. Wheeler was mistaken that Clifford was an adviser to four presidents. The correct number was three: Truman, Kennedy, and Johnson.

96. Hedrick Smith and Neil Sheehan, "Westmoreland Requests 206,000 More Men," *New York Times,* March 10, 1968, p. 1. The *Times* figure was slightly higher than the actual request of 205,179.

97. Clifford Oral History, July 14, 1969, LBJL.

98. Clifford handwritten notes, March 14, 1968, Clifford Papers, Box 1, LBJL.

99. Nitze to Johnson, March 16, 1968, Clifford Papers, Box 1, LBJL; Isaacson and Thomas, *The Wise Men,* 691.

100. Hoopes to Clifford, March 14, 1968, Clifford Papers, Box 1, LBJL; Brzezinski to Clifford, March 14, 1968, Clifford Papers, Box 1, LBJL.

101. McPherson Oral History, March 24, 1969, LBJL.

102. Isaacson and Thomas, *The Wise Men,* 686–87; Townsend Hoopes, "The Fight for the President's Mind and the Men Who Won It," *Atlantic Monthly,* October 1969, 107.

103. Isaacson and Thomas, *The Wise Men,* 696.

104. Notes of the President's meeting with his foreign advisers at the Tuesday luncheon, March 19, 1968, *FRUS, January–August 1968,* vol. 6; Clifford handwritten notes, March 19, 1968, Clifford Papers, Box 2, LBJL.

105. Telephone conversation between Johnson and Clifford, March 20, 1968, *FRUS, January–August 1968,* vol. 6.

106. Ibid.

107. Clifford with Holbrooke, *Counsel,* 508.

108. Notes of meeting, March 20, 1968, *FRUS, January–August 1968,* vol. 6.

109. Ibid.

110. Ibid.

111. Harry McPherson, *A Political Education* (Boston: Little, Brown and Co., 1972), 431.

112. Robert H. Phelps, "U.S. to Put More Men in Vietnam," *New York Times,* March 17, 1968, p. 1.

113. "Excerpts from Speech by President," *New York Times,* March 19, 1968, p. 35.

114. Ibid.

115. Notes of Meeting, March 22, 1968, *FRUS, January–August 1968,* vol. 6.

116. Isaacson and Thomas, *The Wise Men,* 699.

117. Ibid., 699–700.

118. George Ball Oral History, July 9, 1971.

119. Isaacson and Thomas, *The Wise Men,* 700.

120. Ball, *The Past,* 408.

121. Isaacson and Thomas, *The Wise Men,* 701.

122. Notes of Meeting, March 26, 1968, *FRUS, January–August 1968,* vol. 6; Ball, *The Past,* 408; Isaacson and Thomas, *The Wise Men,* 702.

123. Clifford with Holbrooke, *Counsel,* 518; Ball, *The Past,* 409; Hoopes, "The Fight for the President's Mind," 111. In a notable dissent, historian Robert Dallek concluded that Johnson's anger was feigned and that he was merely posturing as a hawk while quietly pursuing a peace strategy. Robert Dallek, *Flawed Giant: Lyndon Johnson and His Times, 1961–1973* (New York: Oxford University Press, 1998), 511–12.

124. McPherson Oral History, March 24, 1969, LBJL.

125. Hoopes, "The Fight for the President's Mind," 11.

126. McPherson Oral History, March 24, 1969, LBJL.

127. Clifford with Holbrooke, *Counsel,* 521.

128. "Transcript of the President's Address on the Vietnam War and His Political Plans," *New York Times,* April 1, 1968, p. 26.

129. Clifford Oral History, August 7, 1969, LBJL.

130. Clifford with Holbrooke, *Counsel,* 525.

131. Gardner, *Pay Any Price,* 458.

132. "Transcript of the President's Address on the Vietnam War and His Political Plans," *New York Times,* April 1, 1968, p. 26.

133. Hoopes, "The Fight for the President's Mind," 114.

## 10. I Search for Why I Find Myself Constantly Alone

1. Notes of meeting, April 2, 1968, *FRUS, January–August 1968,* vol. 6; Draft of Clifford Statement regarding bombing incident north of DMZ, Clifford Papers, Box 3, LBJL.

2. Editorial Note, April 3, 1968, *FRUS, January–August 1968,* vol. 6.

3. Notes of Meeting, April 3, 1968, ibid.

4. Notes of the President's Meeting with General Westmoreland, April 6, 1968, ibid.

5. Ibid.

6. Notes of Meeting, April 8, 1968, ibid.

7. Notes of the President's Meeting at Camp David, April 9, 1968, ibid.

8. Ibid.

9. William Beecher, "Sets G.I. Ceiling at 549,500," *New York Times,* April 12, 1968, p. 1.

10. Rostow to Johnson, April 13, 1968, *FRUS, January–August 1968,* vol. 6.

11. Neil Sheehan, "Clifford Emerges as the President's Chief Spokesman on Vietnam," *New York Times,* April 28, 1968, p. 3.

12. Clifford quoted in Gardner, *Pay Any Price,* 468.

13. Elsey notes, May 6, 1968, Elsey Papers, Box 1, LBJL.

14. Notes of meeting, May 6, 1968, *FRUS, January–August 1968,* vol. 6.

15. Notes on Tuesday Luncheon, May 6, 1968, ibid.

16. Notes of meeting, May 8, 1968, ibid.

17. Notes on Tuesday Luncheon, May 14, 1968, ibid.

18. Elsey notes, May 18, 1968, Elsey Papers, Box 1, LBJL.

19. Ibid.

20. Ibid.

21. Ibid.

22. Ibid.

23. Notes of Meeting, May 21, 1968, *FRUS, January–August 1968,* vol. 6. Clifford made the same argument about the San Antonio formula in a May 20, 1968, memo to the president.

24. Elsey notes, May 22, 1968, Elsey Papers, Box 1, LBJL.

25. Notes of Meeting, May 21, 1968, *FRUS, January–August 1968,* vol. 6.

26. Ibid.; Elsey notes, May 22, 1968, Elsey Papers, Box 1, LBJL.

27. Notes of Meeting, May 21, 1968, *FRUS, January–August 1968,* vol. 6.

28. Elsey notes, May 22, 1968, Elsey Papers, Box 1, LBJL.

29. Notes of Meeting, May 21, 1968, *FRUS, January–August 1968,* vol. 6; Elsey notes, May 22, 1968, Elsey Papers, Box 1, LBJL.

30. Rostow to Johnson, May 22, 1968, *FRUS, January–August 1968,* vol. 6; Clifford to Rostow, May 24, 1968, Clifford Papers, Box 4, LBJL.

31. Elsey notes, May 29, 1968, Elsey Papers, Box 1, LBJL.

32. Clifford to Wheeler, June 8, 1968, Clifford Papers, Box 5, LBJL; Elsey notes, June 7, 1968, Elsey Papers, Box 1, LBJL.

33. Elsey notes, June 8, 1968, Elsey Papers, Box 1, LBJL.

34. Notes of Meeting, June 9, 1968, *FRUS, January–August 1968,* vol. 6.

35. Memorandum Prepared by Ambassador at Large Harriman—General Review of the Last Six Months, December 14, 1968, ibid.

36. Notes of Meeting, June 9, 1968, ibid; Rostow to Johnson, June 11, 1968, ibid; Elsey notes, June 11, 1968, Elsey Papers, Box 1, LBJL.

37. Elsey notes, June 12, 1968, Elsey Papers, Box 1, LBJL.

38. Neil Sheehan, "Clifford Detects Slight Paris Gains," *New York Times,* June 21, 1968, p. 1.

39. Peter Grose, "Rusk Sees No Gain in the Substance of Vietnam Talks," *New York Times,* June 22, 1968, p. 1.

40. Elsey notes, June 24, 1968, Elsey Papers, Box 1, LBJL.

41. Clifford Oral History, August 7, 1969, LBJL; Elsey notes, June 27, 1968, September 11, 1968, September 12, 1968, September 14, 1968, Elsey Papers, Box 1, LBJL; Clifford with Holbrooke, *Counsel,* 554–59.

42. Clifford to Johnson, July 18, 1968, Clifford Papers, Box 2, LBJL.

43. Elsey notes, July 22, 1968, Elsey Papers, Box 1, LBJL.

44. Ibid.

45. Ibid.; Notes for U.S. briefing on Honolulu meetings and Joint Communiqué, July 19, 1968, *FRUS, January–August 1968,* vol. 6.

46. Elsey notes, July 22, 1968, Elsey Papers, Box 1, LBJL.

47. Taylor to Johnson, July 17, 1968, Elsey Papers, Box 1, LBJL.

48. Elsey notes, July 24, 1968, Elsey Papers, Box 1, LBJL.

49. Ibid.

50. Taylor to Johnson, July 30, 1968, Elsey Papers, Box 1, LBJL.

51. Telegram from the Embassy in France to the Department of State, July 29, 1968, *FRUS, January–August 1968,* vol. 6.

52. Elsey notes, August 1, 1968, Elsey Papers, Box 1, LBJL; Notes of the President's Meeting with Foreign Policy Advisers, July 30, 1968, *FRUS, January–August 1968,* vol. 6.

53. Elsey notes, July 31, 1968, and August 1, 1968, Elsey Papers, Box 1, LBJL.

54. Clifford to Johnson, August 1, 1968, Clifford Papers, Box 3, LBJL; Elsey notes, August 1, 1968, Elsey Papers, Box 1, LBJL.

55. Elsey notes, August 1, 1968, Elsey Papers, Box 1, LBJL.

56. Elsey notes, August 5, 1968, Elsey Papers, Box 1, LBJL.

57. Ibid.

58. Merle Miller, *Lyndon: An Oral Biography* (New York: Putnam Books, 1980), 503.

59. Elsey notes, August 8, 1968, Elsey Papers, Box 1, LBJL.

60. Elsey notes, August 9, 1968, Elsey Papers, Box 1, LBJL.

61. Elsey notes, July 29, 1968, Elsey Papers, Box 1, LBJL.

62. Elsey notes, July 30, 1968, Elsey Papers, Box 1, LBJL.

63. Memorandum Prepared by Ambassador at Large Harriman—General Review of the Last Six Months, December 14, 1968, *FRUS, January–August 1968,* vol. 6.

64. Notes of the President's Luncheon Meeting, July 24, 1968, ibid.

65. Elsey notes, August 12, 1968, Elsey Papers, Box 1, LBJL.

66. Ibid.

67. Elsey notes, August 13, 1968, Elsey Papers, Box 1, LBJL.

68. "Democrats on Vietnam," *New York Times,* August 19, 1968, p. 36.

69. Elsey notes, August 19, 1968, Elsey Papers, Box 1, LBJL.

70. Rostow to Clifford, August 19, 1968, *FRUS, January–August 1968,* vol. 6.

71. Elsey notes, August 21, 1968, Elsey Papers, Box 1, LBJL.

72. Elsey notes, August 23, 1968, Elsey Papers, Box 1, LBJL; Clifford with Holbrooke, *Counsel,* 564.

73. Elsey notes, August 30, 1968, Elsey Papers, Box 1, LBJL.

74. Abrams to Rostow, August 23, 1968, *FRUS, January–August 1968,* vol. 6.

75. John W. Finney, "Defeat for Doves Reflects Deep Division in the Party," *New York Times,* August 29, 1968, p. 1.

76. Elsey notes, August 23, 1968, Elsey Papers, Box 1, LBJL.

77. Clifford with Holbrooke, *Counsel,* 565.

78. Telephone conversation between Johnson and Clifford, September 2, 1968, *FRUS, September 1968–January 1969,* vol. 7 (Pittsburgh, Pa.: U.S. Government Printing Office, 2003).

79. Elsey notes, September 11, 1968, Elsey Papers, Box 1, LBJL; Notes of meeting, September 12, 1968, *FRUS, September 1968–January 1969,* vol. 7.

80. Clifford with Holbrooke, *Counsel,* 570.

81. Elsey notes, September 16, 1968, Elsey Papers, Box 1, LBJL.

82. Ibid.

83. Elsey notes, September 17, 1968, Elsey Papers, Box 1, LBJL.

84. Elsey notes, September 19, 1968, Elsey Papers, Box 1, LBJL.

85. Elsey notes, September 20, 1968, Elsey Papers, Box 1, LBJL.

86. Elsey notes, September 23, 1968, Elsey Papers, Box 1, LBJL.

87. Elsey notes, September 24, 1968, Elsey Papers, Box 1, LBJL.

88. Elsey notes, September 25, 1968, Elsey Papers, Box 1, LBJL.

89. Ibid.

90. Notes of the 591st Meeting of the National Security Council, September 25, 1968, *FRUS, September 1968–January 1969*, vol. 7. Elsey notes, September 25, 1968, Elsey Papers, Box 1, LBJL.

91. Elsey notes, September 30, 1968, Elsey Papers, Box 1, LBJL.

92. R. W. Apple Jr., "Humphrey Vows Halt in Bombing If Hanoi Reacts," *New York Times,* October 1, 1968, p. 1.

93. Notes of Meeting, September 25, 1968, *FRUS, September 1968–January 1969*, vol. 7.

94. Elsey notes, October 1, 1968, Elsey Papers, Box 1, LBJL.

95. Elsey notes, October 8, 1968, Elsey Papers, Box 1, LBJL.

96. Telegram from the Embassy in France to the Department of State, October 11, 1968, *FRUS, September 1968–January 1969*, vol. 7.

97. Notes of meeting, October 14, 1968, *FRUS, September 1968–January 1969*, vol. 7.

98. Ibid.

## 11. OCTOBER SURPRISE

1. Gardner, *Pay Any Price*, 495–97.

2. Notes of Meeting and Notes of the President's Tuesday Luncheon Meeting, October 22, 1968, *FRUS, September 1968–January 1969*, vol. 7; Elsey notes, October 23, 1968, Elsey Papers, Box 1, LBJL.

3. Telephone Conversation between Johnson and Clifford, October 22, 1968, *FRUS, September 1968–January 1969*, vol. 7.

4. Gardner, *Pay Any Price*, 499.

5. Notes of Meeting, October 27, 1968, *FRUS, September 1968–January 1969*, vol. 7.

6. Ibid.

7. Notes of Meeting, October 29, 1968, *FRUS, September 1968–January 1969*, vol. 7.

8. Ibid.

9. Gardner, *Pay Any Price,* 502.

10. Notes of Meeting, October 29, 1968, *FRUS, September 1968–January 1969*, vol. 7.

11. Notes on Tuesday Luncheon, October 29, 1968, *FRUS, September 1968–January 1969*, vol. 7.

12. Notes of Meeting, October 29, 1968, *FRUS, September 1968–January 1969*, vol. 7; Elsey notes, October 30, 1968, Elsey Papers, Box 1, LBJL.

13. Elsey notes, October 30, 1968, Elsey Papers, Box 1, LBJL; Notes of Meeting, October 29, 1968, *FRUS, September 1968–January 1969*, vol. 7.

14. Elsey notes, October 31, 1968, Elsey Papers, Box 1, LBJL.

15. Transcript of Telephone Conversation among President Johnson, Vice President Humphrey, Richard Nixon, and George Wallace, October 31, 1968, *FRUS, September 1968–January 1969*, vol. 7.

16. Neil Sheehan, "Attacks on North Vietnam Halt Today," *New York Times,* November 1, 1968, p. 1.

17. Clifford to Johnson, November 1, 1968, Clifford Papers, Box 10, LBJL.

18. Elsey notes, November 2, 1968, Elsey Papers, Box 1, LBJL.

19. Editorial Note, November 2, 1968, *FRUS, September 1968–January 1969,* vol. 7.

20. Telephone conversation between Johnson and Nixon, November 3, 1968, ibid.

21. Telephone conversation among Johnson, Clifford, Rusk, and Rostow, November 5, 1968, ibid.

22. Hubert Humphrey, *The Education of a Public Man* (Garden City, N.Y.: Doubleday & Co., 1976), 7.

23. Notes of the President's Meeting with President-Elect Nixon, November 11, 1968, *FRUS, September 1968–January 1969,* vol. 7.

24. Elsey notes, November 9, 1968, Elsey Papers, Box 1, LBJL.

25. William Beecher, "Clifford Asserts Talks May Go On Without Saigon," *New York Times,* November 13, 1968, pp. 1, 14.

26. Editorial Note, November 12, 1968, *FRUS, September 1968–January 1969,* vol. 7.

27. Elsey notes, November 17, 1968, Elsey Papers, Box 1, LBJL.

28. Memorandum Prepared in the Central Intelligence Agency, November 19, 1968, *FRUS, September 1968–January 1969,* vol. 7.

29. Elsey notes, January 4, 1969, and January 6, 1968, Elsey Papers, Box 1, LBJL.

30. Editorial Note, January 7, 1969, *FRUS, September 1968–January 1969,* vol. 7.

31. McGeorge Bundy to Clifford, December 31, 1968, Elsey Papers, Box 1, LBJL.

32. Johnson to Clifford, December 24, 1968, Clifford Papers, Box 10, LBJL.

33. Clifford with Holbrooke, *Counsel,* 488.

34. Joseph A. Califano, *The Triumph and Tragedy of Lyndon Johnson: The White House Years* (New York: Simon & Schuster, 1991), 264.

35. Clifford Oral History, August 7, 1969, LBJL.

36. David Halberstam, *The Best and the Brightest* (New York: Random House, 1972), 650.

## 12. The Wise Man

1. William Safire, *Before the Fall* (Garden City, N.Y.: Doubleday, 1975), 108.

2. Clifford with Holbrooke, *Counsel,* 607.

3. Clark Clifford, "A Viet Nam Reappraisal," 601–22.

4. Ibid., 613, 622.

5. Ibid., 619–22.

6. James Reston, "Pray Silence for Mr. Clifford," *New York Times,* June 20, 1969, sec. 1, p. 40.

7. Patrick Anderson, "Clifford Sounds the Alarm," *New York Times,* August 8, 1971, sec. Magazine, p. 55.

8. Ibid.

9. H. R. Haldeman: *The Haldeman Diaries: Inside the White House* (New York: G. P. Putnam's Sons, 1994), 65.

10. Clark Clifford, "Set a Date in Vietnam. Stick to It. Get Out," *Life,* May 22, 1970, 34.

11. Ibid., 35–36.

12. Ibid.

13. Haldeman, *Diaries*, 169.

14. James M. Naughton, "Agnew Asserts Eight Leading Antiwar Critics Prescribe Defeat to Achieve Peace in Indochina," *New York Times*, June 21, 1970, sec. 1, p. 39.

15. Clifford quoted in David L. DiLeo, *George Ball, Vietnam, and the Rethinking of Containment* (Chapel Hill: University of North Carolina Press, 1991), 119.

16. Terrence Smith, "Clifford Offers Formula for U.S. to Quit War in '71," *New York Times*, June 9, 1971, sec. 1, p. 1; Terrence Smith, "Prisoners: Will Hanoi Free Them in Exchange for a Date Certain," *New York Times*, June 13, 1971, p. E3.

17. Patrick Anderson, "Clifford Sounds the Alarm," p. 9.

18. Clark Clifford, "Open Peace Covenants, Openly Arrived At," *New York Times*, January 30, 1972, p. E13.

19. Safire, *Before the Fall*, 310–11.

20. James Naughton, "Data on Politicians Traced to Wiretaps for 'Security,'" *New York Times*, June 7, 1974, sec. 1 p. 1.

21. Haldeman, *Diaries*, 305.

22. Frantz and McKean, *Friends in High Places*, 267.

23. "The Talk of the Town," *The New Yorker*, July 16, 1973.

24. "Text of Memo to Ehrlichman from Young on Plans for Investigation of Disclosure of Pentagon Papers," *New York Times*, July 25, 1973, sec. 1, p. 30.

25. John Herbers, "Nixon Aides Move against War Foes," *New York Times*, February 4, 1973, sec. 1, p. 29.

26. James M. Naughton, "Muskie Reported Ready to End Active Candidacy," *New York Times*, April 27, 1972, sec. 1, p. 1.

27. James M. Naughton, "McGovern Asserts Nixon Misleads Nation on Peace," *New York Times*, November 6, 1972, sec. 1, p. 1.

28. Clark Clifford, "A Government of National Unity," *New York Times*, June 4, 1973, sec. 1, p. 36.

29. Frantz and McKean, *Friends in High Places*, 268.

30. Clark Clifford, "A Government of National Unity," p. 36.

31. "What They Are Saying of Mr. Clifford's Plan," *New York Times*, June 16, 1973, sec. 1, p. 27; Arthur H. Dean, "The Clifford Plan (Cont.)," *New York Times*, June 15, 1973, sec. 1, p. 37.

32. Christopher Lydon, "Reaction to Nixon Speech: Less in It Than Expected," *New York Times*, August 16, 1973, sec. 1, p. 26. The "Checkers" speech refers to the 1952 campaign speech in which Nixon salvaged his position as the Republican vice presidential nominee following allegations of his accepting illegal campaign donations. During the speech he attested to his austere lifestyle, but he admitted receiving as a gift a cocker spaniel, which his daughter named "Checkers."

33. C. L. Sulzberger, "Challenges to Democracy," *New York Times*, June 10, 1973, sec. Week in Review, p. 229.

34. Nicholas M. Horrock, "Senate Panel on Spying Accepts Compromise on Top Secret Data," *New York Times*, April 17, 1975, sec. 1. p. 8.

35. Laurence Stern, "Intelligence Network Overhaul Suggested," *Washington Post*, December 6, 1975, p. A3; Leslie H. Gelb, "Should We Play Dirty Tricks in the World," *New York Times*, December 21, 1975, sec. Magazine, p. 209; Anthony Lewis, "A Test of Seriousness," *New York Times*, February 9, 1976, sec. 1, p. 27.

36. Clifford with Holbrooke, *Counsel,* 619–20.

37. Christopher Lydon, "Connally Calls Carter Remarks on Johnson an 'Insult,'" *New York Times,* September 29, 1976, sec. 1, p. 23.

38. Clifford with Holbrooke, *Counsel,* 620; Eileen Shanahan, "Carter Gets Two Plans for Tax Reductions and Creation of Jobs," *New York Times,* December 10, 1976, sec. The Week in Review, p. 53.

39. "Clifford Concludes Talks about Cyprus and Arms with Leaders of Turkey," *New York Times,* February 23, 1977, sec. 1, p. 7.

40. Steven B. Roberts, "Cyprus Trip Evokes Memories for Clifford of Truman Doctrine," *New York Times,* February 25, 1977, sec. 1, p. 3.

41. Steven B. Roberts, "Clifford Says Solution Is Possible to the Cyprus Problem This Year," *New York Times,* February 26, 1977, sec. 1, p. 4; "Clifford Sees Chance of Cyprus Pact in '77," *New York Times,* March 11, 1977, sec. 1, p. 6.

42. Carter to Clifford, March 4, 1977, White House Central File—Clark Clifford Name File, Jimmy Carter Library, Atlanta, Georgia.

43. Clifford to Carter, August 30, 1977, ibid.

44. Aaron Latham, "Clark Clifford: Capital Manipulator," *Life,* March 14, 1978, 33–34.

45. William Safire, "Carter's Broken Lance," *New York Times,* July 21, 1977, sec. 1, p. 23.

46. Latham, "Clark Clifford: Capital Manipulator," 35.

47. Clifford with Holbrooke, *Counsel,* 629.

48. Latham, "Clark Clifford: Capital Manipulator," 35.

49. Clifford with Holbrooke, *Counsel,* 631.

50. Wendell Rawls Jr., "Lance, Rebuking Critics, Defends Integrity and Banking Actions," *New York Times,* September 16, 1977, sec. 1, p. 1.

51. Marjorie Hunter, "Elegant Counsel to Lance," *New York Times,* September 17, 1977, sec. 1, p. 13; Russell Baker, "A Crisis in Search of a Theme," *New York Times,* September 20, 1977, sec. 1, p. 41; Latham, "Clark Clifford: Capital Manipulator," 35.

52. James Reston, "Lance Wins Round One," *New York Times,* September 16, 1977, sec. 1, p. 24.

53. Clifford to Brzezinski, December 15, 1977, White House Central File—Clark Clifford Name File, Jimmy Carter Library.

54. Clifford to Brzezinski, November 29, 1978, ibid.

55. Terrence Smith, "Carter Using Old-Lineup Democrats for Advice on Wooing Congress," *New York Times,* June 28, 1978, sec. NJ, p. 21.

56. Richard Burt, "Money Is Already Starting to Flow in Both Sides in Treaty Debate," *New York Times,* January 23, 1979, p. A12; Fred Warner Neal, "Inertia on Salt," *New York Times,* January 22, 1979, p. A21.

57. Carter to Clifford, May 9, 1979, White House Central File—Clark Clifford Name File, Jimmy Carter Library.

58. Carter to Clifford, June 12, 1979, ibid.

59. Wexler to Clifford, June 21, 1979, ibid.

60. Nicholas M. Horrock, "Ex-C.I.A. Directors Urge Senate Panel to Protect Secrets and Agents," *New York Times,* April 6, 1978, p. B11; George Lardner Jr., "Clifford Hits 'Enshrinement' of CIA Curbs," *Washington Post,* April 5, 1978, p. A6.

61. Reginald Stuart, "Firestone Reportedly Will Propose Recall of Tires," *New*

York Times, August 8, 1978, p. A12; "Terms Are Announced for Recall of 7.5 Million Tires by Firestone," *New York Times,* November 30, 1978, p. D23; "Firestone Radial Recall Brings $127 Million Loss," *New York Times,* December 20, 1978, p. D1; Frantz and McKean, *Friends in High Places,* 296–98.

62. "U.S. and I.B.M. Meet over Suit," *New York Times,* October 11, 1979, p. D8; Clifford to Onek, November 23, 1979, and Onek to Clifford, November 27, 1979, White House Central File—Clark Clifford Name File, Jimmy Carter Library; Steven B. Roberts, "Arab Lobby's Specialty: Soft Sell, Tough Message," *New York Times,* April 30, 1978, p. E4.

63. Martin Schram and Edward Walsh, "Camp David Talks Cover Wide Range," *Washington Post,* July 10, 1979, p. A1.

64. Hedrick Smith, "Carter's Aim: Balancing Politics and Foreign Policy," *New York Times,* October 2, 1979, p. A19; Richard Burt, "Carter Has Precedent in Use of 'Wise Men,'" *New York Times,* September 30, 1979, p. 3.

65. Michael T. Kaufman, "Carter Envoy Says India Seeks Soviet Pullout in Kabul," *New York Times,* February 1, 1980, p. D15.

66. Clifford to Carter, August 12, 1980, Clifford Papers, Box 15, Manuscript Division, Library of Congress.

67. Marjorie Hunter, "Elegant Counsel to Lance," *New York Times,* September 17, 1977, sec. 1, p. 13.

# 13. BCCI

1. Roxanne Roberts, "Clifford's Upbeat Night," *Washington Post,* May 23, 1991, p. D1.

2. Frantz and McKean, *Friends in High Places,* 299–301.

3. Ibid., 301–2.

4. Ibid., 291.

5. Ibid., 302–3.

6. Ibid., 307–9.

7. This was the second attempt, the first being rejected on a technicality.

8. Marjorie Williams, "The Man Who Banked on His Good Name," *Washington Post,* May 9, 1991, p. D1.

9. Ibid.

10. Ibid.

11. Frantz and McKean, *Friends in High Places,* 323, 326.

12. Ibid., 320; Williams, "The Man Who Banked on His Good Name," p. D1.

13. Frantz and McKean, *Friends in High Places,* 327.

14. Jeffrey Schmalz, "Bank Is Charged by U.S. With Money-Laundering," *New York Times,* October 12, 1988, p. 1.

15. Frantz and McKean, *Friends in High Places,* 355.

16. Jim McGee and Sharon Walsh, "Foreign Bank Financed Stock Deal," *Washington Post,* May 5, 1991, p. A1.

17. Frantz and McKean, *Friends in High Places,* 355.

18. Jim McGee, "Who Controls First American Bankshares?" *Washington Post,* February 3, 1991, p. A1.

19. Jim McGee, "Foreign Bank Must Sell First American Stake," *Washington Post,* March 5, 1991, p. A1.

20. McGee and Walsh, "Foreign Bank Financed Stock Deal," p. A1.

21. Marjorie Williams, "The Rise of a Reputation," *Washington Post,* May 8, 1991, p. D1; Neil Lewis, "Washington at Work; Clark Clifford, Symbol of the Permanent Capital, Is Faced with a Dilemma," *New York Times,* April 5, 1991.

22. Williams, "The Man Who Banked on His Good Name," p. D1.

23. Lewis, "Washington at Work."

24. Williams, "The Rise of a Reputation," p. D1.

25. Michael Beschloss, "Clifford Speaks," *The New Yorker,* September 6, 1993, 45.

26. Ibid., 45.

27. George Elsey letter to author, March 17, 2007.

28. Author interview with a partner at the Newark firm McCarter & English, who requested anonymity, April 16, 2008. This contradicts Frantz and McKean, who reported that Clifford would be allowed to stay on "of counsel" (*Friends in High Places,* 366).

29. Frantz and McKean, *Friends in High Places,* 366; Beschloss, "Clifford Speaks," 46.

30. Marjorie Williams, "The Performance of a Lifetime," *Washington Post,* September 12, 1991, p. D1.

31. Ibid.

32. Ibid.

33. David E. Rosenbaum, "Clifford Again Denies Knowledge of BCCI Link," *New York Times,* October 25, 1991; Sharon Walsh and Mark Potts, "Altman: He and Clifford Regret Loan," *Washington Post,* October 25, 1991, p. F1; Frantz and McKean, *Friends in High Places,* 368.

34. Frantz and McKean, *Friends in High Places,* 375.

35. Beschloss, "Clifford Speaks," 46; Sharon Walsh, "Clifford's, Altman's Assets Frozen," *Washington Post,* August 11, 1992, p. A1.

36. Sharon Walsh, "Clark Clifford for the Defense; Emotional Elder Statesman Pleads His Case," *Washington Post,* July 31, 1992, p. A1.

37. Beschloss, "Clifford Speaks," 48.

38. Frantz and McKean, *Friends in High Places,* 387.

39. Beschloss, "Clifford Speaks," 49.

40. Sharon Walsh, "Altman Acquitted on BCCI Counts," *Washington Post,* August 15, 1993, p. A1.

41. Frantz and McKean, *Friends in High Places,* 372–73.

42. Williams, "The Man Who Banked on His Good Name," p. D1.

43. Lewis, "Washington at Work."

44. Warren I. Cohen, "The Fall of Clark Clifford," *The Nation,* October 5, 1992, p. 356.

## CONCLUSION

1. Spingarn Oral History, March 20, 1967, HSTL.

2. Allen and Shannon, *The Truman Merry-Go-Round,* 58.

3. Irwin Ross, *The Loneliest Campaign: The Truman Victory of 1948* (Westport, Conn.: Greenwood Press, 1977) 19.

4. Valenti, *A Very Human President,* 229–30.

5. Blumenthal, "Clark Clifford: The Ultimate Insider and the Presidents He's Known," 9.

6. Donovan quoted in Frantz and McKean, *Friends in High Places,* 90.

7. Keyserling Oral History, May 10, 1971, HSTL.

8. Spingarn Oral History, March 20, 1967, HSTL.

9. Sorensen quoted in Frantz and McKean, *Friends in High Places,* 181.

10. "Little Accident," 28.

11. Sidey quoted in Frantz and McKean, *Friends in High Places,* 155.

12. Coffin, "Harry Truman's Bright Young Man," 16.

13. Robert H. Ferrell, ed., *Off the Record: The Private Papers of Harry S. Truman* (New York: Harper & Row, 1980), 149. The quote is from Truman's diary entry on September 13, 1948.

14. Allen and Shannon, *The Truman Merry-Go-Round,* 61.

15. Phillips, *The Truman Presidency,* 137, 135.

16. Spingarn Oral History, March 20, 1967, HSTL.

17. Ibid.

18. Ibid.

19. Phillips, *The Truman Presidency,* 135.

20. Hechler Oral History, November 29, 1985, HSTL.

21. Spingarn Oral History, March 20, 1967, HSTL.

22. Ferrell, ed., *Truman in the White House,* 165.

23. Ibid., 260.

24. Hamby, *Man of the People,* 304.

25. Richard Cohen, "Calling Clark Clifford Is Washington Folkway," *Washington Post,* September 11, 1977, p. 37.

26. George Reedy, *Lyndon B. Johnson: A Memoir* (New York: Andrews and McMeel, 1982), 151.

# Sources

## Manuscript Collections and Oral Histories

Dean Acheson Oral History, Harry S. Truman Library, Independence, Missouri

Eben Ayers Oral History, Harry S. Truman Library, Independence, Missouri

George Ball Oral History, Lyndon B. Johnson Library, Austin, Texas

William Batt Oral History, Harry S. Truman Library, Independence, Missouri

David Bell Oral History, Harry S. Truman Library, Independence, Missouri

David Bell Papers, John F. Kennedy Library, Boston, Massachusetts

Zbigniew Brzezinski Papers, Jimmy Carter Library, Atlanta, Georgia

Jimmy Carter Papers, Jimmy Carter Library, Atlanta, Georgia

Oscar Chapman Oral History, Harry S. Truman Library, Independence, Missouri

Clark M. Clifford Oral History, Lyndon B. Johnson Library, Austin, Texas

Clark M. Clifford Oral History, John F. Kennedy Library, Boston, Massachusetts

Clark M. Clifford Oral History, Harry S. Truman Library, Independence, Missouri

Clark M. Clifford Papers, Lyndon B. Johnson Library, Austin, Texas

Clark M. Clifford Papers, John F. Kennedy Library, Boston, Massachusetts

Clark M. Clifford Papers, Manuscript Division, Library of Congress, Washington, D.C.

Clark M. Clifford Papers, Harry S. Truman Library, Independence, Missouri

Jonathan Daniels Papers, Harry S. Truman Library, Independence, Missouri

Frederick Dutton Oral History, John F. Kennedy Library, Boston, Massachusetts

George M. Elsey Oral History, Harry S. Truman Library, Independence, Missouri

George M. Elsey Papers, Lyndon B. Johnson Library, Austin, Texas

George M. Elsey Papers, Harry S. Truman Library, Independence, Missouri

Oscar Ewing Oral History, Harry S. Truman Library, Independence, Missouri

Oscar Ewing Papers, Harry S. Truman Library, Independence, Missouri

J. William Fulbright Oral History, John F. Kennedy Library, Boston, Massachusetts

Arthur Goldberg Oral History, John F. Kennedy Library, Boston, Massachusetts

Albert Gore Oral History, John F. Kennedy Library, Boston, Massachusetts

Kenneth Hechler Oral History, Harry S. Truman Library, Independence, Missouri

Kenneth Hechler Papers, Harry S. Truman Library, Independence, Missouri

Loy Henderson Oral History, Harry S. Truman Library, Independence, Missouri

Lyndon B. Johnson Papers, Lyndon B. Johnson Library, Austin, Texas

John F. Kennedy Papers, John F. Kennedy Library, Boston, Massachusetts

John F. Kennedy Presidential Recordings, John F. Kennedy Library, Boston, Massachusetts

Robert F. Kennedy Oral History, John F. Kennedy Library, Boston, Massachusetts

Robert S. Kerr Papers, Carl Albert Center, University of Oklahoma, Norman, Oklahoma

Leon Keyserling Oral History, Harry S. Truman Library, Independence, Missouri

Marx Leva Oral History, Harry S. Truman Library, Independence, Missouri

Max Lowenthal Oral History, Harry S. Truman Library, Independence, Missouri

Harry McPherson Oral History, Lyndon B. Johnson Library, Austin, Texas

Samuel Rosenman Oral History, Harry S. Truman Library, Independence, Missouri

Samuel Rosenman Papers, Harry S. Truman Library, Independence, Missouri

James Rowe Papers, Franklin D. Roosevelt Library, Hyde Park, N.Y., and Harry S. Truman Library, Independence, Missouri

Stephen Spingarn Oral History, Harry S. Truman Library, Independence, Missouri

Stuart Symington Oral History, John F. Kennedy Library, Boston, Massachusetts

Harry S. Truman Papers, Harry S. Truman Library, Independence, Missouri

Paul Warnke Papers, Lyndon B. Johnson Library, Austin, Texas

## INTERVIEWS

Clark M. Clifford, interview on *Meet the Press,* February 4, 1950, Recorded Sound Division, Library of Congress.

George M. Elsey, interviews with author, June 14, 2001, March 19, 2002, and May 7, 2004.

## PUBLISHED WORKS

Abell, Tyler, ed. *Drew Pearson Diaries: 1949–1959.* New York: Holt, Rinehart and Winston, 1974.

Acheson, Dean. *Present at the Creation: My Years in the State Department.* New York: Norton, 1969.

Allen, Robert S., and William V. Shannon. *The Truman Merry-Go-Round.* New York: Vanguard Press, 1950.

Anderson, Patrick. "Clifford Sounds the Alarm." *New York Times,* August 8, 1971, sec. Magazine, p. 5.

———. "The New Defense Secretary Thinks Like the President." *New York Times,* January 28, 1968, sec. 6, p. 20.

———. *The President's Men.* Garden City, N.Y.: Doubleday, 1968.

Ball, George W. *The Past Has Another Pattern.* New York: Norton, 1982.

Barrett, David M. *Uncertain Warriors: Lyndon Johnson and His Vietnam Advisers.* Lawrence: University Press of Kansas, 1993.

Benson, Michael. *Harry S. Truman and the Founding of Israel.* Westport, Conn.: Praeger, 1997.

Berman, Larry. *Lyndon Johnson's War: The Road to Stalemate in Vietnam.* New York: Norton, 1989.

———. *Planning a Tragedy: The Americanization of the War in Vietnam.* New York: Norton, 1982.

Beschloss, Michael. "Clifford Speaks." *The New Yorker,* September 6, 1993, 44–50.

———. *The Crisis Years: Kennedy and Khrushchev, 1960–1963.* New York: HarperCollins, 1991.

———, ed. *Reaching for Glory: Lyndon Johnson's Secret White House Tapes, 1964–1965.* New York: Simon & Schuster, 2001.

———, ed. *Taking Charge: The Johnson White House Tapes, 1963–1964.* New York: Simon & Schuster, 1997.

Blumenthal, Sidney. "Clark Clifford: The Ultimate Insider and the Presidents He's Known." *Washington Post National Weekly Edition,* March 6–12, 1989, 8–11.

Bohlen, Charles. *Witness to History, 1929–1969.* New York: Norton, 1973.

Borklund, Carl W. *Men of the Pentagon: From Forrestal to McNamara.* New York: Frederick A. Praeger, 1966.

Brands, H. W. *Inside the Cold War: Loy Henderson and the Rise of the American Empire, 1918–1961.* New York: Oxford University Press, 1991.

Brzezinski, Zbigniew. *Power and Principle: Memoirs of a National Security Advisor, 1977–1981.* New York: Farrar, Straus and Giroux, 1983.

Byrnes, James F. *All in One Lifetime.* New York: Harper, 1958.

Califano, Joseph A. *The Triumph and Tragedy of Lyndon Johnson: The White House Years.* New York: Simon & Schuster, 1991.

Carter, Jimmy. *Keeping Faith: Memoirs of a President.* New York: Bantam Books, 1982.

"Carter at the Crossroads." *Time,* July 23, 1979, 20–22.

Clifford, Clark. "Business and Government: Greater Teamwork to Expand U.S. Economy." *Vital Speeches of the Day* 16, no. 14 (May 1950): 426–30.

———. "Set a Date in Vietnam. Stick to It. Get Out." *Life,* May 22, 1970, 34.

———. "A Viet Nam Reappraisal: The Personal History of One Man's View and How It Evolved." *Foreign Affairs* 47, no. 4 (July 1969): 601–22.

Clifford, Clark, with Richard Holbrooke. *Counsel to the President.* New York: Random House, 1991.

Cochran, Bert. *Harry Truman and the Crisis Presidency.* New York: Funk & Wagnalls, 1973.

Coffin, Tris. "Harry Truman's Bright Young Man." *The New Republic,* January 6, 1947, 14–17.

Cohen, Michael J. *Truman and Israel.* Berkeley: University of California Press, 1990.

Cohen, Warren I. "The Fall of Clark Clifford." *The Nation,* October 5, 1992, 354–56.

Dallek, Robert. *Flawed Giant: Lyndon Johnson and His Times, 1961–1973.* New York: Oxford University Press, 1998.

———. *An Unfinished Life: John F. Kennedy, 1917–1963.* New York: Little, Brown and Co., 2003.

Daniels, Jonathan. *The Man of Independence.* Port Washington, N.Y.: Kennikat Press, 1950.

DiLeo, David L. *George Ball, Vietnam, and the Rethinking of Containment.* Chapel Hill: University of North Carolina Press, 1991.

Divine, Robert A., ed. *Exploring the Johnson Years:* Austin: University of Texas Press, 1981.

Divine, Robert A. *Foreign Policy and U.S. Presidential Elections, 1940–1948.* New York: New Viewpoints, 1974.

————. *Since 1945: Politics and Diplomacy in Recent American History.* New York: Wiley, 1979.

Dobbs, Charles M. *The Unwanted Symbol: American Foreign Policy, the Cold War, and Korea, 1945–1950.* Kent, Ohio: Kent State University Press, 1981.

Donaldson, Gary A. *Truman Defeats Dewey.* Lexington: University Press of Kentucky, 1999.

Donovan, Robert J. *Conflict and Crisis: The Presidency of Harry S. Truman, 1945–1948.* New York: Norton, 1977.

————. *Tumultuous Years: The Presidency of Harry S. Truman, 1949–1953.* New York: Norton, 1982.

Elsey, George McKee. *An Unplanned Life.* Columbia: University of Missouri Press, 2005.

————. "Some White House Recollections, 1942–53." *Diplomatic History* 12, no. 3 (Summer 1988): 357–64.

Farrar, Ronald T. *Reluctant Servant: The Story of Charles Ross.* Columbia: University of Missouri Press, 1969.

Ferrell, Robert H., ed. *Off the Record: The Private Papers of Harry S. Truman.* New York: Harper & Row, 1980.

————. *Truman and Pendergast.* Columbia: University of Missouri Press, 1999.

————, ed. *Truman in the White House: The Diary of Eben Ayers.* Columbia: University of Missouri Press, 1991.

Frantz, Douglas, and David McKean. *Friends in High Places: The Rise and Fall of Clark Clifford.* New York: Little, Brown and Co., 1995.

Gaddis, John L. *The Long Peace: Inquiries into the History of the Cold War.* New York: Oxford University Press, 1987.

Gardner, Lloyd C. *Pay Any Price: Lyndon Johnson and the Wars for Vietnam.* Chicago: Ivan R. Dee, 1995.

Goldman, Eric F. *The Crucial Decade: America, 1945–1955.* Westport, Conn.: Greenwood Press, 1981.

Goodwin, Doris Kearns. *Lyndon Johnson and the American Dream.* New York: Harper & Row, 1976.

Goulden, Joseph C. *The Superlawyers: The Small and Powerful World of the Great Washington Law Firms.* New York: Dell Publishing Co., 1972.

Goulding, Phil G. *Confirm or Deny: Informing the People on National Security.* New York: Harper & Row, 1970.

Gullan, Harold I. *The Upset That Wasn't: Harry S. Truman and the Crucial Election of 1948.* Chicago: Ivan R. Dee, 1998.

Guthman, Edwin O., and Jeffrey Shulman, eds. *Robert Kennedy: In His Own Words.* New York: Bantam Books, 1988.

Halberstam, David. *The Best and the Brightest.* New York: Random House, 1972.

————. *The Unfinished Odyssey of Robert Kennedy*. New York: Random House, 1968.

Haldeman, H. R. *The Haldeman Diaries: Inside the White House*. New York: G. P. Putnam's Sons, 1994.

Hamby, Alonzo L. *Man of the People: A Life of Harry S. Truman*. New York: Oxford University Press, 1995.

Harper, Alan D. *The Politics of Loyalty: The White House and the Communist Issue, 1946–1952*. Westport, Conn.: Greenwood Publishing Corp., 1969.

Hartmann, Susan M. *Truman and the 80th Congress*. Columbia: University of Missouri Press, 1971.

Havemann, Ernest. "Clark Clifford." *Life*, January 27, 1947, 45–53.

Hechler, Kenneth. *Working with Truman*. New York: G. P. Putnam's Sons, 1982.

Heller, Francis, ed. *The Truman White House: The Administration of the Presidency, 1945–1953*. Lawrence: Regents Press of Kansas, 1980.

Hellmann, John. *The Kennedy Obsession: The American Myth of JFK*. New York: Columbia University Press, 1997.

Helsing, Jeffrey W. *Johnson's War/Johnson's Great Society: The Guns and Butter Trap*. Westport, Conn.: Praeger, 2000.

Herring, George C. *LBJ and Vietnam: A Different Kind of War*. Austin: University of Texas Press, 1994.

Hersey, John. *Aspects of the Presidency*. New York: Ticknor and Fields, 1980.

Heymann, C. David. *A Woman Named Jackie*. New York: Penguin Books, 1989.

Hoopes, Townsend. "The Fight for the President's Mind and the Men Who Won It." *Atlantic Monthly*, October 1969, 97–114.

Hoopes, Townsend, and Douglas Brinkley. *Driven Patriot: The Life and Times of James Forrestal*. New York: Knopf, 1992.

Howard, Clive. "The Clark Cliffords." *Redbook*, June 1949, 28–31, 82–83.

Humphrey, Hubert. *The Education of a Public Man*. Garden City, N.Y.: Doubleday, 1976.

Ireland, Timothy P. *Creating the Entangling Alliance: The Origins of the North Atlantic Treaty Organization*. Westport, Conn.: Greenwood Press, 1981.

Isaacson, Walter, and Evan Thomas. *The Wise Men: Six Friends and the World They Made: Acheson, Bohlen, Harriman, Kennan, Lovett, McCloy*. New York: Simon & Schuster, 1986.

Johnson, Lyndon. *The Vantage Point: Perspectives of the Presidency, 1963–1969*. New York: Holt, Rinehart and Winston, 1971.

Jones, Howard. *"A New Kind of War": America's Global Strategy and the Truman Doctrine in Greece*. New York: Oxford University Press, 1989.

Jones, Joseph. *The Fifteen Weeks (February 21–June 4, 1947)*. New York: Viking, 1955.

Kennan, George F. *Memoirs: 1925–1950*. Boston: Little, Brown and Co., 1967.

Kernell, Samuel, and Samuel L. Popkin, eds. *Chief of Staff: Twenty-Five Years of Managing the Presidency*. Berkeley: University of California Press, 1986.

Krock, Arthur. *Memoirs: Sixty Years on the Firing Line*. New York: Funk & Wagnalls, 1968.

Kuniholm, Bruce R. *The Origins of the Cold War in the Near East: Great Power Conflict and Diplomacy in Iran, Turkey, and Greece*. Princeton: Princeton University Press, 1980.

Larkin, Al. "The Campaign and the Presidency: An Interview with Richard Neustadt." *Boston Globe Magazine,* November 2, 1980, 13.

Latham, Aaron. "Clark Clifford: Capital Manipulator." *Life,* March 14, 1978, 33–34.

Leffler, Melvyn P. *A Preponderance of Power: National Security, the Truman Administration, and the Cold War*. Stanford, Calif.: Stanford University Press, 1992.

Lilienthal, David. *The Journals of David Lilienthal,* vol. 2, *The Atomic Energy Years, 1945–1950*. New York: Harper & Row, 1964.

———. *The Journals of David Lilienthal,* vol. 3, *The Venturesome Years, 1950–1955*. New York: Harper & Row, 1966.

———. *The Journals of David Lilienthal,* vol. 6, *Creativity and Conflict, 1964–1967*. New York: Harper & Row, 1976.

"Little Accident." *Time,* March 15, 1948, 26–29.

Manchester, William. *The Death of a President*. New York: Harper & Row, 1967.

McCormick, Thomas J., and Walter LaFeber, eds. *Behind the Throne: Servants of Power to Imperial Presidents, 1898–1968*. Madison: University of Wisconsin Press, 1993.

McCoy, Donald. *The Presidency of Harry S. Truman*. Lawrence: University Press of Kansas, 1984.

McCullough, David. *Truman*. New York: Simon & Schuster, 1992.

McDonald, Donald. "Counseling the President: An Interview with Clark M. Clifford." *Center Magazine,* May–June 1974, 22–26.

McNamara, Robert S., with Brian VanDeMark. *In Retrospect: The Tragedy and Lessons of Vietnam*. New York: Times Books, 1995.

McPherson, Harry. *A Political Education*. Boston: Little, Brown and Co., 1972.

Medved, Michael. *The Shadow Presidents: The Secret History of the Chief Executives and Their Top Aides*. New York: Times Books, 1979.

Miller, Merle. *Lyndon: An Oral Biography*. New York: Putnam Books, 1980.

Millis, Walter, ed. *The Forrestal Diaries.* New York: Viking Press, 1951.

Nitze, Paul. *From Hiroshima to Glasnost: At the Center of Decision: A Memoir.* New York: Grove Weidenfeld, 1989.

Nixon, Richard. *The Memoirs of Richard Nixon.* New York: Grosset & Dunlap, 1978.

Parmet, Herbert S. *The Presidency of John F. Kennedy.* Norwalk, Conn.: Easton Press, 1983.

Pearson, Drew, and Jack Anderson. *The Case against Congress.* New York: Simon & Schuster, 1968.

Phillips, Cabell B. H. *The Truman Presidency: The History of a Triumphant Succession.* New York: Macmillan, 1966.

Pogue, Forrest C. *George C. Marshall: Statesman, 1945–1959.* New York: Viking, 1987.

"The Presidency: It's Truman in '52, Plus Clifford." *Newsweek,* August 15, 1949, 15–17.

"Problems of President's Right-Hand Man." *U.S. News and World Report,* December 20, 1946, 60–62.

Reedy, George. *Lyndon B. Johnson: A Memoir.* New York: Andrews and McMeel, 1982.

Reeves, Richard. *President Kennedy: Profile of Power.* New York: Simon & Schuster, 1993.

Reeves, Thomas. *A Question of Character: A Life of John F. Kennedy.* New York: Free Press, 1991.

Ross, Irwin. *The Loneliest Campaign: The Truman Victory of 1948.* Westport, Conn.: Greenwood Press, 1977.

Safire, William. *Before the Fall.* Garden City, N.Y.: Doubleday, 1975.

Salinger, Pierre. *With Kennedy.* Garden City, N.Y.: Doubleday, 1966.

Savage, Sean J. *Truman and the Democratic Party.* Lexington: University Press of Kentucky, 1997.

Schandler, Herbert Y. *The Unmaking of a President: Lyndon Johnson and Vietnam.* Princeton: Princeton University Press, 1977.

Schlesinger, Arthur M., Jr. *A Thousand Days: John F. Kennedy in the White House.* Boston: Houghton Mifflin Co., 1965.

Schoenbaum, Thomas J. *Waging Peace and War: Dean Rusk in the Truman, Kennedy, and Johnson Years.* New York: Simon & Schuster, 1988.

Sherwood, Robert E. *Roosevelt and Hopkins: An Intimate History.* New York: Harper & Brothers, 1948.

Sidey, Hugh. *John F. Kennedy, President.* New York: Atheneum, 1964.

Smith, Gaddis. *Morality, Reason, and Power.* New York: Hill and Wang, 1986.

Snetsinger, John. *Truman, the Jewish Vote, and the Creation of Israel.* Stanford, Calif.: Hoover Institution Press, 1974.

Sorensen, Theodore C. *Kennedy.* New York: Harper & Row, 1965.

Spragens, William C., ed. *Popular Images of American Presidents*. New York: Greenwood Press, 1988.

Strout, Richard L. "CIA Reform Suggested by Clifford." *Christian Science Monitor,* July 24, 1975, p. 1.

"The Talk of the Town." *The New Yorker,* July 16, 1973, p. 21.

Thompson, Francis H. *The Frustration of Politics: Truman, Congress, and the Loyalty Issue, 1945–1953*. Rutherford, N.J.: Fairleigh Dickinson University Press, 1979.

Troy, Thomas F. *Donovan and the CIA: A History of the Establishment of the Central Intelligence Agency*. Frederick, Md.: Aletheia Books, 1981.

Underhill, Robert. *The Truman Persuasions*. Ames: Iowa State University Press, 1981.

U.S. Department of State. *Foreign Relations of the United States, 1948*. Vol. 5. Pittsburgh, Pa.: U.S. Government Printing Office, 1975.

———. *Foreign Relations of the United States, 1949*. Vol. 5. Pittsburgh, Pa.: U.S. Government Printing Office, 1976.

———. *Foreign Relations of the United States, 1949*. Vol. 9. Pittsburgh, Pa.: U.S. Government Printing Office, 1974.

———. *Foreign Relations of the United States, 1965*. Vol. 3. Pittsburgh, Pa.: U.S. Government Printing Office, 1996.

———. *Foreign Relations of the United States, 1966*. Vol. 4. Pittsburgh, Pa.: U.S. Government Printing Office, 1998.

———. *Foreign Relations of the United States, 1967*. Vol. 5. Pittsburgh, Pa.: U.S. Government Printing Office, 2002.

———. *Foreign Relations of the United States, January–August 1968*. Vol. 6. Pittsburgh, Pa.: U.S. Government Printing Office, 2002.

———. *Foreign Relations of the United States, September 1968–January 1969*. Vol. 7. Pittsburgh, Pa.: U.S. Government Printing Office, 2003.

Valenti, Jack. *A Very Human President*. New York: W. W. Norton, 1975.

Vance, Cyrus. *Hard Choices: Critical Years in America's Foreign Policy*. New York: Simon & Schuster, 1983.

VanDeMark, Brian. *Into the Quagmire: Lyndon Johnson and the Escalation of the War in Vietnam*. New York: Oxford University Press, 1991.

Wallace, Mike, and Gary Paul Gates. *Close Encounters*. New York: William Morrow and Co., 1984.

Welsh, David, with David Horowitz. "Clark Clifford: Attorney at War." *Ramparts,* August 24, 1968, 43–50.

Westerfield, Bradford H. *Foreign Policy and Party Politics: Pearl Harbor to Korea*. New Haven, Conn.: Yale University Press, 1955.

White, Theodore. *The Making of the President, 1960*. New York: Atheneum Publishers, 1961.

Wills, Garry. "Keeper of the Seal." *New York Review of Books,* July 18, 1991, 19–22.

# Index